ST GEORGE'S
CHAPEL,
WINDSOR
A PORTRAIT

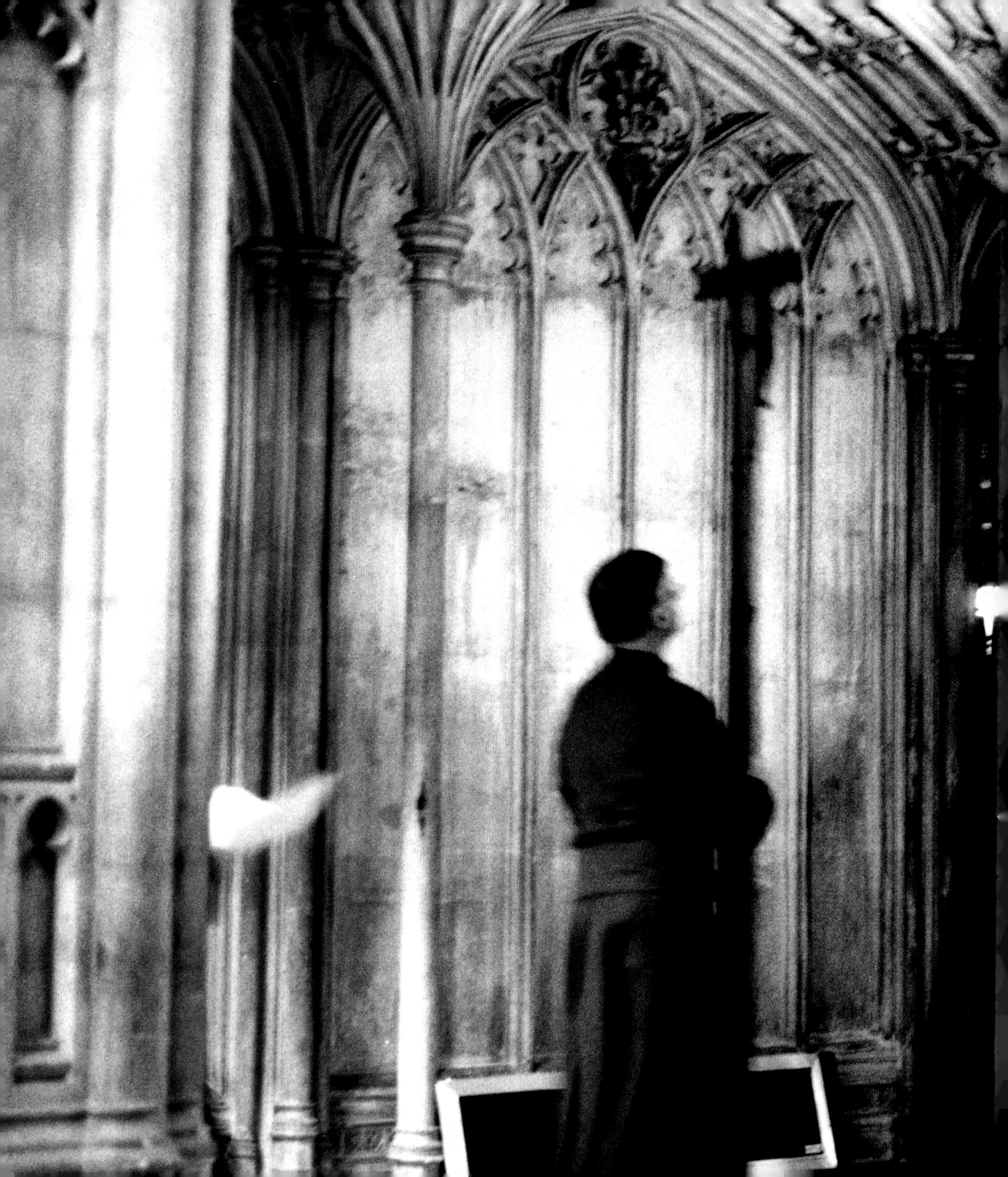

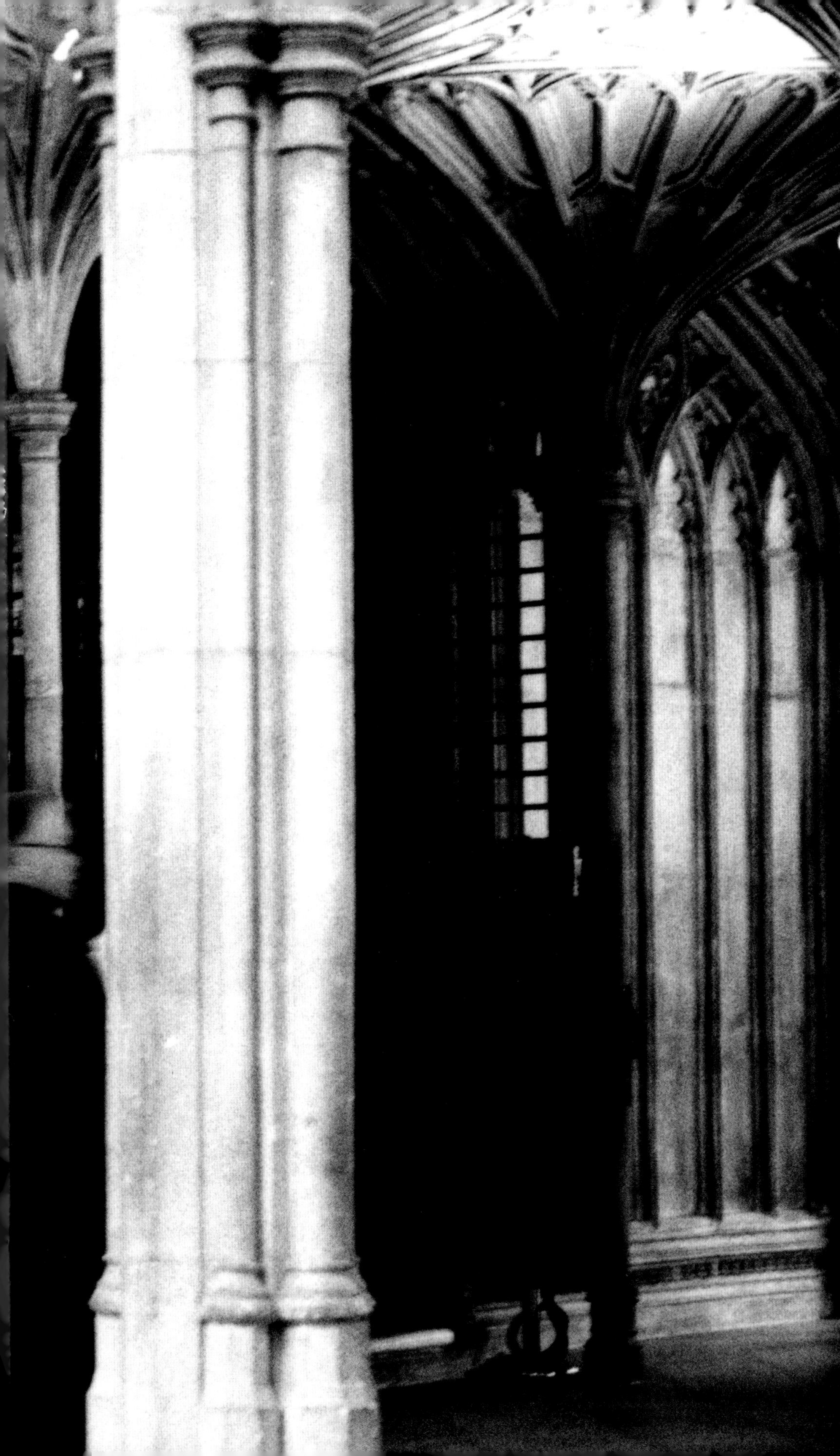

ST GEORGE'S CHAPEL, WINDSOR

A PORTRAIT

Eleanor Curtis

D. Giles Limited,
London

First published in 2008 by GILES
An imprint of D Giles Limited
2nd Floor, 162–164 Upper Richmond Road,
London, SW15 2SL, UK
www.gilesltd.com

ISBN: 978-1-904832-55-3

Written and edited by Eleanor Curtis
Copy-edited and proof-read by David Rose
Designed by Anikst Design, London
Produced by GILES, an imprint of D Giles Limited, London
Printed and bound in Hong Kong

Publication accompanies the travelling exhibition *St George's Chapel, Windsor: A Portrait*, which opens at St George's Chapel during the Windsor Festival, September 2008.

All photographs reproduced in this volume were taken by Eleanor Curtis at various intervals between 2006 and 2007 using Leica cameras.

Front cover: St George's Chapel in the mist from the south-east. December 2006
Back cover: Members of the Royal Body Guard of the Yeomen of the Guard standing in the Galilee Porch in preparation for the ceremony of the Royal Victorian Order.
Frontispiece: A Minor Canon can be seen carrying a plain wooden cross under the fan vaults of the organ screen to its position for the Good Friday service.

Contents

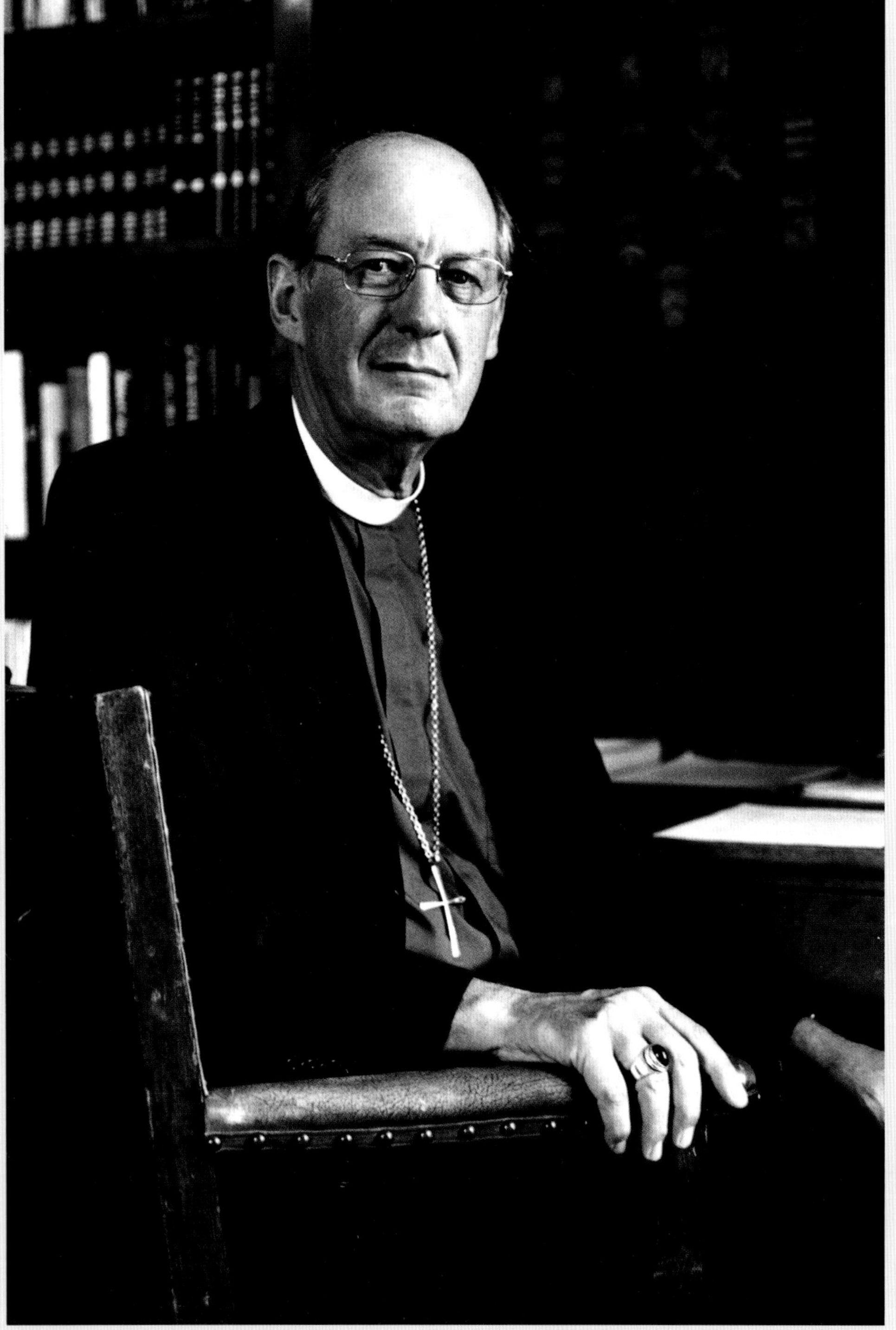

Foreword

by the Dean of Windsor

To those of us who have been living and working at St George's during the last two years, Eleanor Curtis has become a familiar figure and a good friend. As these photographs show, she has frequently been in the thick of things. Her presence, however, has always been sensitive and unobtrusive. She has fitted into life here in a very natural way.

These pictures reveal her deep appreciation of the Chapel's central place in the life of the community of the College of St George. They do so as much by capturing the quiet and prayerful moments of daily routine as by marking some of the great ceremonies that take place within the Chapel every year. They do so too by drawing attention to work that goes on very much behind the scenes, and by showing something of the complexity of the total operation.

At the same time, our eyes are opened once again to the sheer beauty of the place; we are invited to look freshly at the building. While these photographs clearly praise the magnificence of St George's, they do so in a way that I can only call 'respectful'. Some of the images on the pages of this book are very humbling. Moreover, they will remind those whose job it is to care for this wonderful church that their particular responsibility is a great privilege. We at St George's are grateful to the many people who, through their generosity, share both the responsibility and privilege with us.

Eleanor Curtis's photographs also record and express the vitality of life at St George's. Music and ritual and pageantry can provide rich experiences. They are often means that we employ to celebrate some of the attitudes and values that we believe make for a good society: loyalty to the Sovereign, appreciation of the importance of tradition as we embrace the future, and willingness to be of service to others.

There are suggestions here too of the wider life of our community. We are reminded of all the scholarly work that is associated with the Archives. We glimpse a conversation taking place at St George's House, a centre within the College for a large range and number of important consultations every year. The Choristers, very much in evidence, make us aware that, down the hill, St George's School is there to provide them (and hundreds of other children too) with a good education.

It is, however, the 'goings on' within the Chapel that Eleanor Curtis has most focused on. It is the spiritual heart of the community with which she puts us in touch. About many of these beautiful photographs, there is a contemplative air. The subtlety of the photography matches a subtle question that seems to be being asked. Is there here something more to be explored than we might have thought when we began? By what comes to us through a camera lens, is an inner eye opened? For me, the answer is most definitely 'Yes'. I am grateful for this book.

David Conner

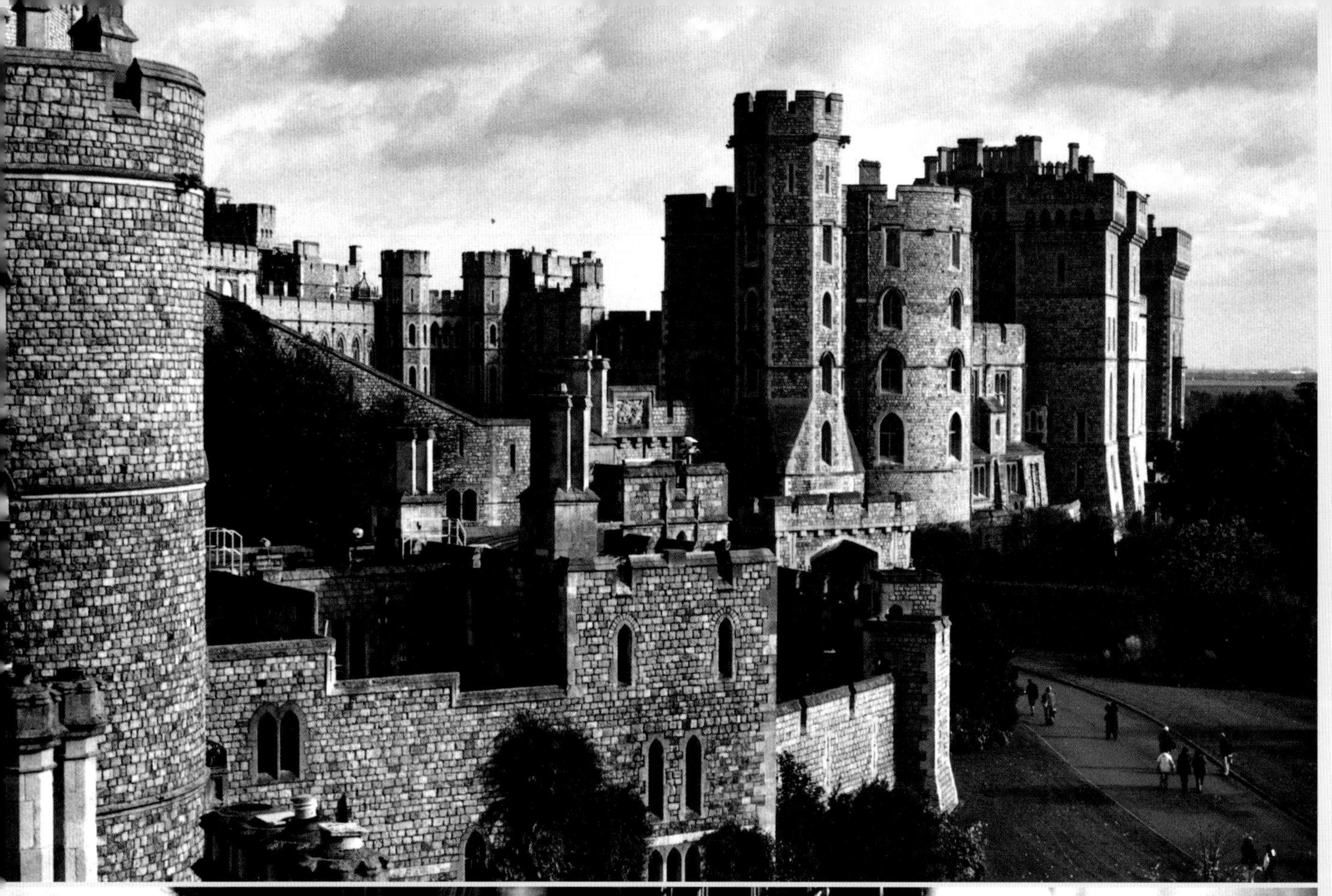

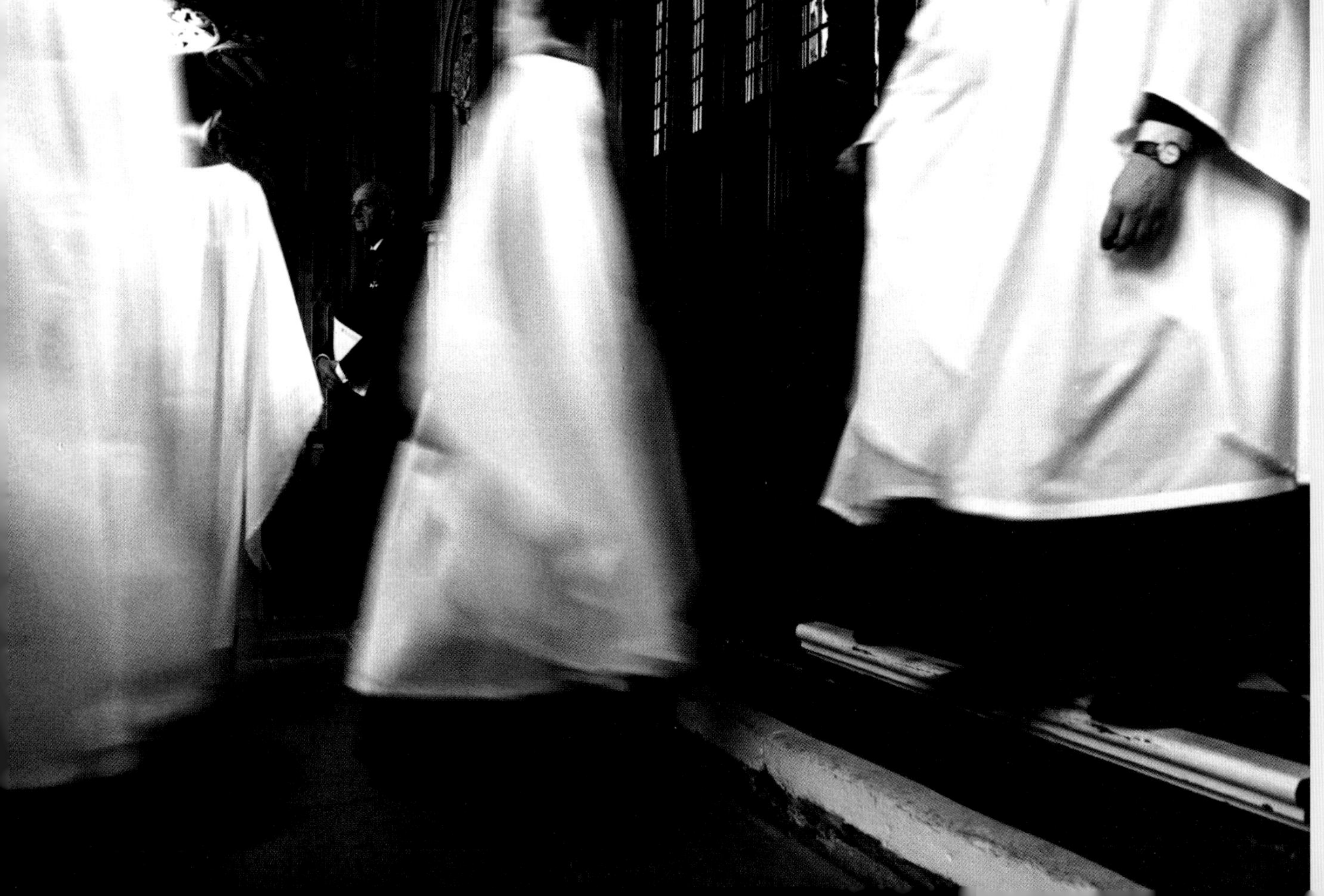

Introduction

My first glimpse of St George's Chapel was in early 2000, when I was invited to meet with one of the Canons in residence to discuss the possibility of a photographic exhibition in the Dean's Cloister. The subject was to be my three-year coverage of the civil war in Angola, with images that depicted scenes far from the peaceful daily workings of the Chapel. A year later, while hanging my photographic show on Angola in the cloister in Summer 2001, my visual wonderment grew as I became better acquainted with the Chapel and the idea of a photographic portrait of St George's Chapel took shape.

During those summer months, my eyes continued to follow the shapes and shades of the robes that flowed through the cloister, as the choristers and Lay Clerks hurried to Evensong in the late afternoon. The accompanying quiet chatter and light footsteps were followed closely by the Dean and Canons in their own dignified liturgical garments and I recall whispers of long white gowns almost brushing the stone floor as they disappeared into the north quire aisle.

From my limited but intimate view, centuries of tradition and ritual seemed to be present in the pattern of the choristers' steps on the path taken from cloister to quire, and from these first impressions the composition of photographs started to take shape in my mind's eye. I saw the white cuffs of gown and robe illuminated by natural light as the figures moved through this architecturally magnificent Chapel; and I can still recall the spirit of those holy voices as they grabbed my attention, causing me to stop and be still, and to reflect upon the Chapel's history and its use today.

The Chapel's incredible history, which is revealed through layer upon layer of stone and heraldic carving, dates back to 1475 and is carried to the present day through the banners and helms that hang overhead representing today's Knights of the Order of the Garter. Here is a timeless capsule of British history, set in a chapel as large as a cathedral, and which hosts three services a day, each day of each year. It is also open daily to the public and is one of the most popular tourist attractions in England with approximately one million visitors each year.

I remained in dialogue with Chapter, the governing body of St George's Chapel, about the idea of a photographic study of the Chapel and continued to convey my enthusiasm for a challenging task – to capture both the contemporary and the traditional in a set of black and white images. Some years on, after much deliberation and debate, I was invited back to the Chapel by the Dean and Canons of Windsor, but this time with permission to bring my cameras.

Over the course of eighteen months, between Spring 2006 and Autumn 2007, I was witness to and photographed an incredible range of events and people at St George's Chapel. It has been a unique opportunity that offered the most privileged access to the daily activities and great festivities of this incredible church. I have been allowed to photograph behind the scenes for most of the services and major events, attempting to capture the essence and spirit of St George's Chapel through image alone. Whether this be the in-depth rehearsals for Garter Day, or the procession itself, an early Mattins service, or even the installation of a new grotesque commissioned to adorn the outer wall of the Chapel, the variety of activities has never ceased to impress. My year here also coincided with the Queen's 80th birthday celebrations, for which the Chapel community again sprang into action to create an exceptional service to mark the importance of the Sovereign having attained such a year.

In contrast, I have enjoyed and witnessed much quieter moments of prayer and contemplation, and have sat in the wonderful silence of the Chapel, both day and night. I have observed seminars taken by a colourful range of people from far and wide during St George's House consultations, and have photographed Chapter at work during its monthly meetings. I have sat in on the most wonderful rehearsals by the choir of St George's and by visiting orchestras, including a unique and moving concert for the three Abrahamic faiths. I have climbed to the top of the organ loft to photograph some of the four thousand pipes that comprise the mighty organ, returning to the console covered in dust; and hung on to ropes while ascending the narrowest of ladders in the belfry to photograph the innards of the clock tower and the medieval timber-framed bell-tower with its eight enormous bells.

I have scanned the height of the west window while balanced on the platform of a cherry picker, photographing details of kings, popes, saints and princes depicted in the stained glass. Exposed to the elements, one gloriously sunny day I donned protective head- and foot-gear and climbed seven storeys of scaffolding on the west front of the Chapel. Down below the guard was changing, looking as small as tin soldiers from that height. As the band played tunes from popular musicals there was much humming and foot tapping high up on the scaffolding.

I have been alone in the dungeon, with its dark corners and cobwebs, and photographed graffiti of the condemned who scratched their initials and year of captivity into the stone as they awaited their fate; and descended through the trap door in the Curfew Tower and down the first few steps of the sallyport, not daring to venture any further as it heads off below street level into darkness.

Throughout these adventures exploring the length and breadth of the Chapel and its vicinity, while attempting to capture both grand features and minute detail, I have remained humbled by its historic associations. As the College of St George and the Order of the Garter prepare to celebrate their 660th anniversary in 2008, my work in the Chapel seems like a mere snapshot of its extended life. The Chapel embodies a deep sense of this nation's history and there never ceases to be more to uncover.

The editing of images during the preparation of this book has been a difficult and arduous task, as editing from a wide choice of images always is. The total of films used for this body of work numbers almost two hundred and many images offering fine details of life at the Chapel remain unrepresented here. During the editorial process the difficulty of finding a single image that might adequately capture what the Chapel is, does, or represents, became obvious. St George's Chapel is incredibly rich in historic texture, performing so many different daily functions: the relationship between the Royal Family, the Church, the military and the general public is one with many facets – both historical and contemporary.

The annual Garter Service is a celebration of this historic relationship and is dressed up in great splendour. It was during a less obvious service, however, that the subtlety of this dynamic between Royalty, the Church, the military and the public came into photographic view: a

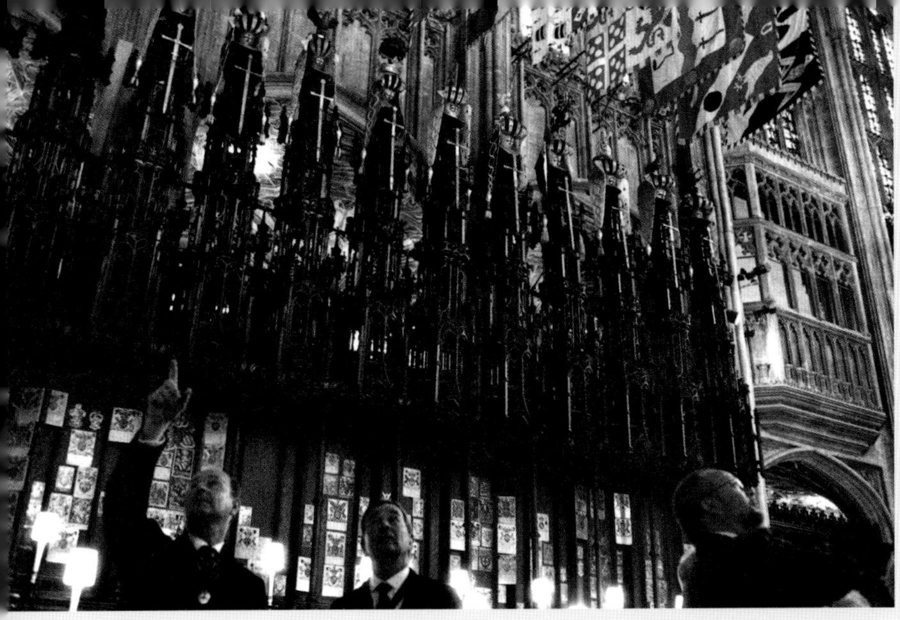

Service of Thanksgiving for the disbanding of a regiment. Within one corner of the frame there is a prominent member of the Royal Family in attendance, the Dean preparing his blessing, the soldiers handing over their colours and the nave packed with members of the public. It was, like all other services, rehearsed with absolute precision and there was a calm and contemplative element to it as the regiment entered the Chapel via the west doors, silhouetted against the outside light. This service, commemorating the disbandment and further amalgamation of some of the army's regiments, seemed to give a contemporary realisation of this unique dynamic of military, Church, Royalty and public at St George's Chapel.

It is hoped that the range of work presented here, divided into seven themes – architecture, history and tradition, festivities, music, military, foundations and daily life – will offer the reader an intimate insight into the life and daily activities of St George's Chapel, and that the fascinating dynamic of tradition and contemporary life as played out through all the functions of the Chapel will be revealed.

St George's Chapel is part of the College of St George and is also known as The Queen's Free Chapel of St George: 'Free' in the sense that the Chapel is a Royal Peculiar coming under the direct authority of the Queen, rather than any of the Church of England's normal structures. Its governing body, the Dean and Canons of Windsor, known collectively as Chapter, is the freehold owner of the Chapel and associated buildings.

The Chapel is not actually a Chapel Royal (in England this term may be applied to those in St James's Palace, Hampton Court Palace and the Tower of London), nor is it the property of the Royal Family, Church of England or the State, but it is a place of worship for the Sovereign and Royal Family, the setting for Royal and State occasions and the Chapel of the Order of the Garter. It is also the burial-place for members of the Royal Family and the final resting-place for ten royal sovereigns, including Henry VIII, Charles I and George VI.

The College of St George was founded under Edward III in 1348 as the spiritual element of the Order of the Garter and as a self-governing community of priests and laymen dedicated to daily prayer for the Sovereign and all the faithful. The term 'College' is used to denote the group of clergy and laity who live and work together as a community at St George's. The Dean and Canons of Windsor govern and are entirely responsible for the College.

The Order of the Garter, also founded in 1348, is both the highest order of chivalry in the gift of the Sovereign and the oldest surviving in the world. The Order consists of the Sovereign, the Prince of Wales, and twenty-four Knights Companion. In addition to the Knights Companion there are now British Royal Knights, Stranger Knights (sovereigns of other countries) and Ladies of the Order (HM The Queen appointed the first Lady Companion

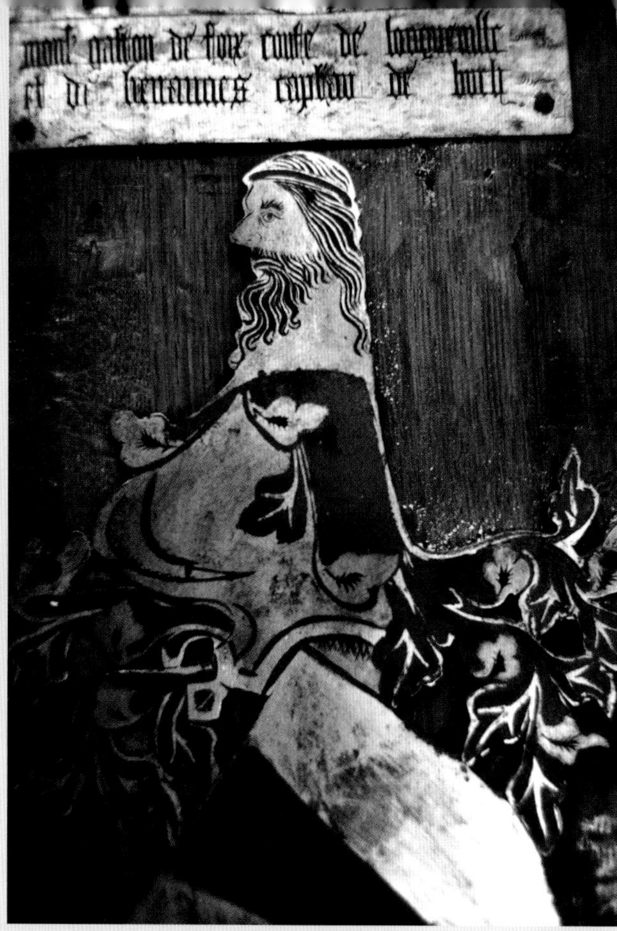

in 1990). Knights were initially drawn exclusively from the fighting nobility close to the king; today, in addition to distinguished former Service personnel, the Knights are chosen from a wider circle of public life, including law, politics and business.

The Sovereign and each Knight Companion has a dedicated stall in the quire of the Chapel, above which is placed a banner, a helm with a crest on top, a part-drawn sword and mantling down either side of the helm. Ladies of the Order each have a banner and a crown or a coronet. Every Knight, but not the Sovereign, has a stallplate, written in Norman French, that remains in place in the Chapel after death. Since 1348 there have been almost a thousand Knights of the Order of the Garter: some seven hundred stallplates remain.

St George's Chapel is a wonderful building that has a special atmosphere of light, height and stillness. It houses an incredible combination of medieval architecture, craftsmanship, heraldry and history. It is essentially a place of worship and still hosts at least three services a day. The Chapel and its surrounding buildings physically make up about one quarter of the area of Windsor Castle. The origins of the first chapel at Windsor date back to the mid-thirteenth century under King Henry III; surviving stonework was later incorporated into what is now the Albert Memorial Chapel on the east side.

The present Chapel buildings were begun in 1475 under King Edward IV as the dedicated Chapel for the Order of the Garter. Edward chose it as his burial-place and now lies with his wife in the north-east corner of St George's. The design of the building, with its large windows and tall pillars, is a magnificent example of Perpendicular architecture. Construction continued under Henry VII, including the vaulting of the nave and the quire. In all it took fifty-three years to complete, by which time Henry VIII was king. His coat of arms is directly above the organ loft and his burial-place is in the centre of the quire.

Refurbishment and changes have been made to the Chapel over the centuries, including those commissioned after the Restoration of Charles II under the direction of Christopher Wren, the architect of St Paul's Cathedral and himself the son of a Dean of Windsor. More recently, King George V oversaw major restoration work in the 1920s and it was George VI who reinstated the annual Thanksgiving Service for the Order of the Garter in 1948.

For almost two centuries the Sovereign and Knights of the Garter met every year at Windsor Castle, usually at St George's-tide in April, for a festival that lasted for three days. They gathered in Chapter, feasted in St George's Hall and occupied their stalls in St George's Chapel for Mattins, the Eucharist, Evensong and a Requiem for departed Knights. From 1674 services were held less frequently, while after 1805, and throughout the remainder of the nineteenth century, the activities of the Order were restricted to Chapter meetings for investitures and elections, which were normally held in London.

In 1948 King George VI commanded the Knights of the Garter to assemble once again at Windsor Castle for a Chapter meeting, to process through the Castle and to attend a Thanksgiving Service in St George's Chapel. Since that year a Garter Day of this type has been regularly held each June. The procession taken by the Garter Knights from the Upper Ward to the Royal Chapel of St George's is testimony to the long tradition of the Sovereign and the leaders of the nation pledging their allegiance and giving thanks to God for creating, renewing and sustaining the World.

From the eighteenth century to 1946, appointments to the Order of the Garter were made on advice from the government. Today the Order has returned to its original function as a mark of Royal favour; Knights of the Garter are chosen personally by the Sovereign to honour those who have held public office, those who have served the Sovereign personally or who have made a particular contribution to national life.

The first Knight of the Garter to be installed was Edward III's eldest son, Edward, Prince of Wales, also known as the Black Prince, around 1348. HM The Queen, who is the thirtieth sovereign since the creation of the Order, has installed almost ninety Knights since 1953. These included some of the most prominent figures from British public life in recent years and many foreign Royals. No fewer than six British Prime Ministers have been among their number – Winston Churchill, Clement Attlee, Anthony Eden, Edward Heath, Harold Wilson and James Callaghan – while Baroness Thatcher was installed as a Lady Companion in 1995. HRH Prince Philip is a Royal

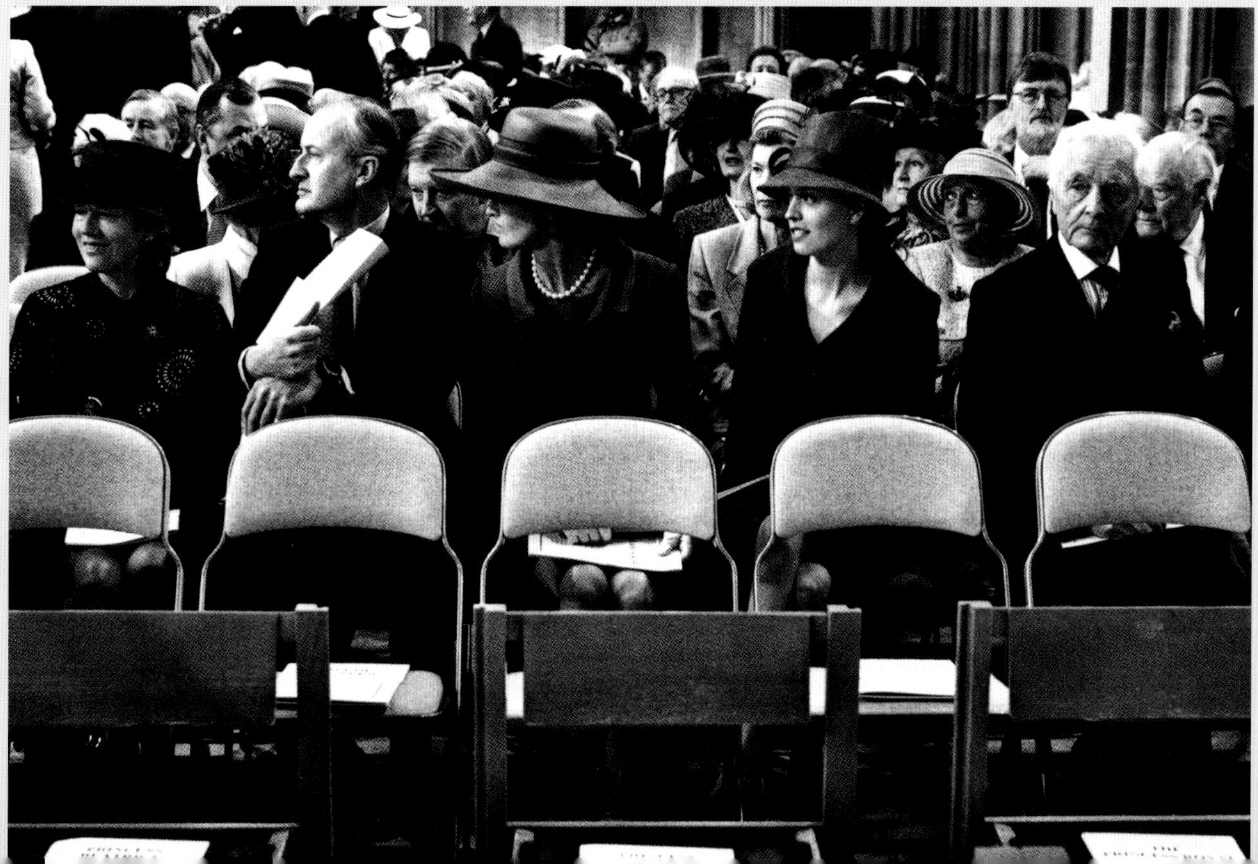

Knight; King Juan Carlos of Spain, King Carl Gustaf of Sweden and King Harald V of Norway became extra Knights Companion, and His Imperial Majesty Emperor Akihito of Japan was made a Garter Knight in 1998.

Another great celebration at the Chapel is that of the Royal Victorian Order. This was instituted in 1896 as an Order entirely within the gift of Queen Victoria to enable her to acknowledge and reward outstanding services to her personally. As the personal gift of the sovereign, admittance to the Order has always been held in high respect. The Chapel of the Royal Victorian Order is the Savoy Chapel in London, but every fourth year a Service of Praise, Remembrance and Dedication is held in St George's, at which members of the Royal Family, Knights and Dames Grand Cross and the Officers of the Order process through the Chapel.

Worship is at the heart of the College of St George: the College's ancient statutes require that it should 'wait eternally upon the Lord'. Through the centuries Sovereigns, Knights, visitors and pilgrims have worshipped at St George's Chapel and this worship forms the spiritual centre of the Castle and its community. The great festivals of Easter, Whitsun and Christmas bring the community of St George's together in celebrations that may last over days and be attended by HM The Queen and members of the Royal Family as well as being open to the public. The atmosphere of the Chapel is almost transformed for these celebrations, especially during the services for Maundy Thursday that merge into the night vigil before Good Friday in one of the smaller chapels, and the Midnight Service of the First Eucharist of Christmas on Christmas Eve. Whitsun (Pentecost) also offers an unusual insight into the Chapel since the current Dean of Windsor, the Right Reverend David Conner, administers the Sacrament of Confirmation at the main service that day as he has been a Bishop in his own right since 1994.

As part of the original College of St George, Edward III established a community of twenty-six impoverished

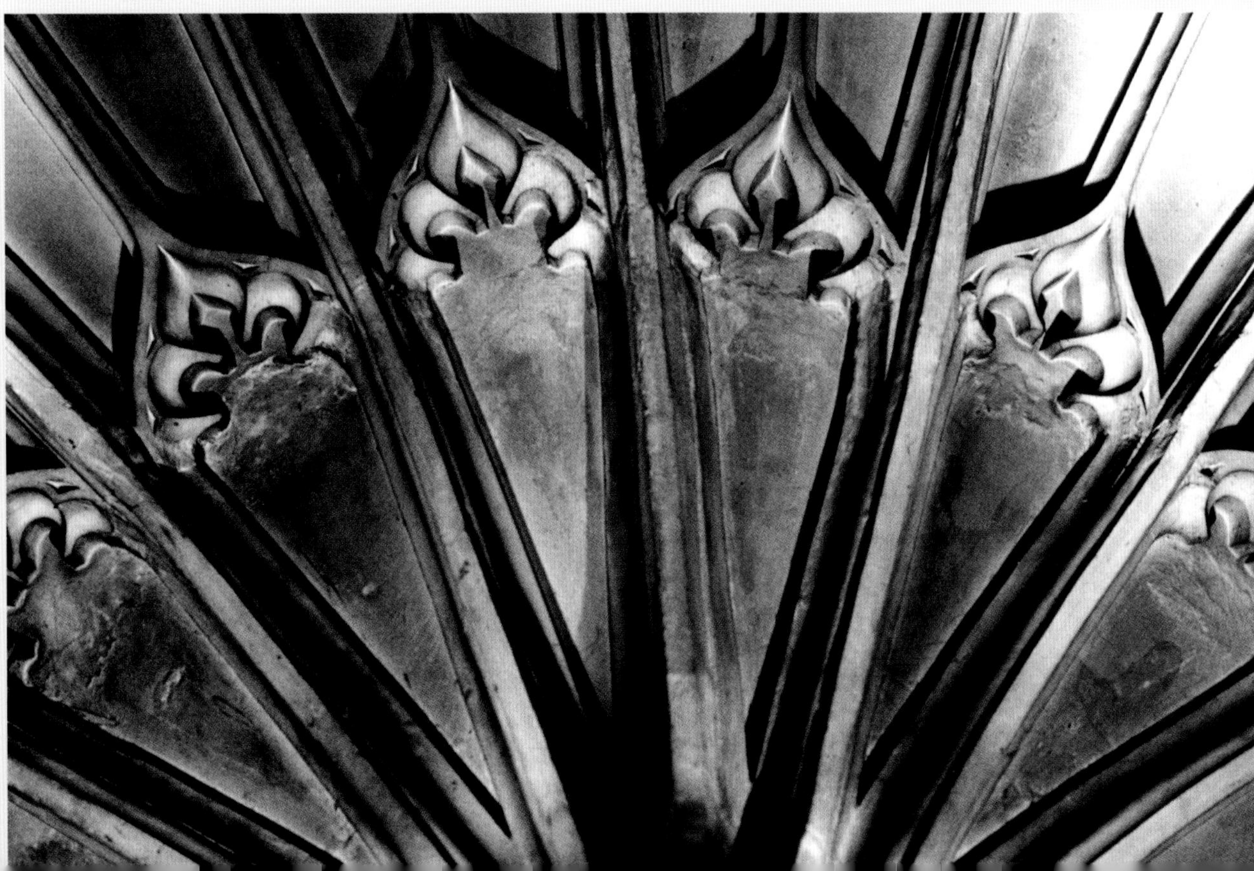

military veterans, known as 'Poor Knights', who were required to pray daily for the Sovereign and the Knights of the Garter during life and also for their souls after death. In return the Poor Knights received maintenance and lodgings in Windsor Castle. Their number was reduced to thirteen by Queen Elizabeth I, following the terms of the will of her father, Henry VIII.

During the early years of the nineteenth century these Poor Knights, all retired army officers, objected to being termed 'poor' and petitioned William IV to be allowed to wear the uniform of Unattached Officers and to change their name. This was subsequently changed to Military Knights in 1834, after which the members no longer had to wear the red cloaks of their original 'uniform', but instead were allowed scarlet swallowtail coats, blue trousers and a plumed cocked hat, the uniform that is still worn today. The Military Knights, who comprise a Governor and twelve officers, still live within the Castle community. They attend services weekly and contribute to the life of the Chapel in various ways. For many, Windsor Castle will be their last home.

The choir of St George's Chapel consists of around twenty boy choristers and twelve Lay Clerks singing alto, tenor and bass. The choir was founded at the same time as the founding of the College in 1348 and has sung for the services of the Chapel throughout its history, except during the Commonwealth (1642–60). The choristers attend St George's School in the Castle grounds, which has a total of about 400 boys and girls; and the Lay Clerks live in the Horseshoe Cloister, to the west of the Chapel.

The choir serves the Chapel and sings for its daily services, the Opus Dei, performing a large repertoire of music drawn from all ages and traditions, including works commissioned from composers such as Benjamin Britten, William Harris and Peter Maxwell Davies. The choir sings frequently in the presence of the HM The Queen during special services at the Chapel and gives many public concerts throughout the year. In addition to the choir's work within the Chapel, it has a worldwide reputation gained through public concerts and collaborations with orchestras, and through its recordings.

The origins of the Chapel's organ date back to the seventeenth century. The instrument given by George III and made by Samuel Green in 1790, however, was drastically rebuilt in 1930 and the instrument moved from the centre of the screen to the sides, allowing an uninterrupted view of the roof vault. There were further rebuilds in 1965 and in 2002, when the instrument was dismantled, cleaned and renovated. It comprises some four thousand pipes that range from a few centimetres to almost two metres in length. Above the organ loft it has been necessary to bend some of the pipes in order that they can be accommodated in the available space.

The Chapel and its buildings have been in almost continual use since they were first built in 1348. The spectacular handiwork of the original master craftsmen has endured daily wear and tear. The Chapel has undergone several major alterations through the centuries, most notably that in the late eighteenth century, which included the reordering of the stalls in the quire and the construction of the present fine Coade stone organ screen. Queen Victoria also made some important changes, including the reconstruction of the remains of Henry III's Chapel at the east end to make the Prince Albert Memorial Chapel and the building of the West Steps, which create a ceremonial entrance to the building.

The Fabric Advisory Committee is responsible for assessing the needs and advising on refurbishment projects and is constantly involved with restoration and conservation work throughout the entire building. St George's, for example, recently commissioned the design of new stone grotesques to be installed on the outer wall of the Chapel, resulting in the development of new stonework projects at the London City and Guilds Institute.

St George's is the Chapel of the Order of the Garter and, primarily, a place of daily worship within the College of St George where the general public are welcome to attend services. The Dean and Canons, however, also oversee many different functions and activities, ranging from the care of the building fabric and fundraising, for both projects and revenue, to the many consultations and courses on international and contemporary issues held at St George's House.

St George's Chapel belongs to no diocese, and is not under any provincial authority. As a place of worship it is open to people from across the world as well as to its local community. Its 'international' dimension is reflected in the membership of the Knights of the Garter and the enormous diversity of those who participate in contemporary consultations at St George's House.

The Archives hold deeds, letters, rolls and other manuscripts dating back to the twelfth century. These reveal the history of not only the Chapel, but also of its former properties spread across some thirty counties in England and Wales. The collection includes some of the most remarkable medieval seals and letters in the country, in addition to those of the Kings and Queens, and among its illuminated manuscripts are richly decorated early registers of the Order of the Garter.

Technical details

Photographing in the Chapel has been a technical challenge from the very start. While the Chapel may have an appearance of light, with a generous number of clerestory windows and the pale Taynton stone of the tall pillars, there is very limited ambient light for the camera. Using artificial light has not been an option and so the photography has been pushed to combine fast fixed lenses, slow shutter speeds, high-speed film and overexposures. For those interested in the fine detail, average exposures have been F2.8, F4 or F5.6 at 1/8, 1/15 or 1/30 second at an ISO rating starting from 1600 and ranging to 6400. The films were then further pushed in the darkroom, up a stop or two, by loyal technicians who came to expect difficult exposures.

The photographs have been taken with two Leica R cameras and one Leica M using standard fixed lenses, one with macro functions. The Leica cameras are fully manual, with no inbuilt computer to calculate exposure or focus, and these particular models are old enough to still have a manual film winder. Using these Leica cameras makes the work both slower and more deliberate than perhaps it would be using a modern high-tech film or digital camera, but this tempo of work has suited the subject. The Leicas continually prove themselves the best cameras for capturing the most subtle of exposures and have produced outstanding results even in the worst of lighting conditions at the Chapel. The cameras are also very quiet, and so have allowed photographs to be taken during Services, even during the 'night watch' on Maundy Thursday.

For the preparation of the book, each image was hand printed onto warm-tone multi-grade photographic fibre paper, and these original prints were then scanned to a high resolution; the printing of the book was made to match the tones of the original hand prints.

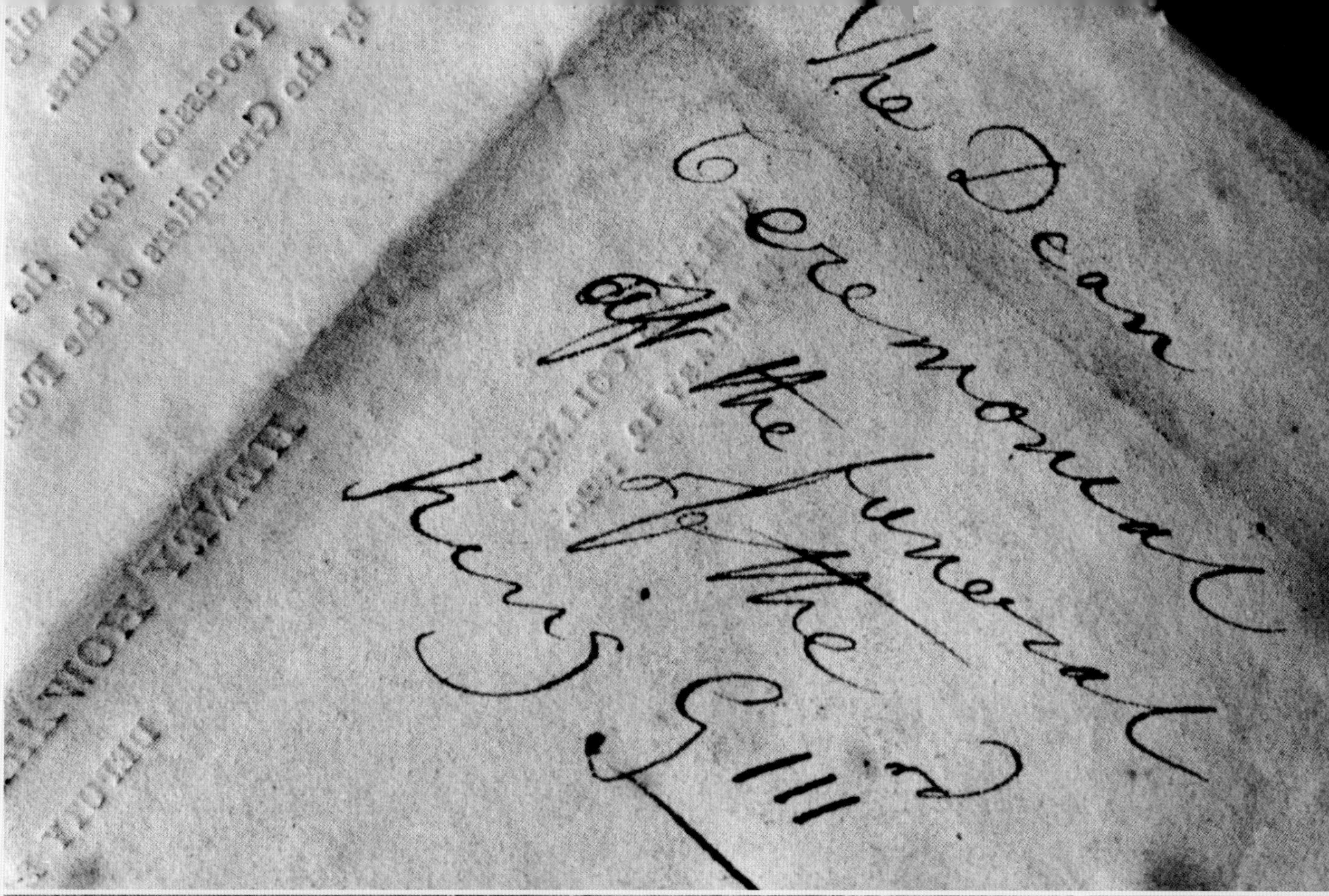
The Dean
Ceremonial
of the funeral
of the
King G III

Ham
Valence

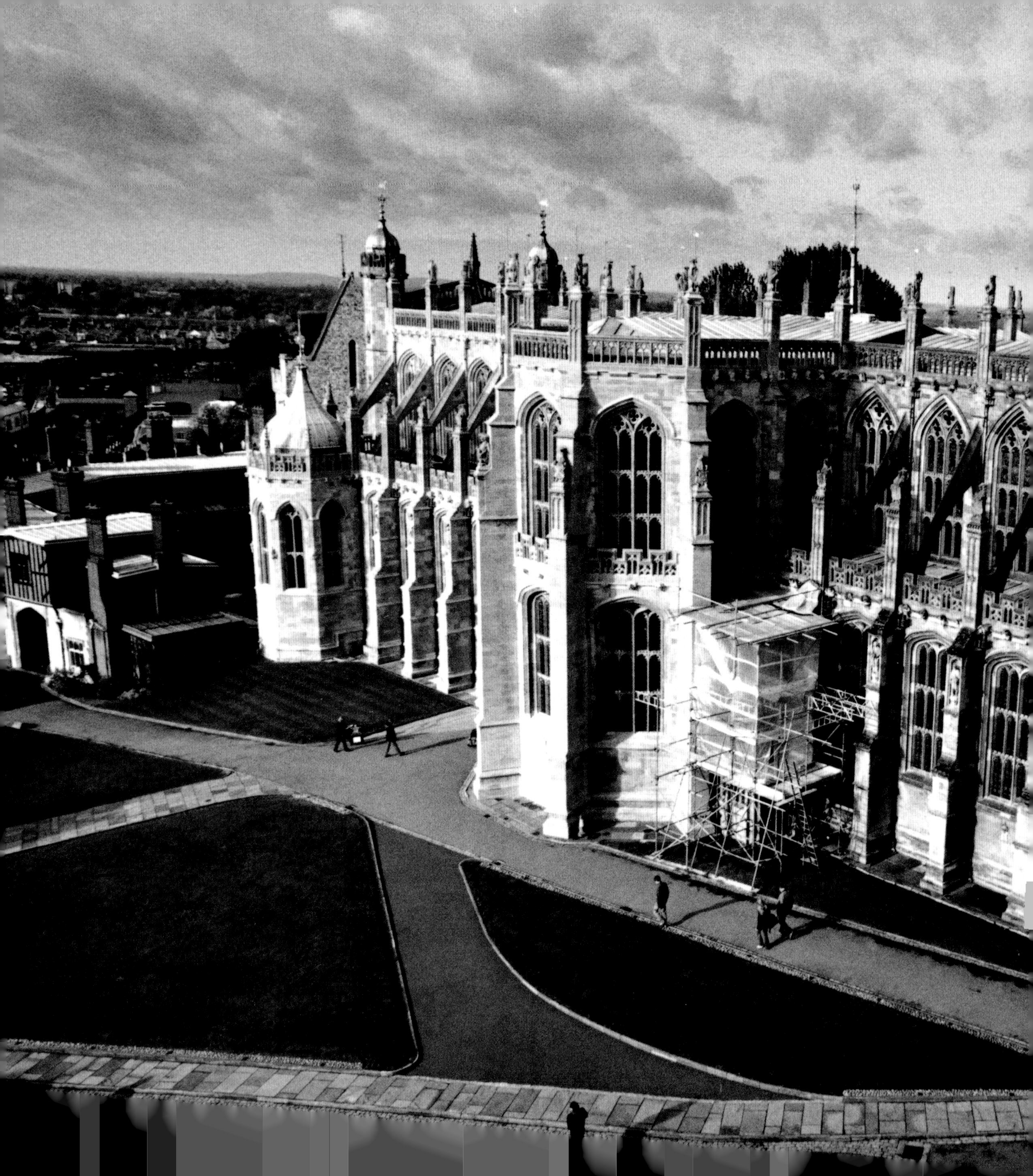

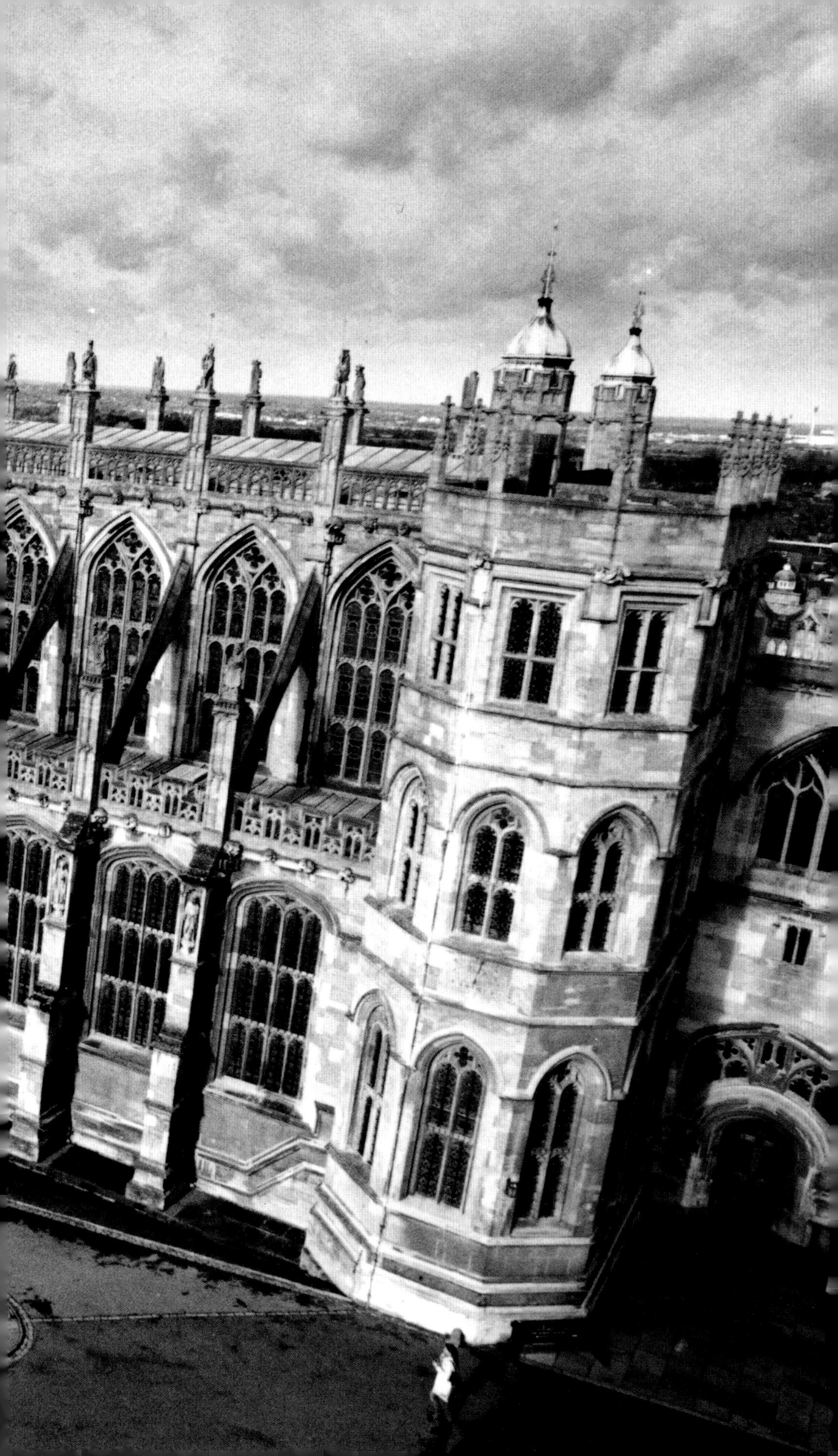

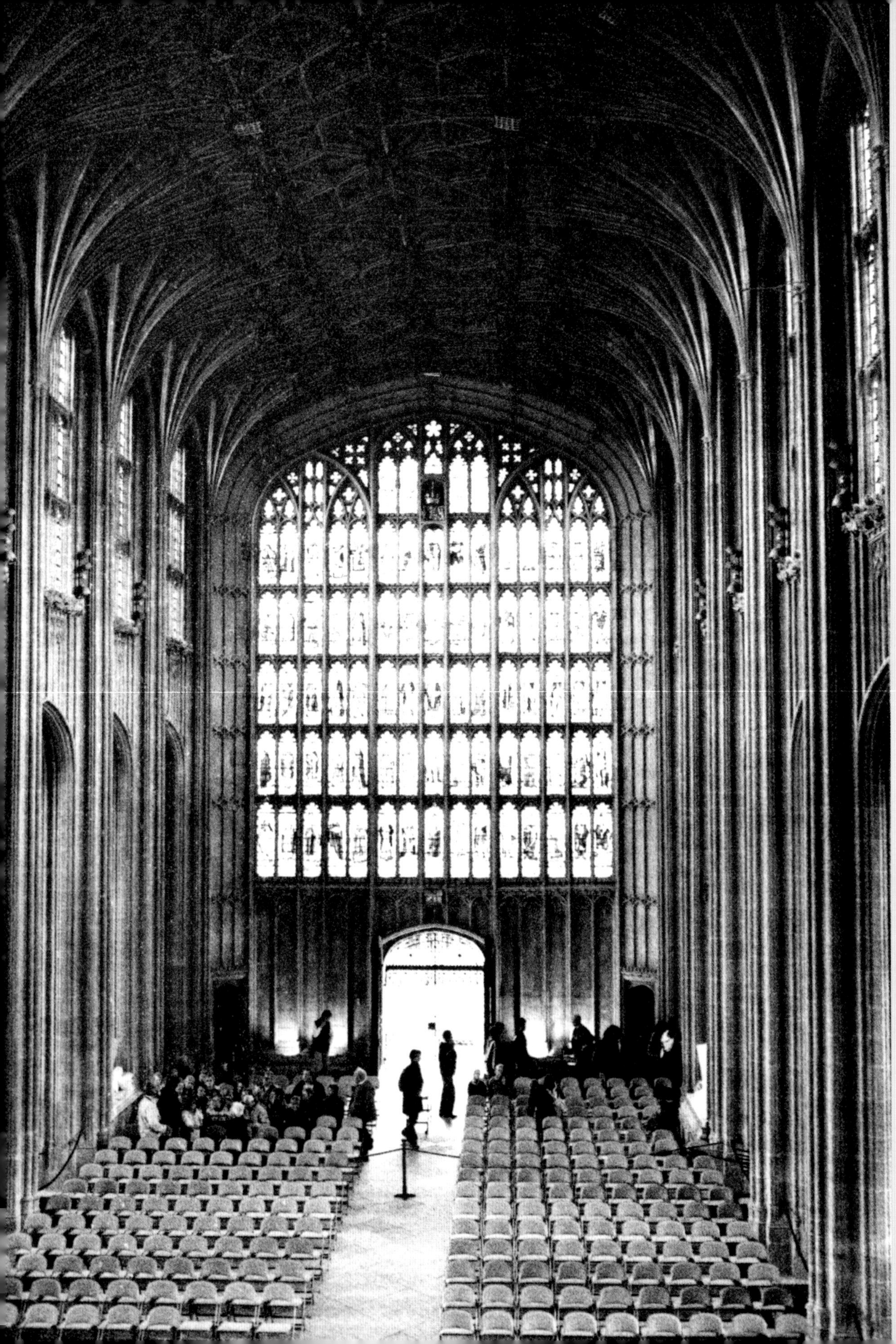

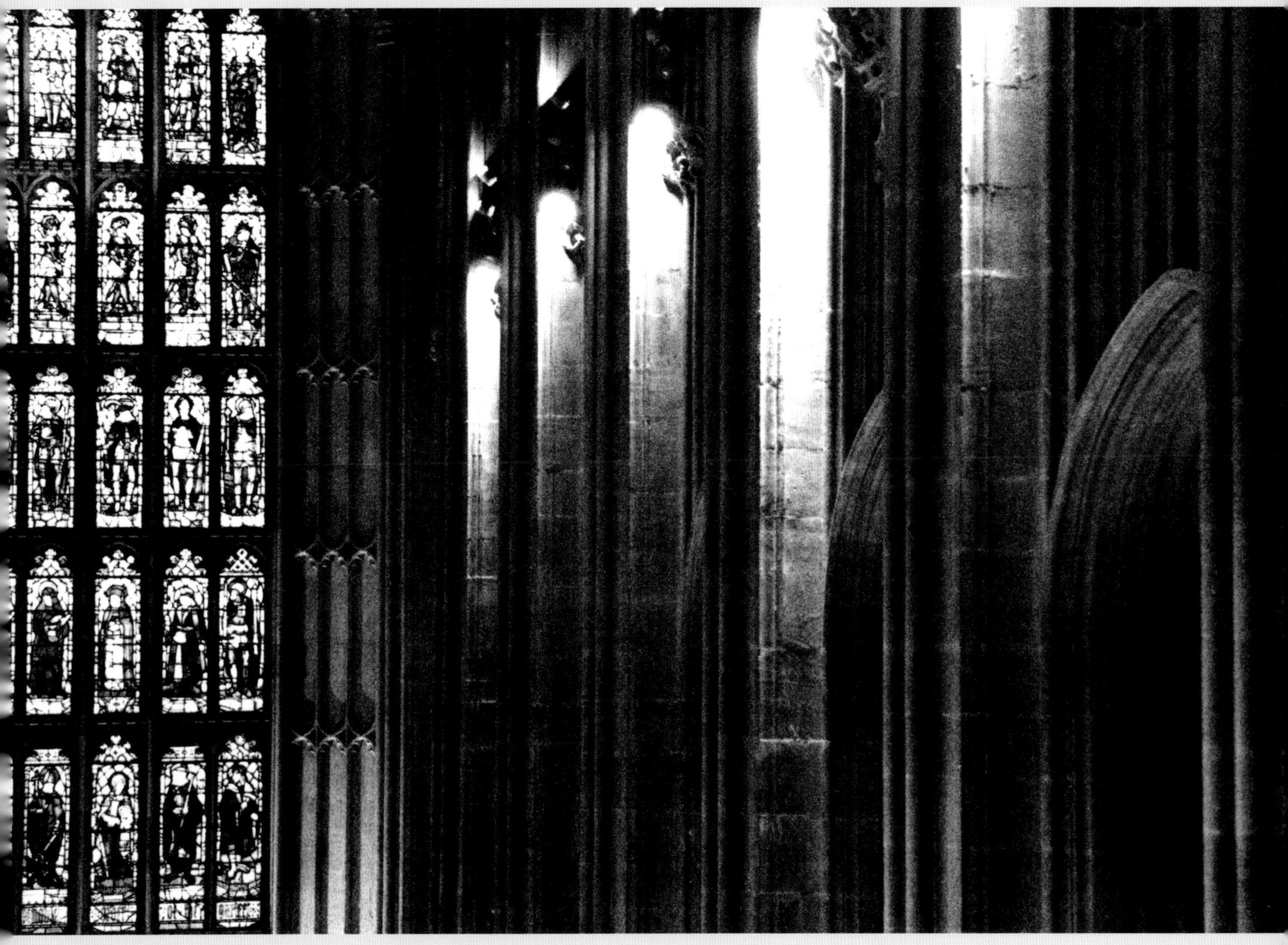

St George's Chapel took over half a century to build (1475 – 1528) and is one of the most remarkable buildings in the late Gothic style to be erected in England.

Preceding pages: St George's Chapel from the south-east.
Left: Long view of the nave and west window.
Above: Detail of the west window and vaulted aisles along the north aisle.

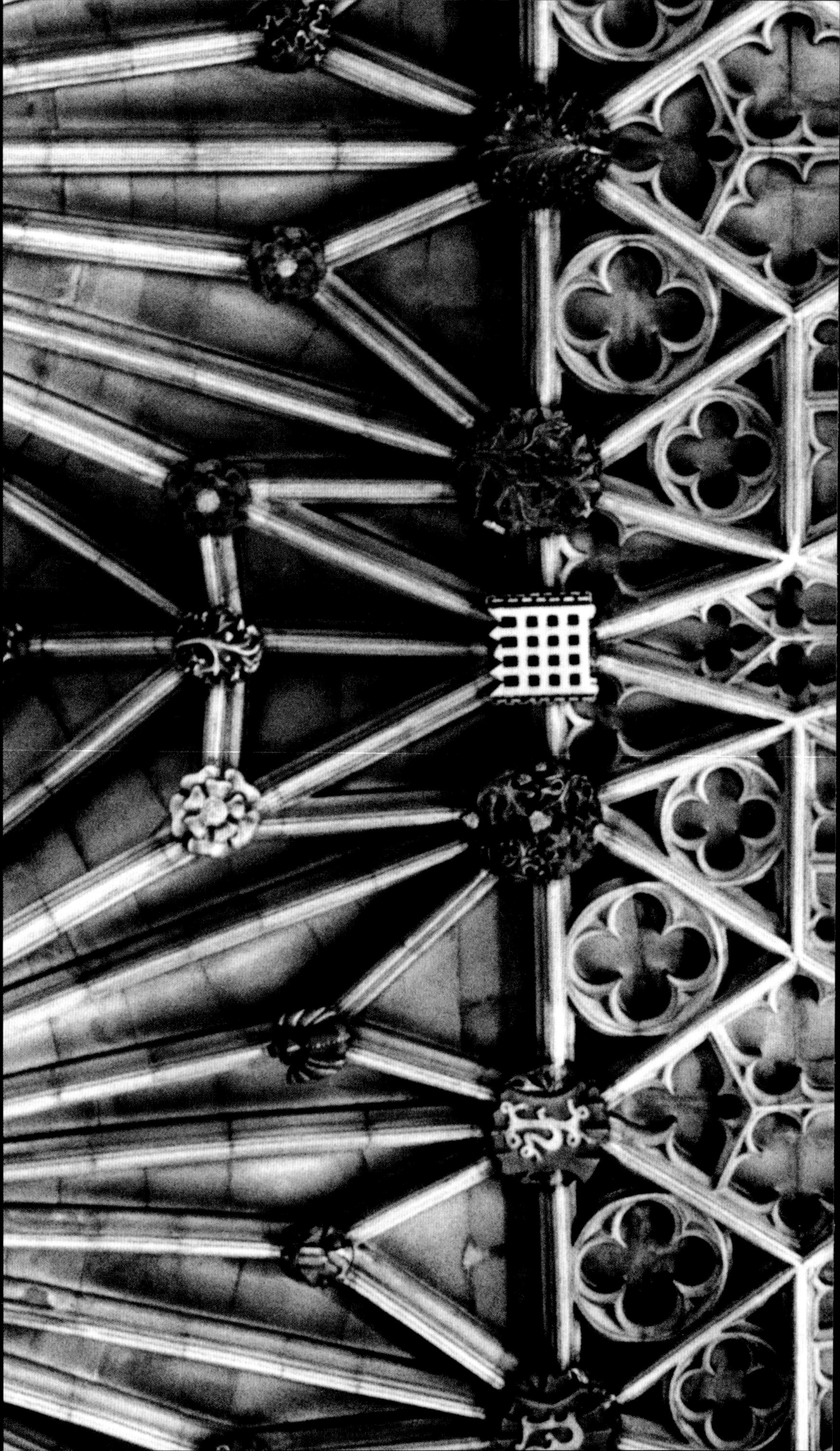

Detail of high vault in the nave showing decorated heraldic bosses. The hempbrake (or bray) badge of Sir Reginald Bray (died 1503) is depicted 175 times throughout the Chapel and can be seen here at the bottom and middle right. Sir Reginald Bray left a large legacy for the completion of the Chapel in the early sixteenth century.

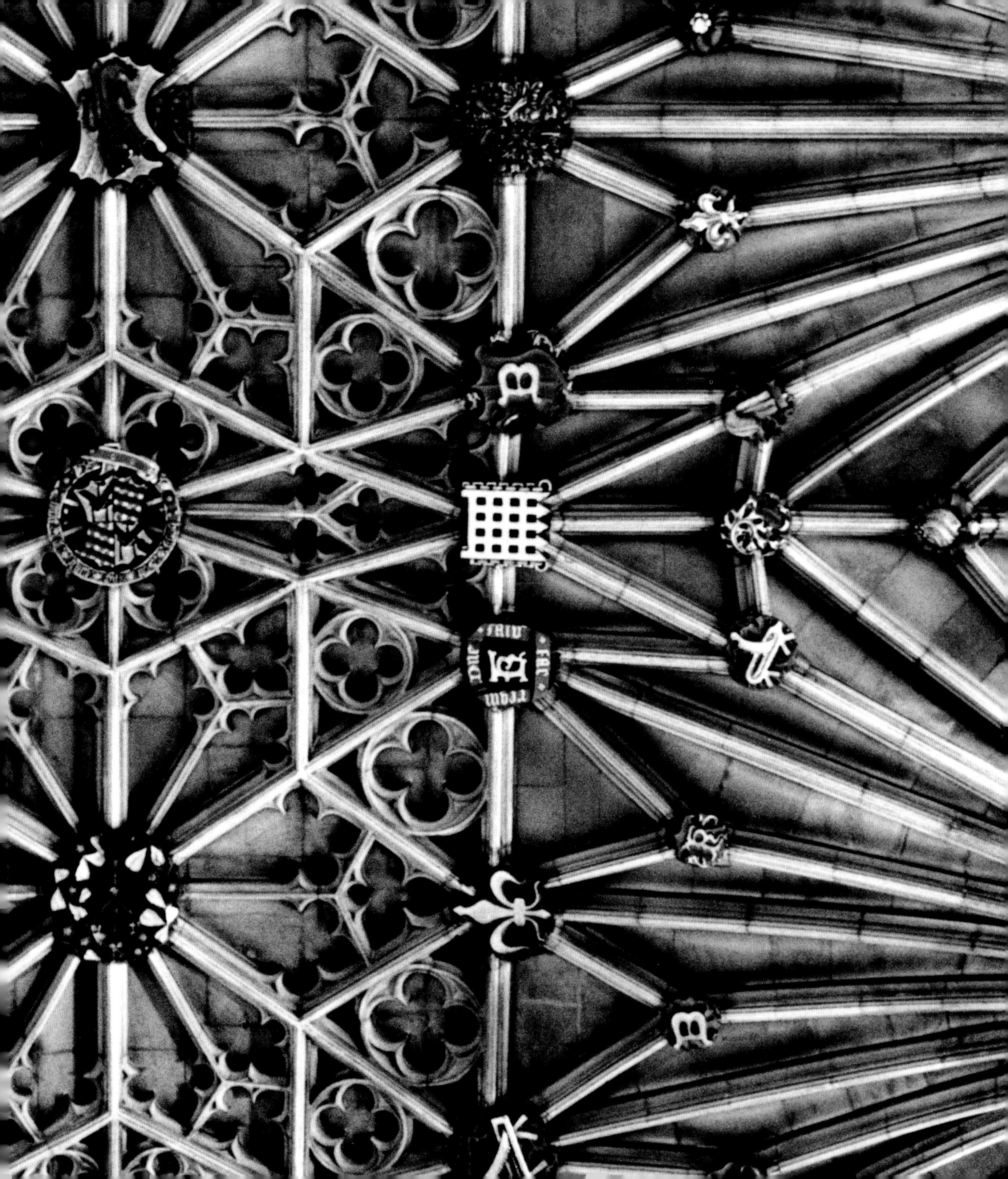

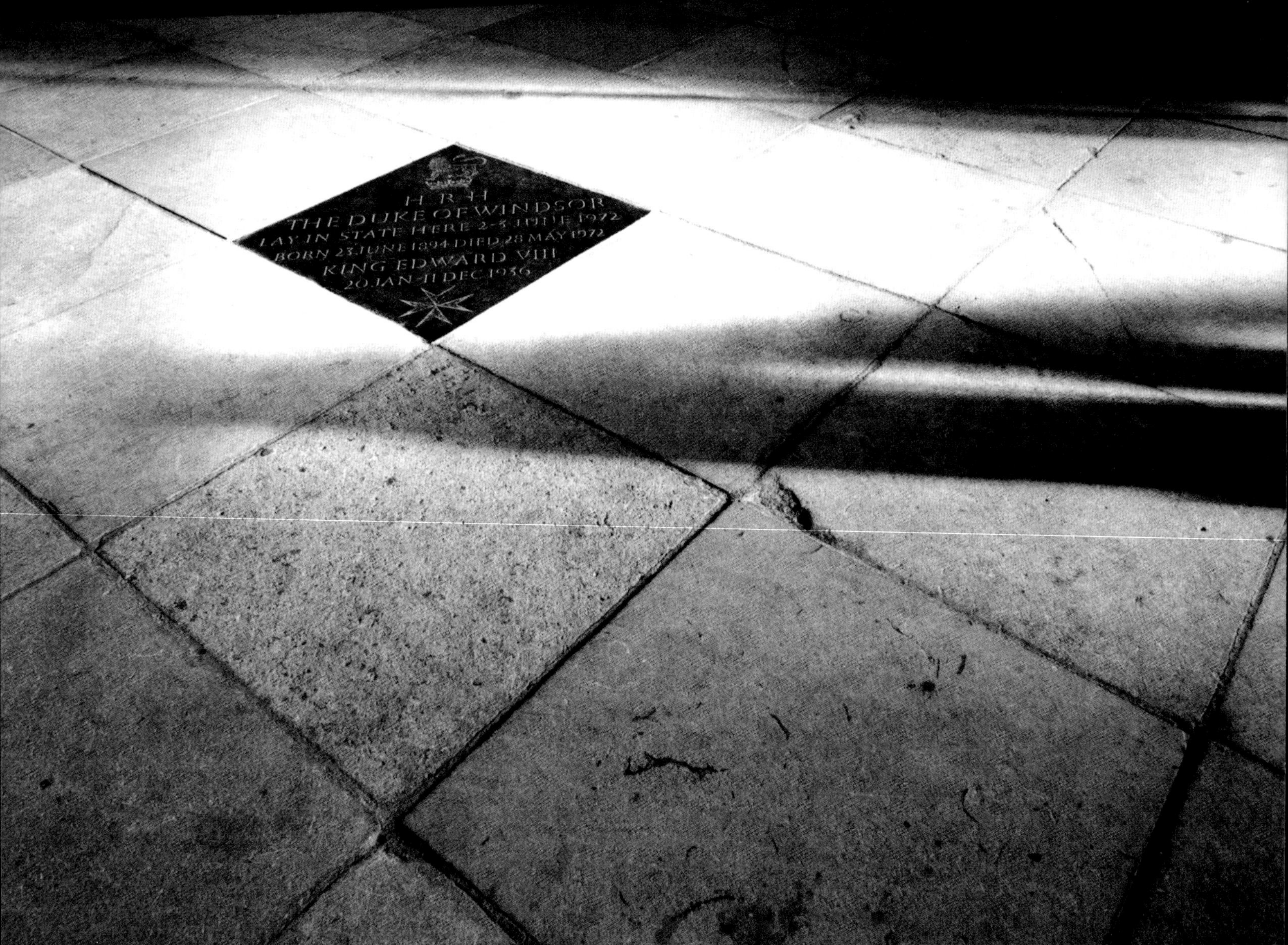

Above: Detail of the inscribed stone in the nave marking the place where the catafalque stood for HRH The Duke of Windsor's lying-in-state, 2-3 June 1972.

Right: Detail of a King. The west window (1509) contains some 75 depictions in stained glass of kings, princes, saints and popes.

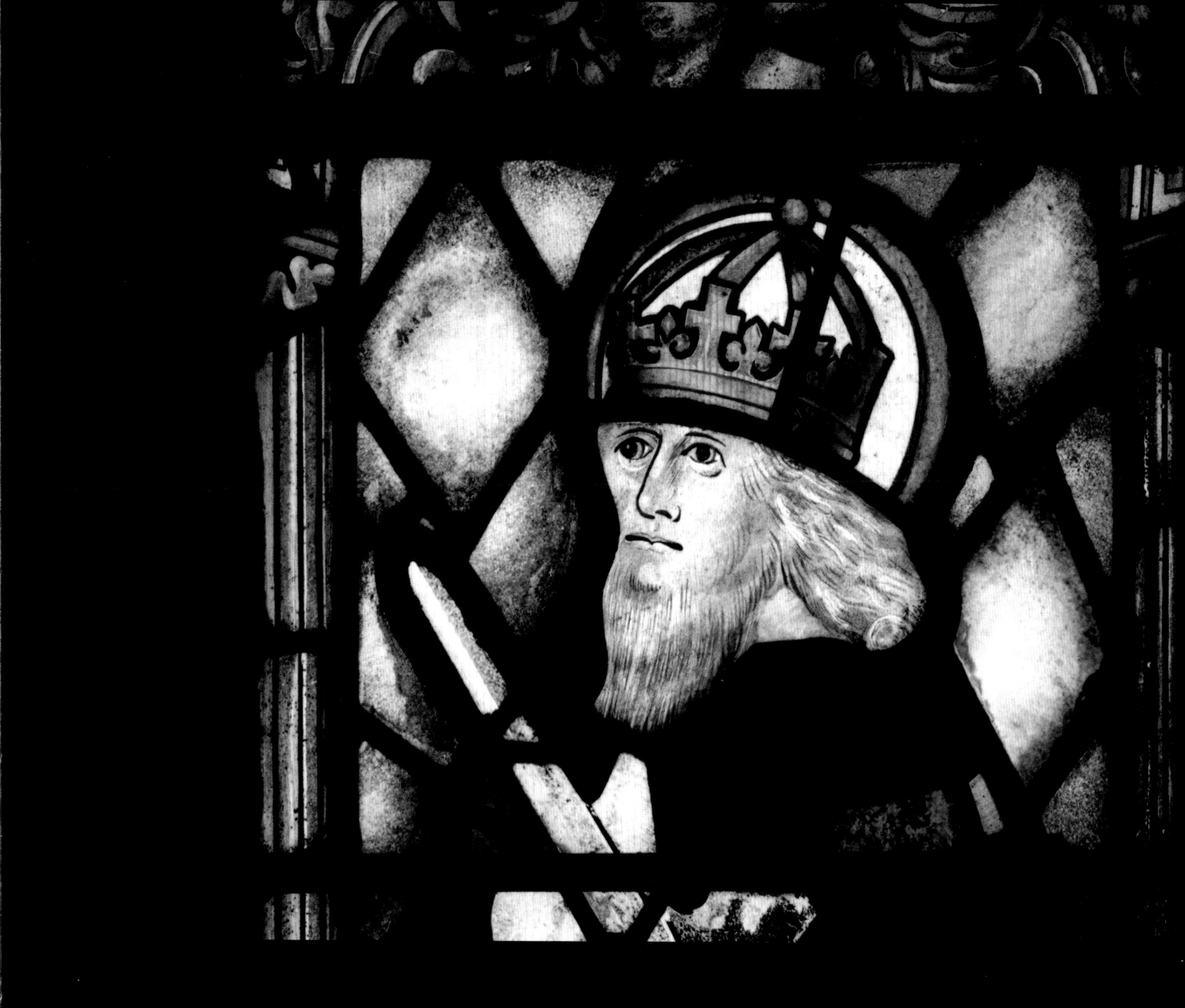

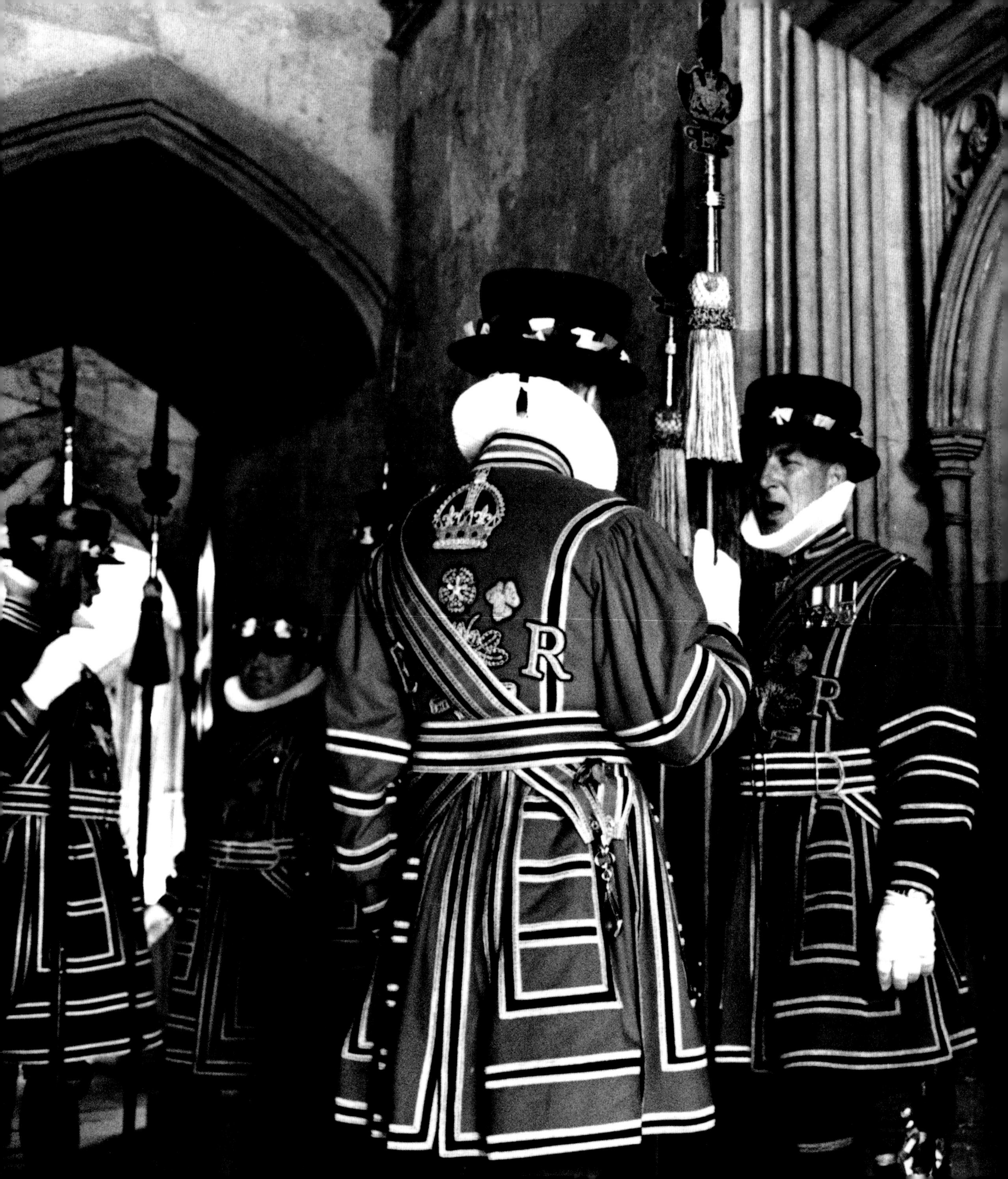

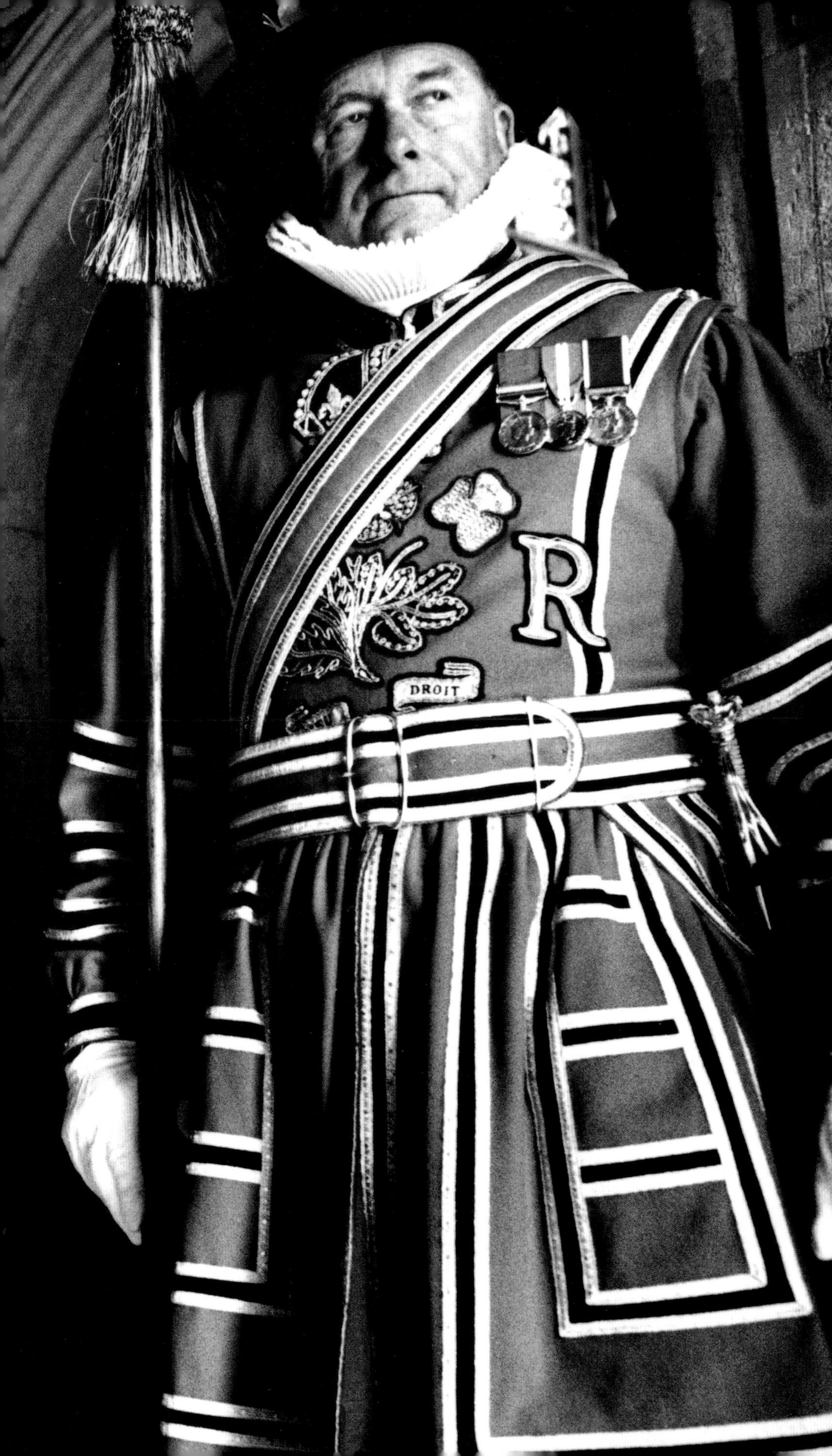

History and Tradition

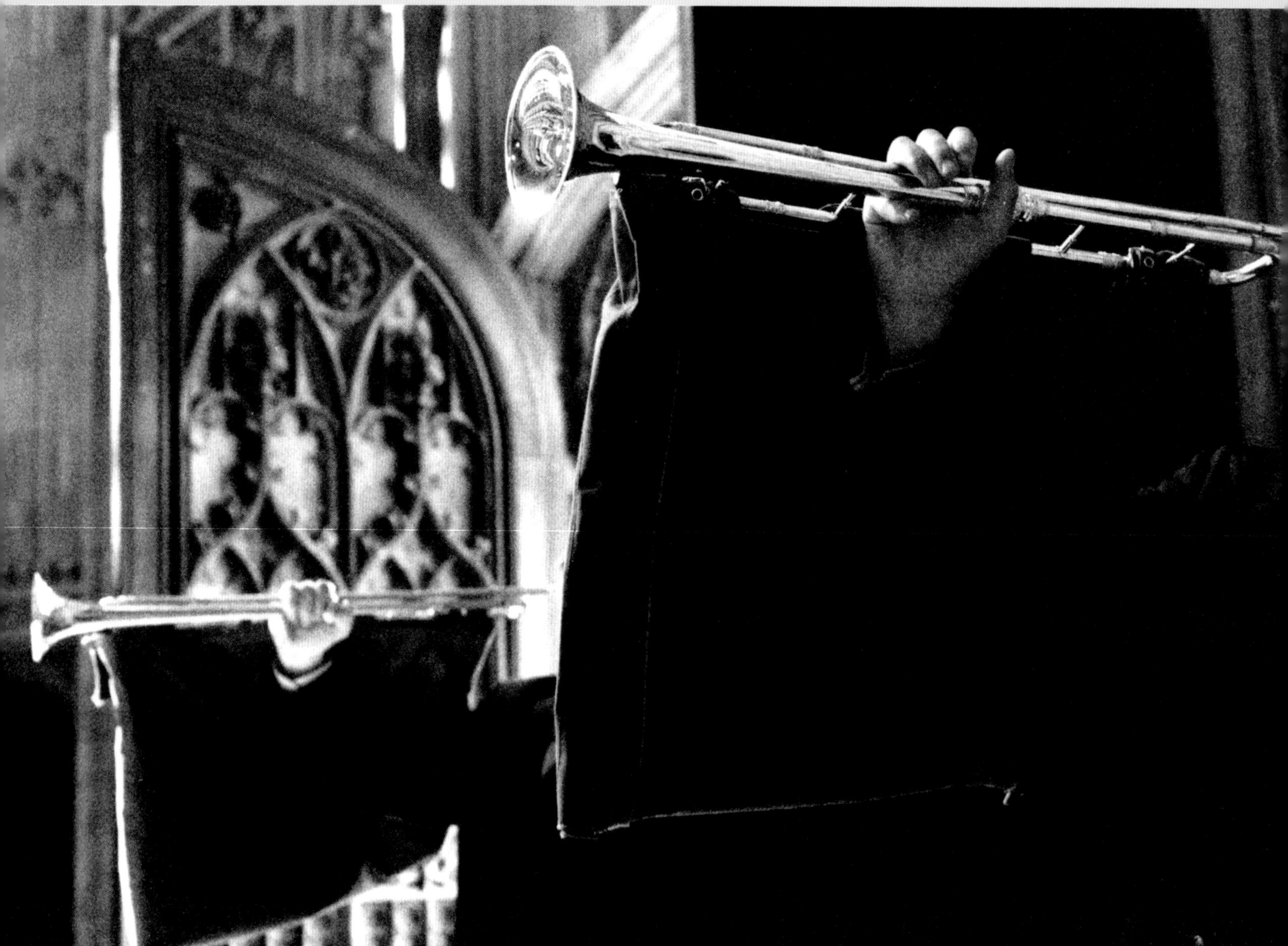

Preceding pages: Members of the Royal Body Guard of the Yeomen of the Guard standing in the Galilee Porch in preparation for the ceremony of the Royal Victorian Order.

Above: Trumpeters in rehearsal for Garter Day standing by the West Door.
Right: Detail of trumpeter's embroidered banner.

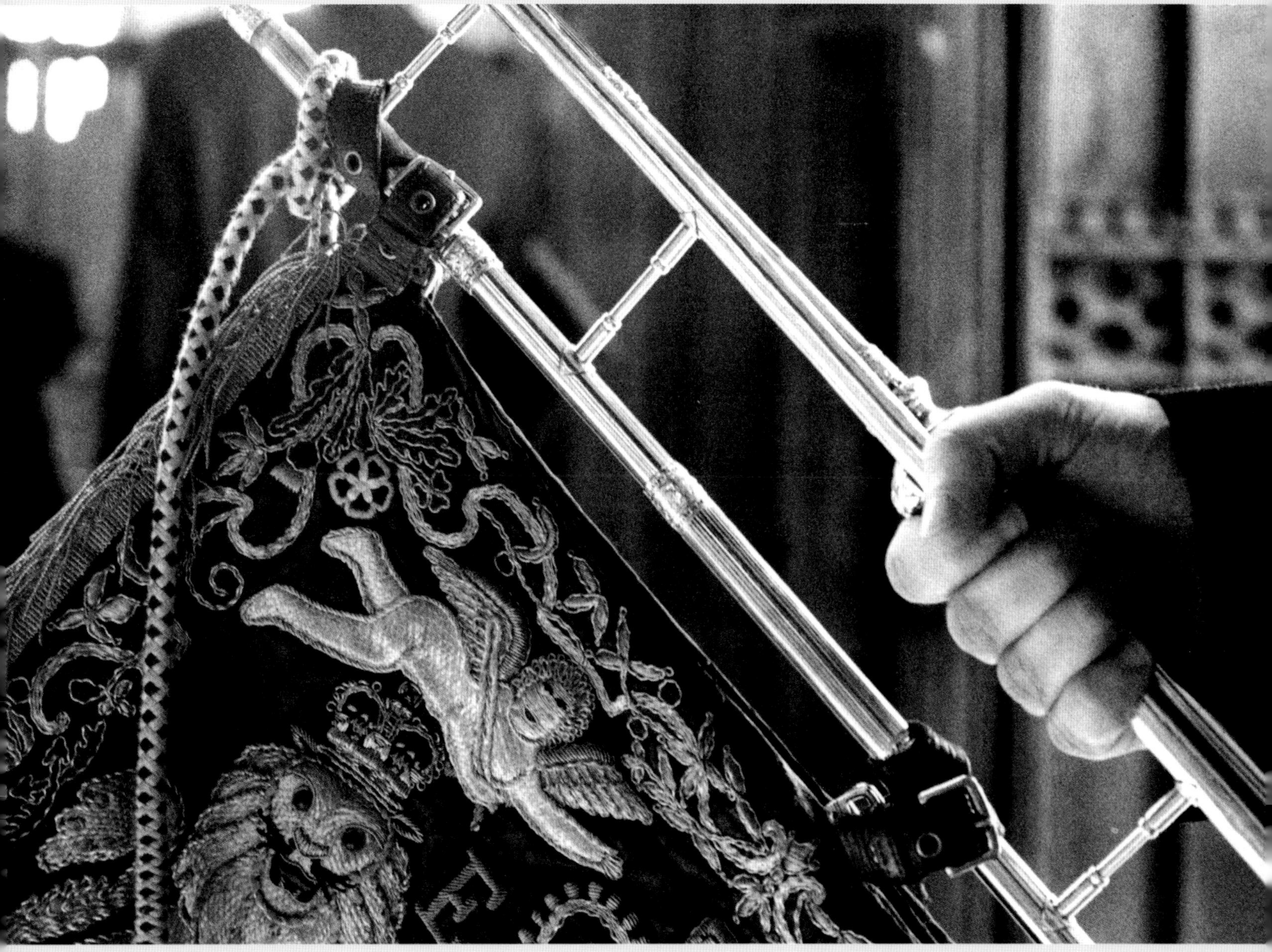

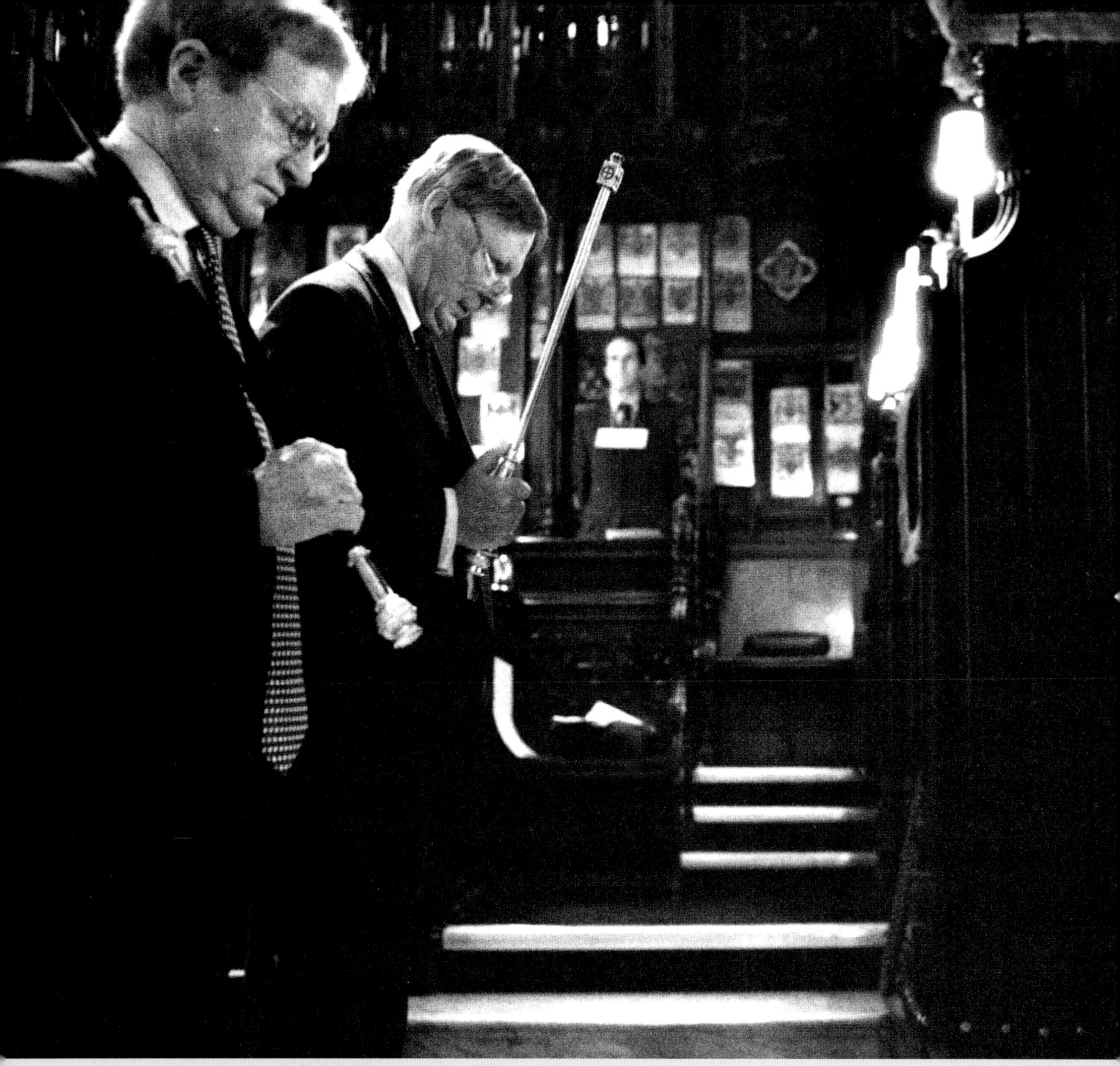

Garter Day: The foundation of the Most Noble Order of the Garter by King Edward III in 1348 served to bring together the Sovereign with twenty-five of the outstanding military leaders of the country. Each year, the Sovereign and Knights came together to feast at Windsor Castle and to occupy their Stalls in St George's Chapel for Mattins, the Eucharist, Evensong and a Requiem for departed Knights. This festival for the Most Noble Order became less frequent during the seventeenth century but was reinstated by King George VI in 1948 to celebrate the six-hundredth anniversary of the Order. Since then, the Thanksgiving Service on Garter Day has been held annually and is a vital expression of the life of the Order.

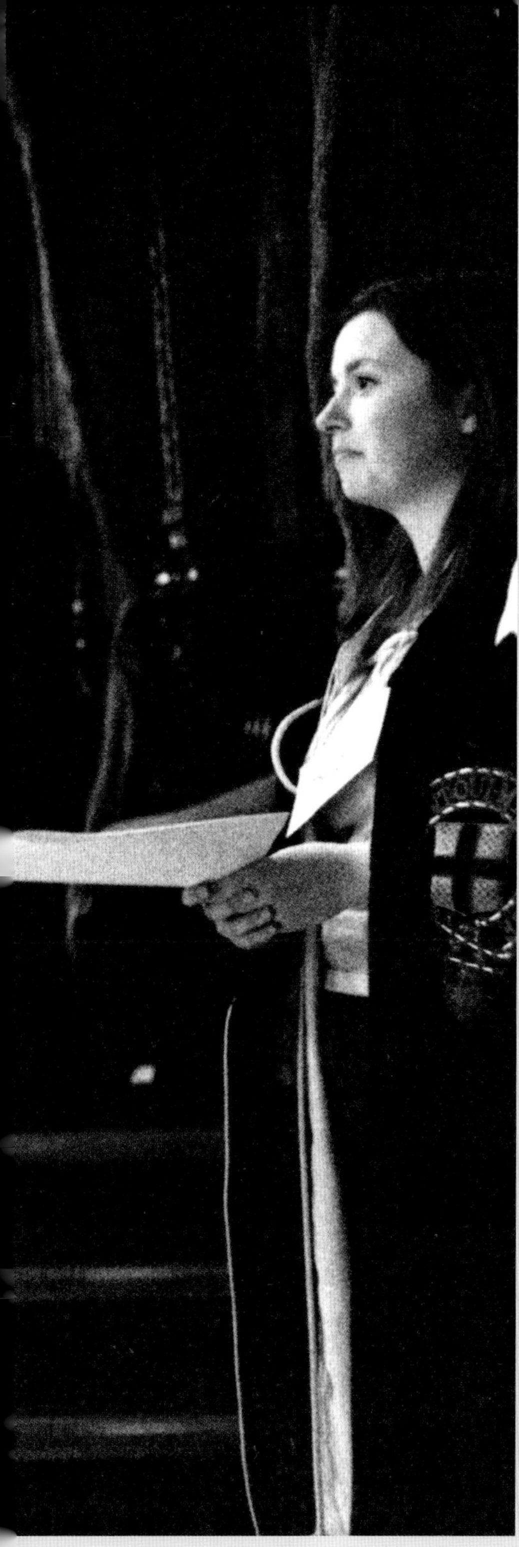

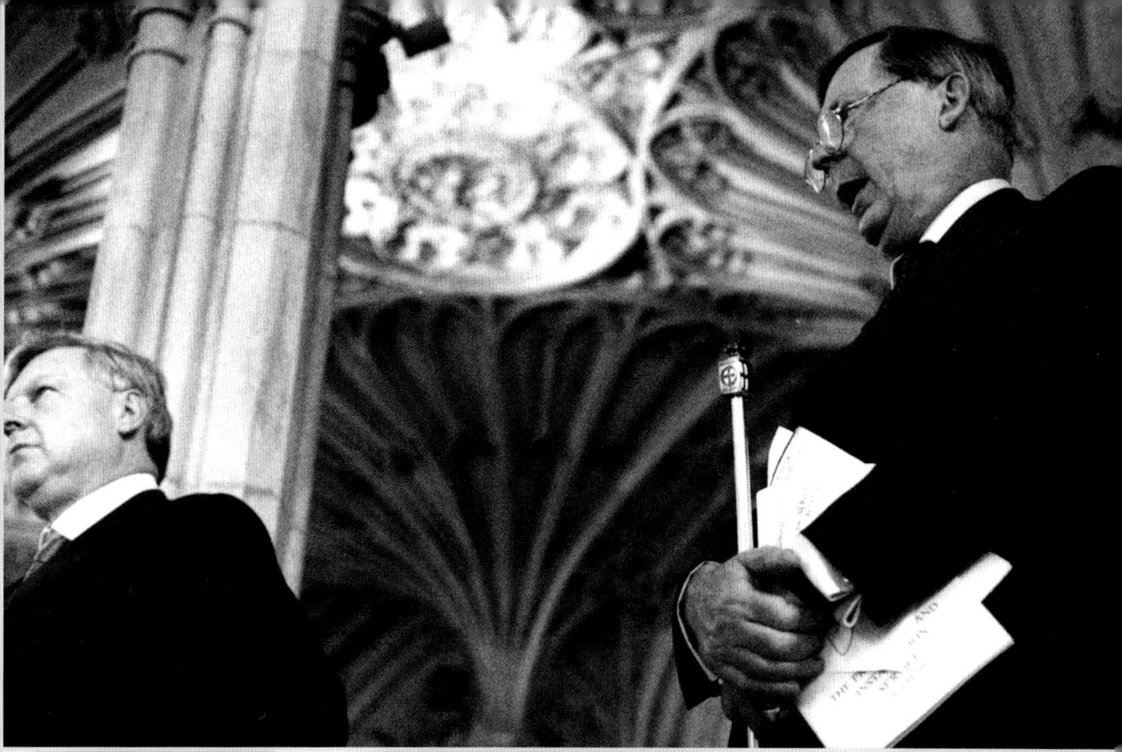

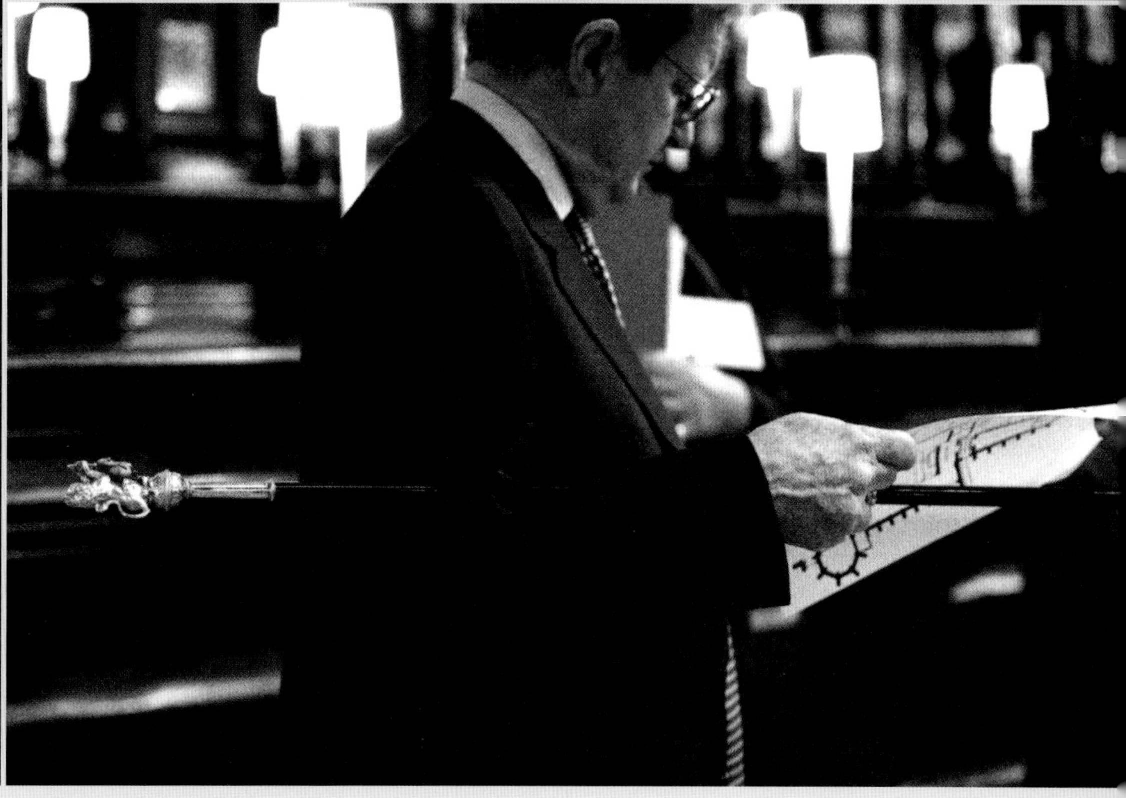

Left: Black Rod, Sir Michael Willcocks, and Garter Principal King of Arms, Peter Gwynn-Jones, bowing to 'the Queen' played by Chessy Russill in rehearsal for the Garter Service, standing by the Sovereign's stall in the quire.

Top Right: Garter giving directions at the beginning of rehearsals in the Nave.

Bottom Right: Black Rod examining the procession plan. Black Rod carries the black rod, which could be used by the Sovereign to demote a Knight by a tap on the shoulder. Black Rod's normal duties are in the House of Lords.

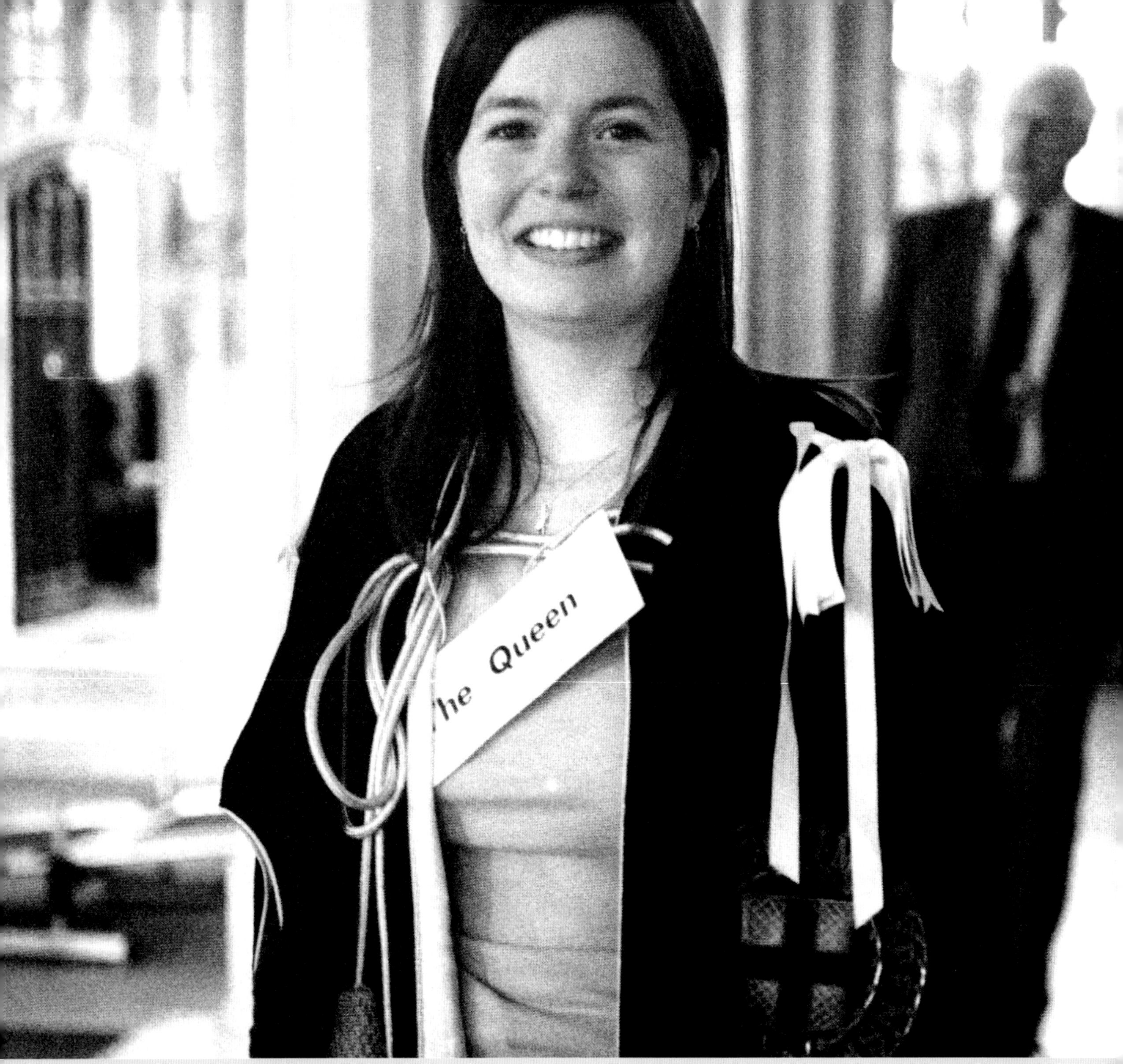

In rehearsal for Garter Day: *Above*: Chessy Russill standing in for 'the Queen' during rehearsals for Garter Day.

Top Right: The Military Knights of Windsor and Heralds processing from the quire through to the nave.
Bottom Right: The Dean and Garter, followed by 'the Queen', processing through the West Door out onto the West Steps.

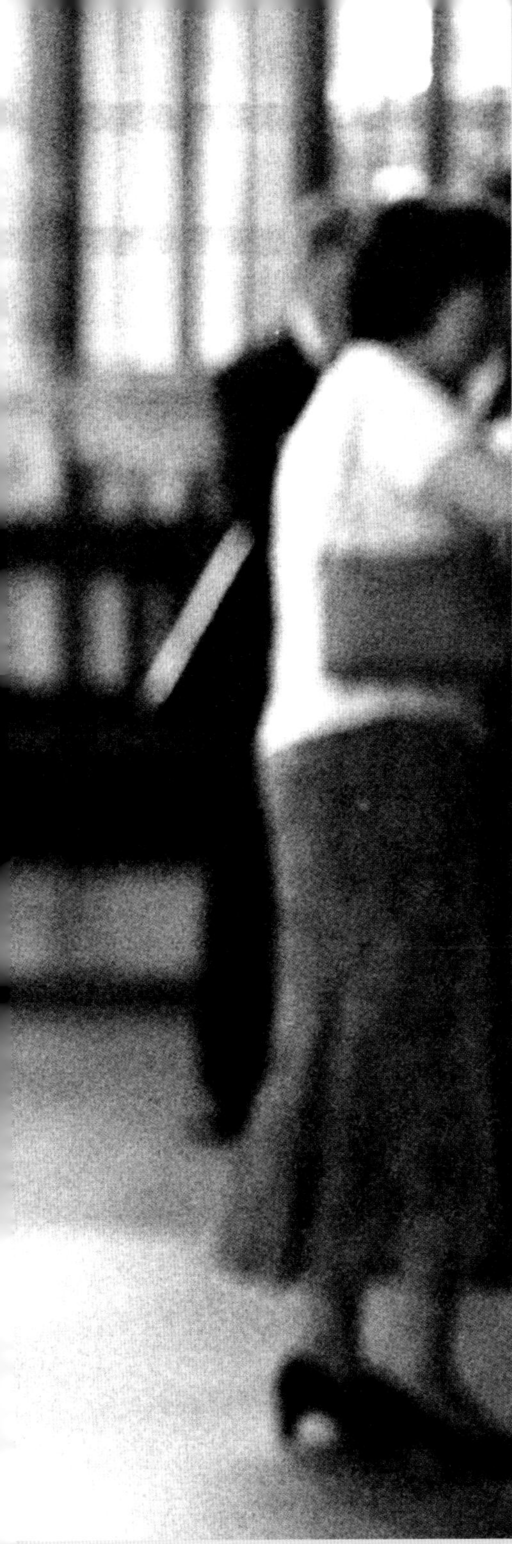

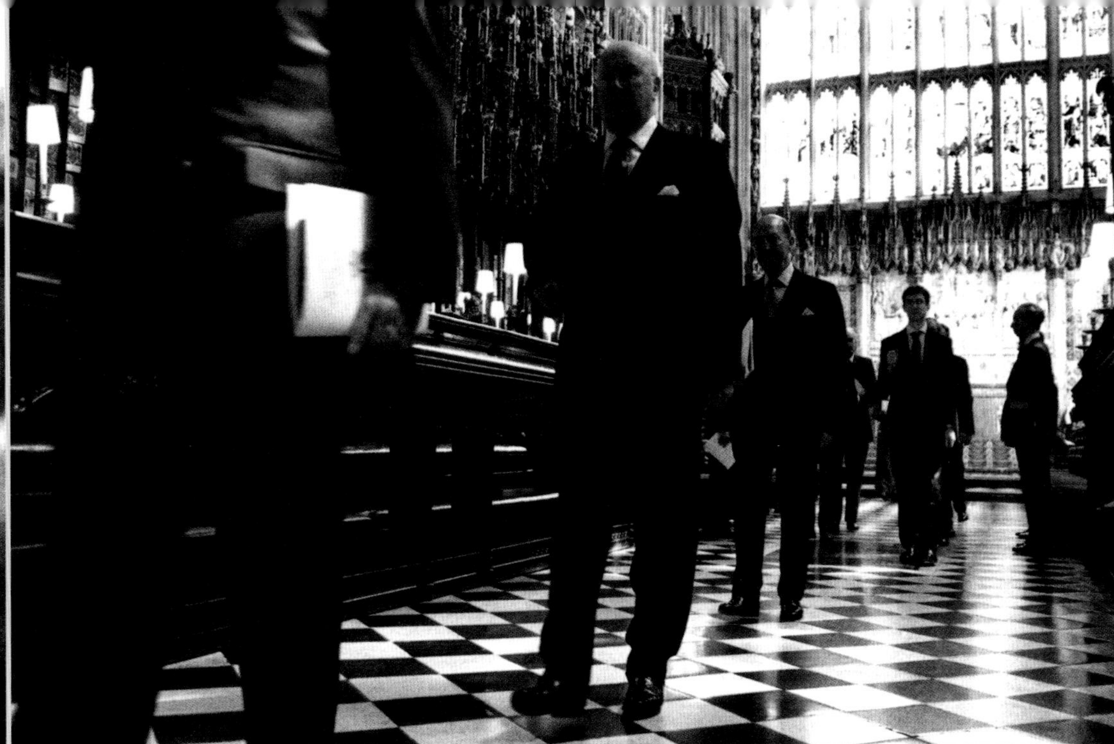

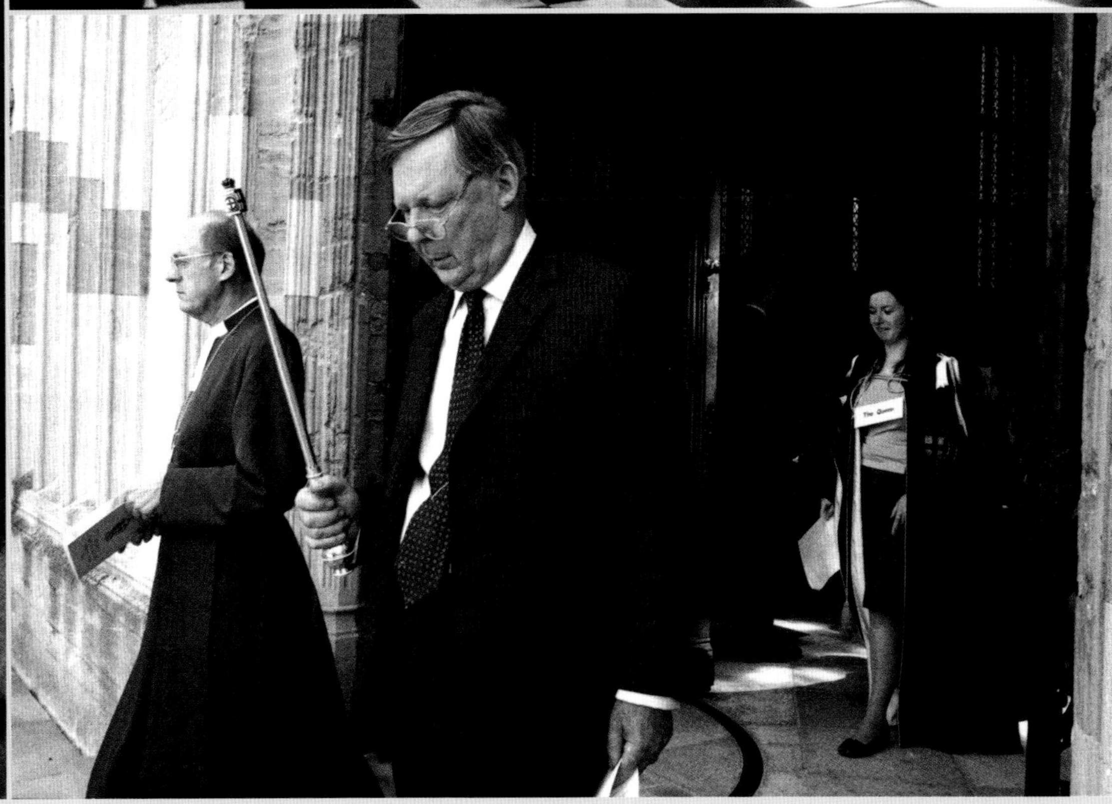

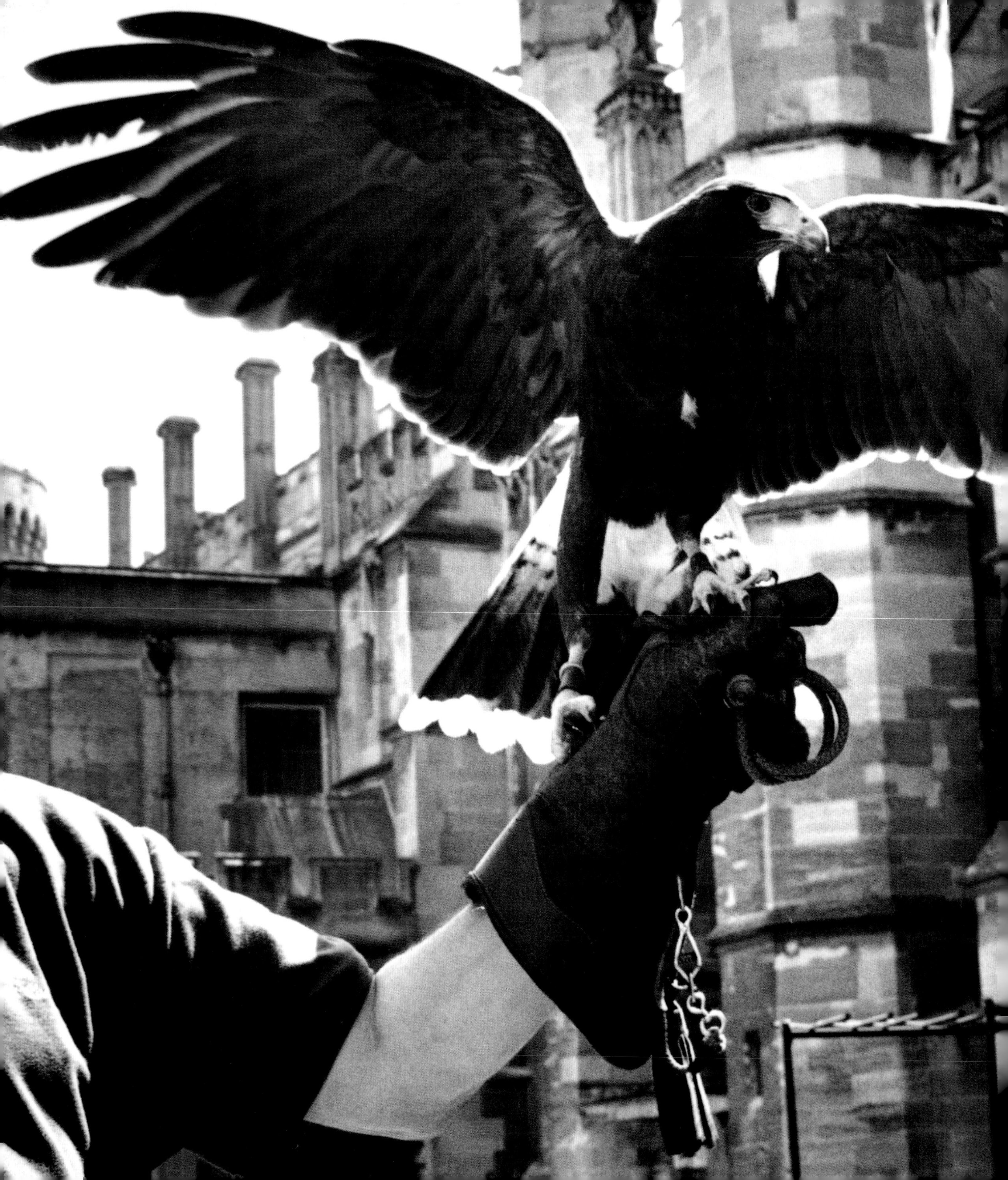

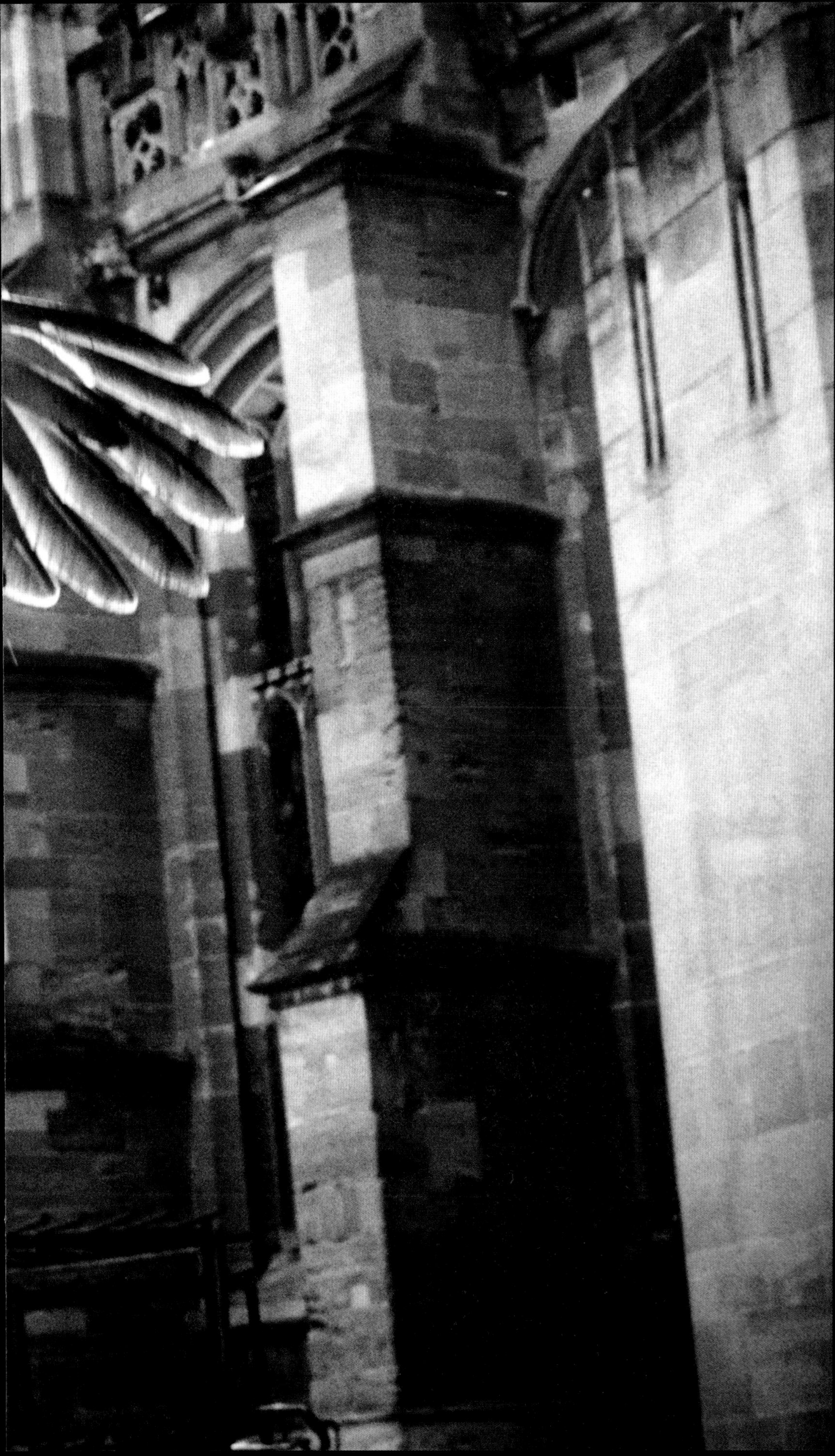

The Harris Hawk spreading its wings before flight . It is frequently used, as here before a Garter Day Service, to clear the roof of the Chapel of pigeons and other birds .

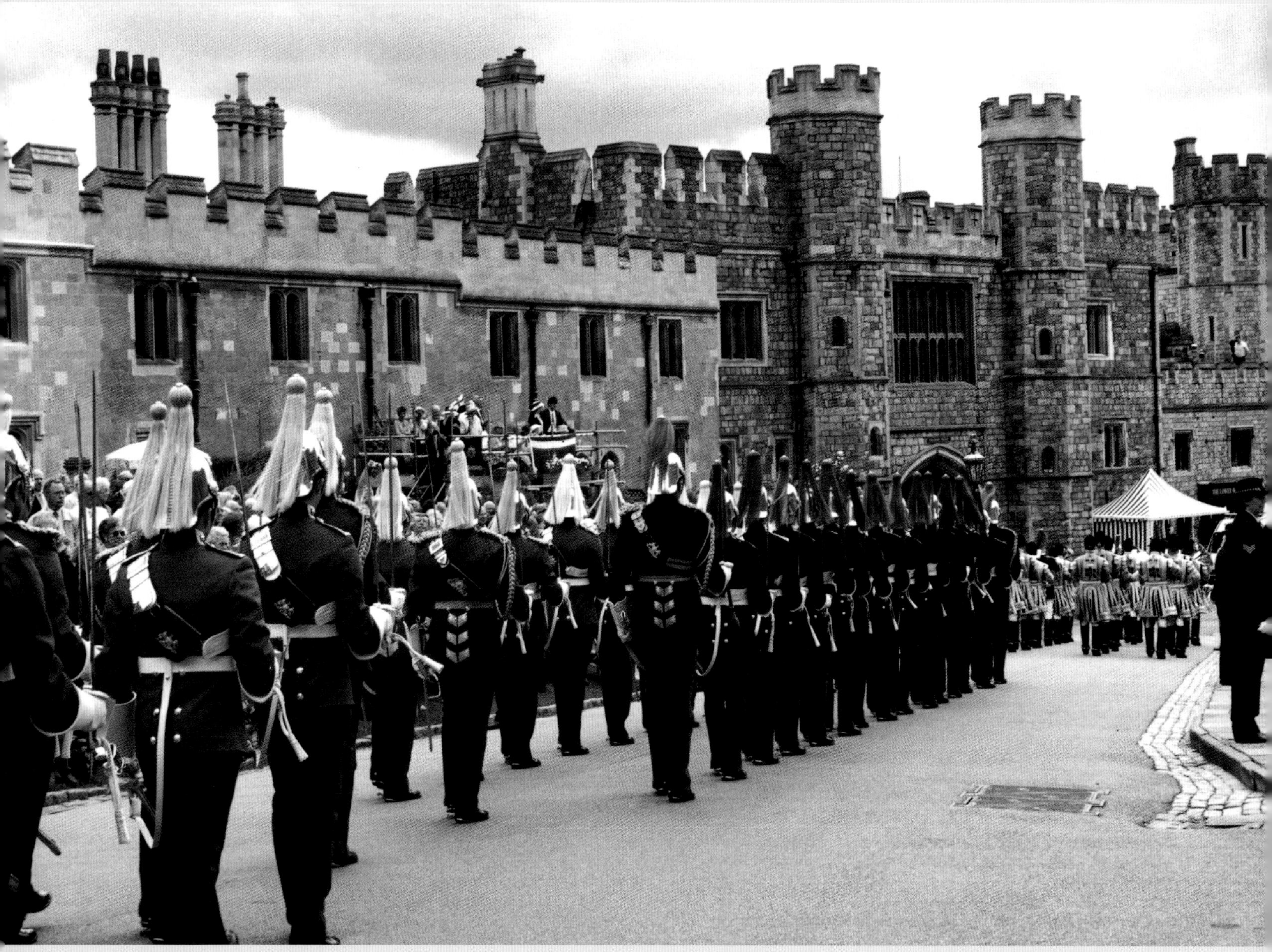

Garter Procession: The Household Cavalry march through the Lower Ward and into the Horseshoe Cloister preceded by the Military Bands.

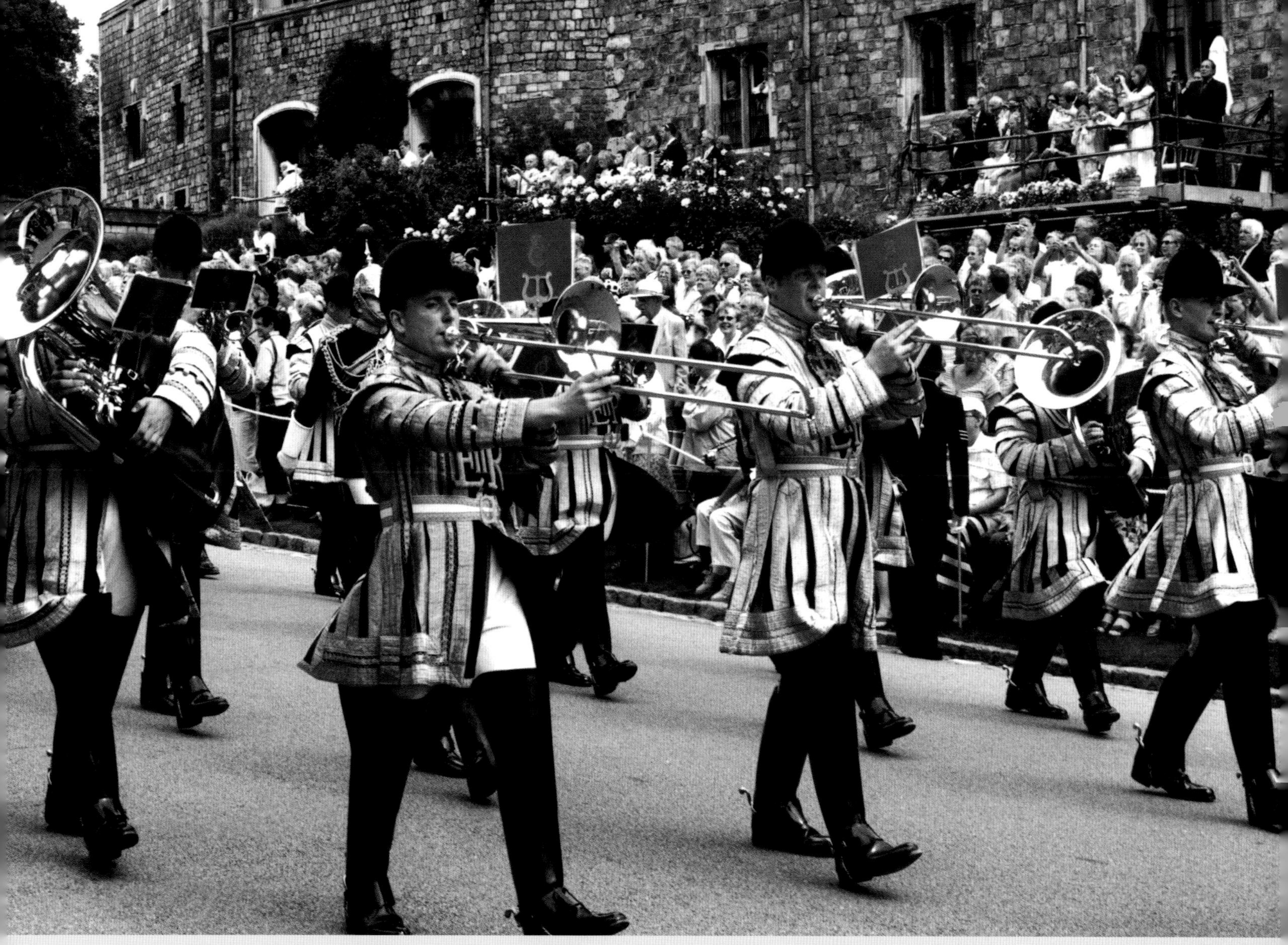

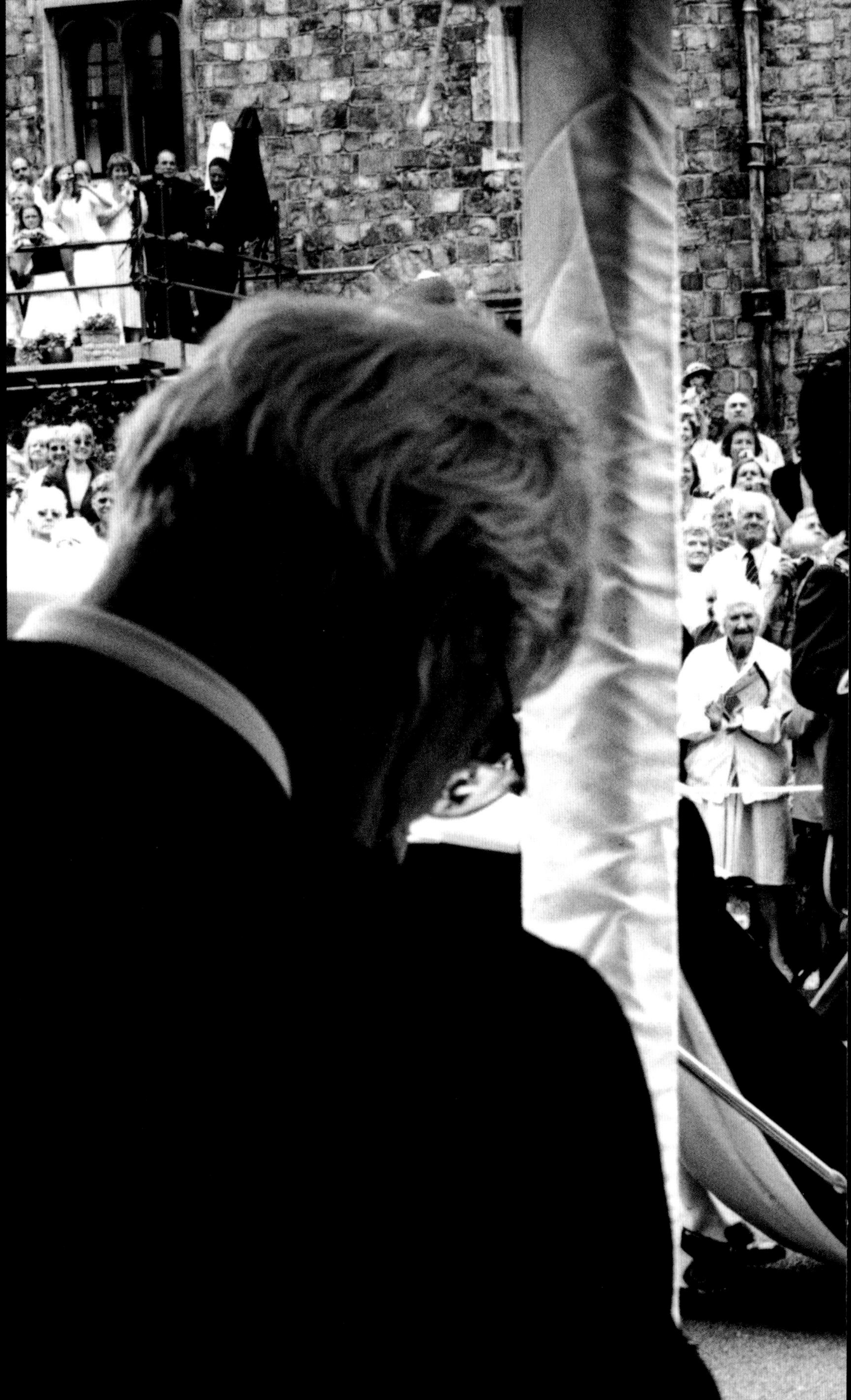

Garter Procession: HM The Queen walking with The Duke of Edinburgh, observed from the Galilee Porch. The Queen's train is carried by two Pages.

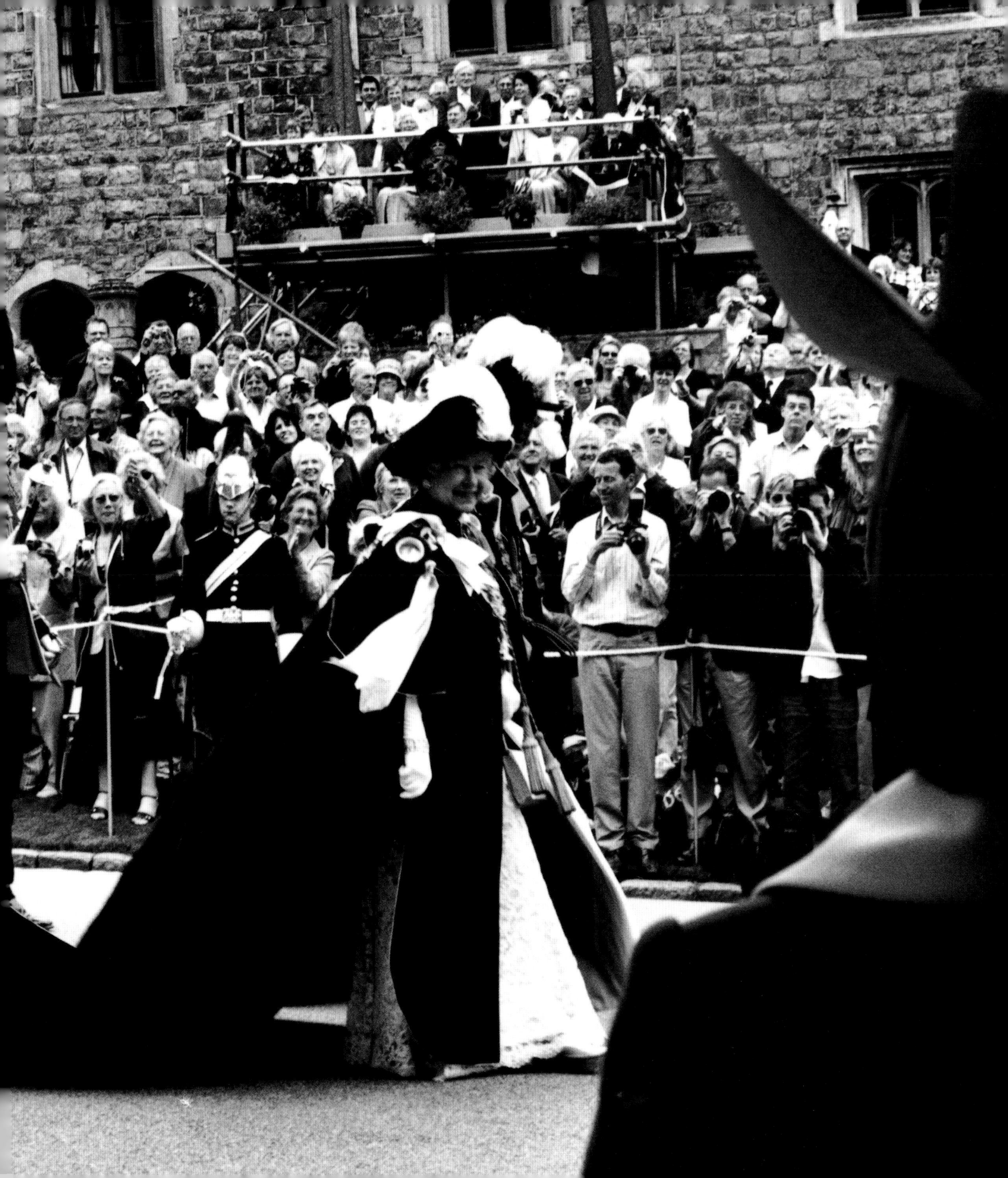

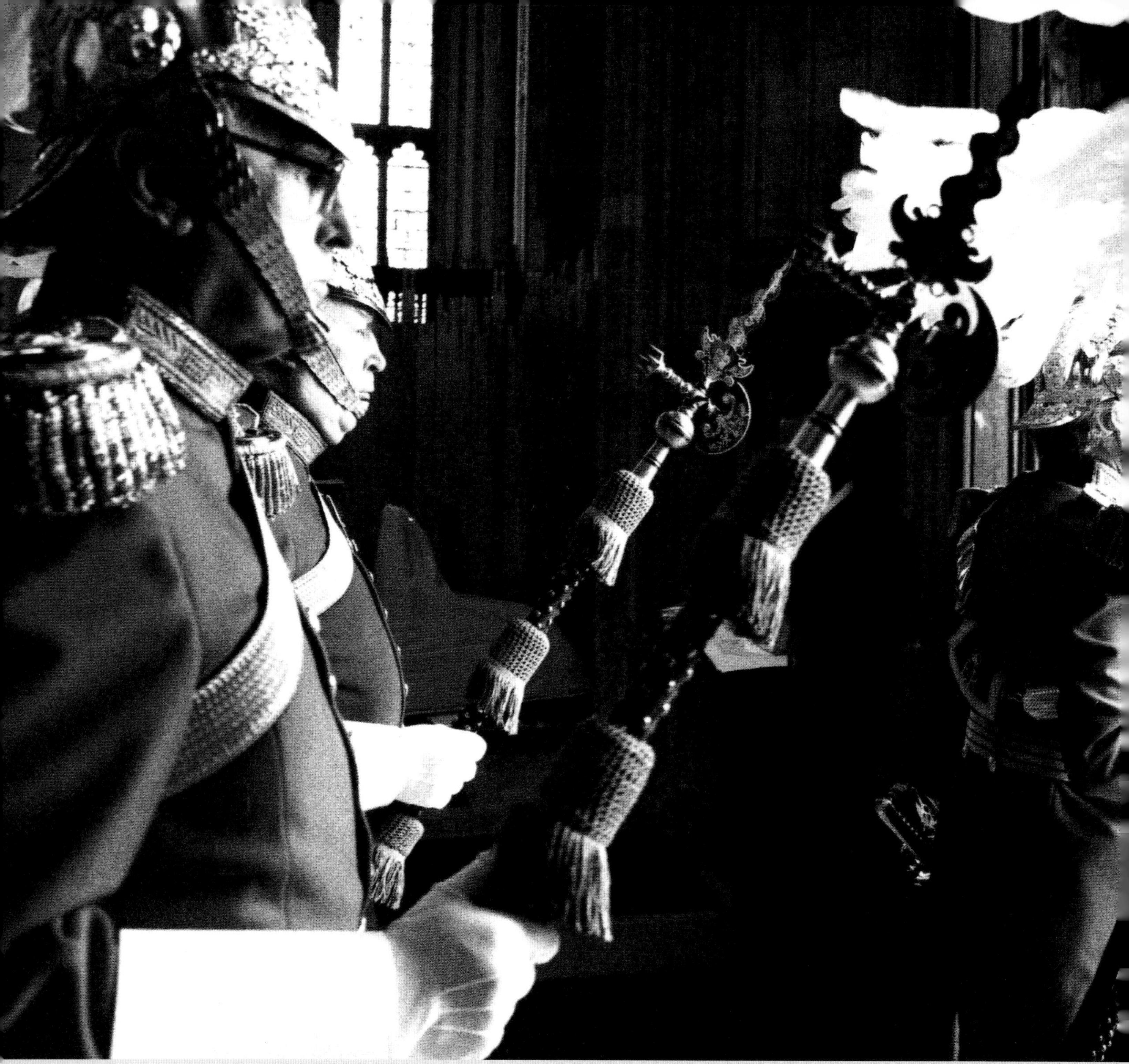

Above and Top Right: Her Majesty's Body Guard of the Honourable Corps of Gentlemen at Arms processing out of the West Door. The Gentlemen at Arms are on duty in the Chapel during the Garter Service.

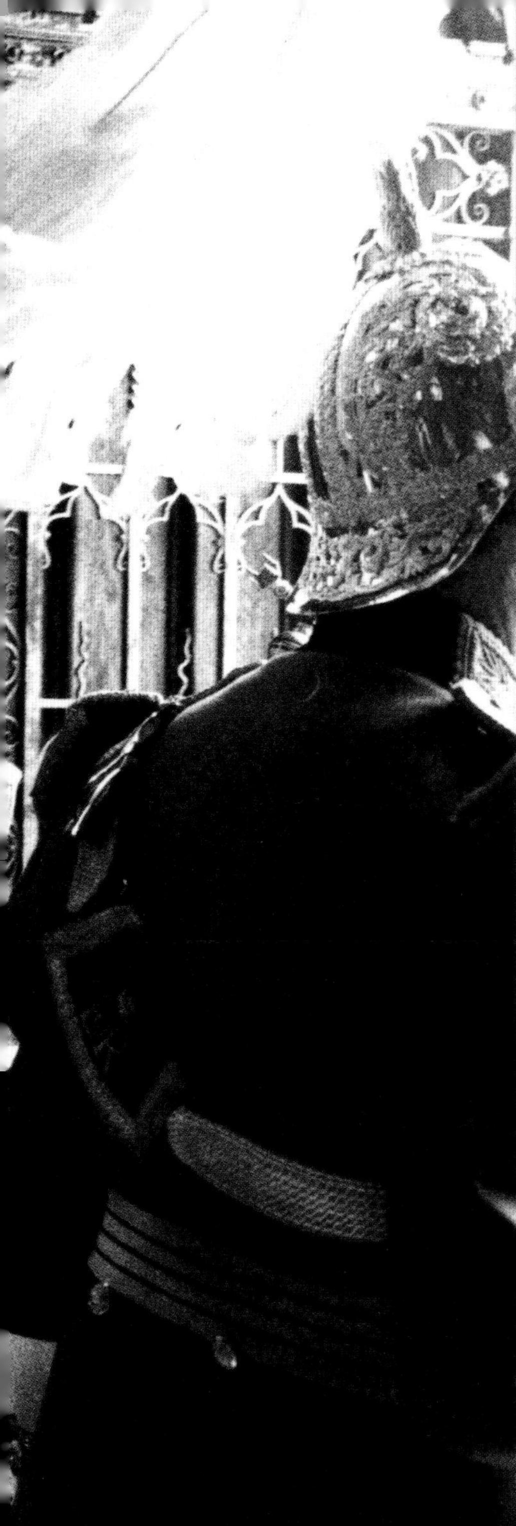

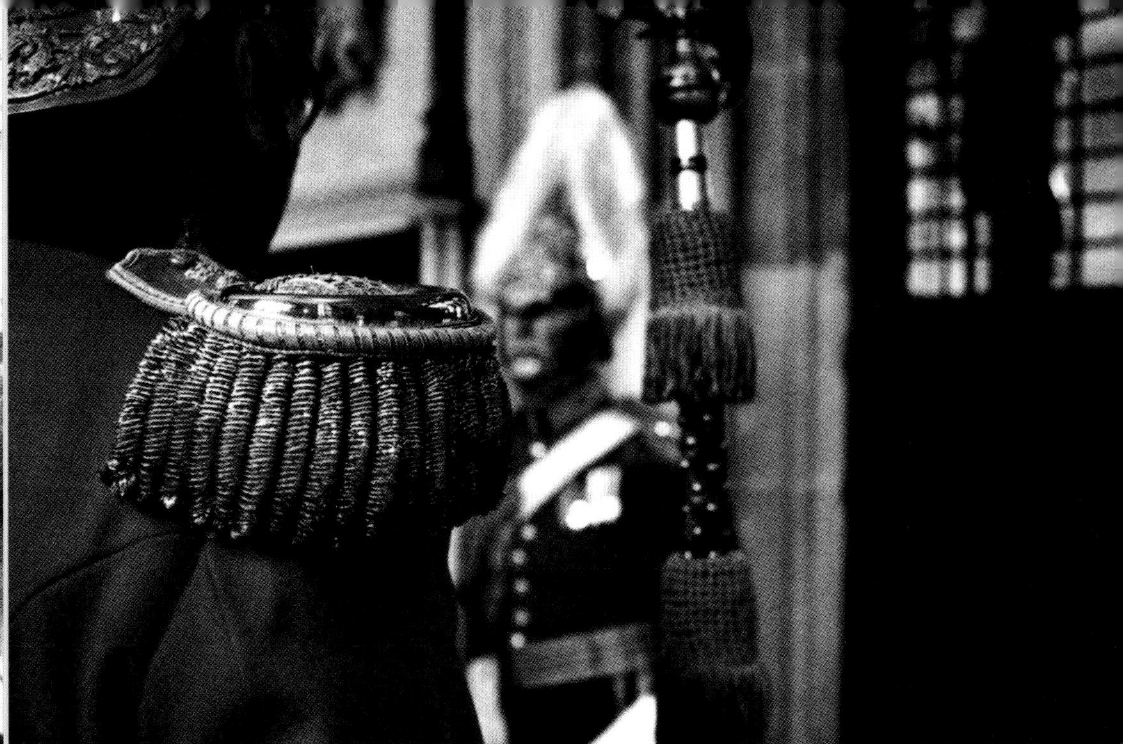

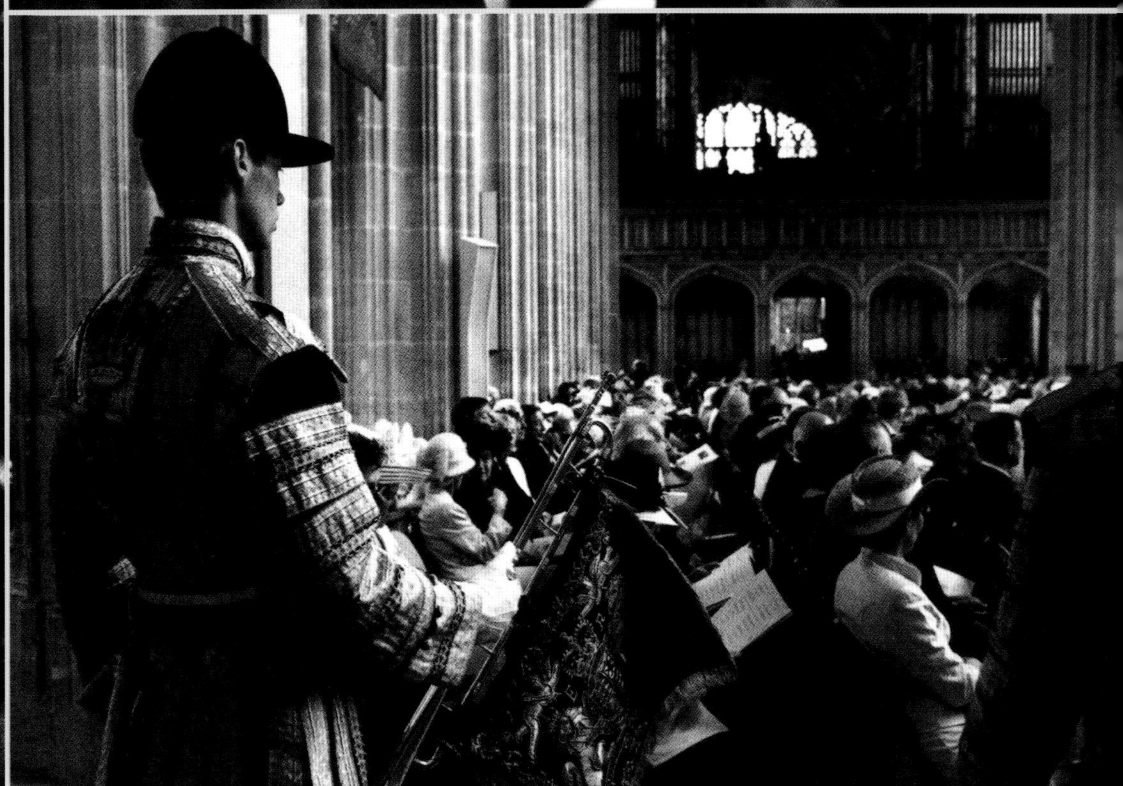

Bottom Right: A State Trumpeter positioned by the West Door ready to sound the fanfare to mark the entrance of the Sovereign.

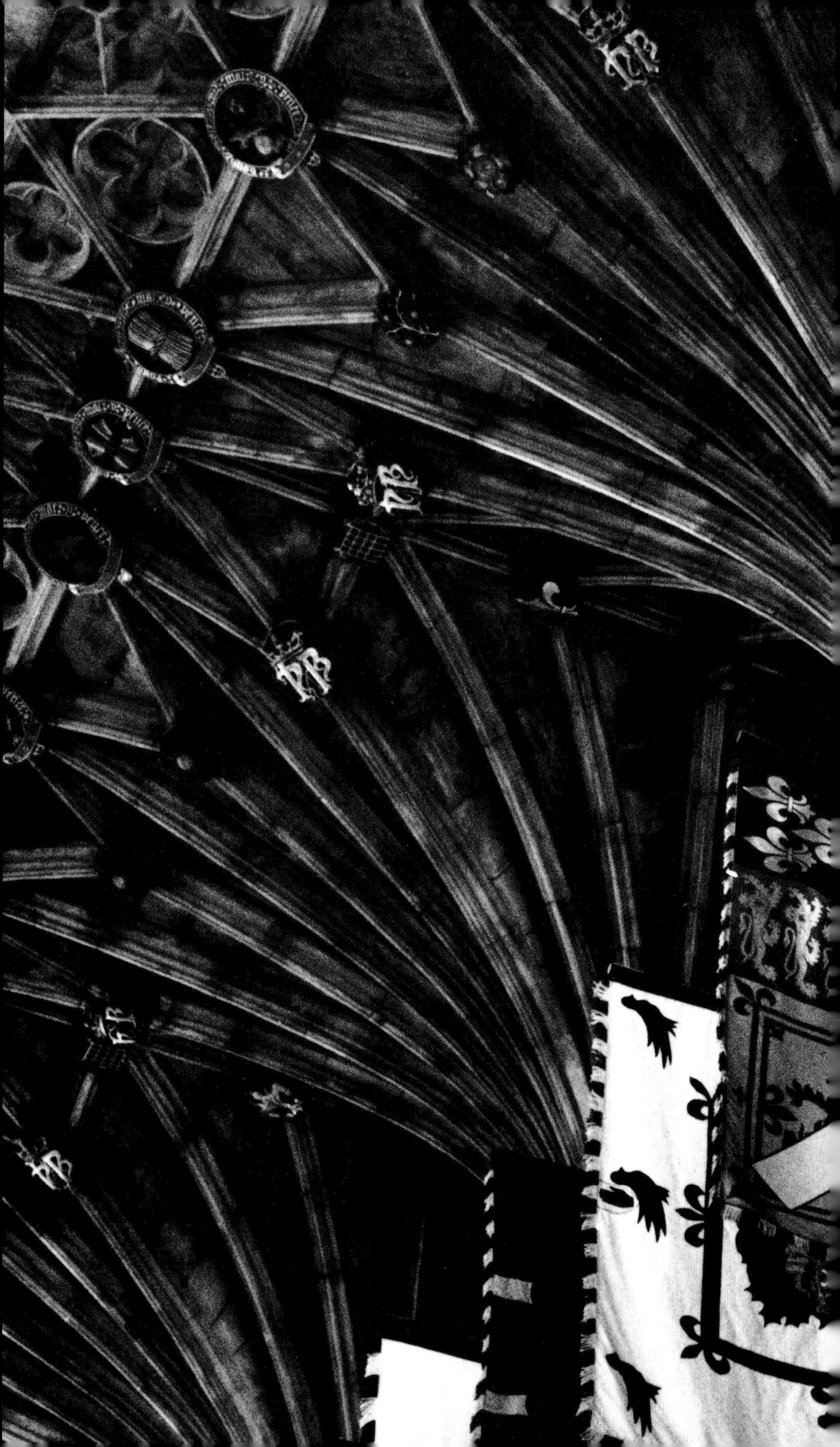

Banners of the Knights of the Garter. Second right is the banner of the late Sir Edmund Hillary (1995), whose heraldic design is derived from the Himalayas and Tibetan prayer wheels. Fourth right is the banner of Lord Carrington, installed in 1985 and also Chancellor to the Order. His banner depicts a chevron with three demi-griffins and has its origins from his eighteenth-century family arms.

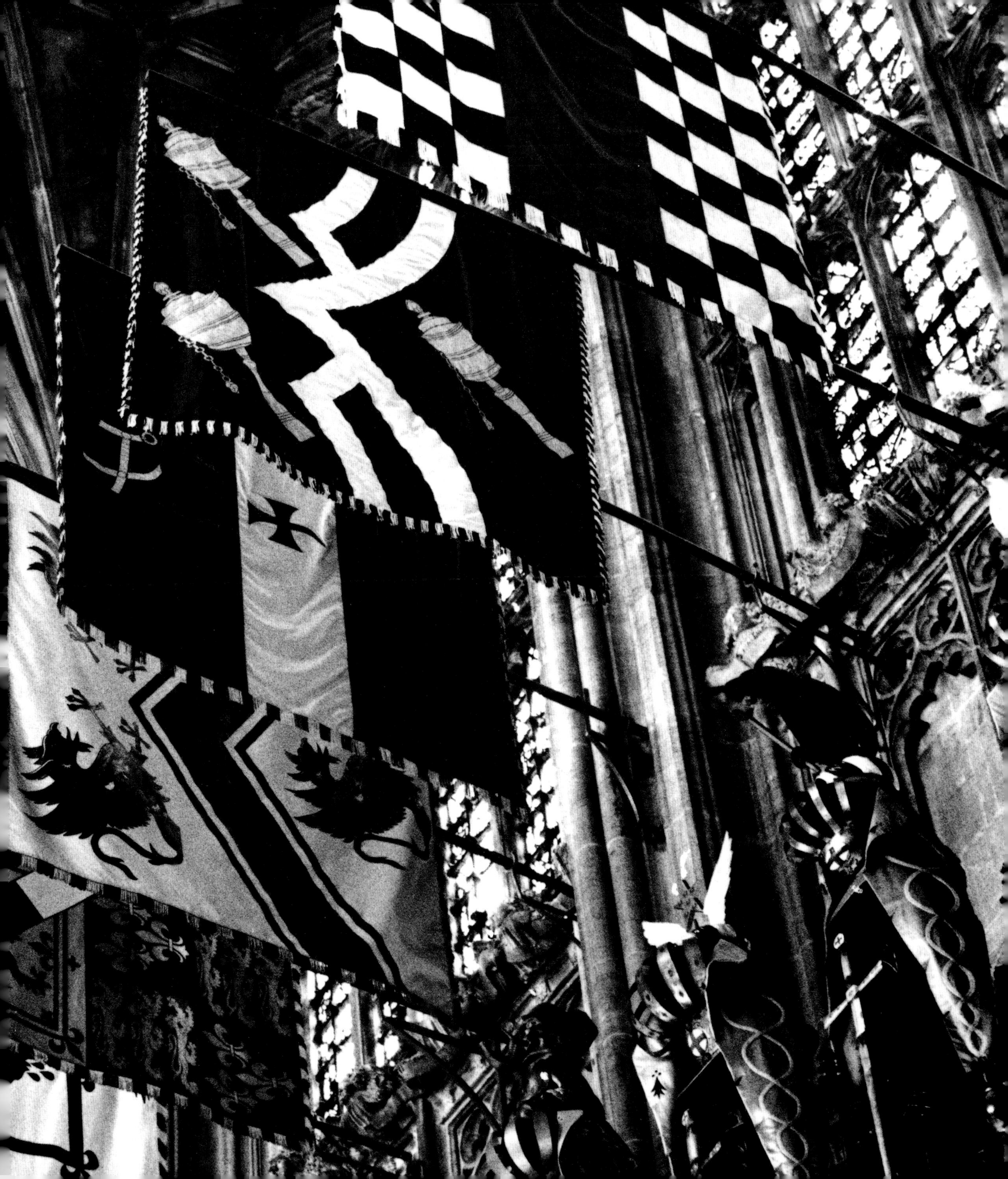

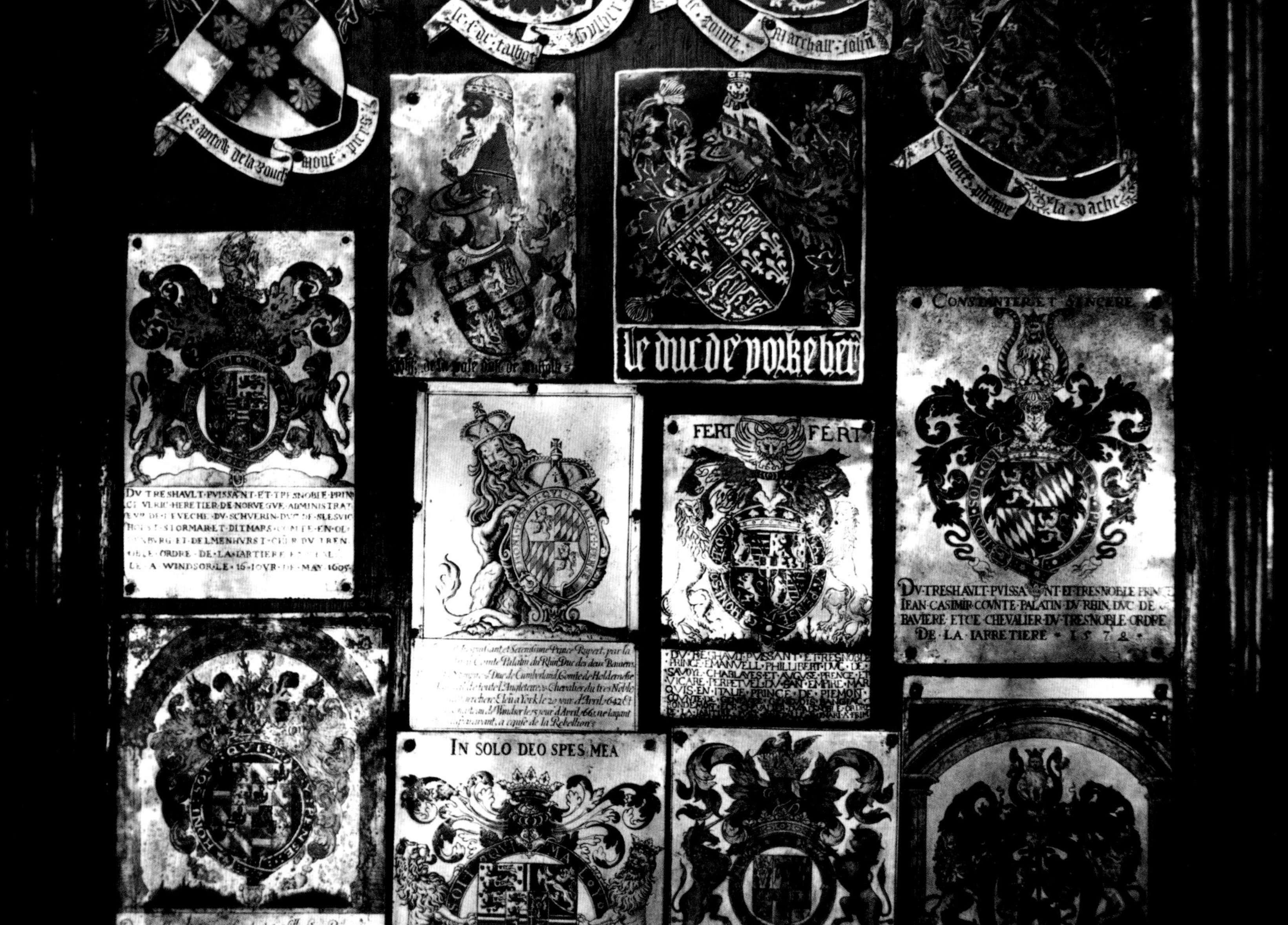

Above: Brass stallplates attached to a Knight's Stall, showing his full coat of arms, title and date of appointment to the Order. These plates remain attached even after the Knight is deceased.

Right: Sir Winston Churchill's stallplate of 1953. The stallplate to the bottom right of the image dates back to 1965 and is of Edward Ettingdere Bridges, Secretary to the Cabinet under Winston Churchill. By tradition the text is in Norman French.

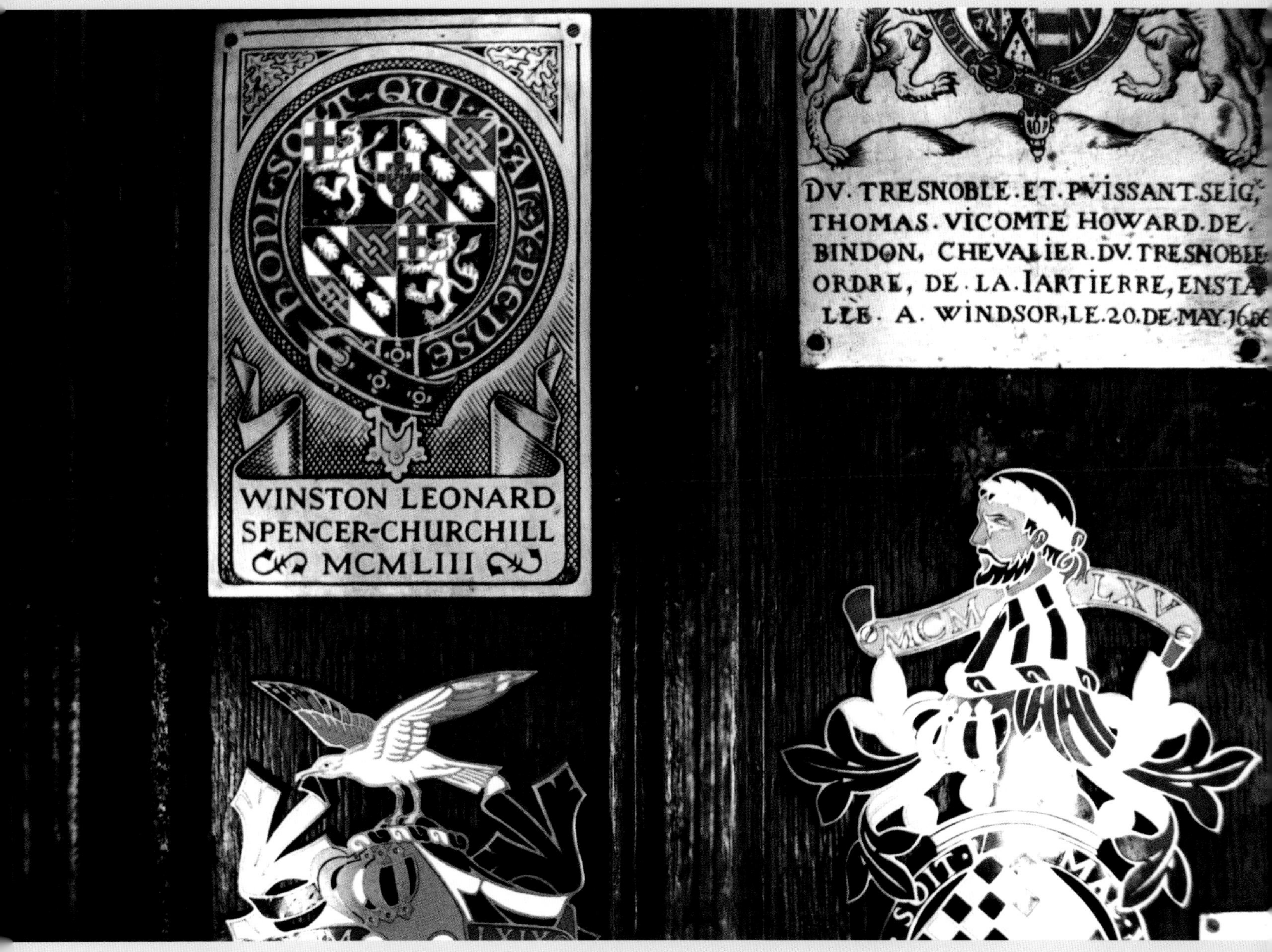
WINSTON LEONARD
SPENCER-CHURCHILL
MCMLIII
DV. TRESNOBLE. ET. PVISSANT. SEIG,
THOMAS. VICOMTE HOWARD. DE.
BINDON, CHEVALIER. DV. TRESNOBLE.
ORDRE, DE. LA. IARTIERRE, ENSTA
LLE. A. WINDSOR, LE. 20. DE. MAY. 1686
MCM LXV

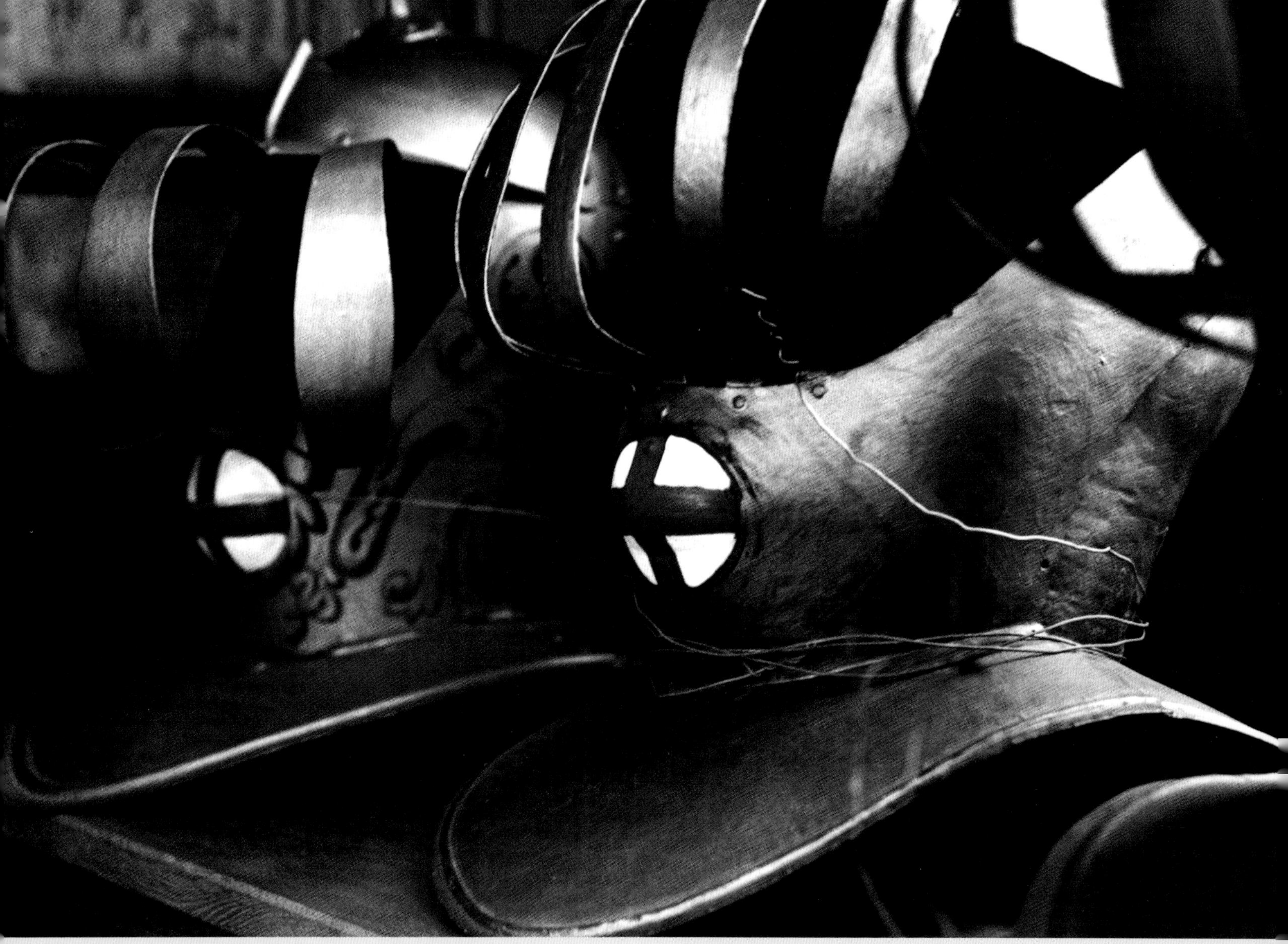

Each Knight of the Garter has his/her own Stall in the quire of St George's Chapel and above it are placed the medieval symbols of chivalry. The Companion has a Banner bearing Arms, a helm (or helmet) upon which sits the heraldic crest, and the half-drawn sword representing the readiness of the Knight of the Garter to use his sword to defend the Sovereign. These heraldic symbols remain above the Knight's Stall until he/she dies.

Above: Details of the Knight's helm (or helmet).
Right: The Knights' stalls in the quire of the Chapel showing the half-drawn sword, the helm and the crest.

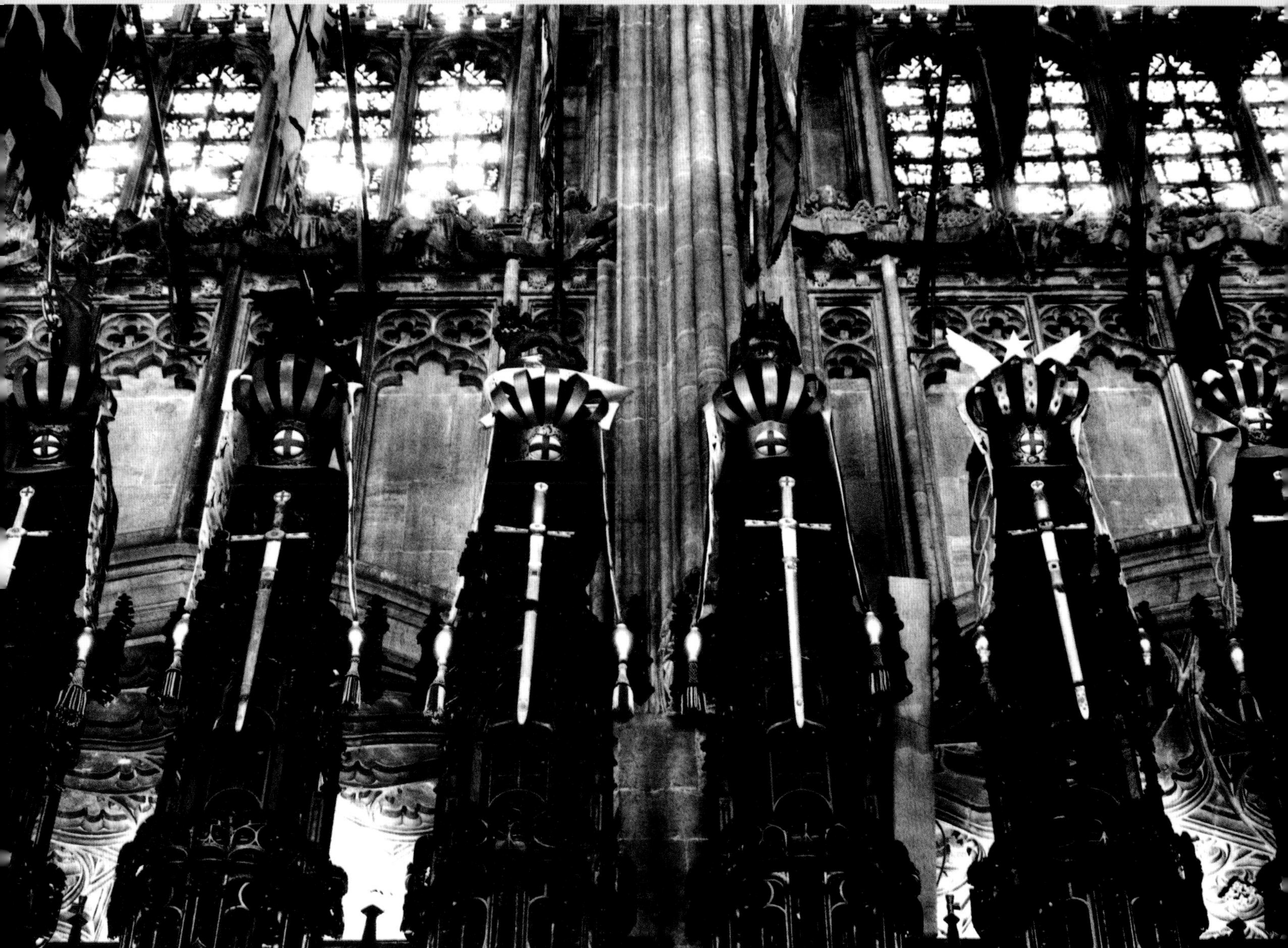

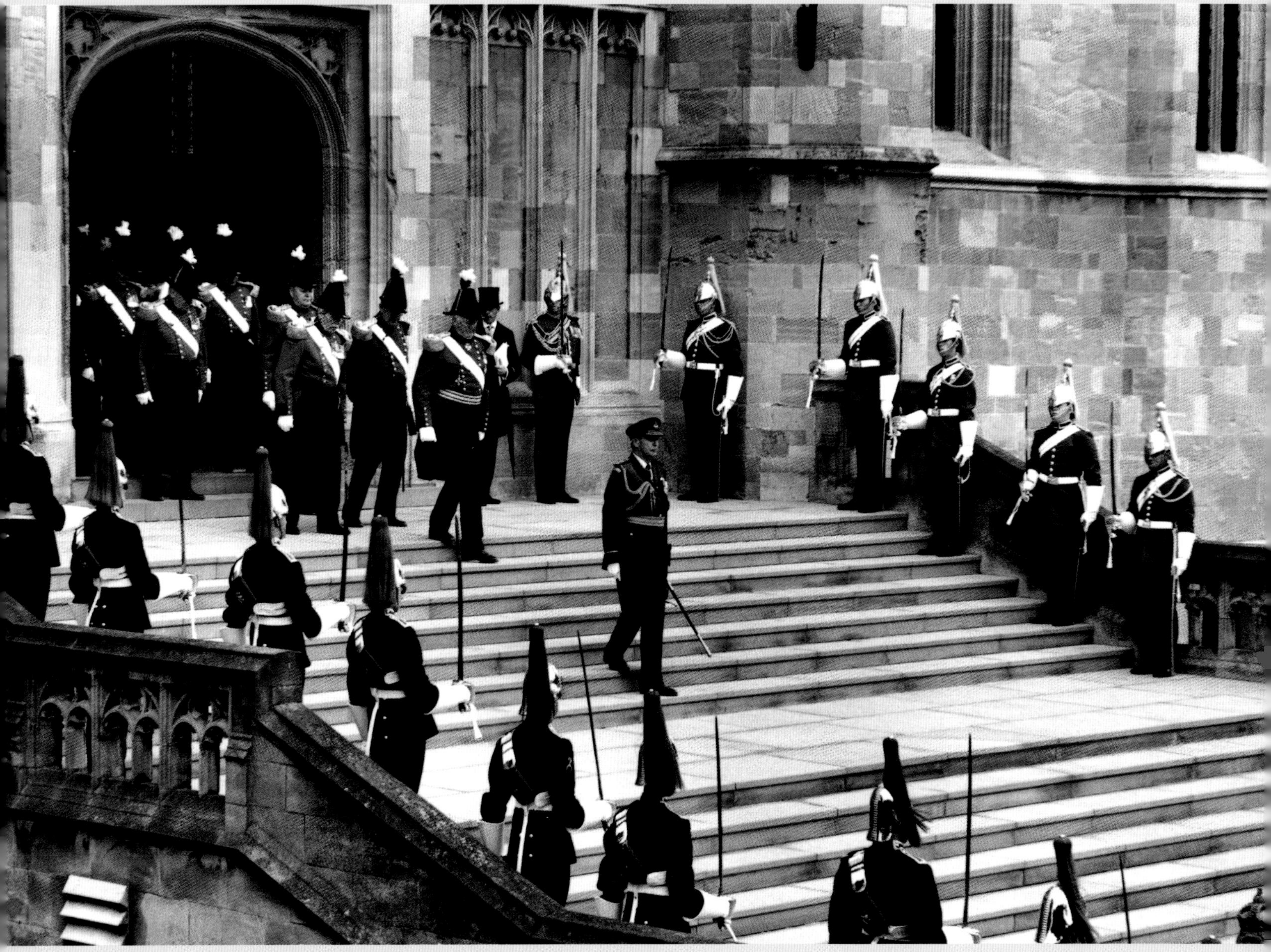

Above: The Procession leaves by the West Door and is led by the Constable and Governor of Windsor Castle, Air Chief Marshal Sir Richard Johns. He is followed by the Military Knights of Windsor led by the Governor of the Military Knights of Windsor, Major General Sir Michael Hobbs.

Right: Members of the Royal Body Guard of the Yeomen of the Guard lining up on the West Steps.

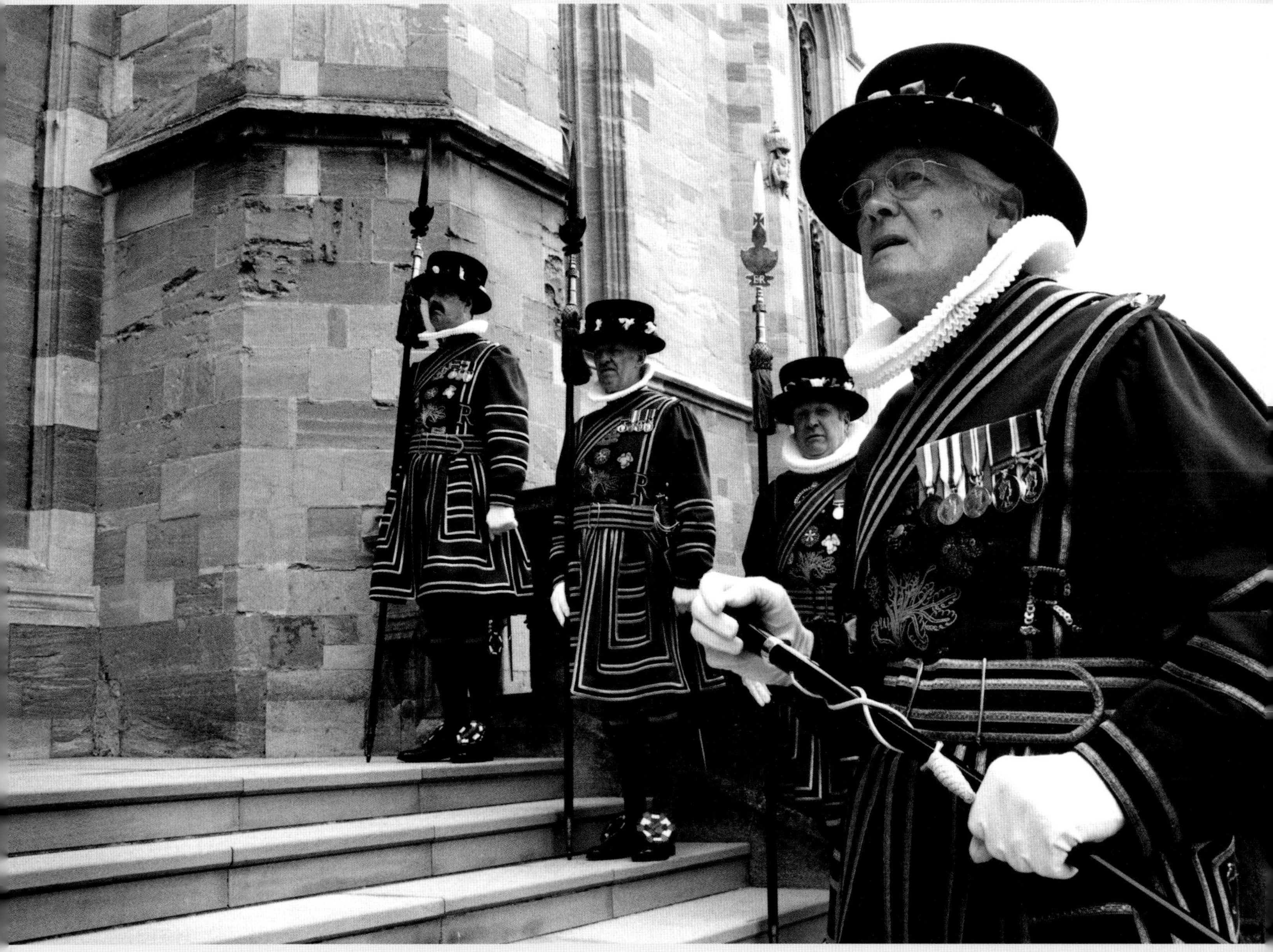

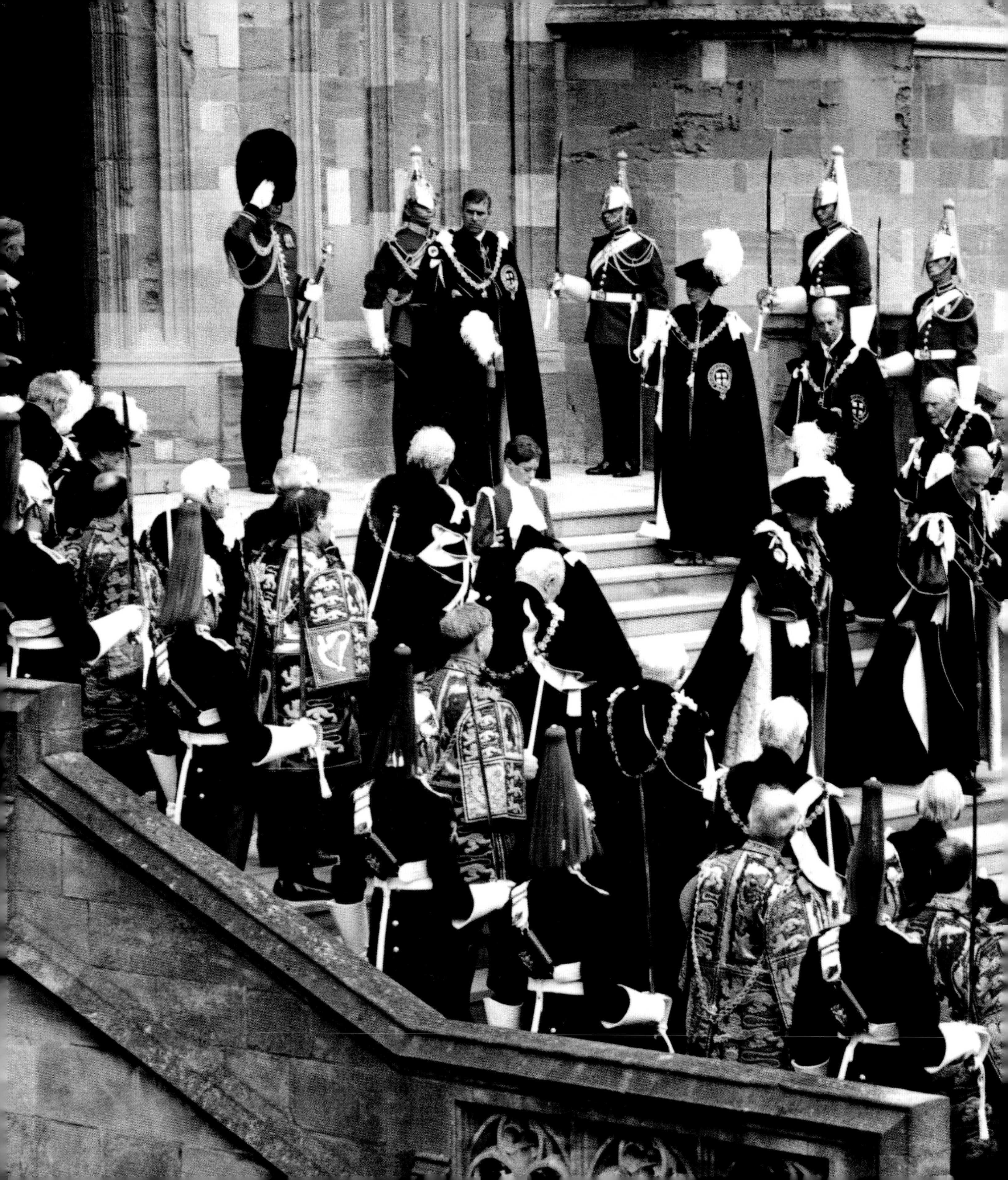

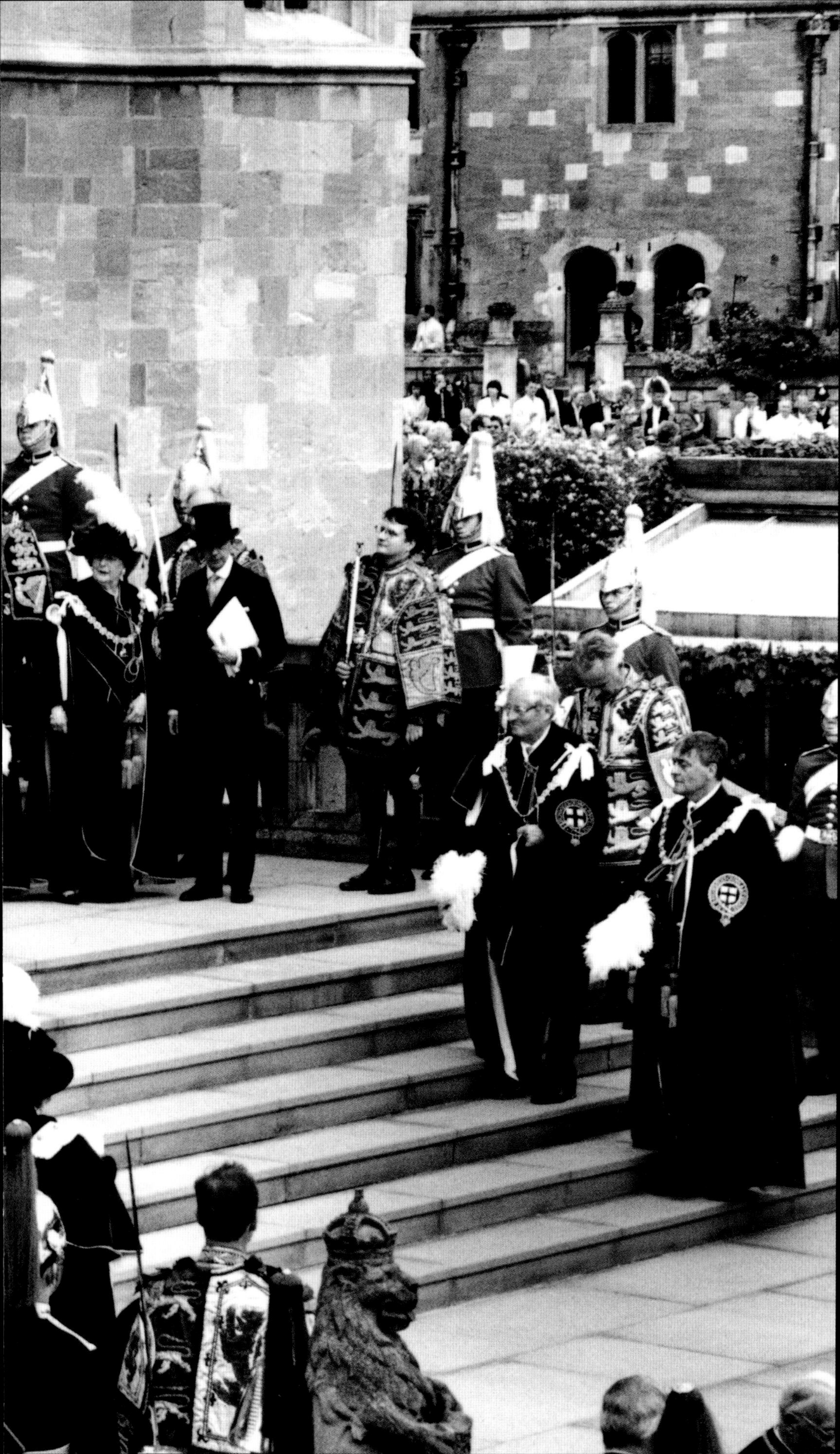

HM The Queen and the Duke of Edinburgh coming down the West Steps after Garter Service, accompanied by the Companions and Officers of the Order and other members of the Royal Family.

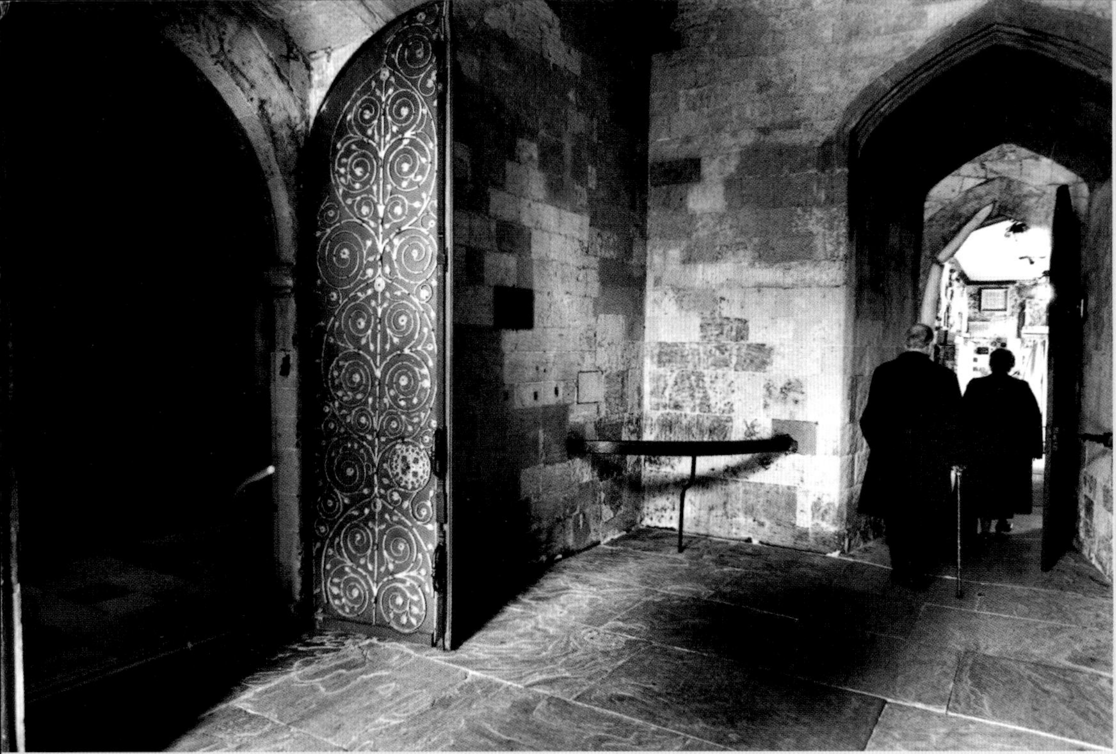

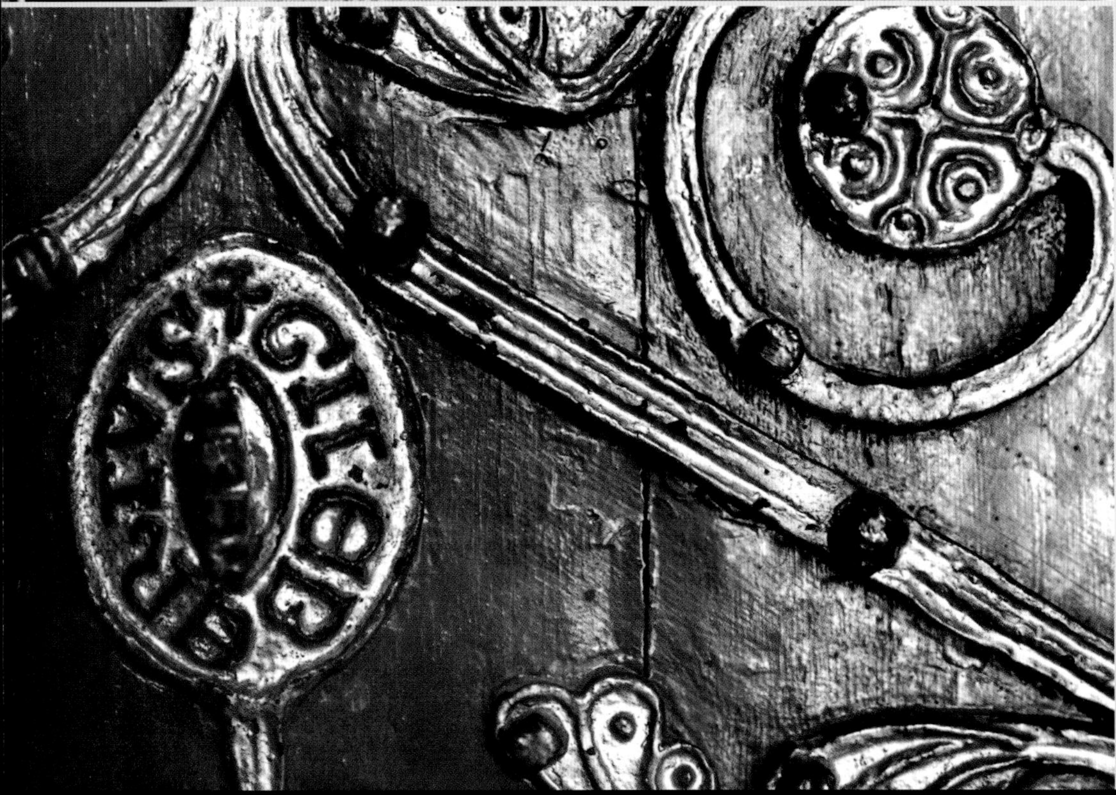

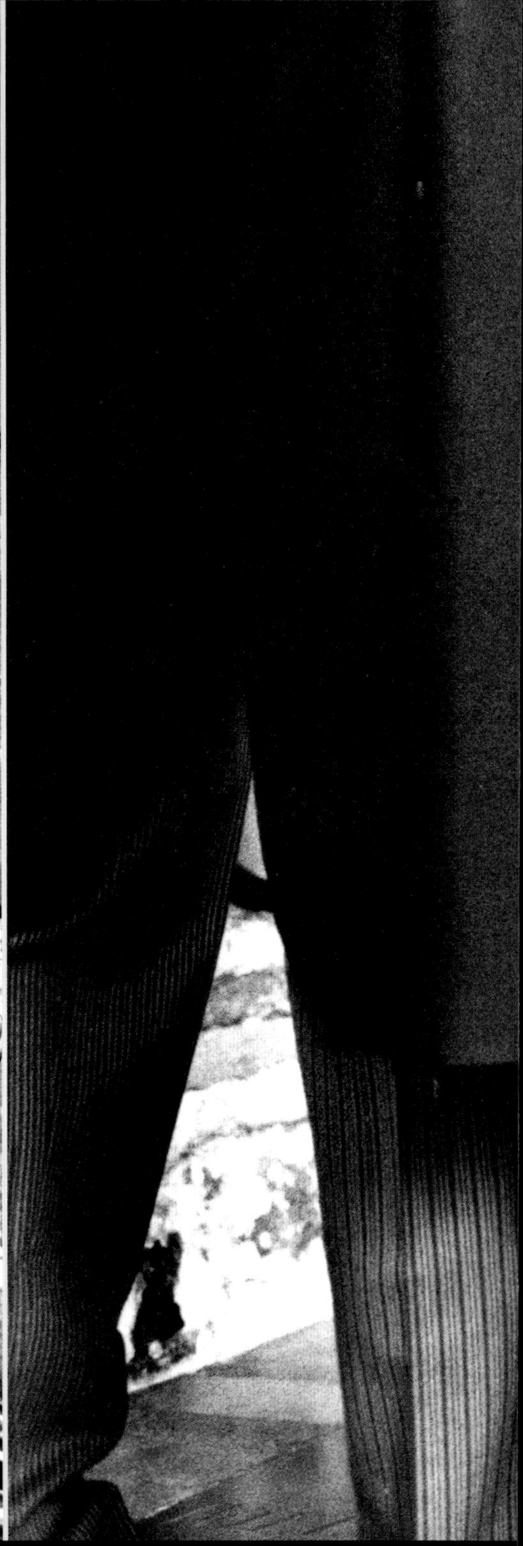

The Royal Victorian Order: The RVO was instituted in 1896 as an Order entirely within the gift of Queen Victoria to enable her to acknowledge and reward outstanding and personal service 'rendered unto her and of which said Order, Her Majesty, her heirs and successors,

from the Monarch admittance was, and continues to be, held in high respect. Every fourth year a Service of Praise, Remembrance and Dedication is held at the Chapel.

Top Left: The Galilee Porch looking through to the Dean's Cloister.

Bottom Left: Detail of the East Doors with their intricate ironwork dating back to 1240. This was the original entrance to King Henry III's Chapel.

Right: A view of the Lay Stewards in the Dean's Cloister as they take instructions from Chapter Clerk in preparation for the RVO service.

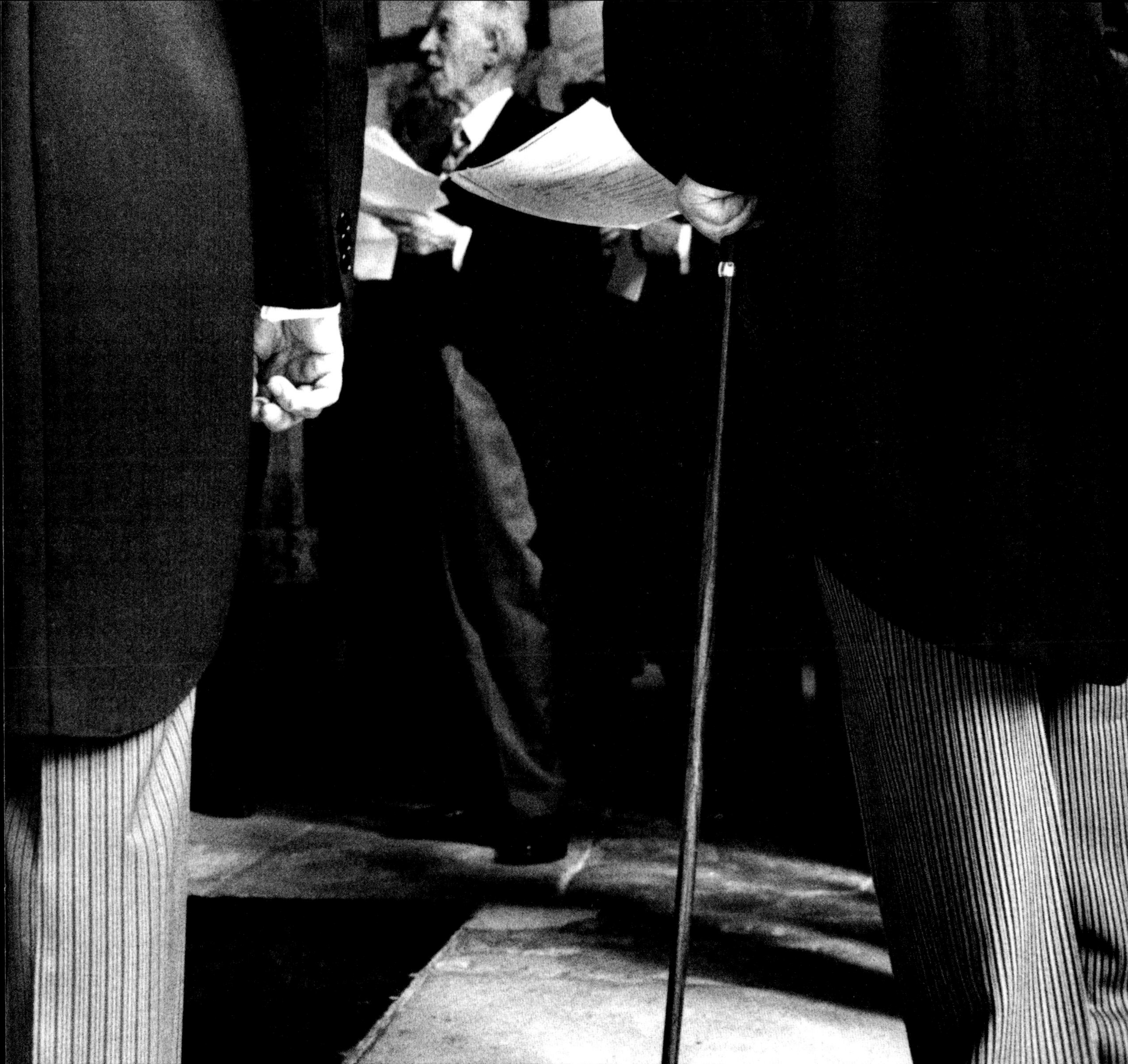

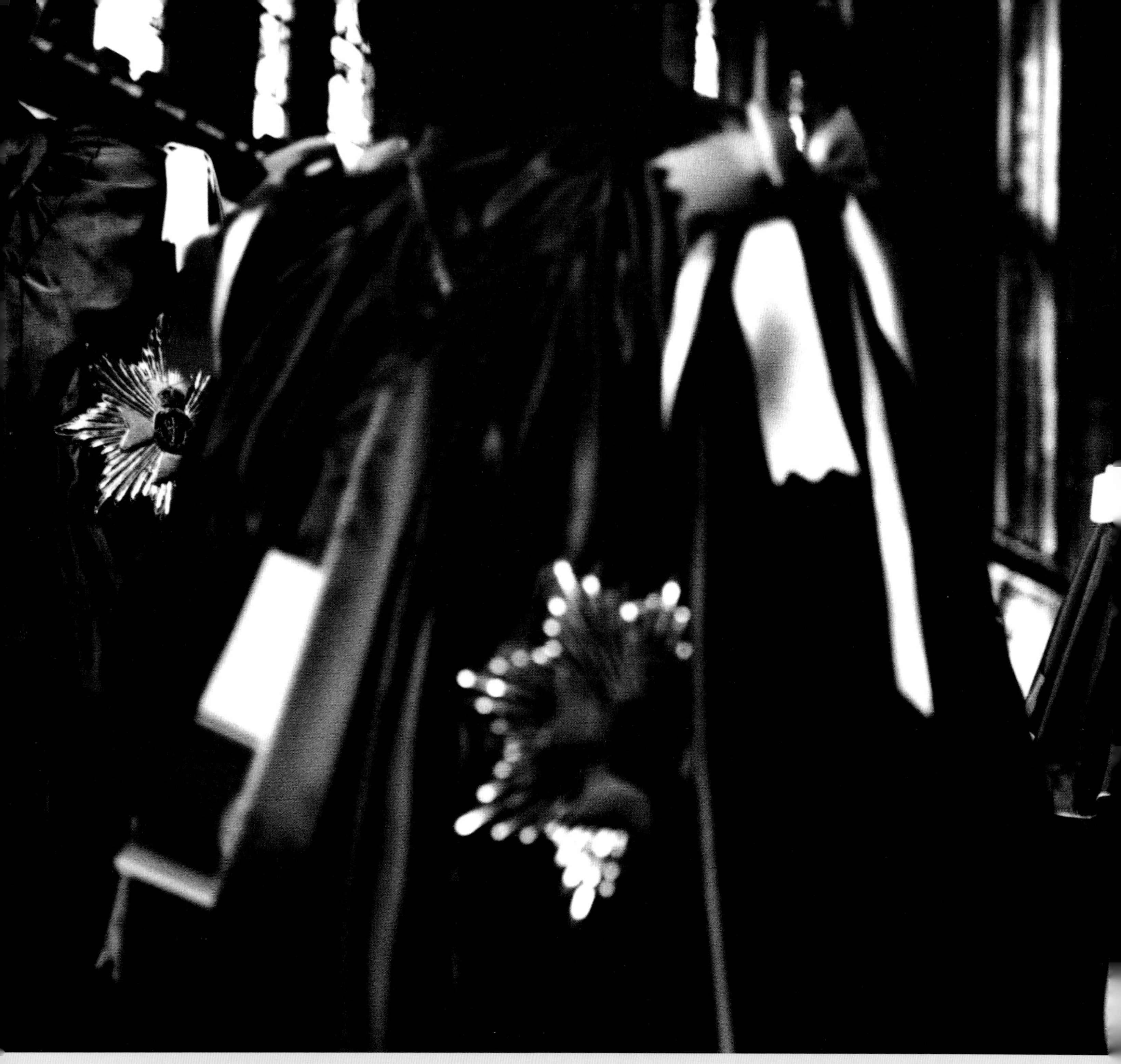

A Procession of Members of the Royal Family, Knights and Dames Grand Cross and the Officers move down the north nave aisle followed by members of the clergy and the choir.

Above: At the far right of the image is Lord Moore of Wolvercote.
Top Right: HRH Princess Alexandra and the Duke of Gloucester.
Bottom Right: Two Minor Canons and a Canon.

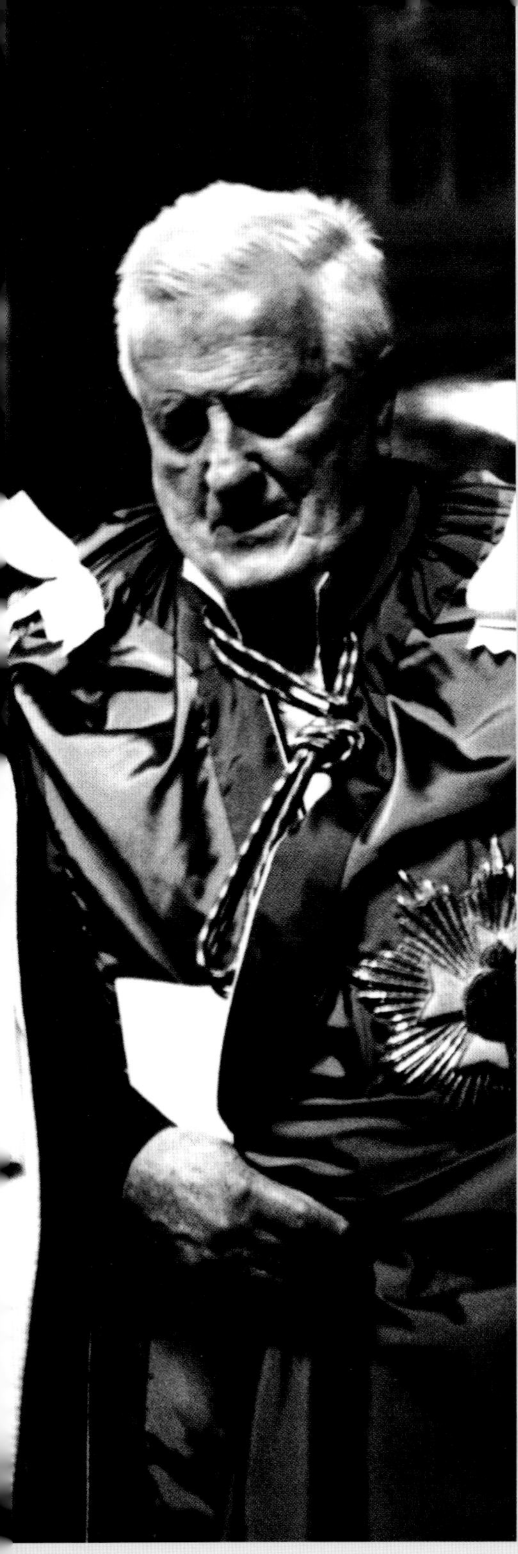
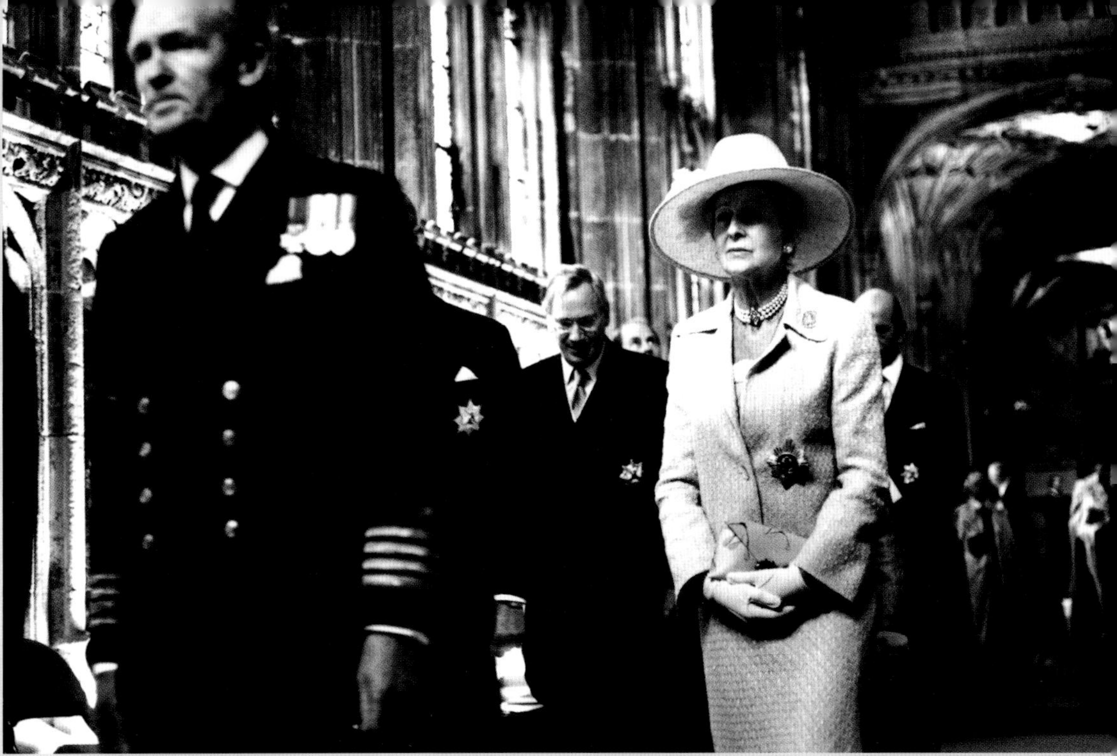
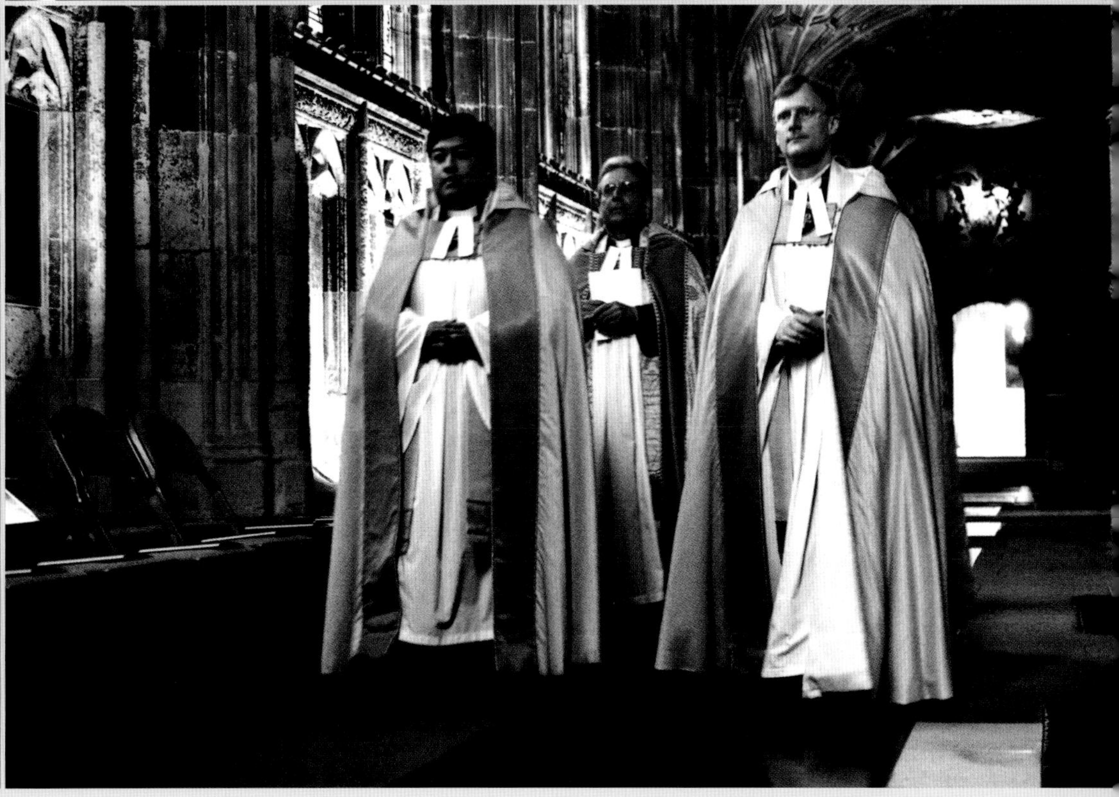

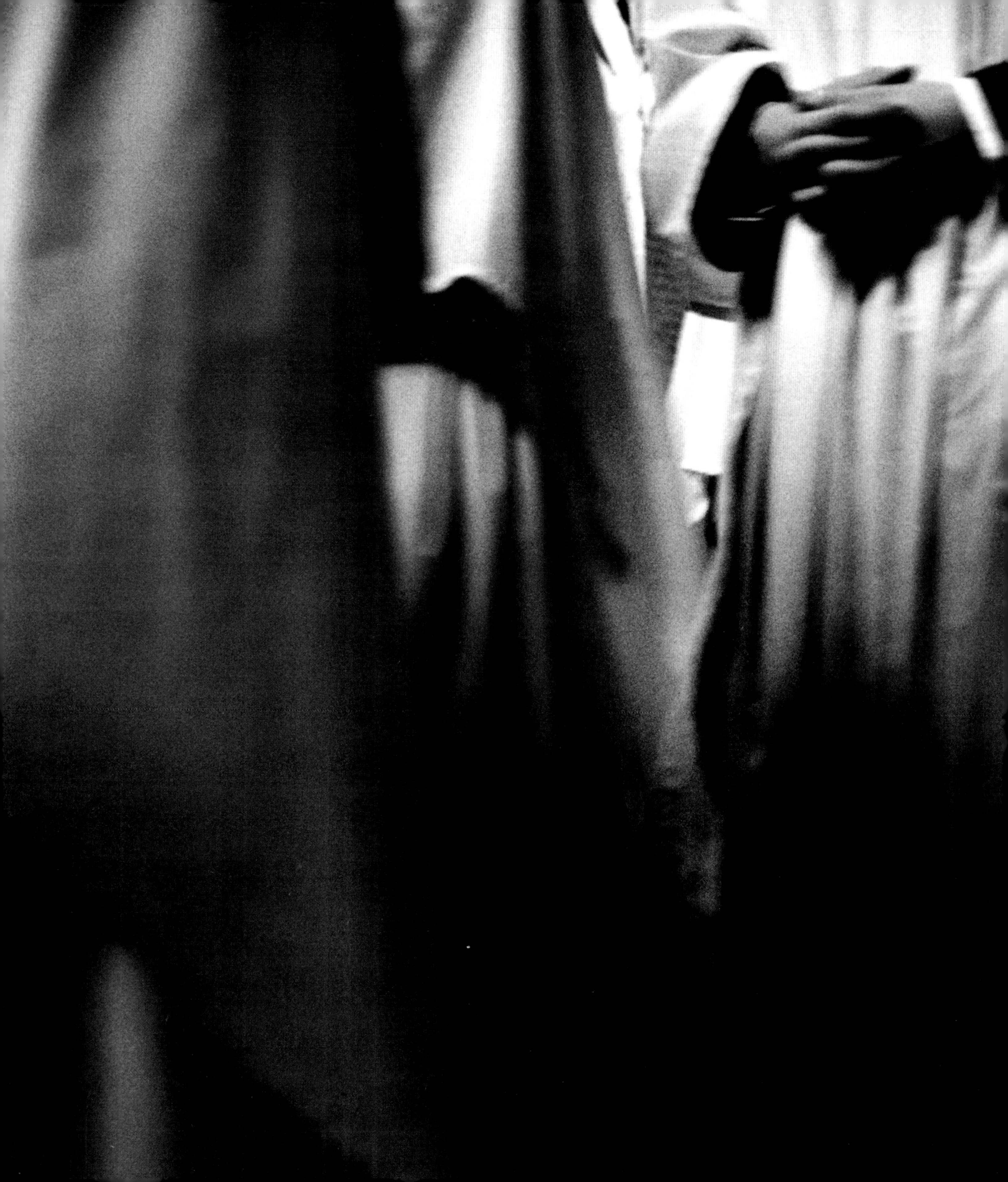

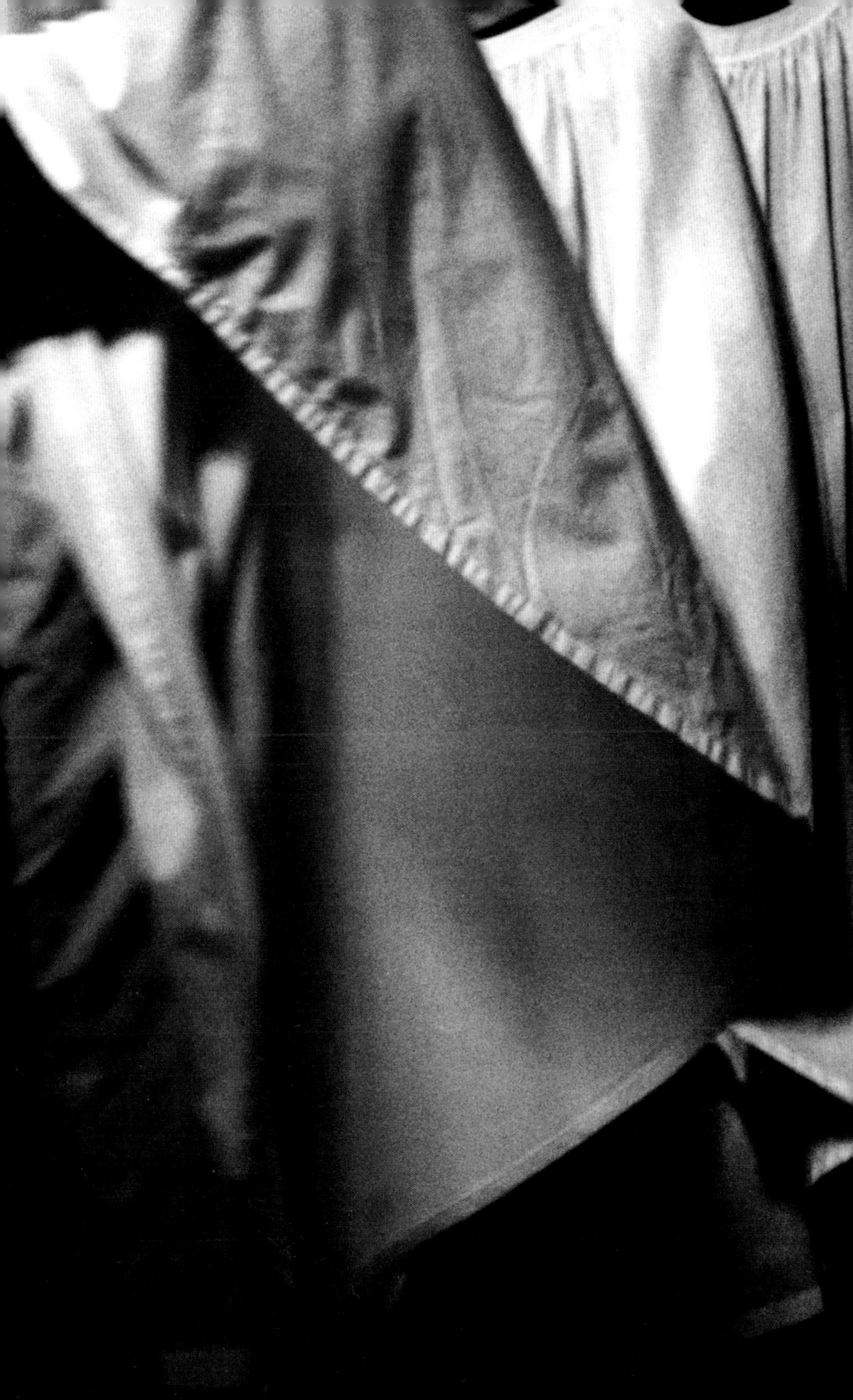

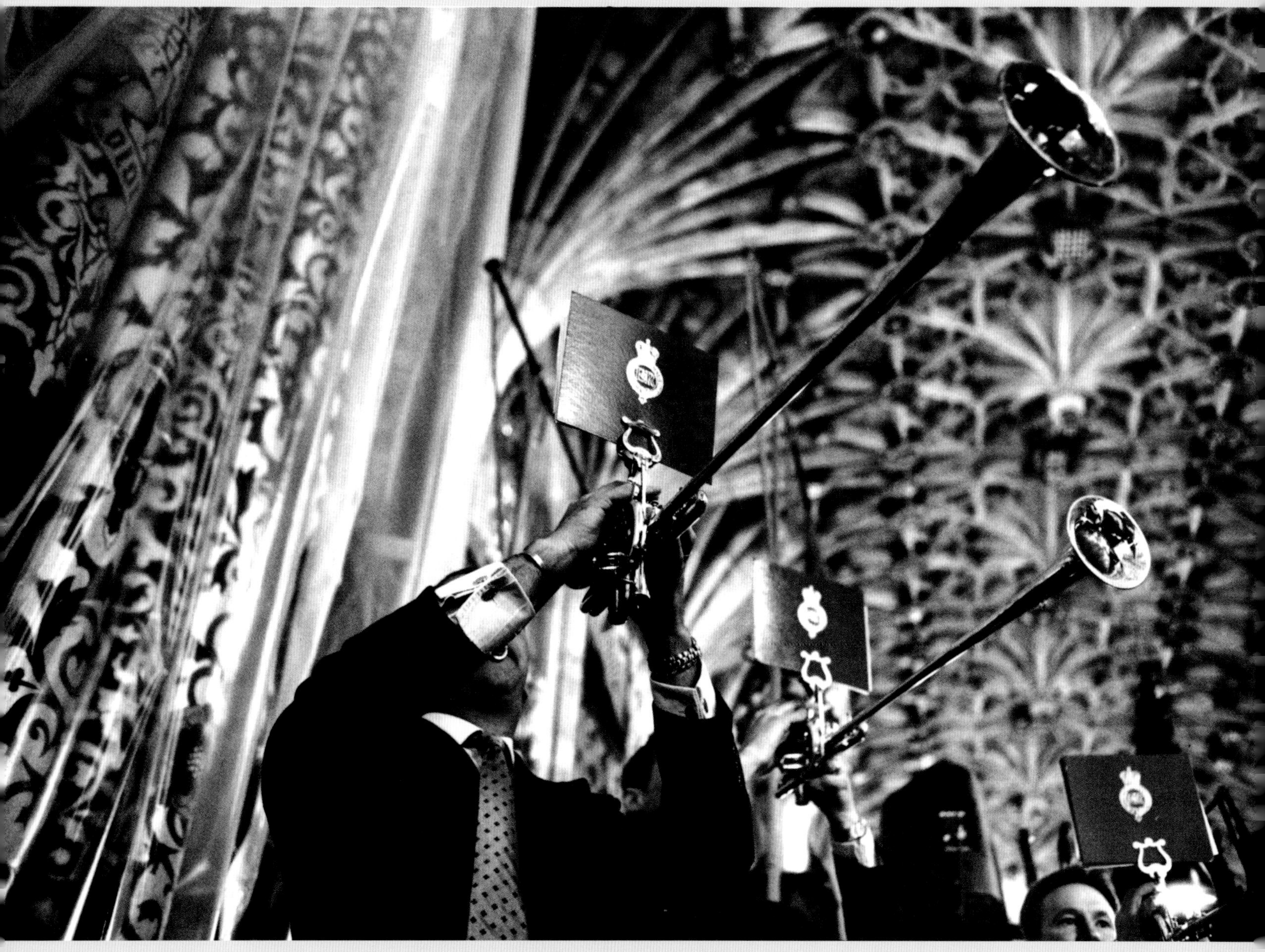

Above: The Trumpeters of the Band of the Life Guards sound fanfares on the arrival of HM The Queen and during the service.

Right: HM The Queen and HRH The Duke of Edinburgh process through the nave. They are led by the Virger of the College of St George and the Dean of Windsor.

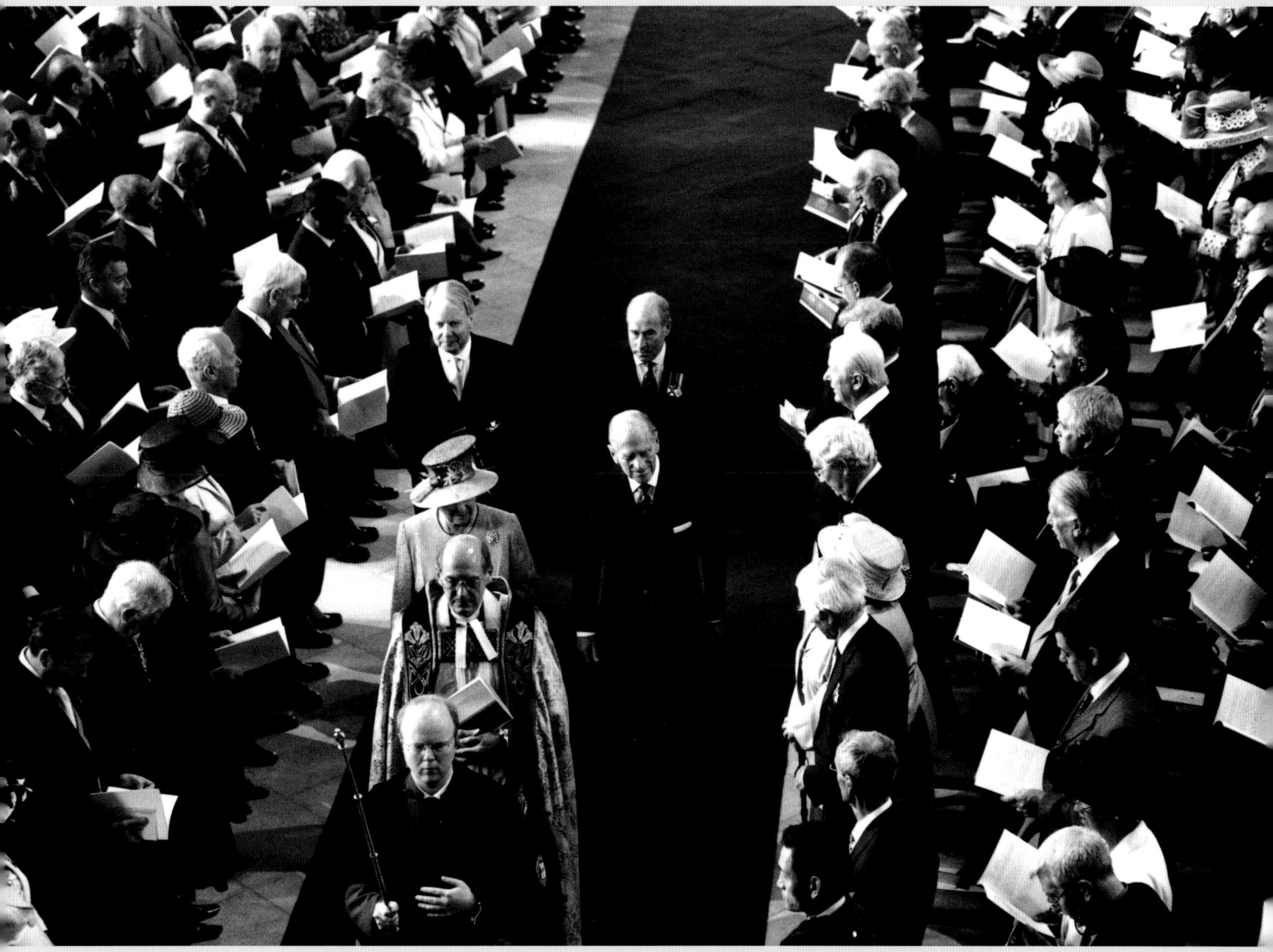

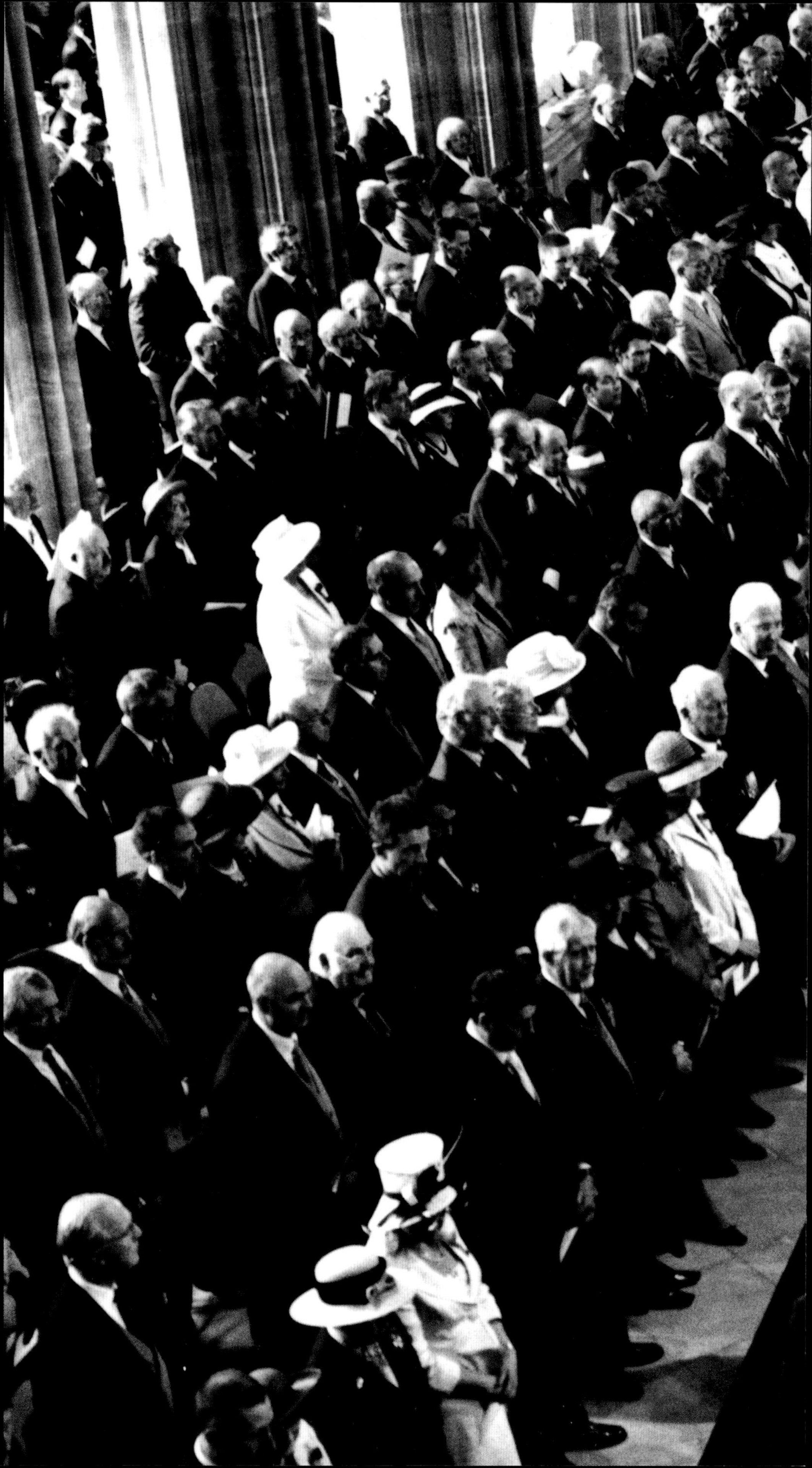

HM The Queen and HRH The Duke of Edinburgh follow the Dean of Windsor, the Virger of the College of St George, Rear Admiral Timothy Laurence, HRH The Princess Royal, and the Chaplain of the Royal Victorian Order.

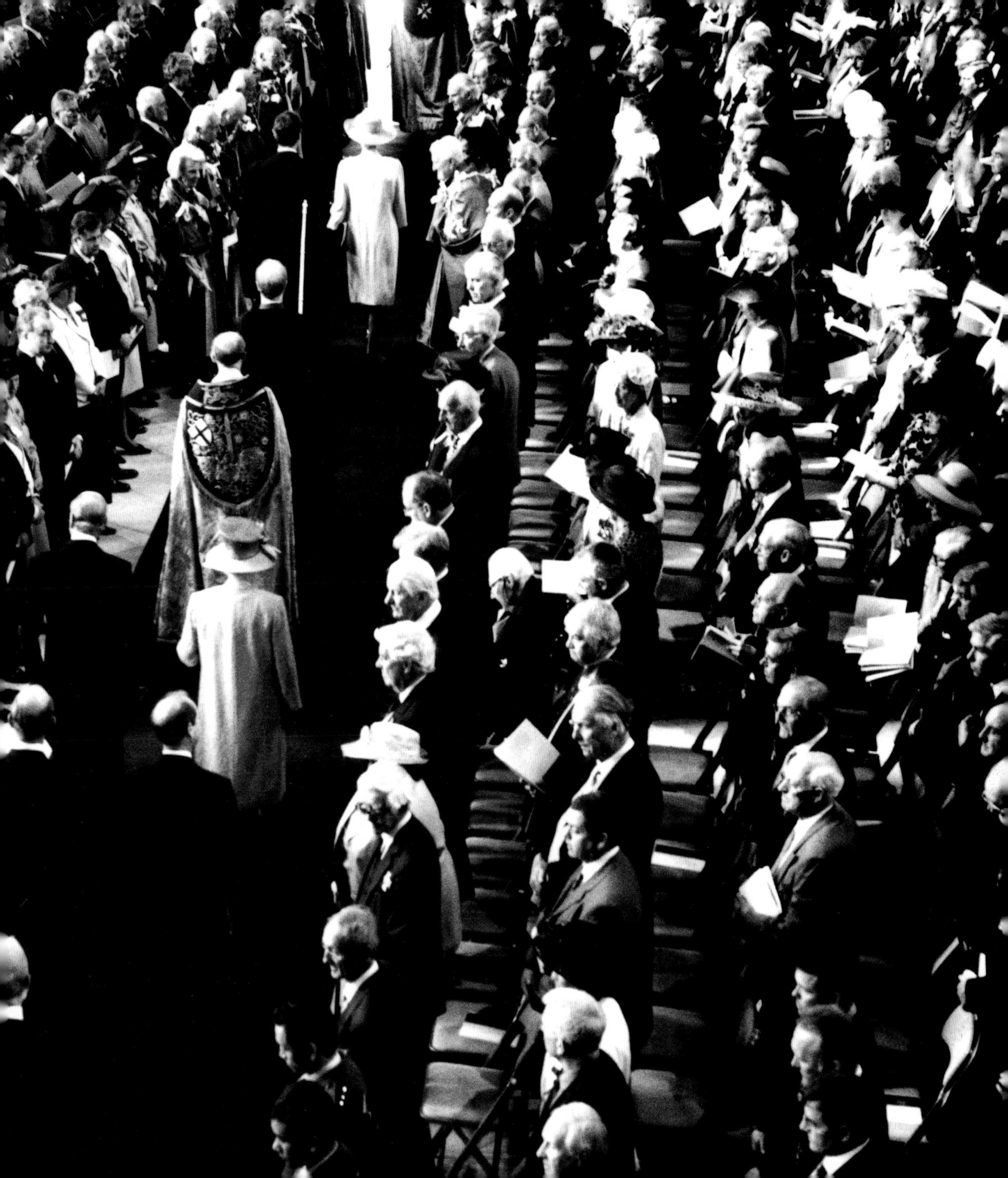

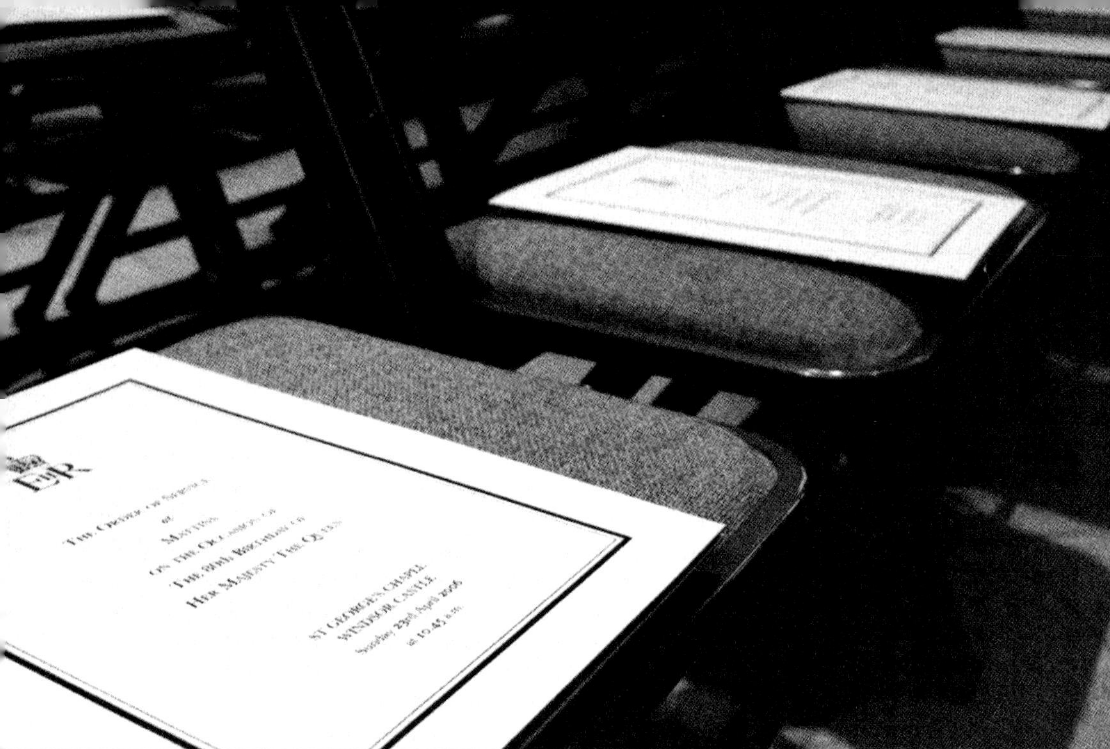

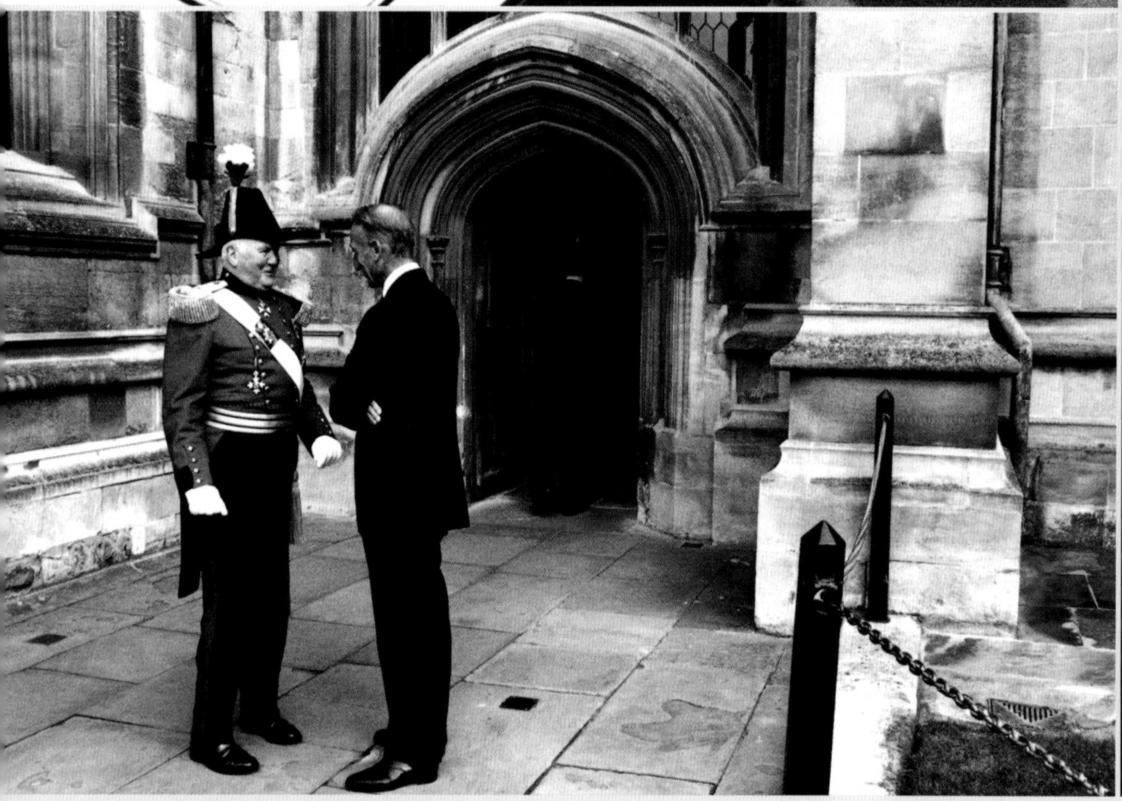

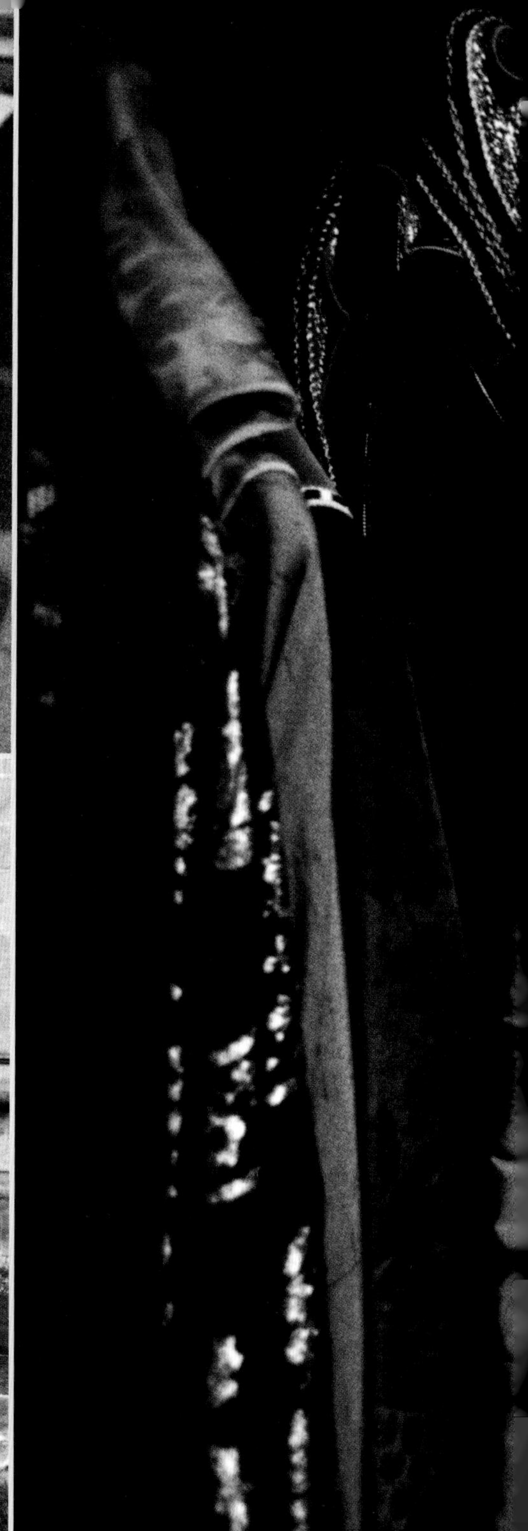

HM The Queen's 80th Birthday, April 2006

Top Left: Service sheets laid out on the seats in the nave in preparation for the Service celebrating HM The Queen's 80th Birthday.

Above Left: The Governor of the Military Knights of Windsor in conversation with a member of the congregation.

Right: Detail of the cope worn by the Dean of Windsor for the Service hung up in the Vestry.

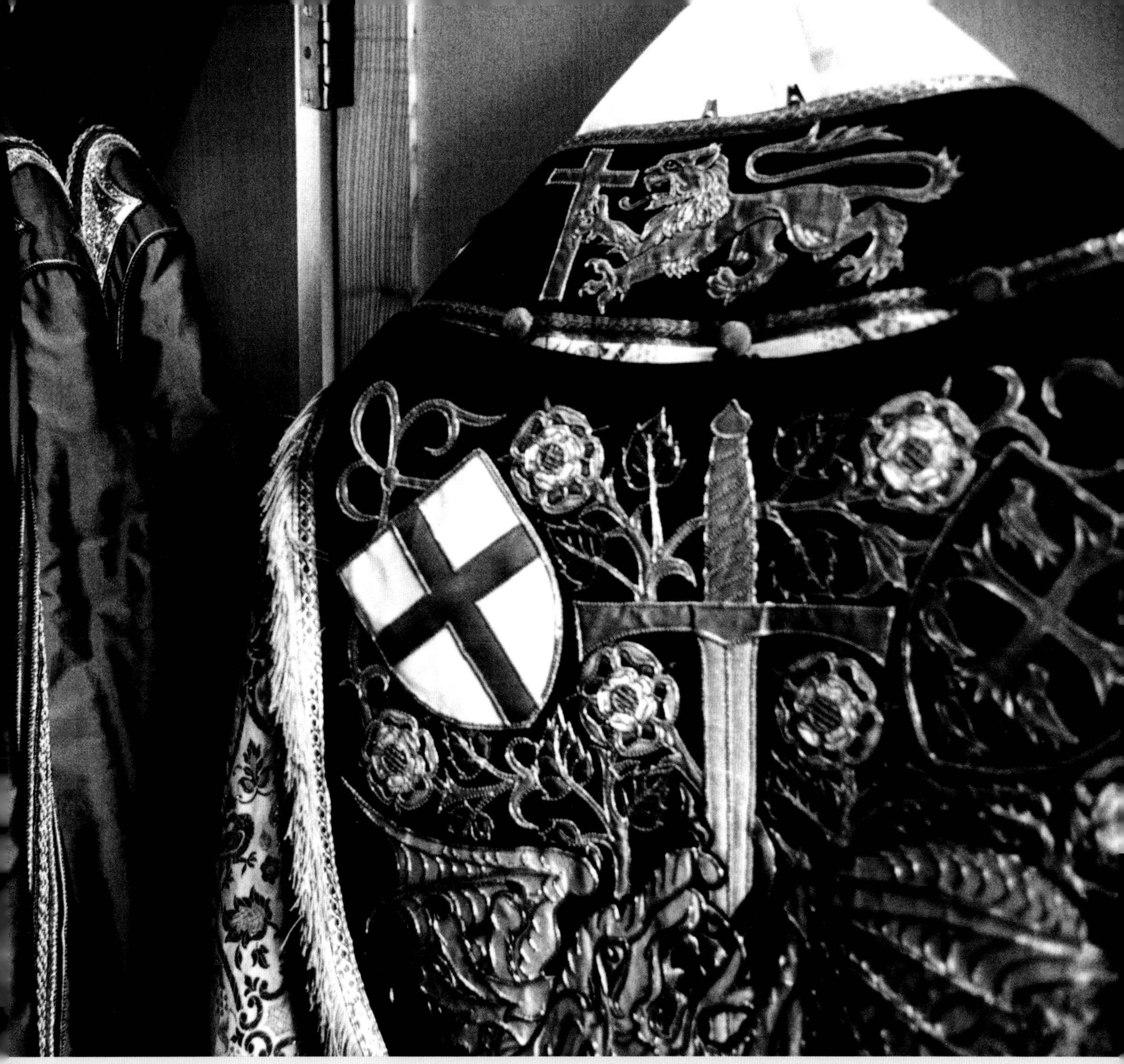

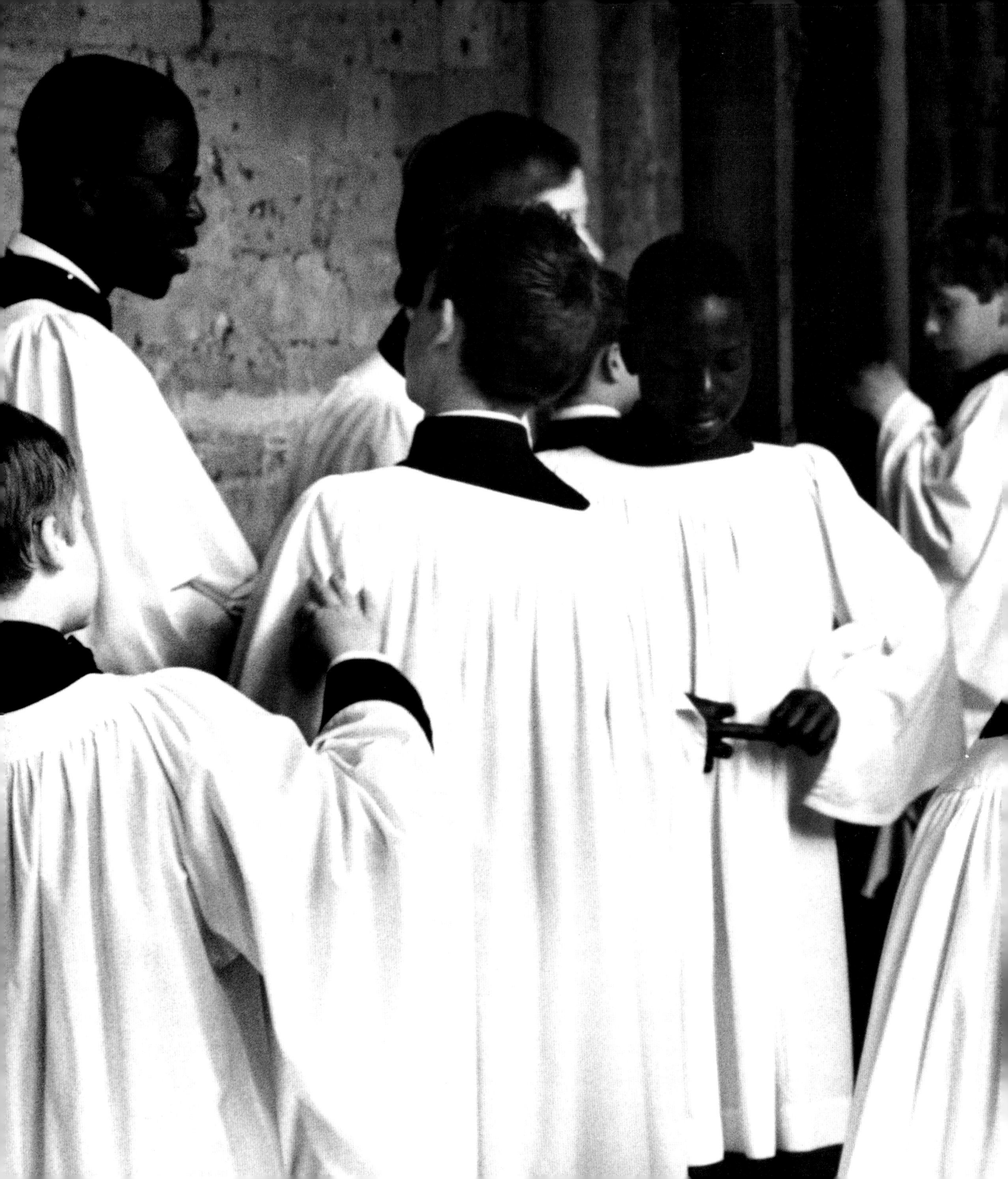

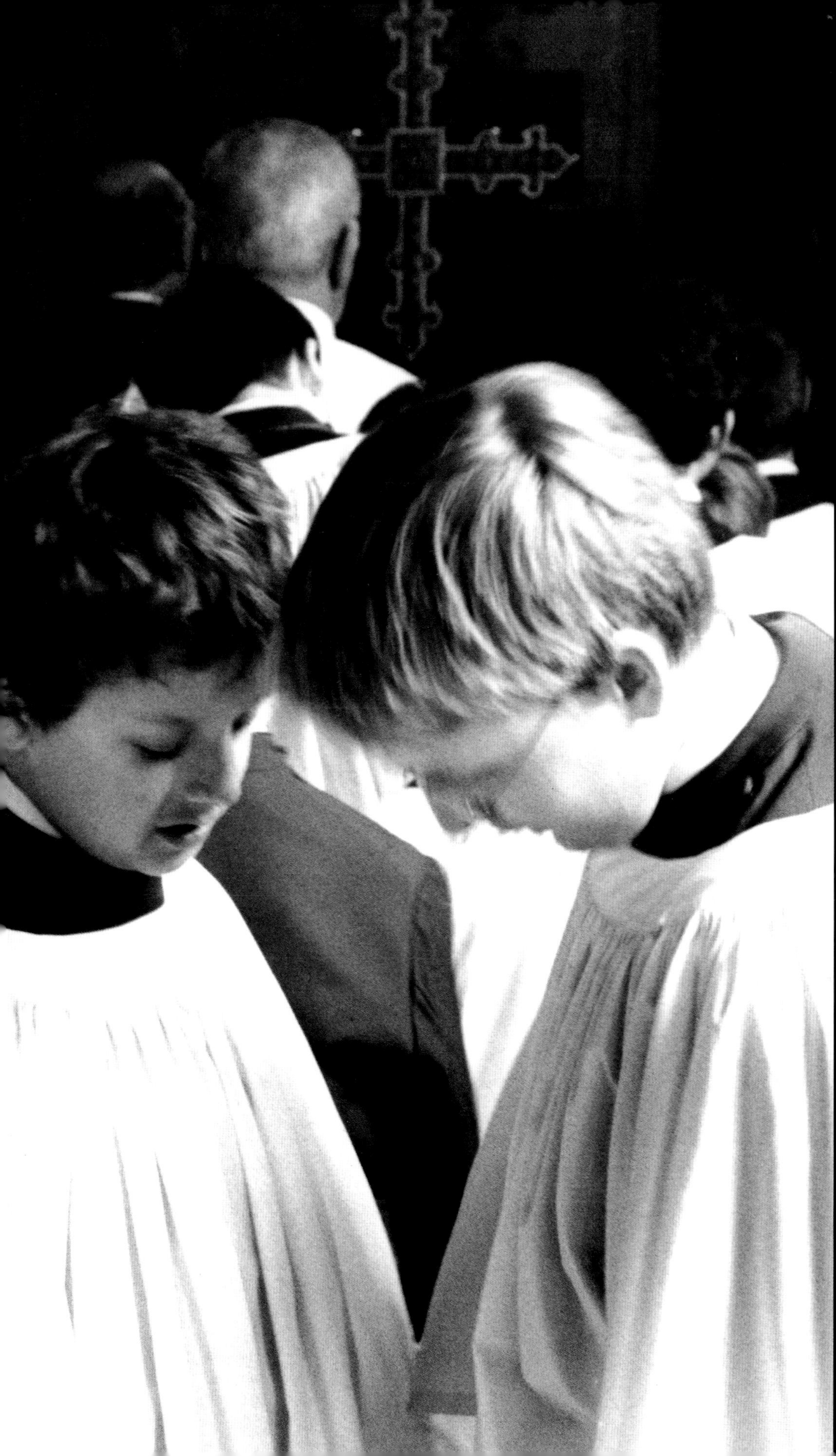

The Choir in the Dean's Cloister form up behind the Crucifer prior to the Service for HM The Queen's 80th Birthday.

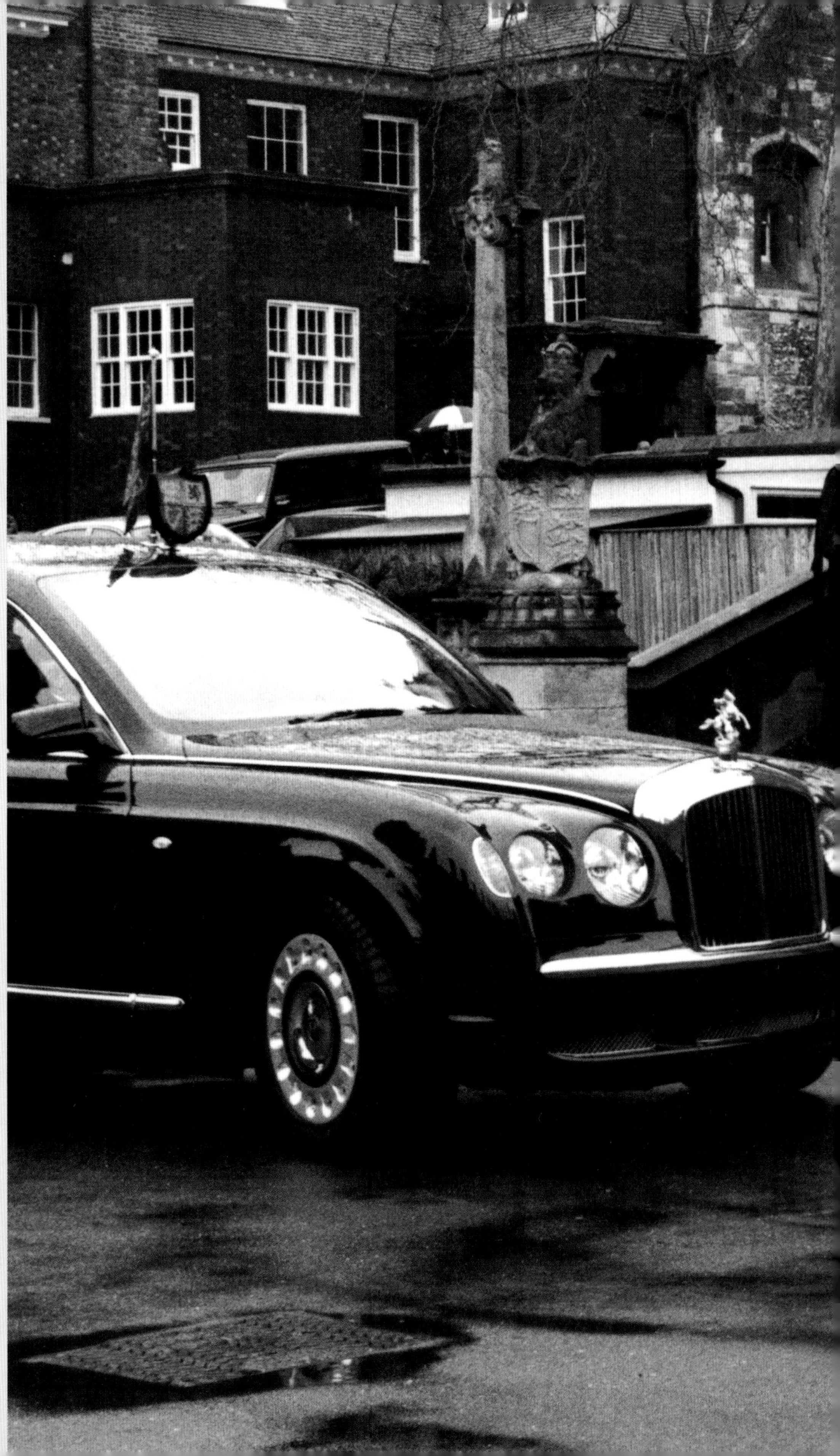

HM The Queen and HRH The Duke of Edinburgh walking down the West Steps followed by members of the Royal Family after the service for her 80th birthday.

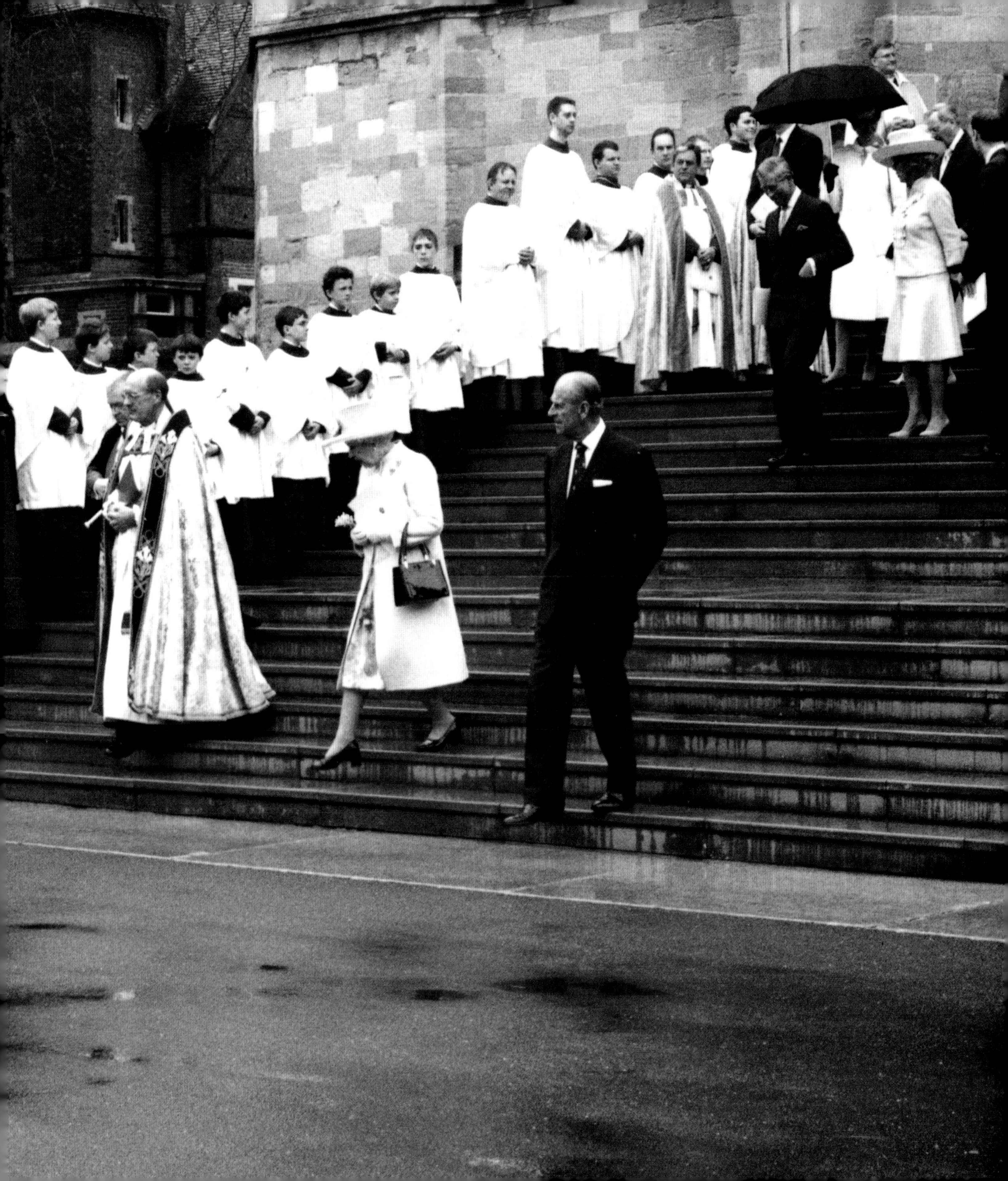

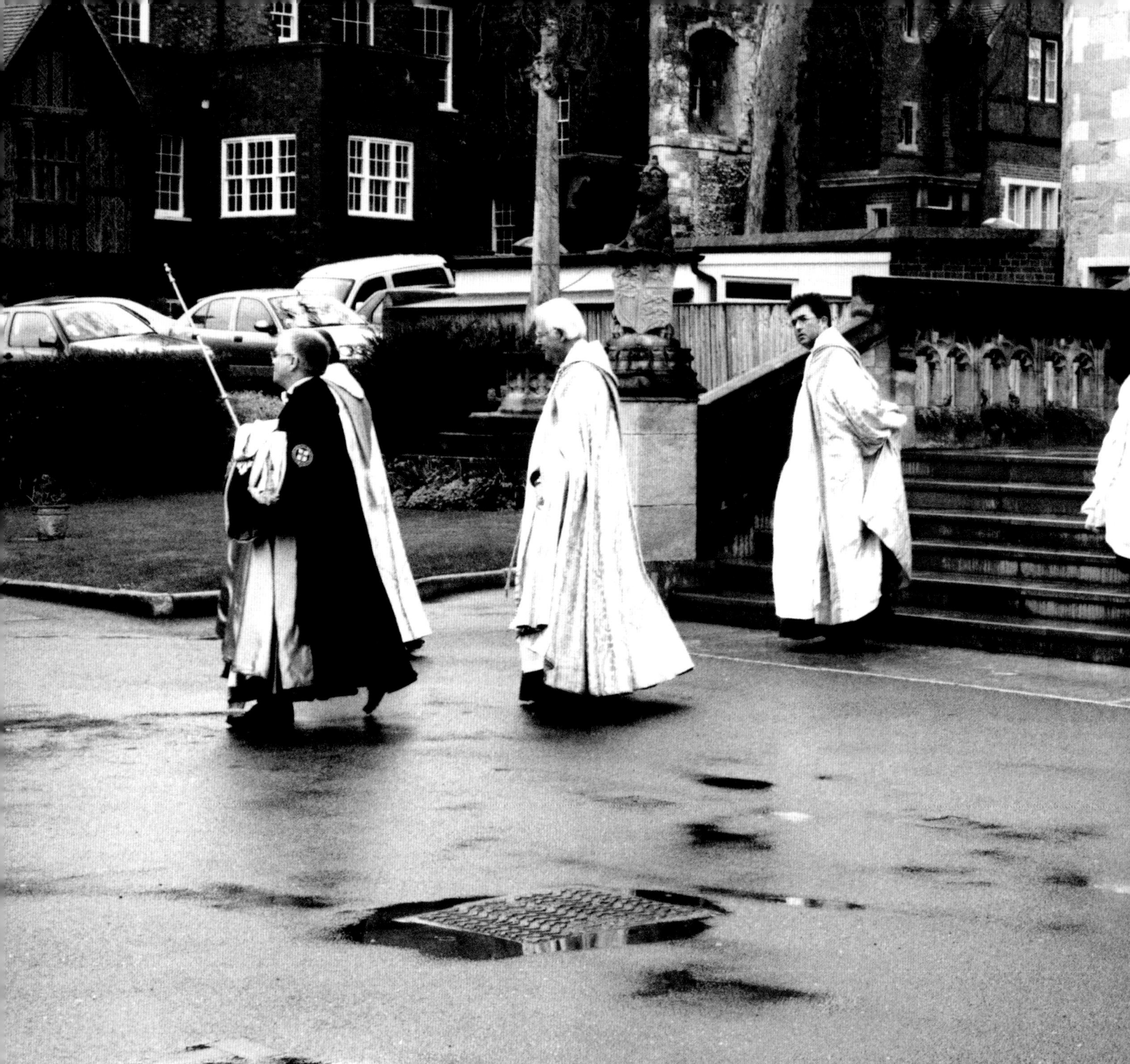

Above: The Virger and Canons of the College of St George's coming down the West Steps after the Service for HM The Queen's 80th Birthday.

Right: Members of the press waiting to film the arrival of the Royal Family on the West Steps after the Service.

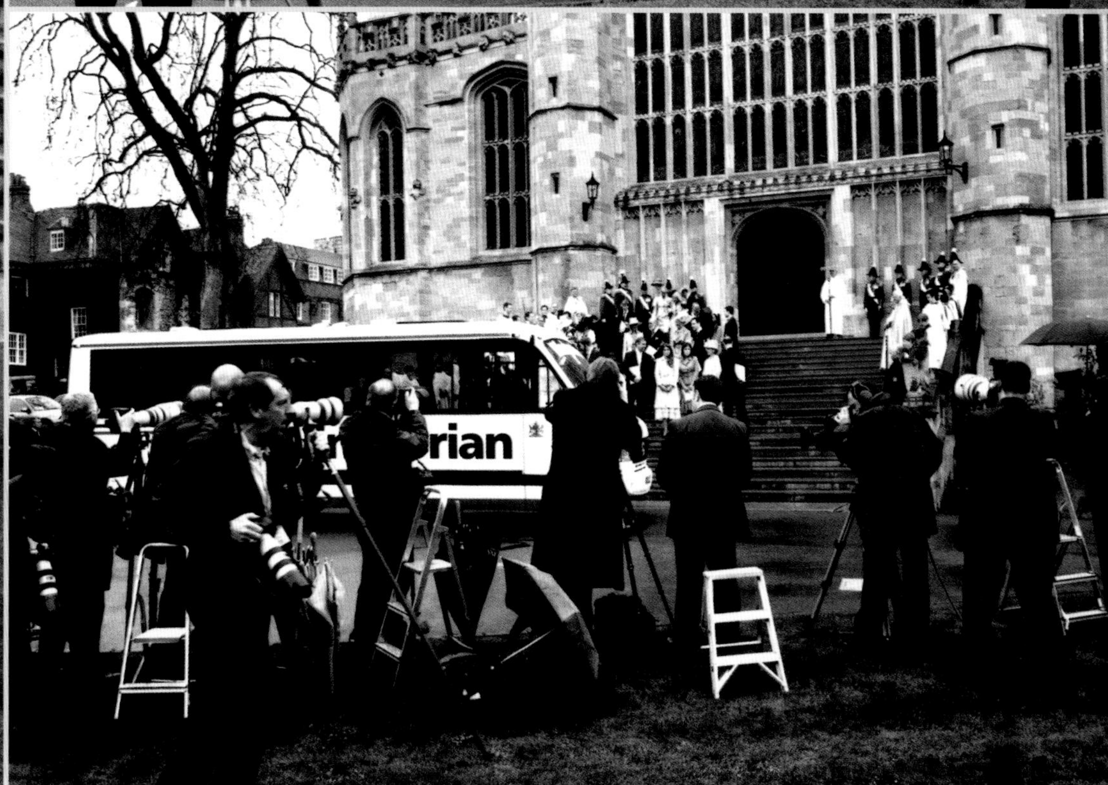

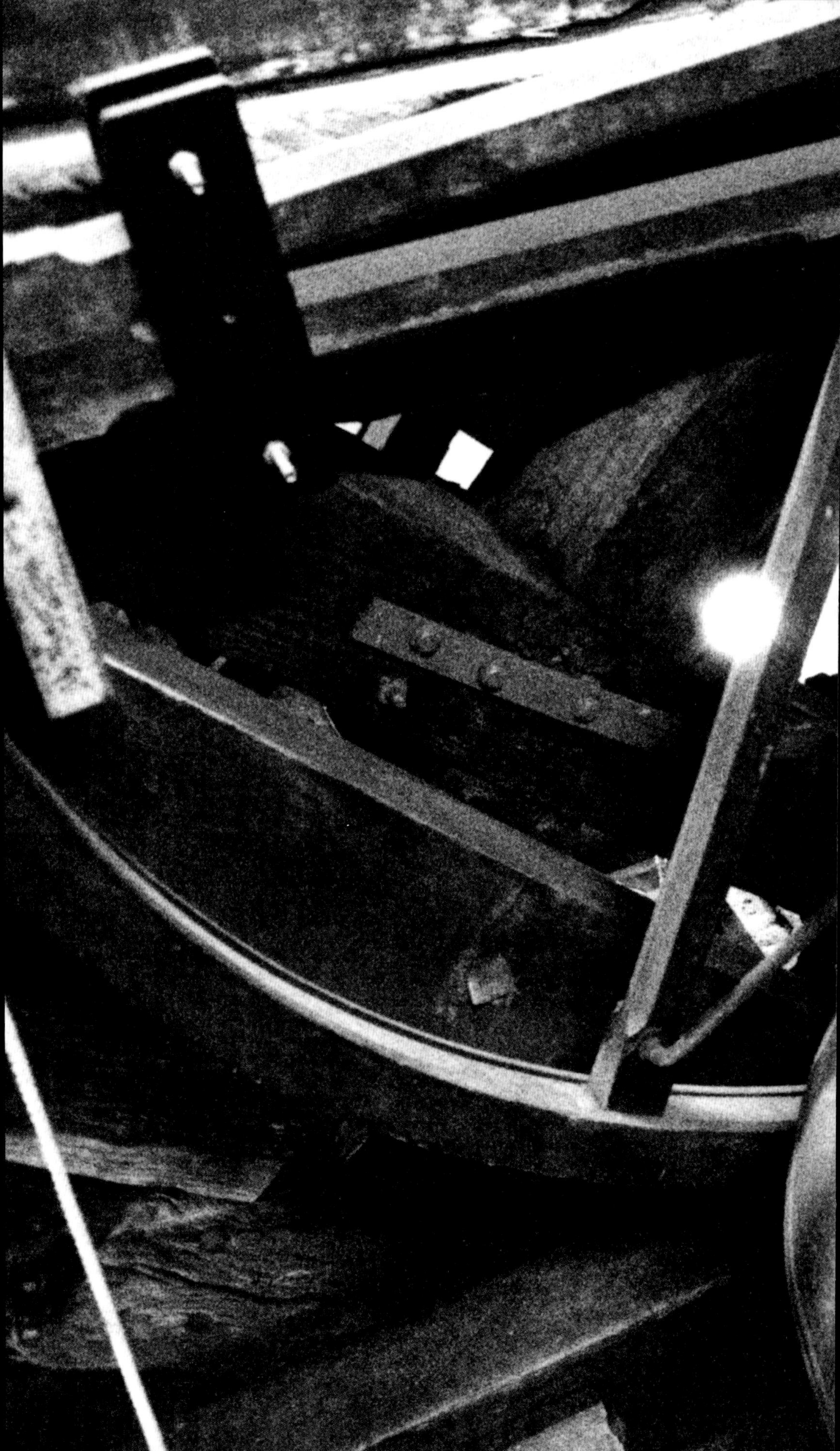

The bell tower inside the Curfew Tower is a magnificent timber-framed structure dating back to the late fifteenth century. It is the principal clock tower and belfry of the Castle, housing eight bells that date from 1612 to 1898. The bells are rung principally for the great Christian Festivals, a feast of title or for Royal birthdays. There are a total of twelve bellringers.

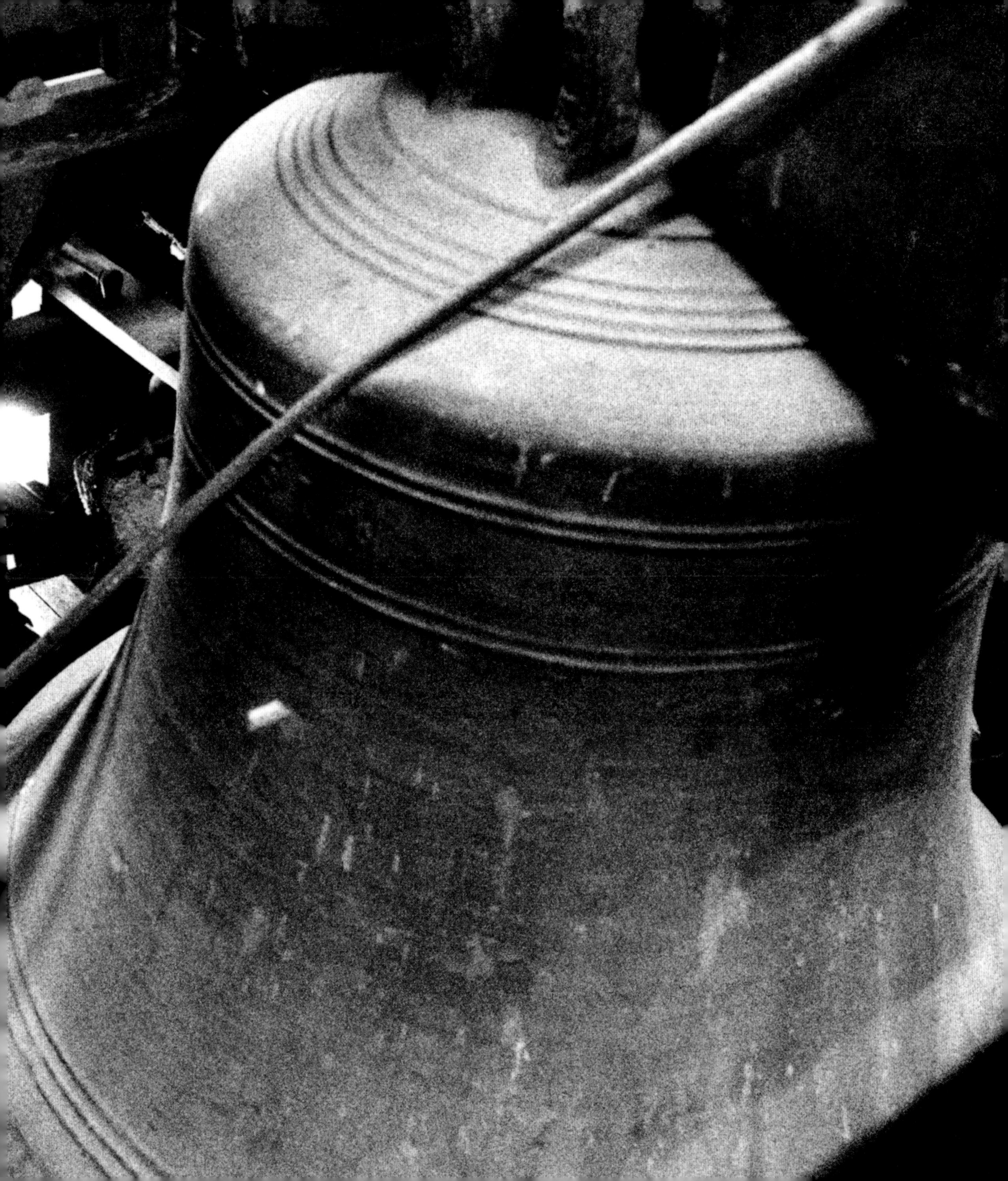

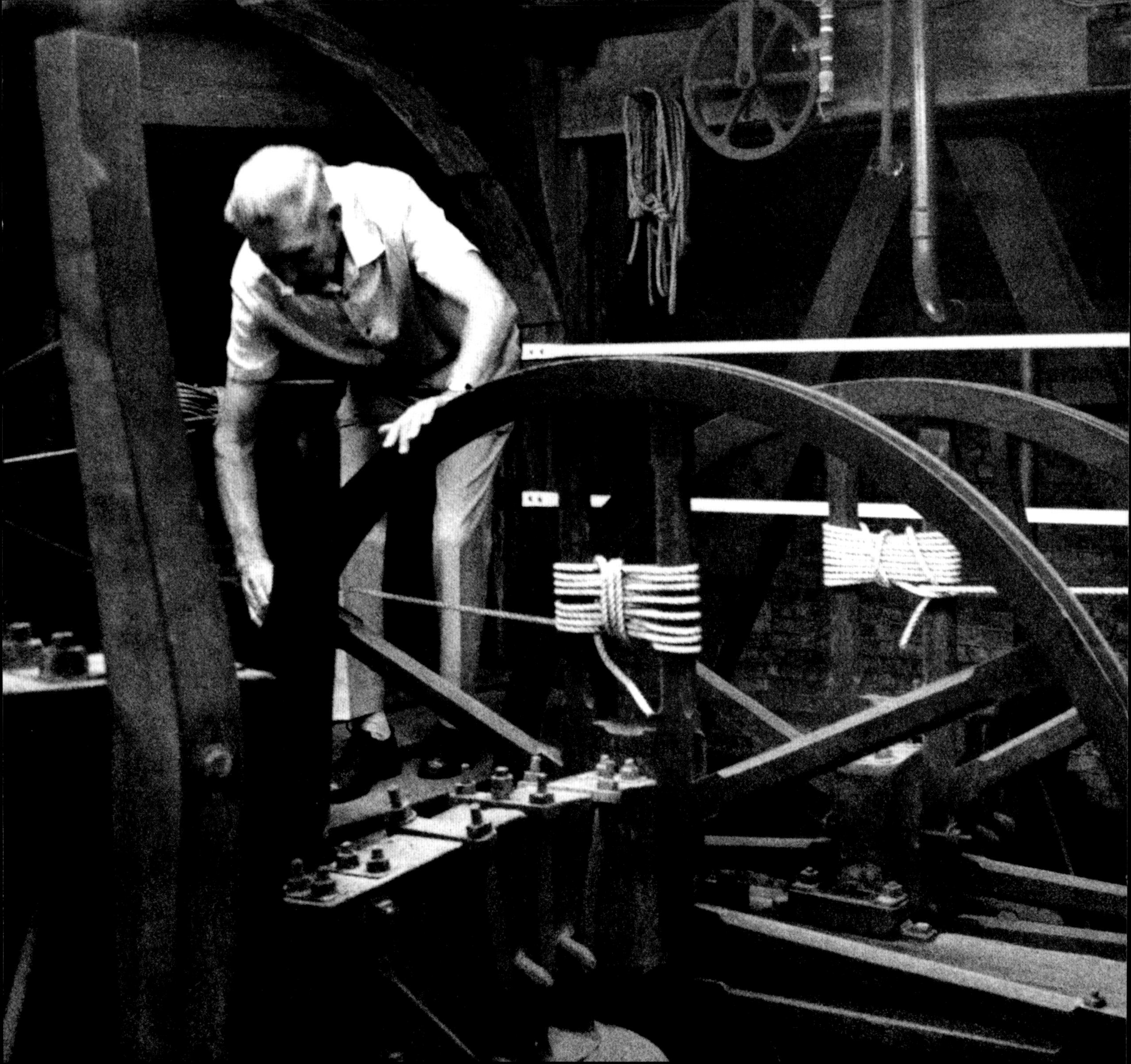

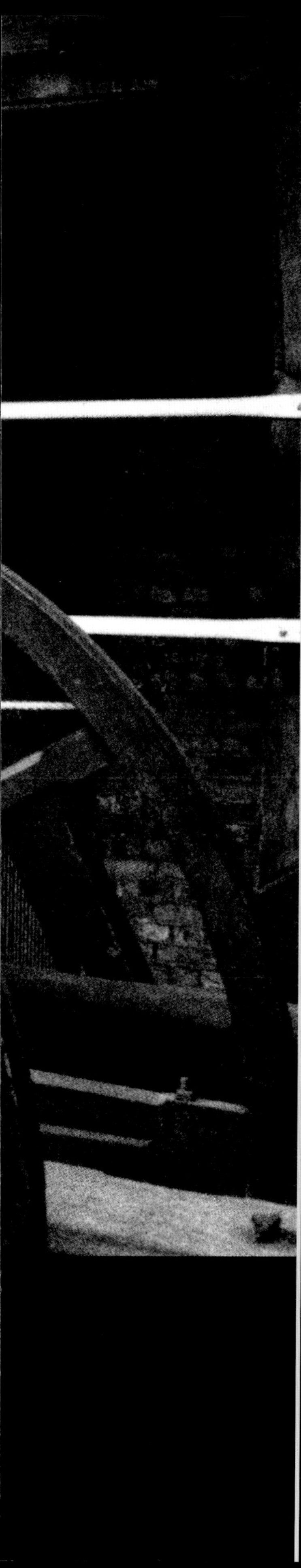

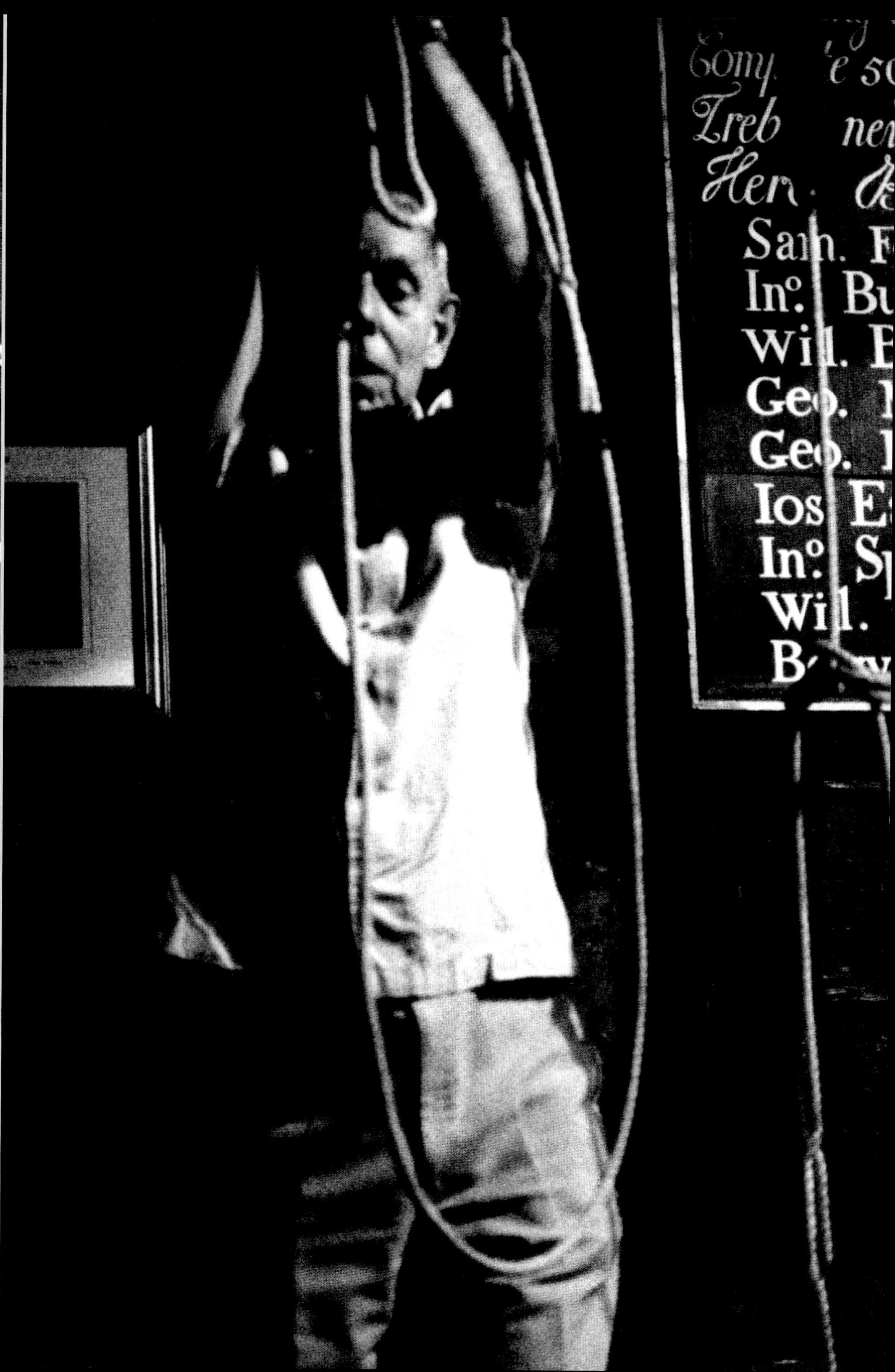

The sallyport is an impressive tunnel dating back to the thirteenth century. Today it is accessed from a trap door in the Curfew Tower. It was built as a secret exit route from the castle and is wide enough for a great number of troops to pass.

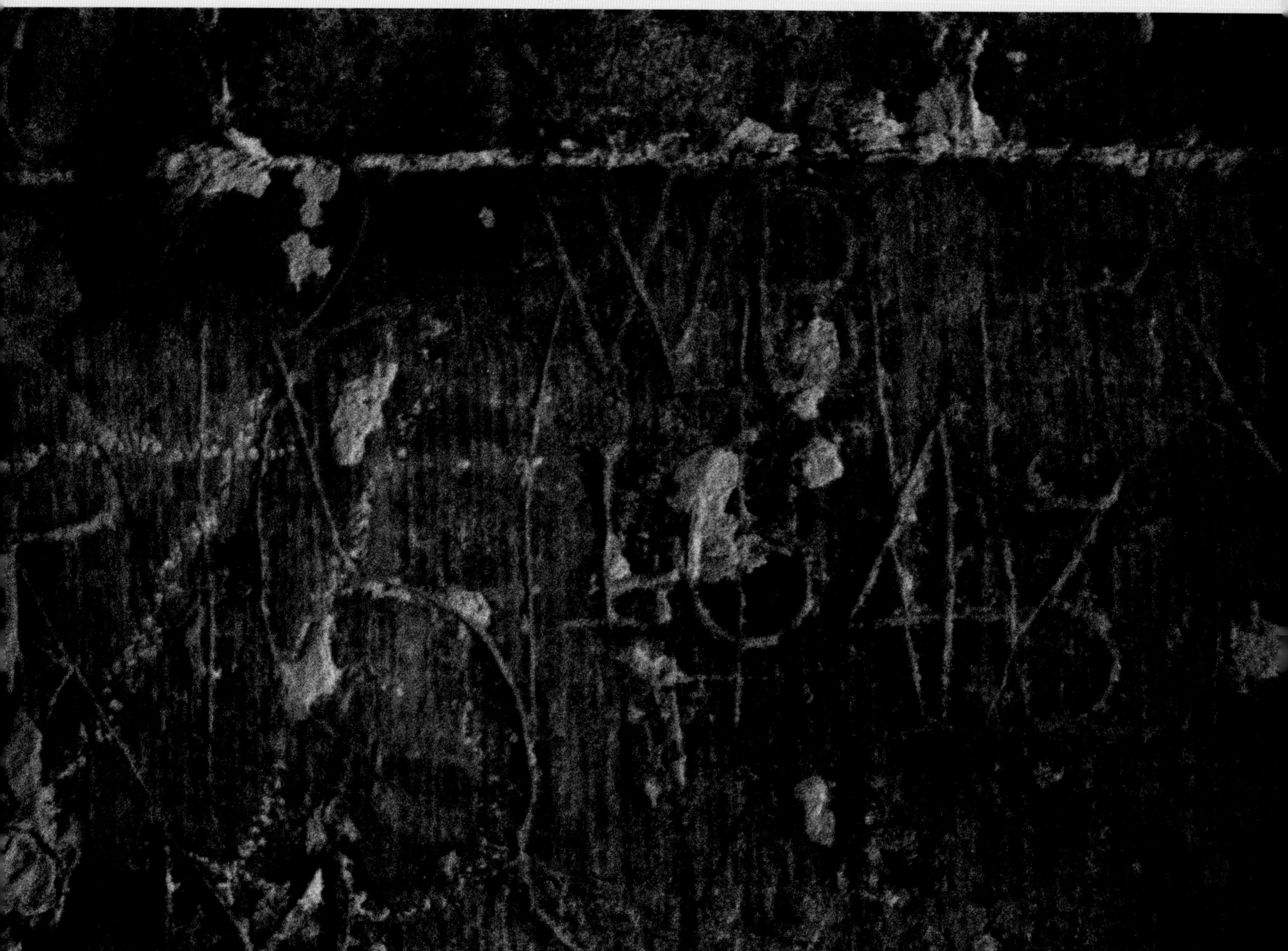

The Dungeon, possibly built for weapon storage rather than as a dungeon, is located at the lower ground level of the Curfew Tower, which itself dates back to the late fifteenth century. During the period from 1642 when Parliament took possession of Windsor Castle until the Restoration of the monarchy in 1660, the Dungeon was used to imprison royalists. Their graffiti has marked their history permanently into the stone walls. Today the Dungeon is used as an occasional venue, but cobwebs remain thick and light is precious.

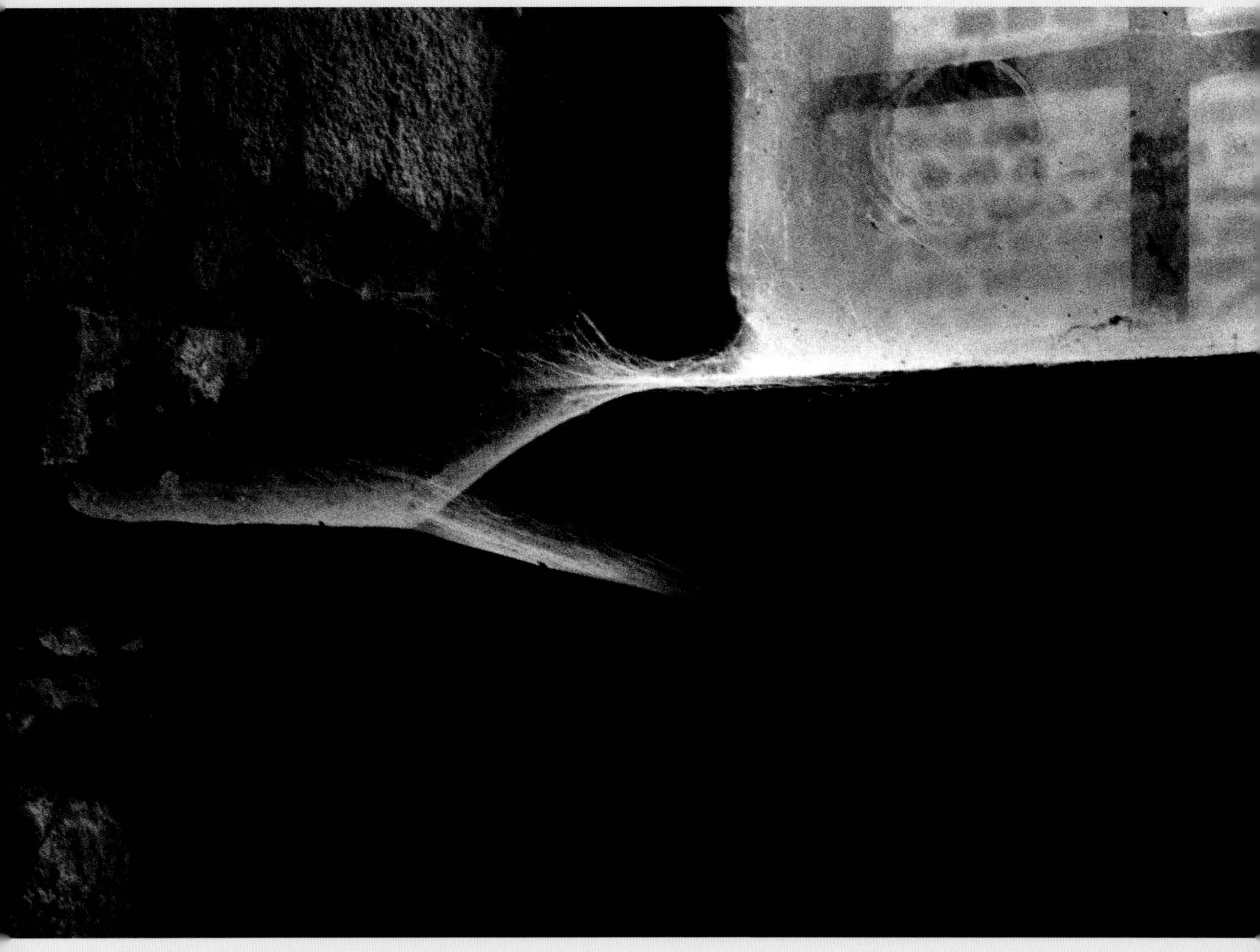

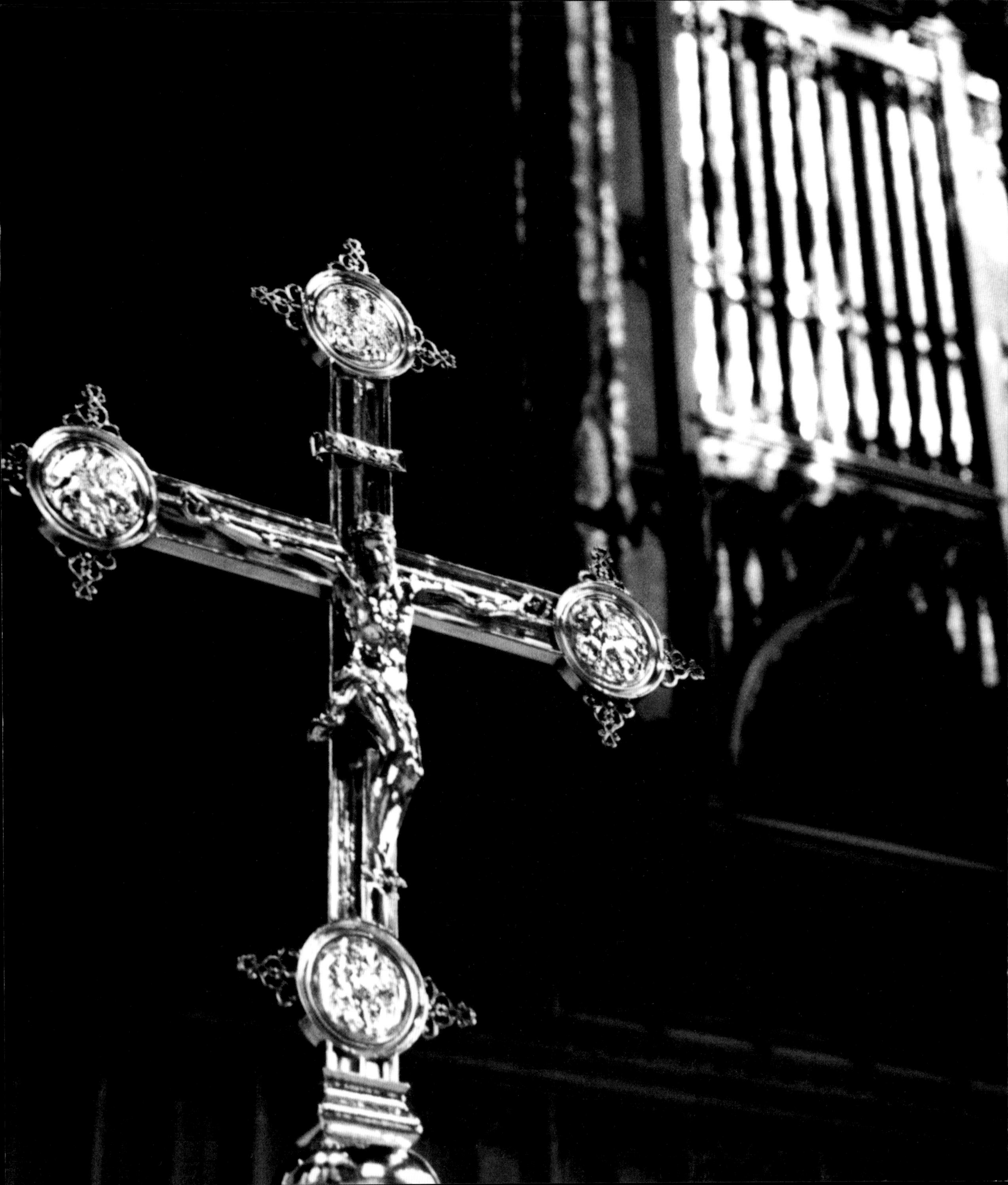

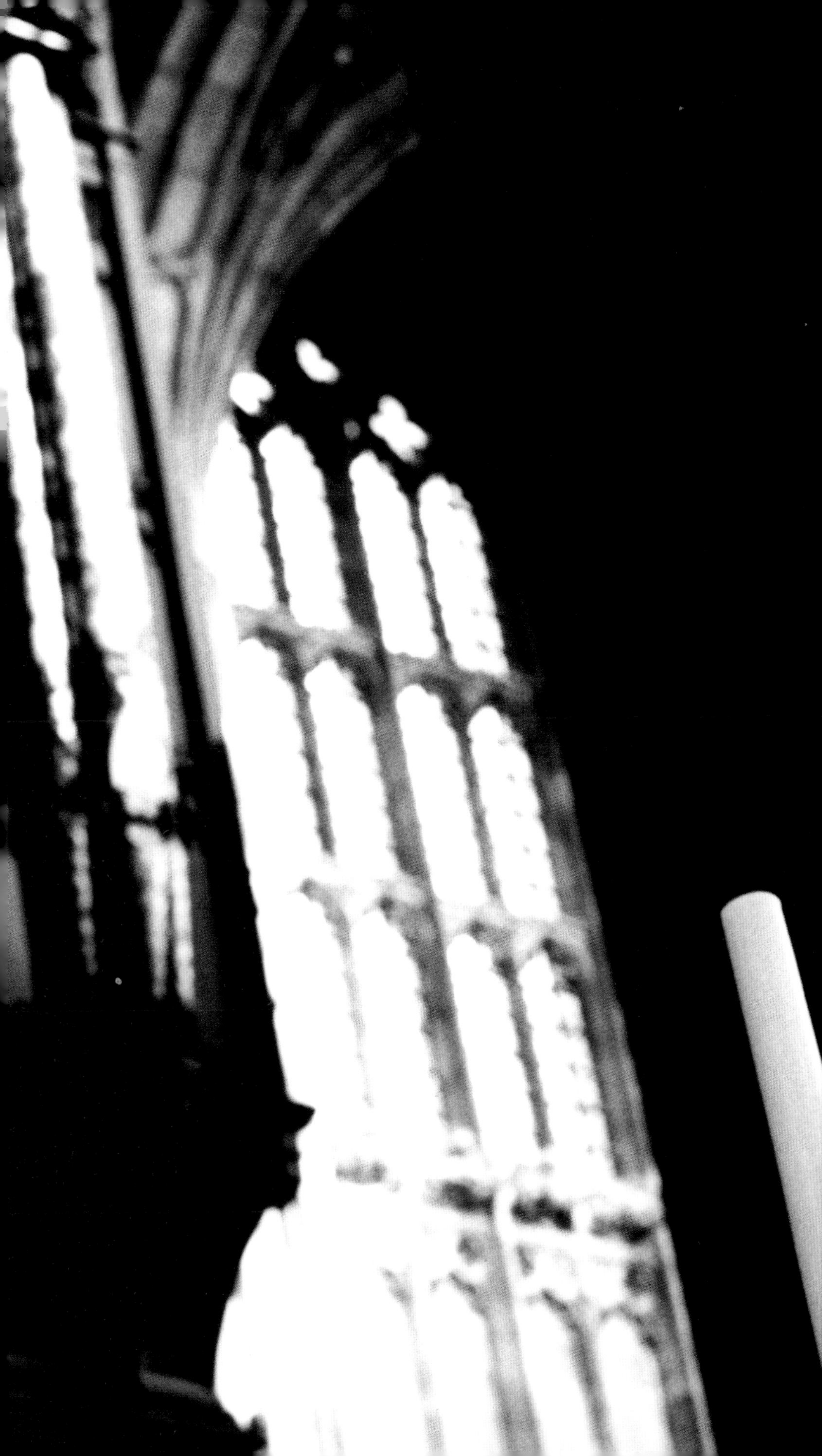

Festivities

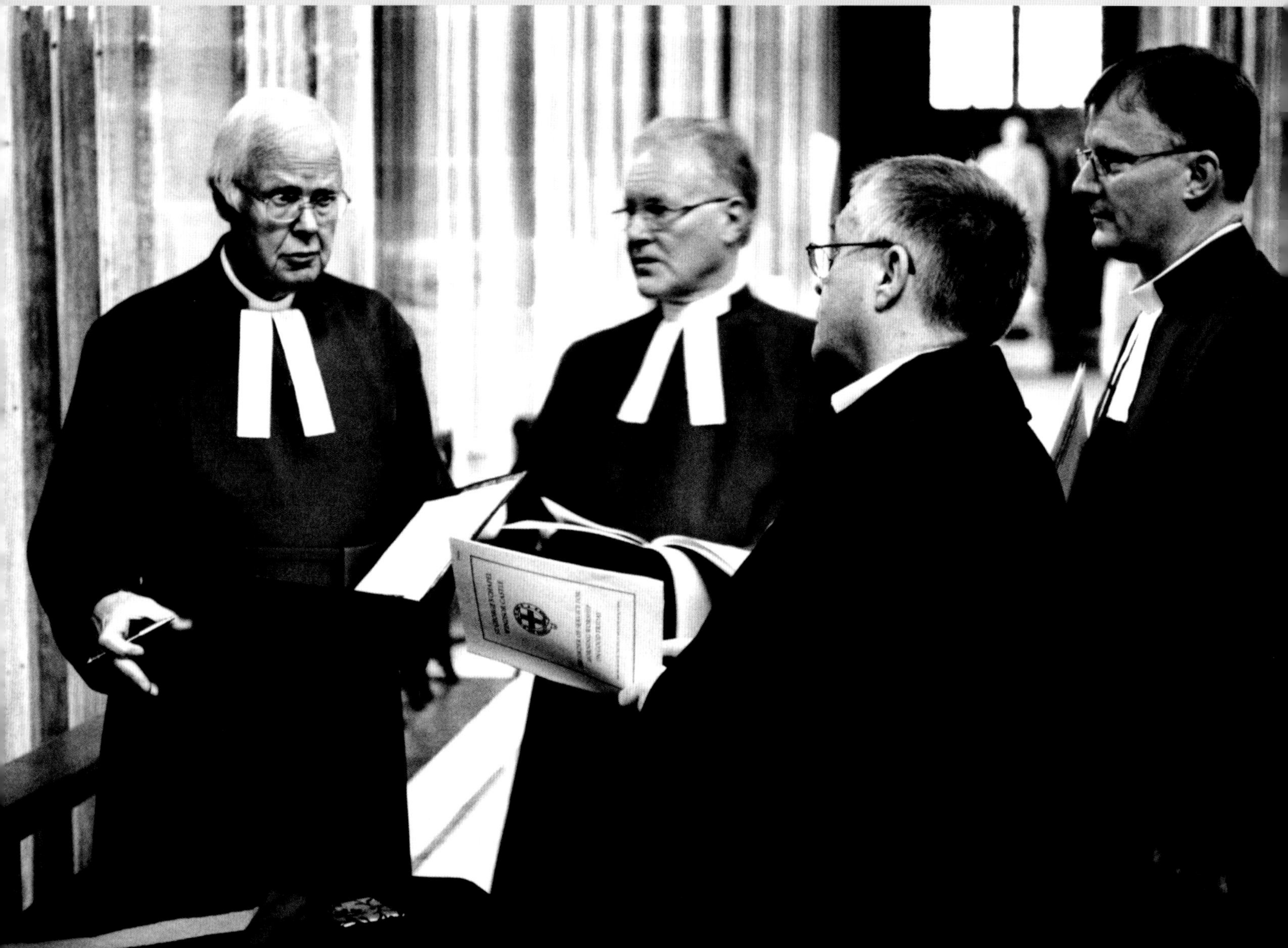

Easter: *Above:* The Virger and Canons of St George's Chapel rehearse for the Eucharist Service on Maundy Thursday and the Liturgy for Good Friday.

Right: A Minor Canon can be seen carrying a plain wooden cross under the fan vaults of the organ screen to its position for a service.

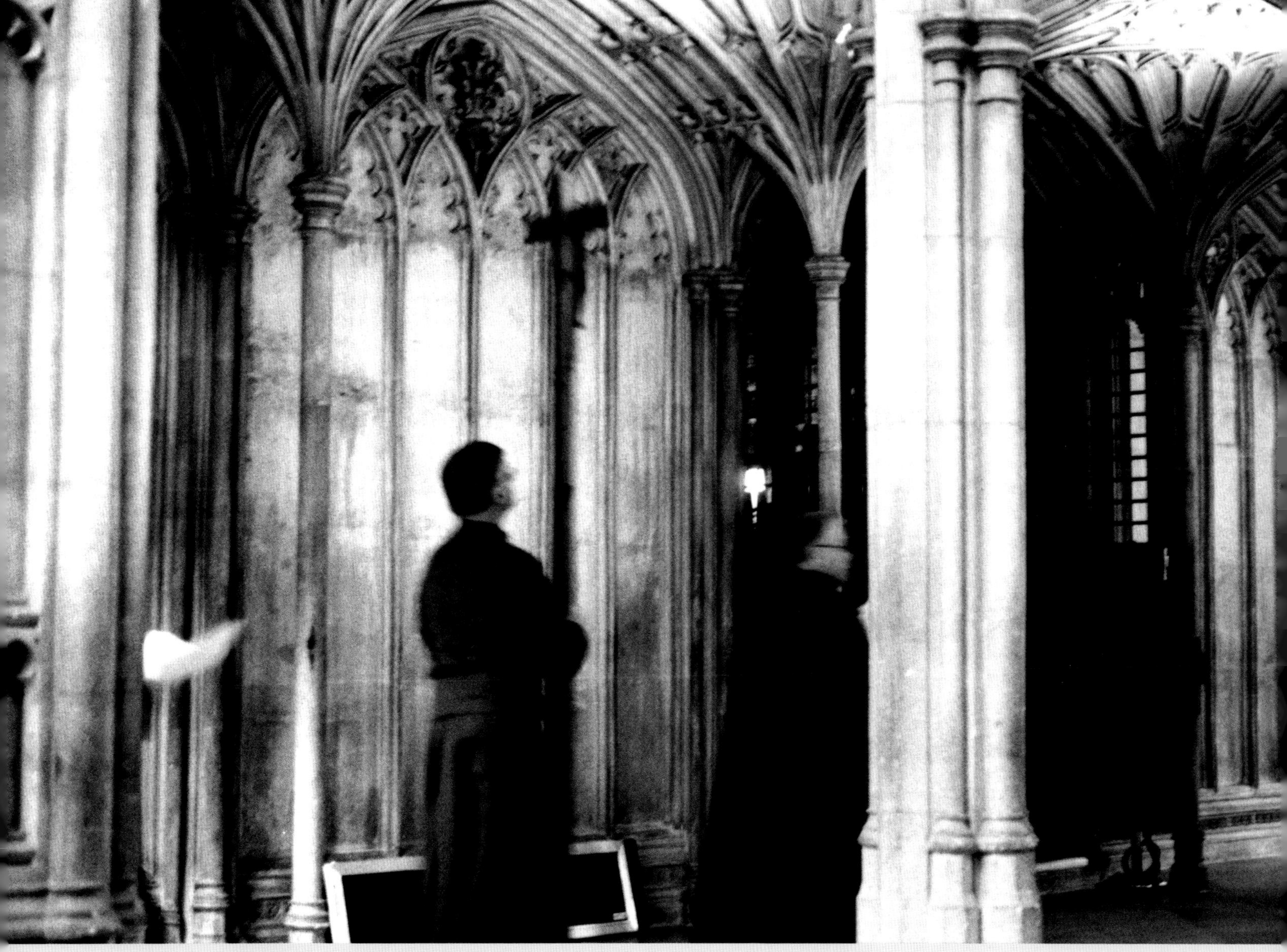

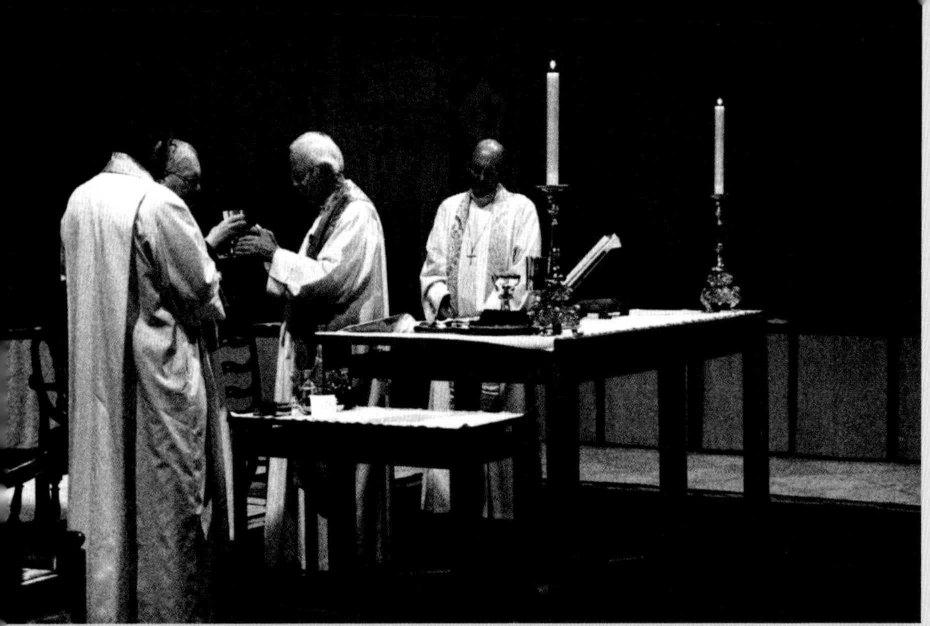

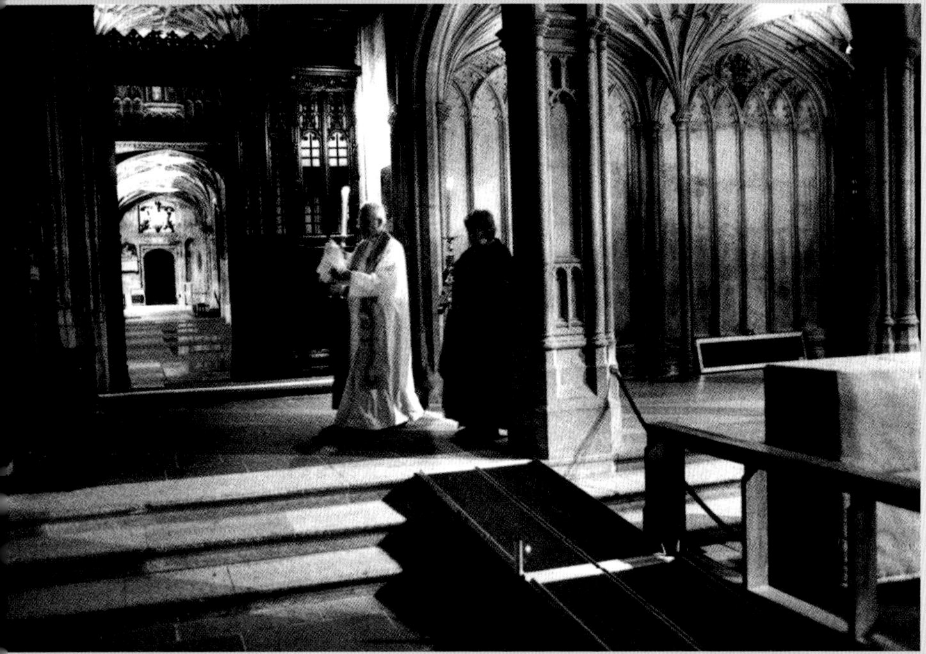

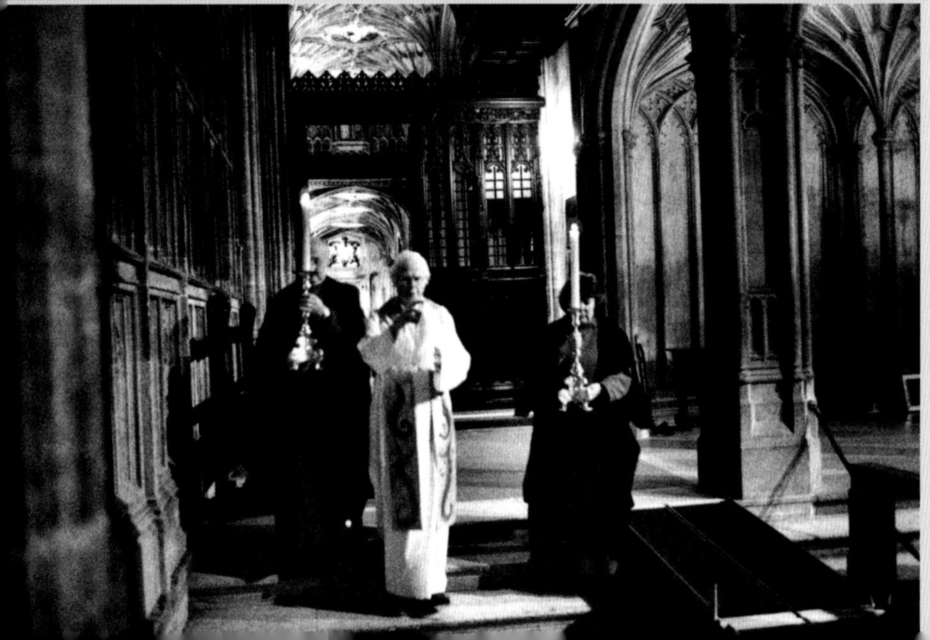

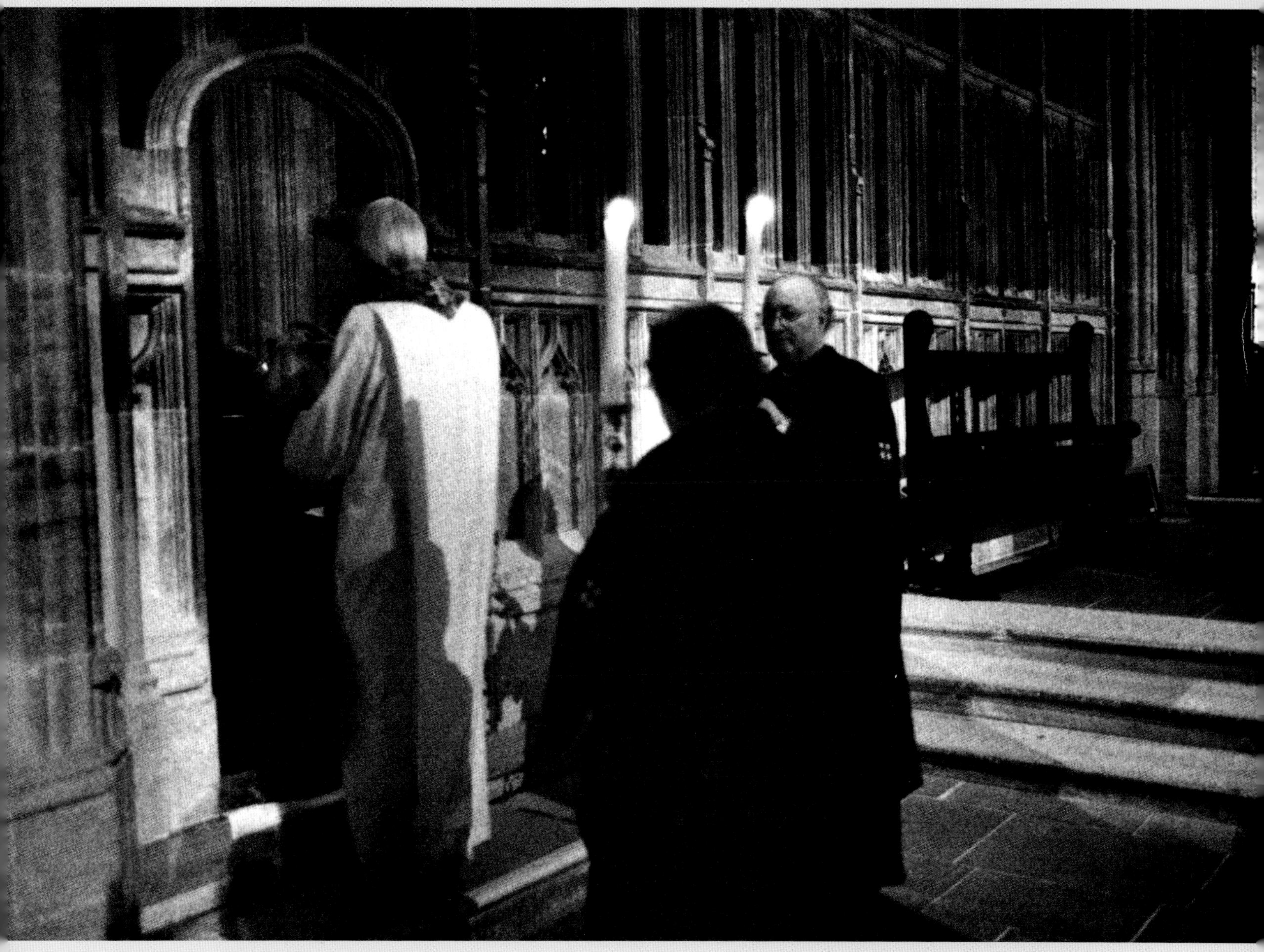

Eucharist Service on Maundy Thursday. The nave is being stripped of all decoration and the clergy are in simple robes. The clergy then carry the ciborium, a vessel for holding communion wafers, and Chapel staff carry candles at the end of the Service into the Rutland Chapel on the north side, where the all-night vigil will take place.

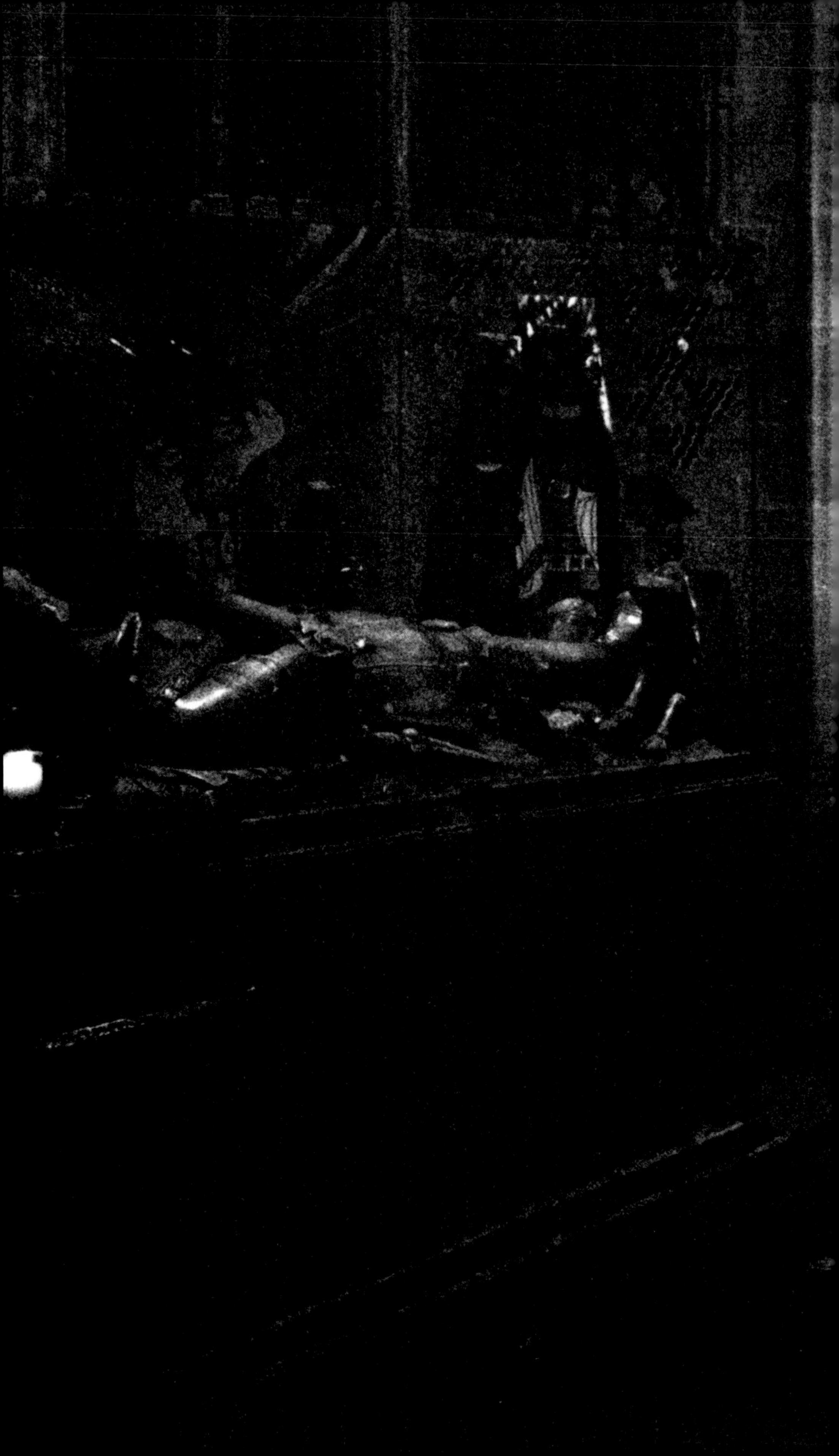

'The night watch'. Members of the College of St George take one-hour turns to 'keep watch' by prayer through the entire night in the Rutland Chapel.

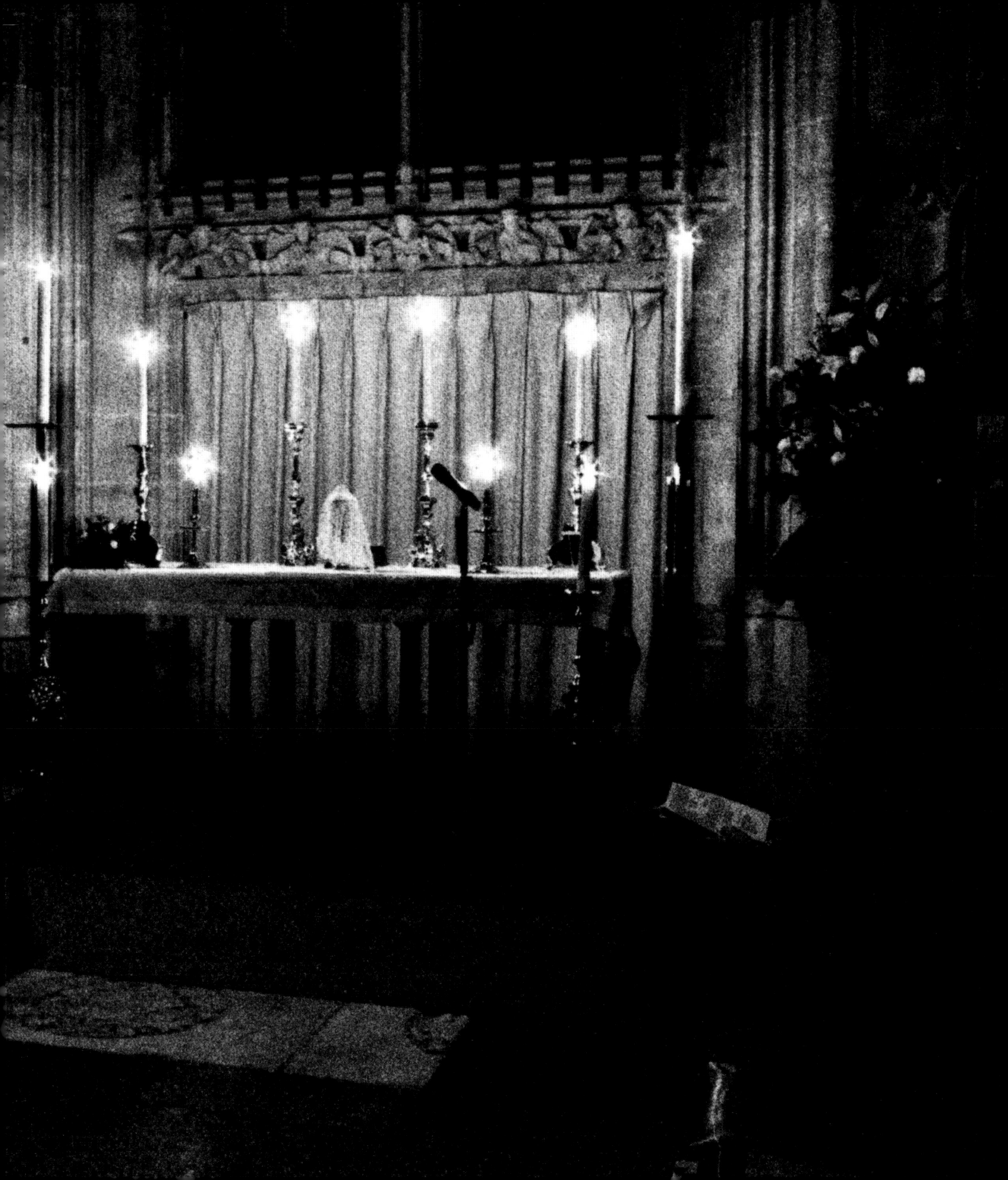

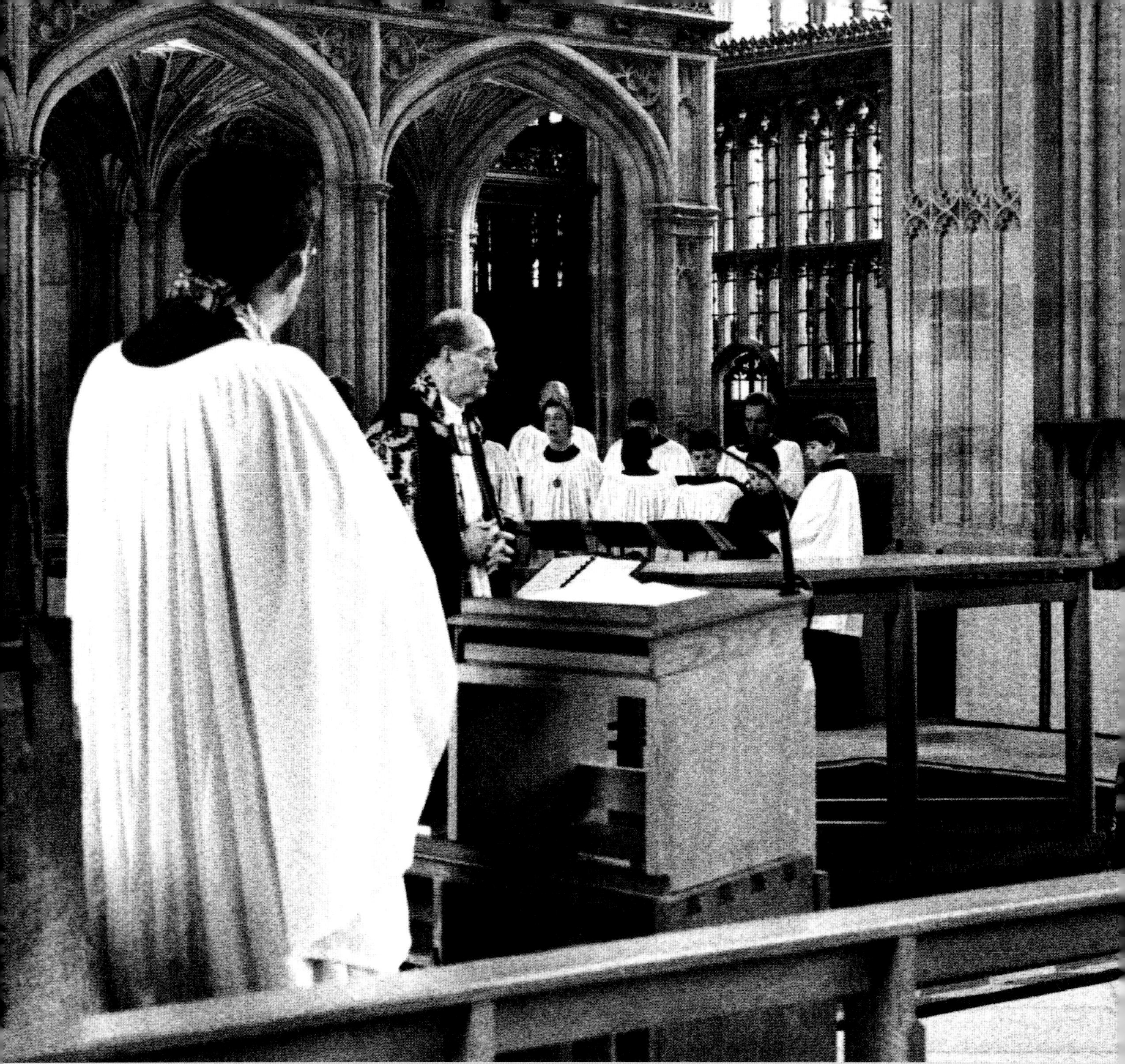

Easter: *Above*: The Minor Canon placing the cross in the nave during the Liturgy for Good Friday.
Top Right: The Canons during the Liturgy for Good Friday.
Bottom Right: Members of the public seated in the nave during a short afternoon service taken in rotation by the Canons of St George's on Good Friday.

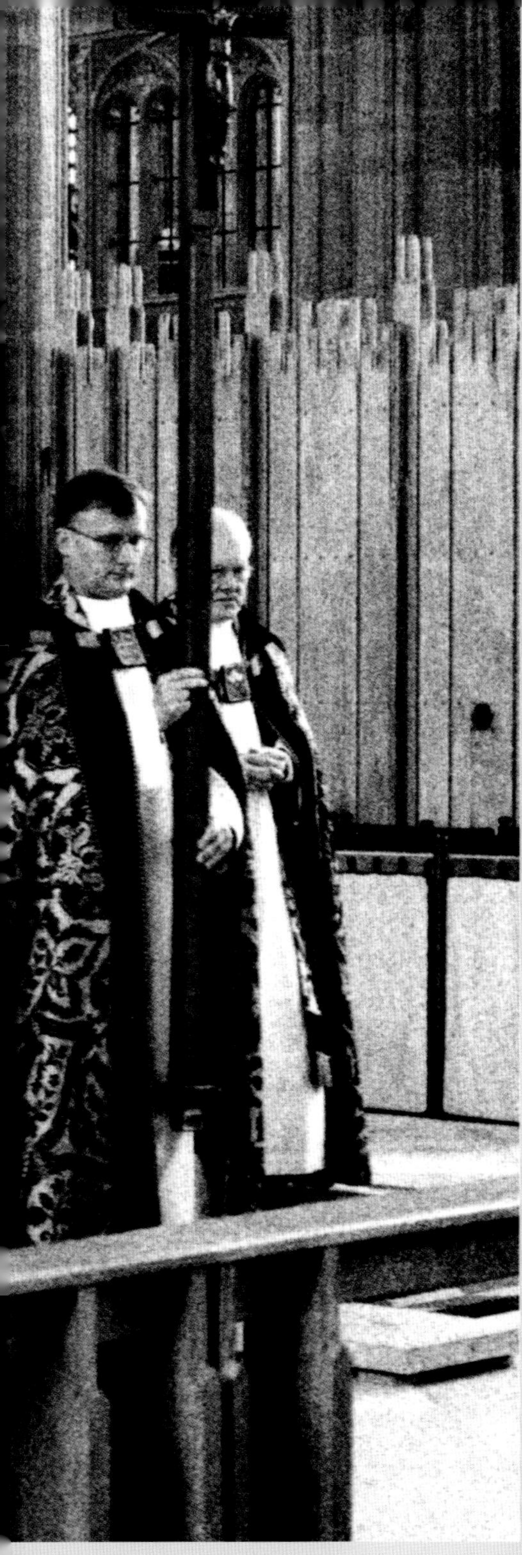

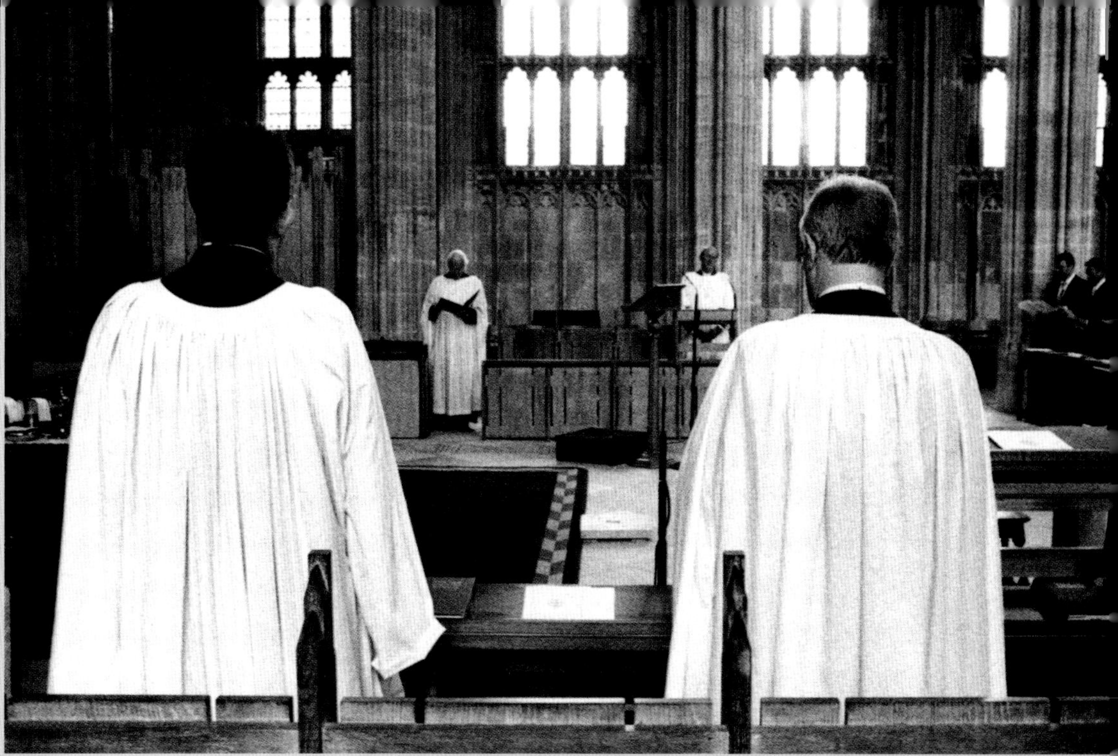

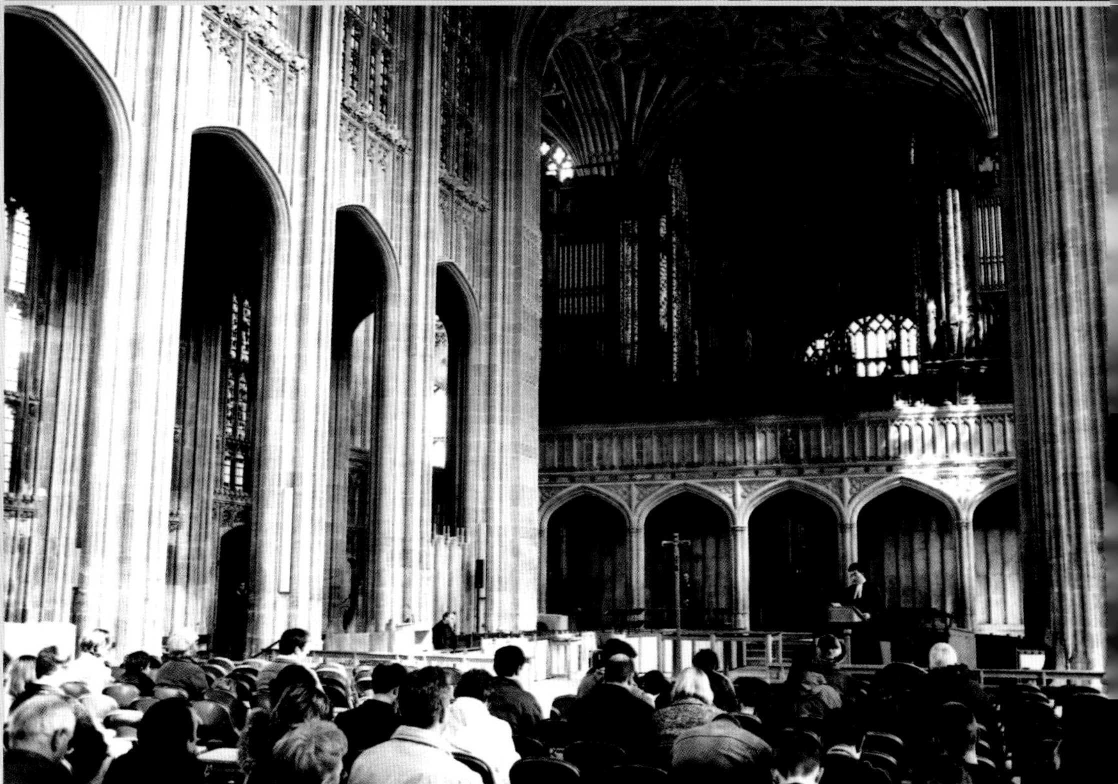

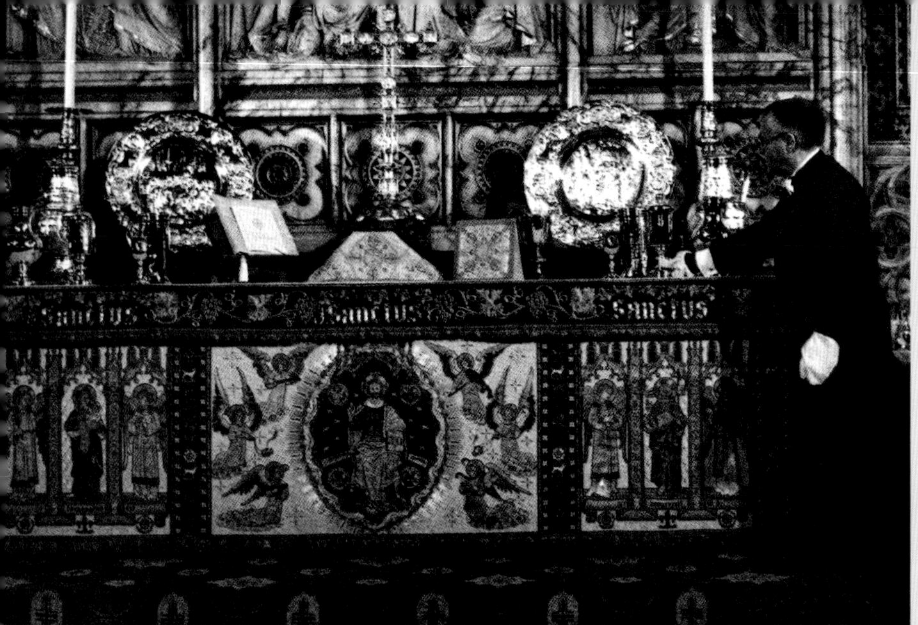
Sanctus Sanctus Sanctus

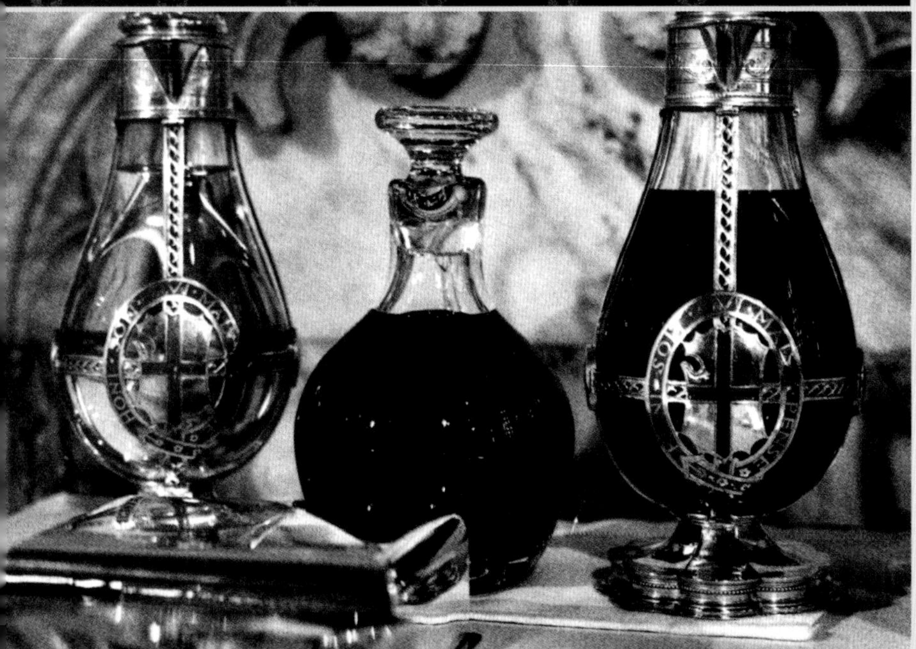

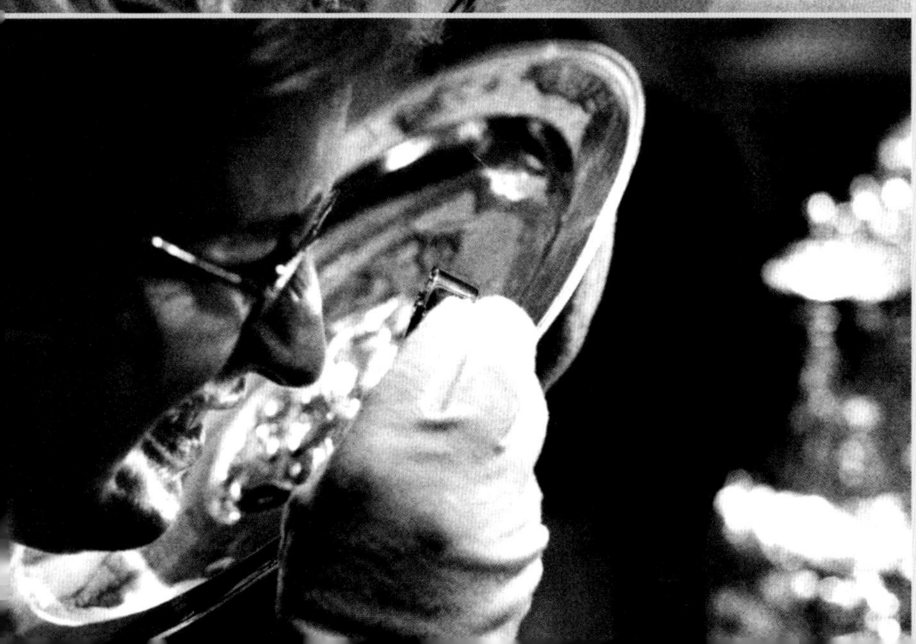

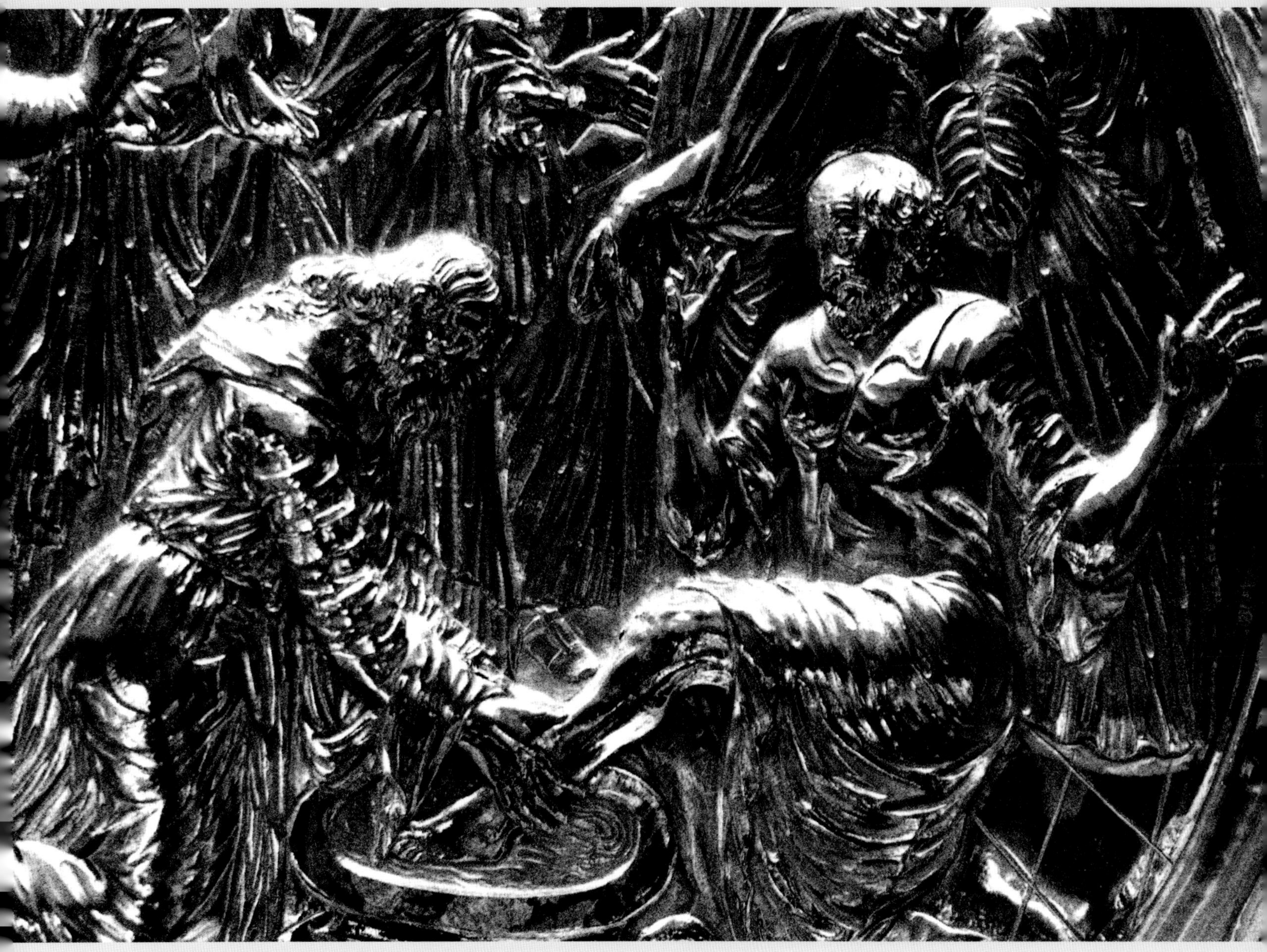

Easter: *Left*: In preparation for Easter Morning, the best plates, communion cruets and chalices are laid out on the altar in the quire.
Bottom Left: A specialist inspects a gold plate dating from 1548.

Above: Detail of a Charles II circular gold dish, circa 1660, representing Christ washing the feet of St Peter.

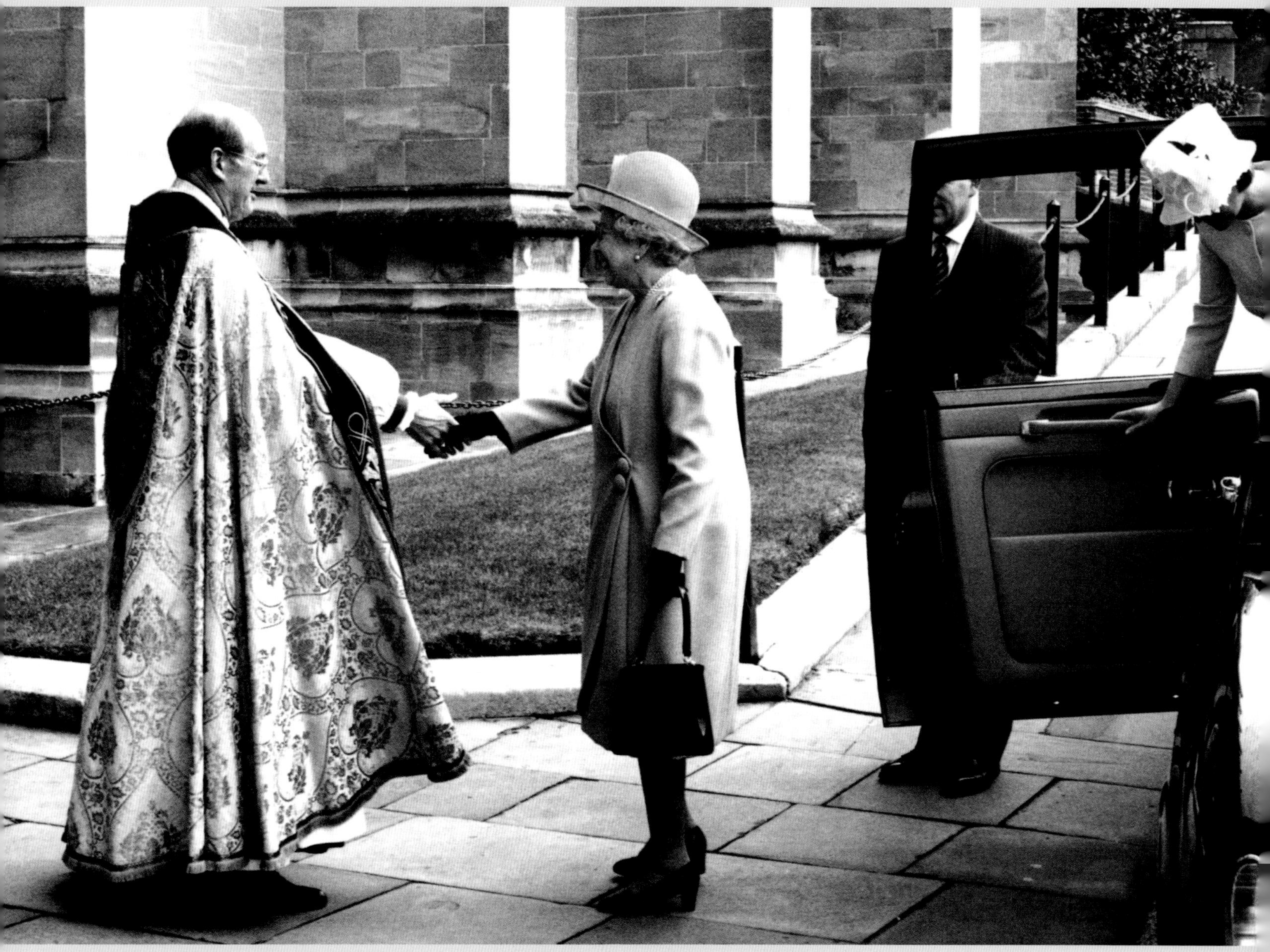

Easter Day: *Above*: The arrival of HM The Queen at the Galilee Porch met by the Dean of Windsor prior to Mattins on Easter Morning.

Right: HM The Queen, HRH The Duke of Edinburgh and members of the Royal Family walk through the Dean's Cloister after the service to the Deanery led by the Virger, and accompanied by the Dean and Canons.

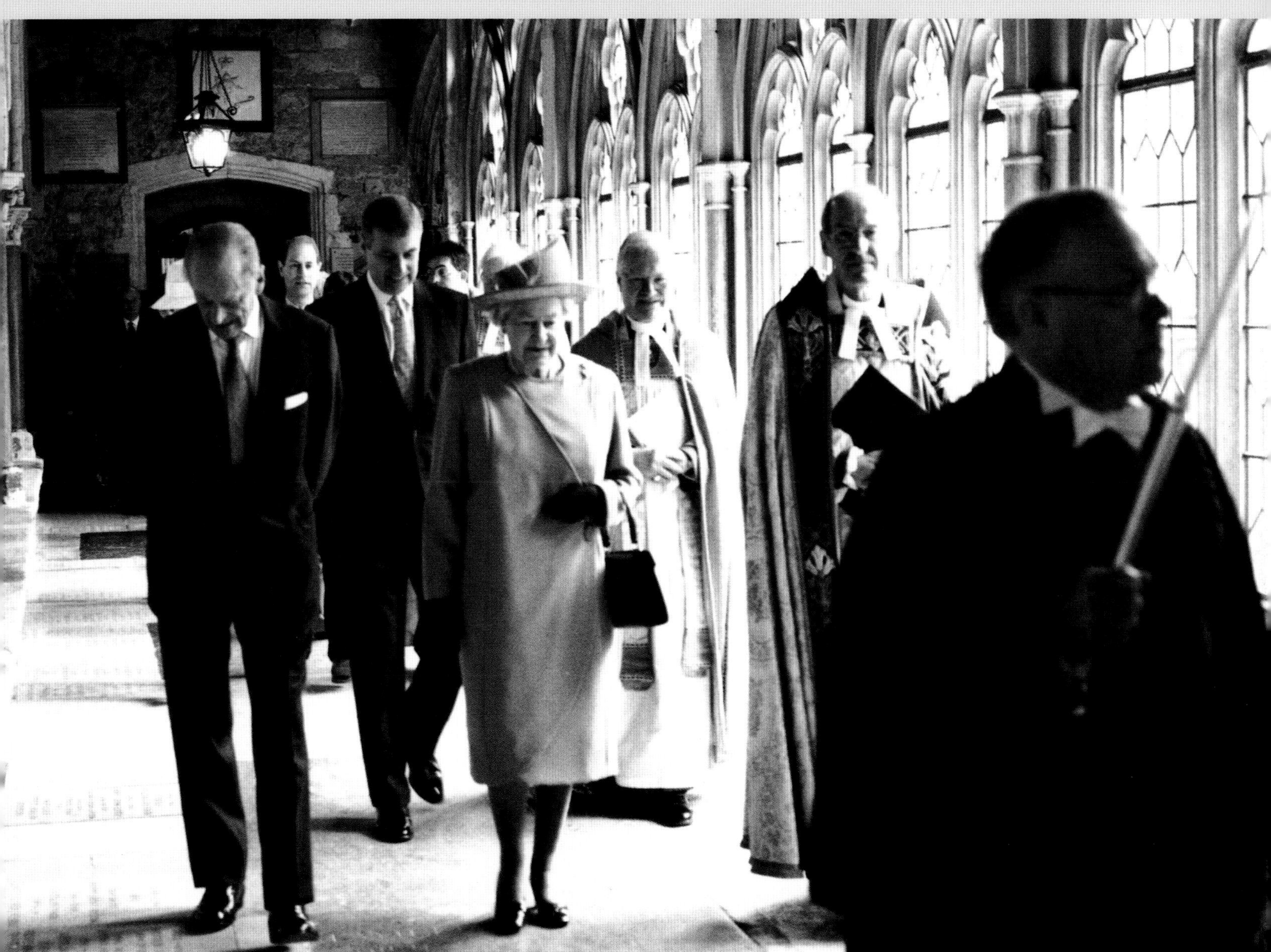

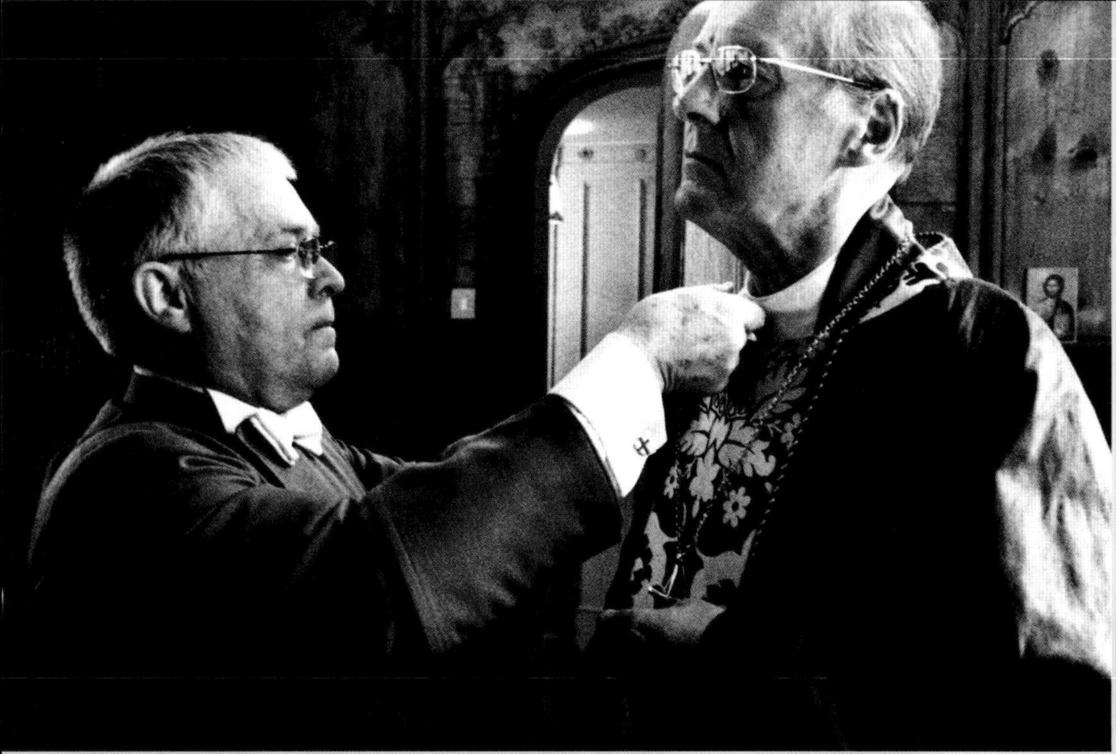

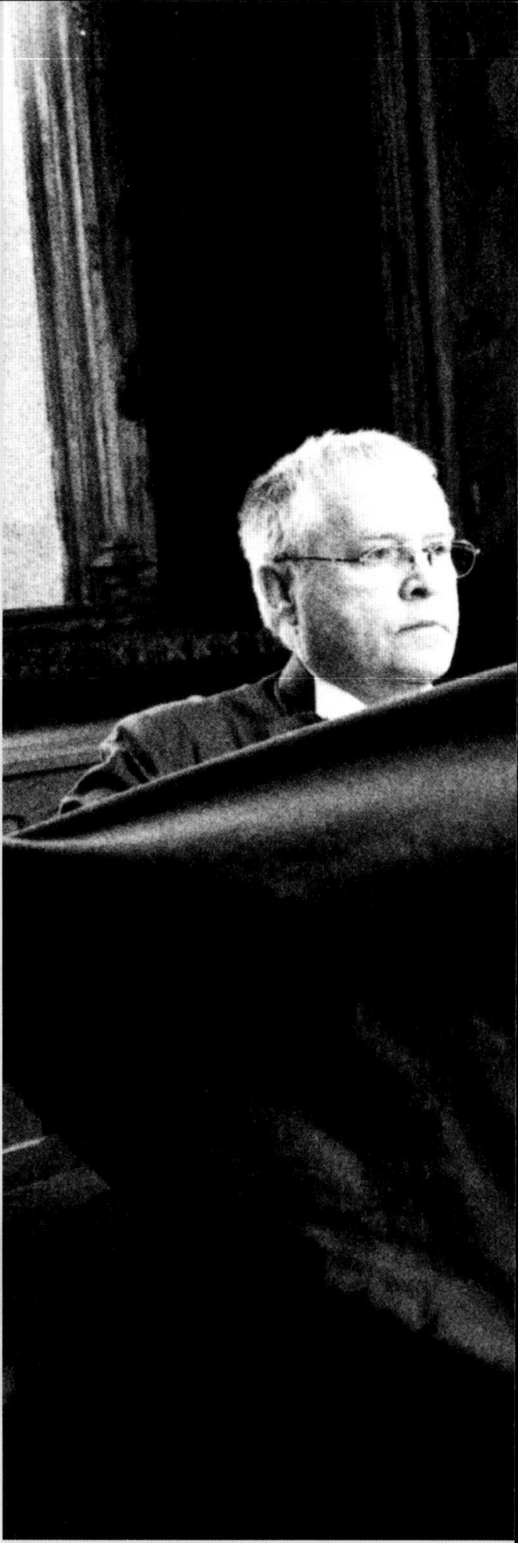

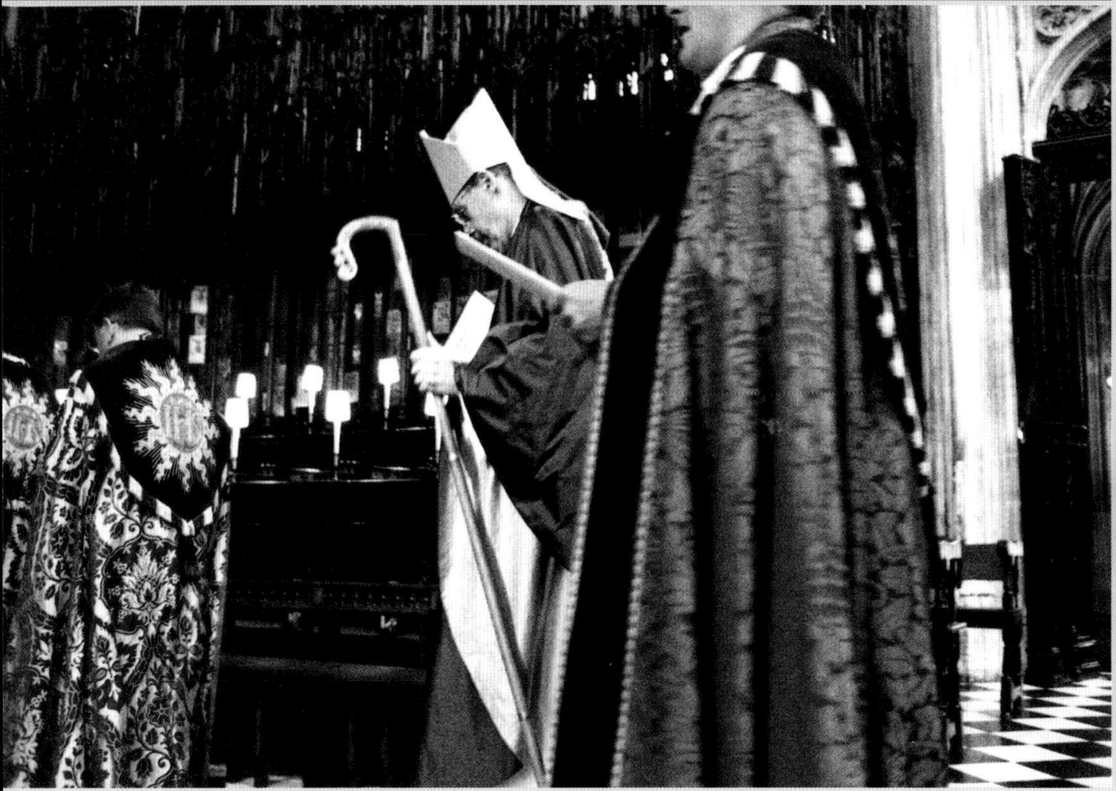

Pentecost: *Top Left and Right*: The Virger assists the Dean with his robes in the Edward IV Chantry Chapel as he takes his role as a Bishop for the Feast of Pentecost.

Above Left: The Bishop, the Right Reverend David Conner, processing through the quire to the nave for the Service of Pentecost.

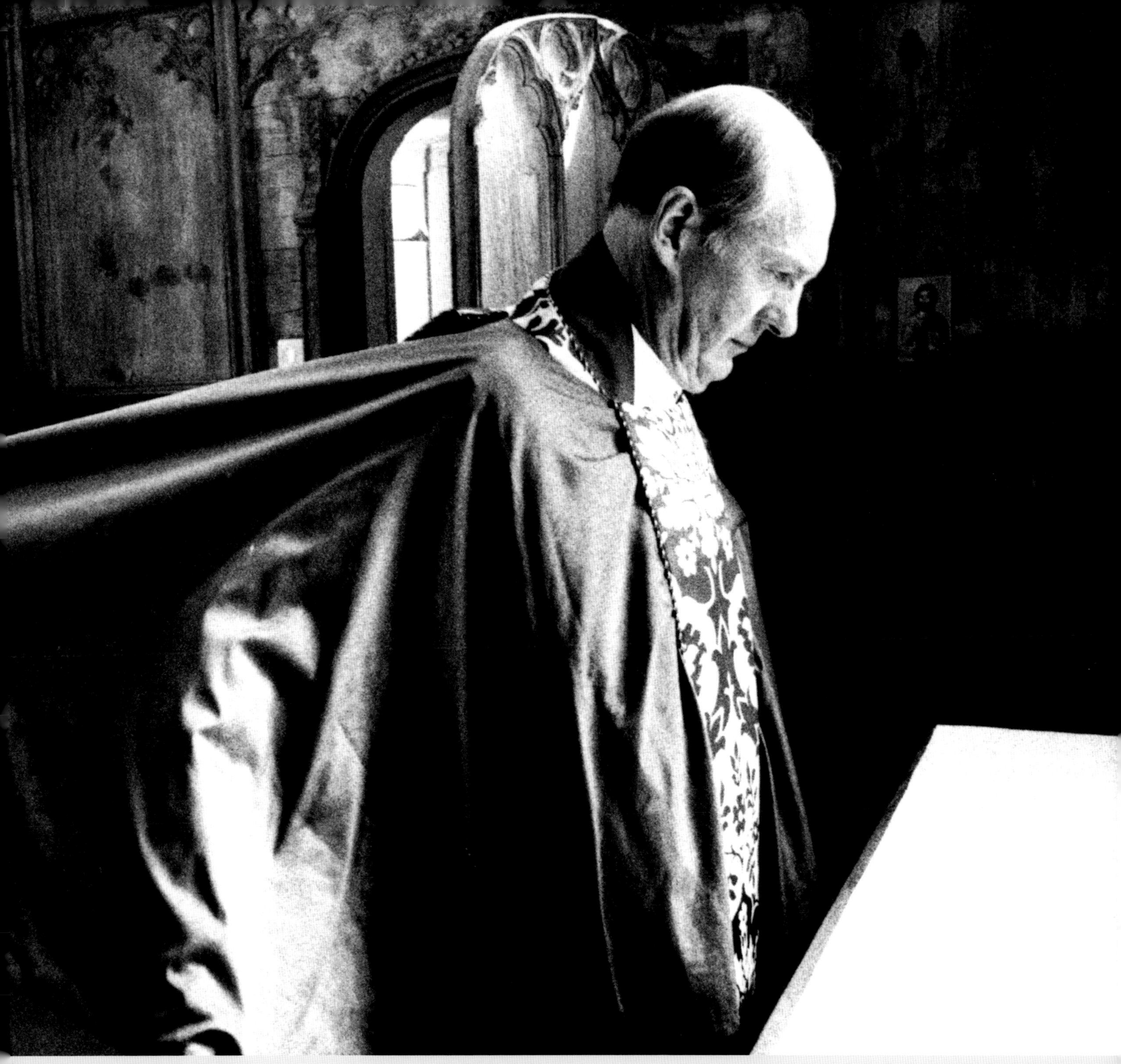

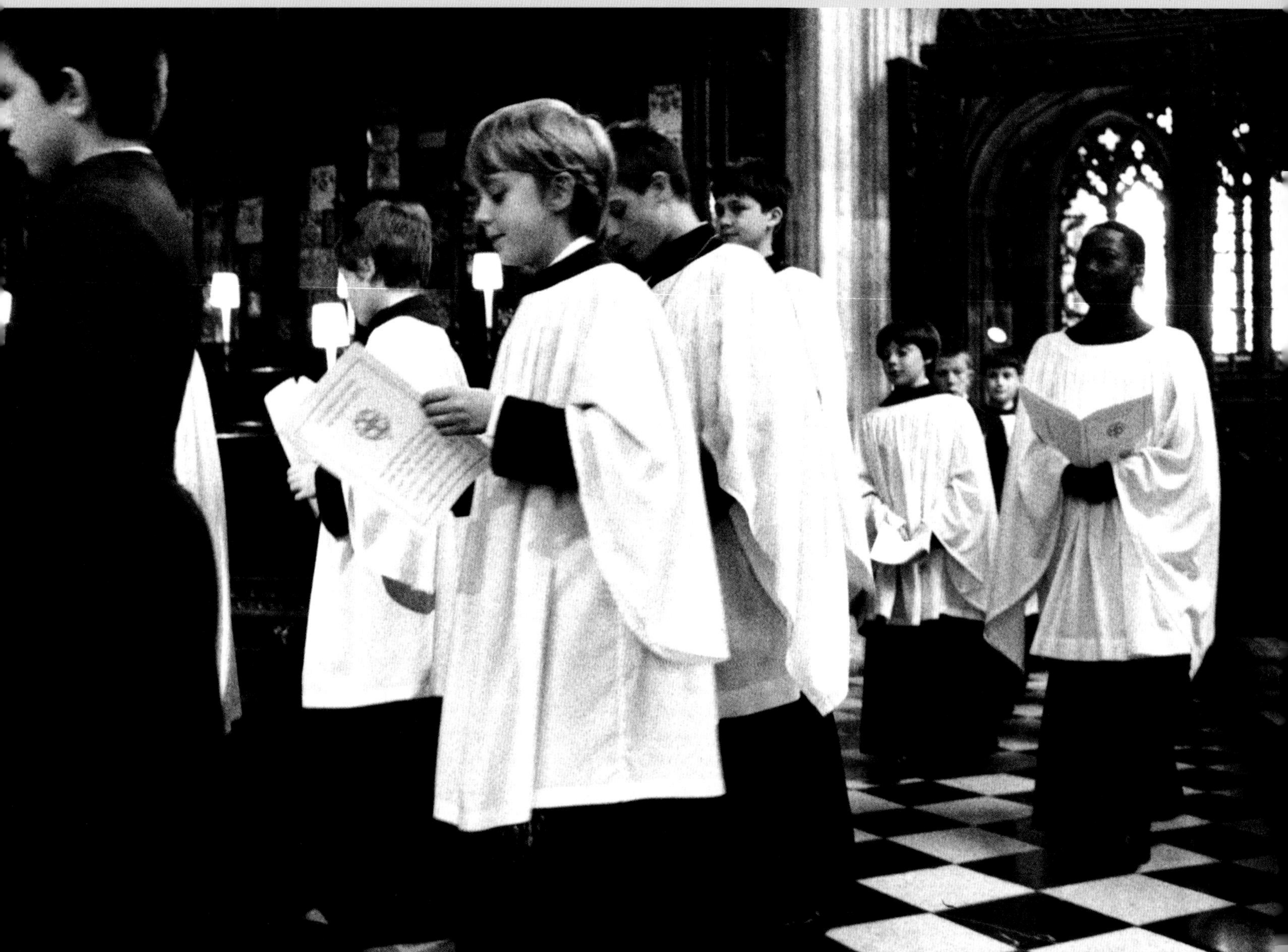

Pentecost: *Above*: The Choir processing through the quire to the nave.
Right: The Bishop and Clergy as they process through the quire to the nave.

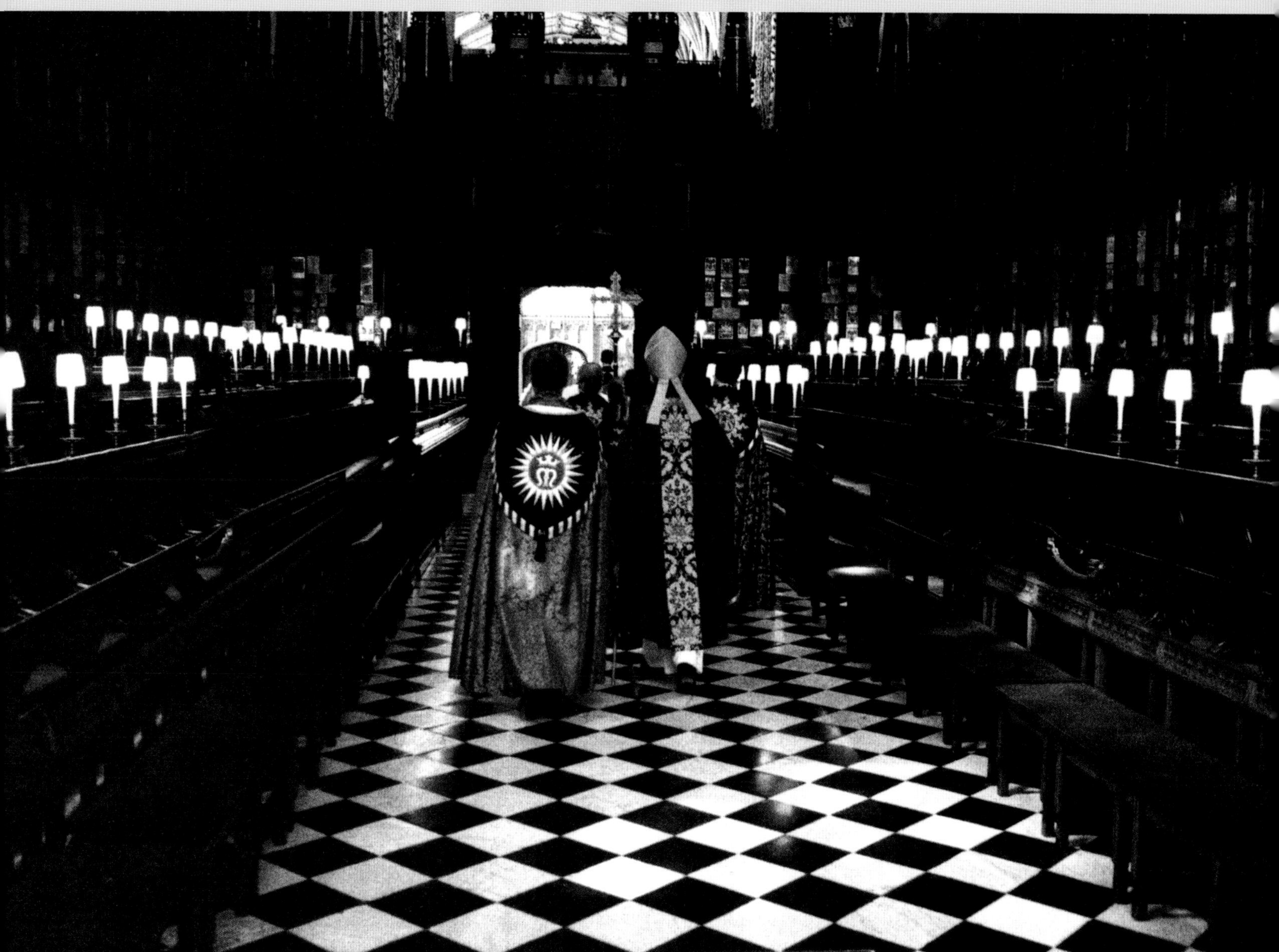

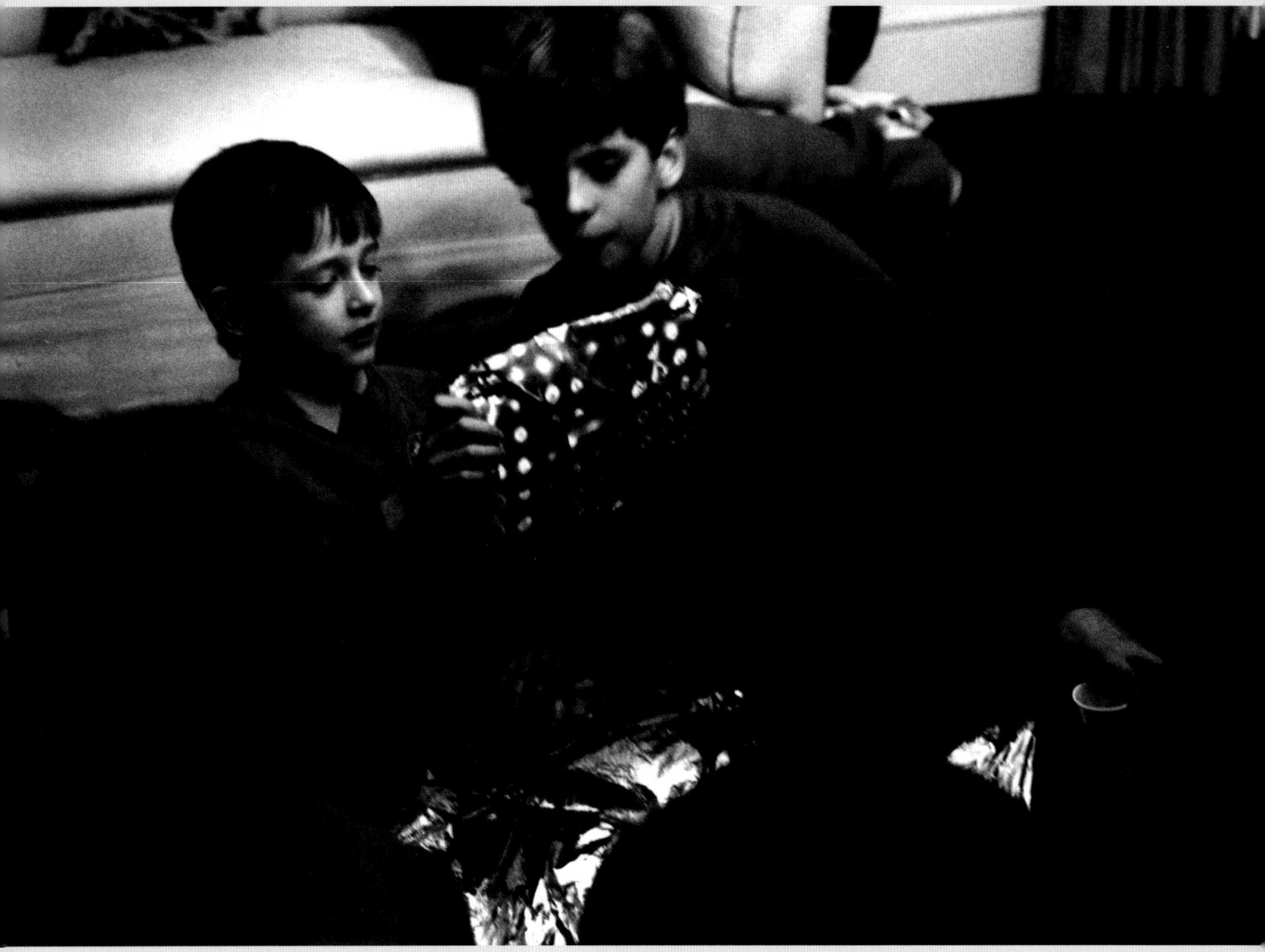

Christmas: The choristers of the Choir of St George's Chapel enjoy their Christmas party with traditional games a few days before Christmas in the Deanery.

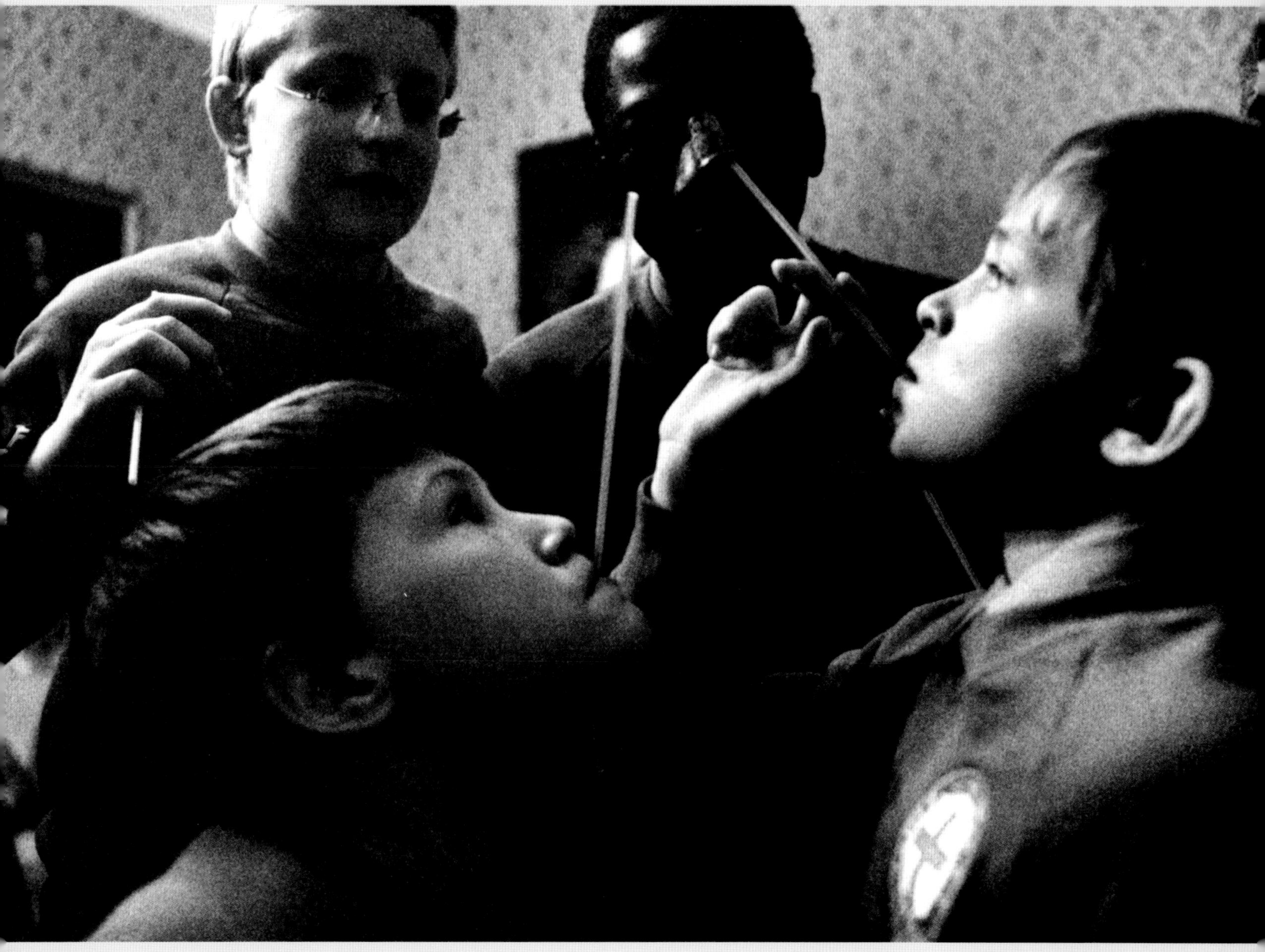

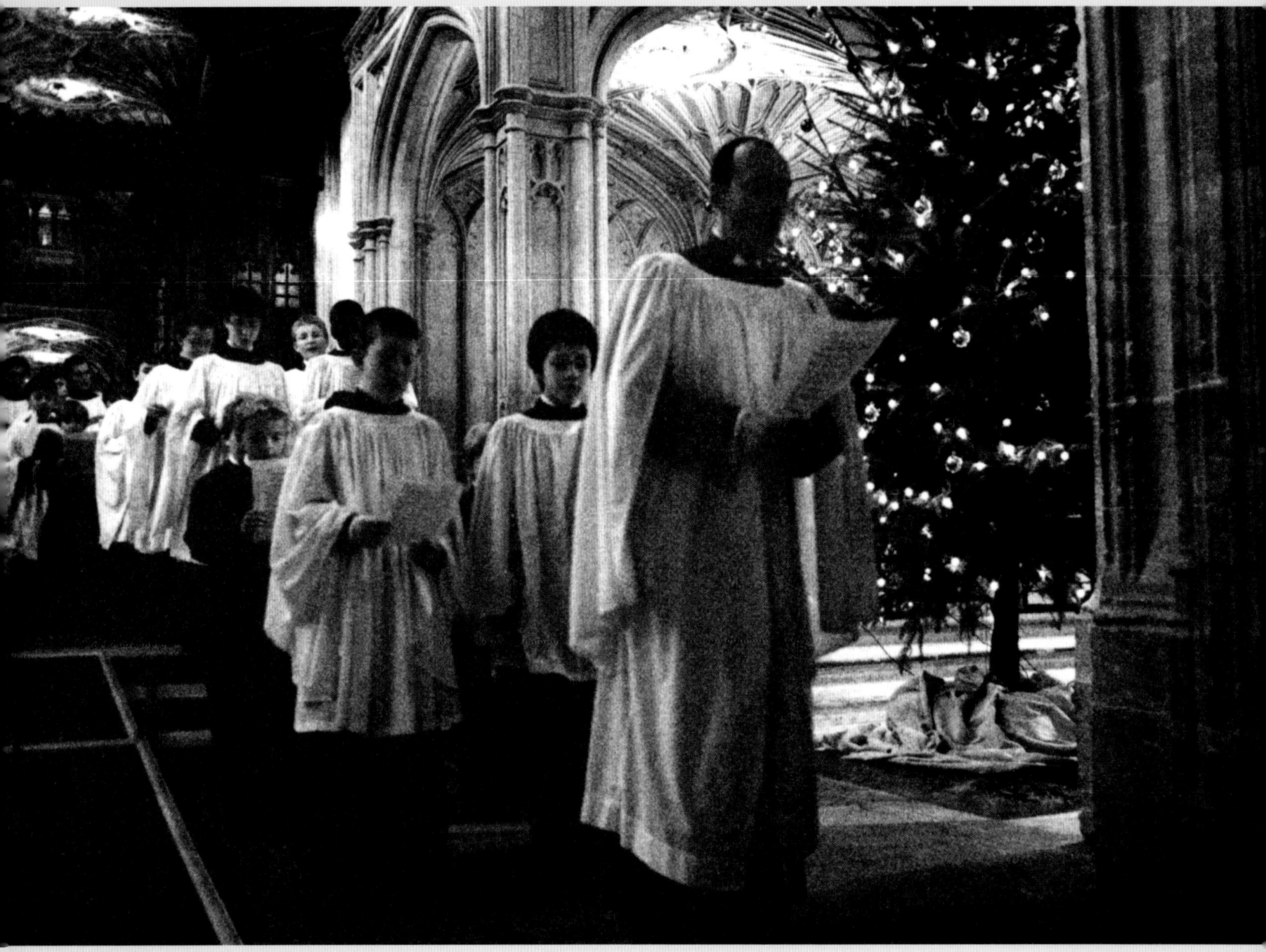

Christmas: *Above*: The choir processing down the north aisle for the Midnight Service of the First Eucharist of Christmas on Christmas Eve.
Right: The Dean and Clergy face the crib at the west end of the Chapel and the Dean blesses the crib.

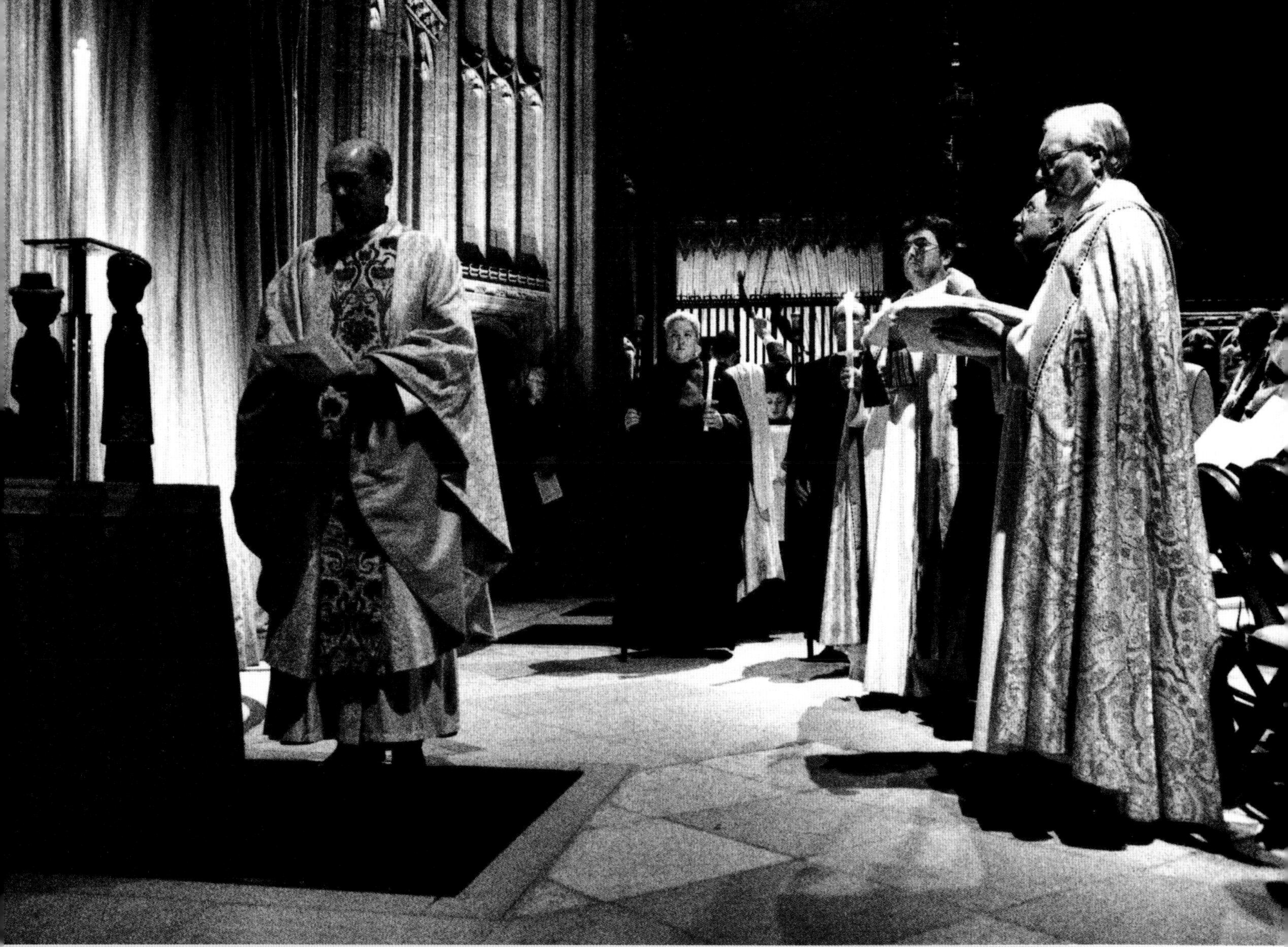

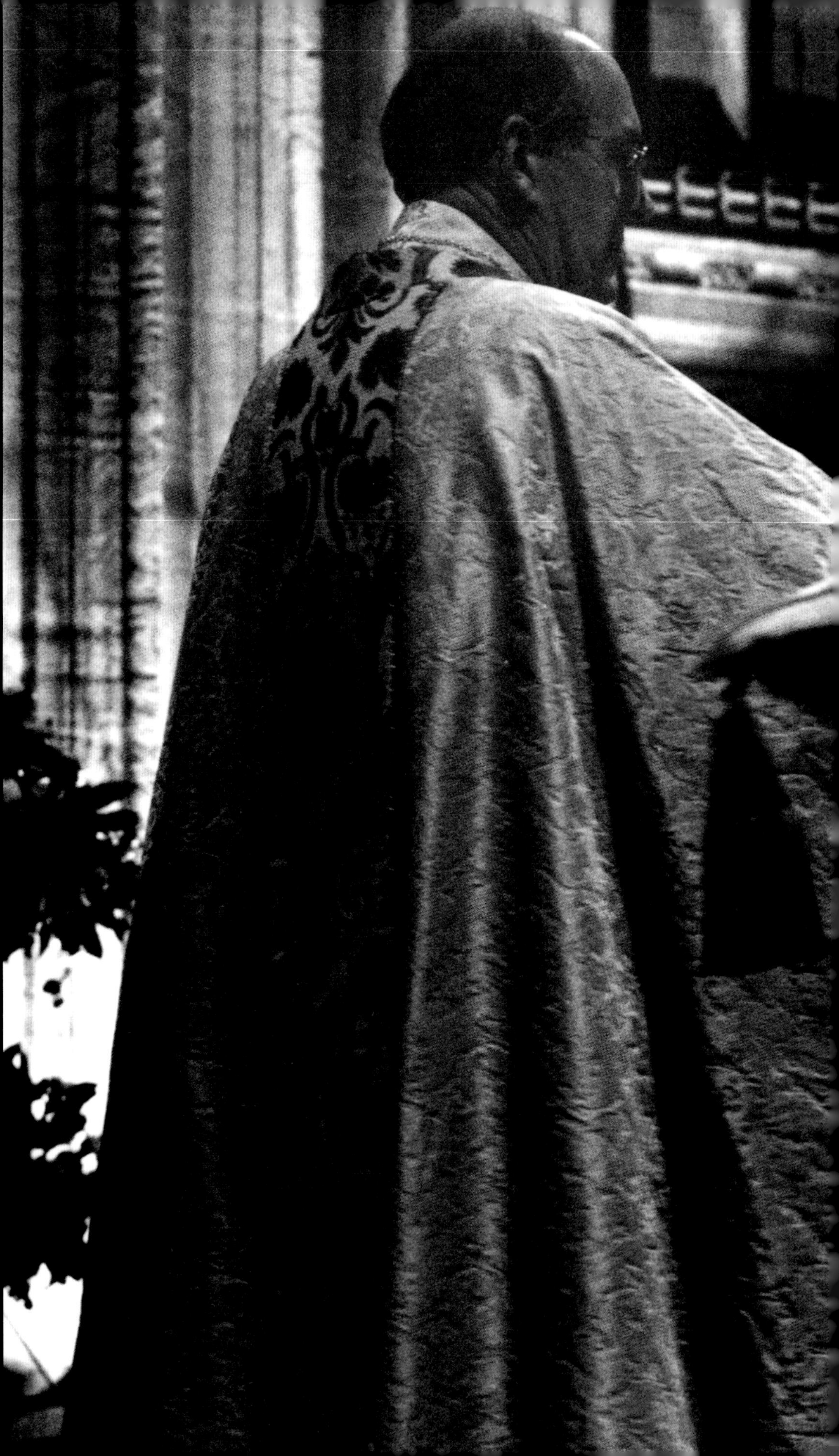

Christmas: The Dean leads the Midnight Service of the First Eucharist of Christmas on Christmas Eve.

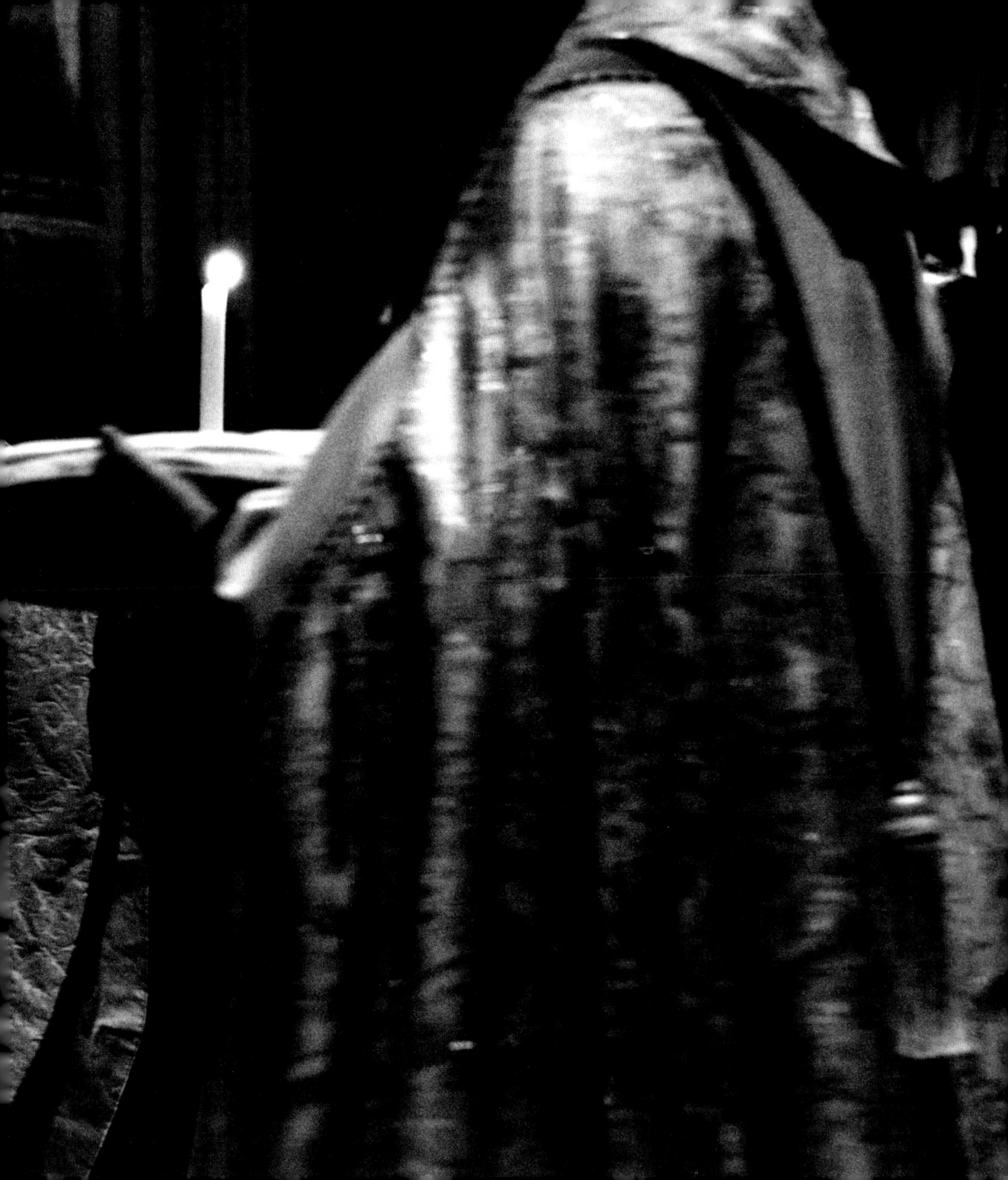

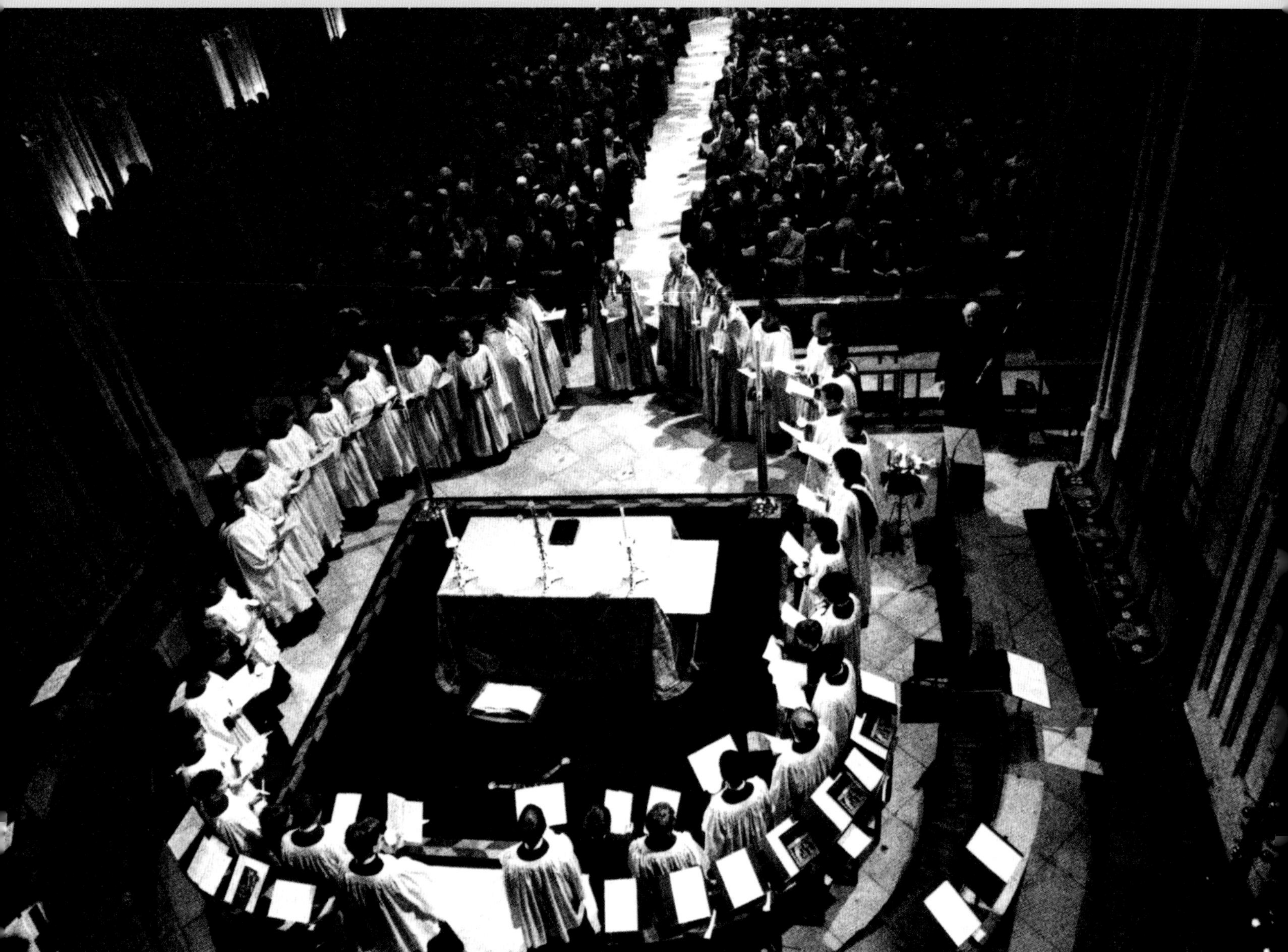

Christmas: *Above*: The choir form a circle in the nave and continue the carols by candlelight during the Service of Nine Lessons and Carols on Christmas Eve. This tradition is to emphasise the great last Gospel lesson that proclaims the doctrine of the Incarnation according to St John; the reader is surrounded by candlelight so that none of us should be unaware of the importance of Light coming into the World.
Right: The choir positioned in the quire during Christmas Day Service.

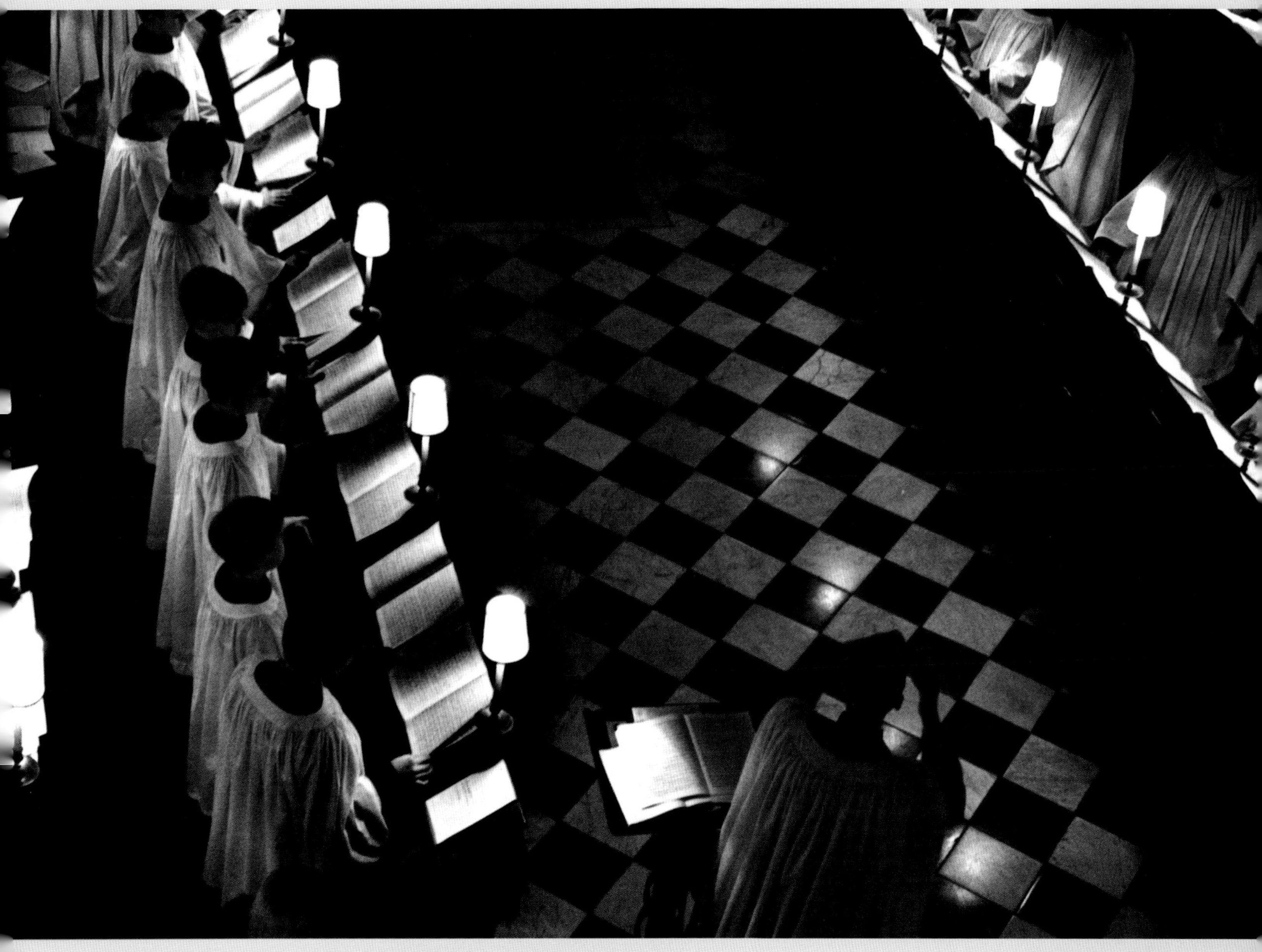

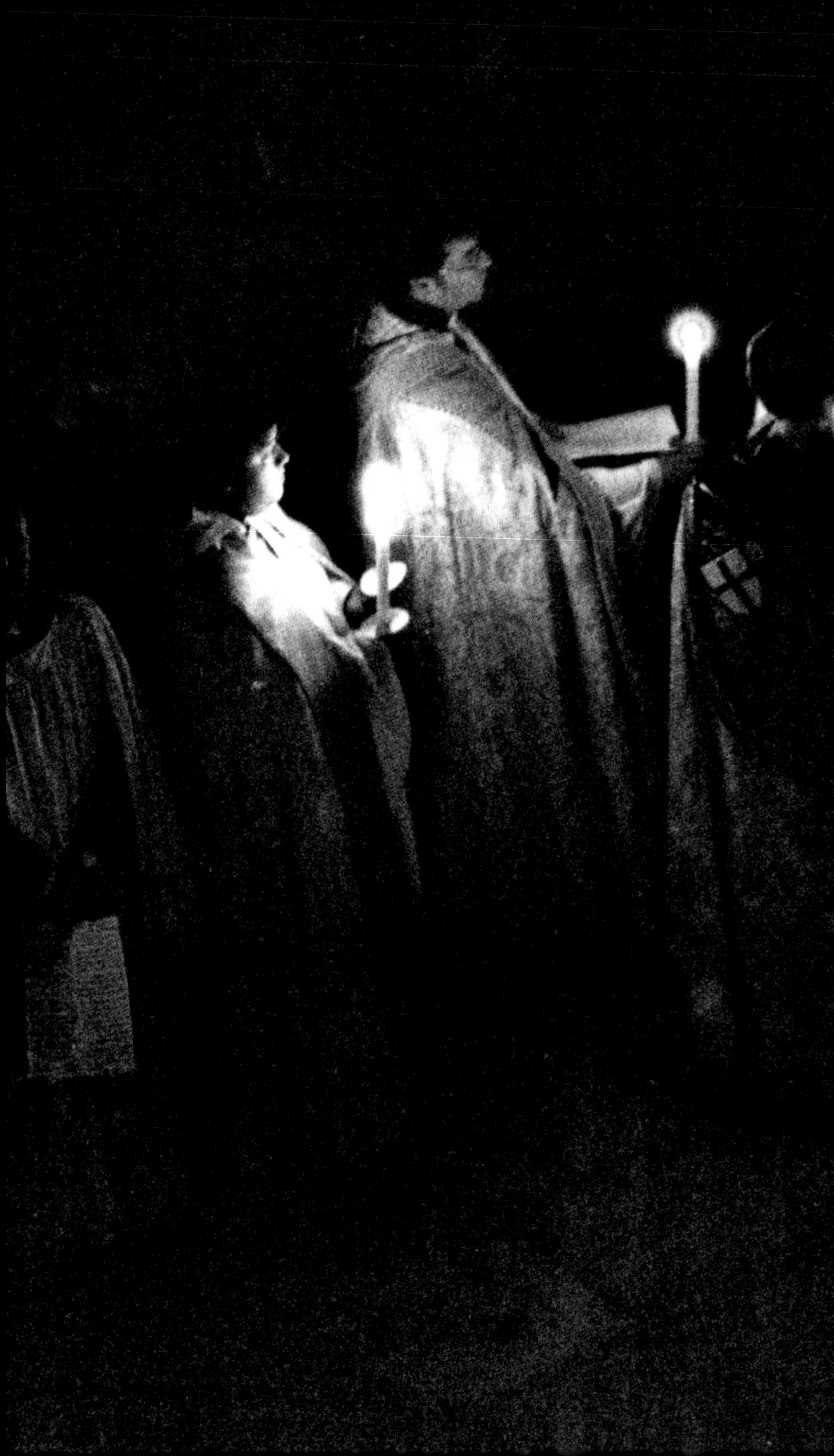

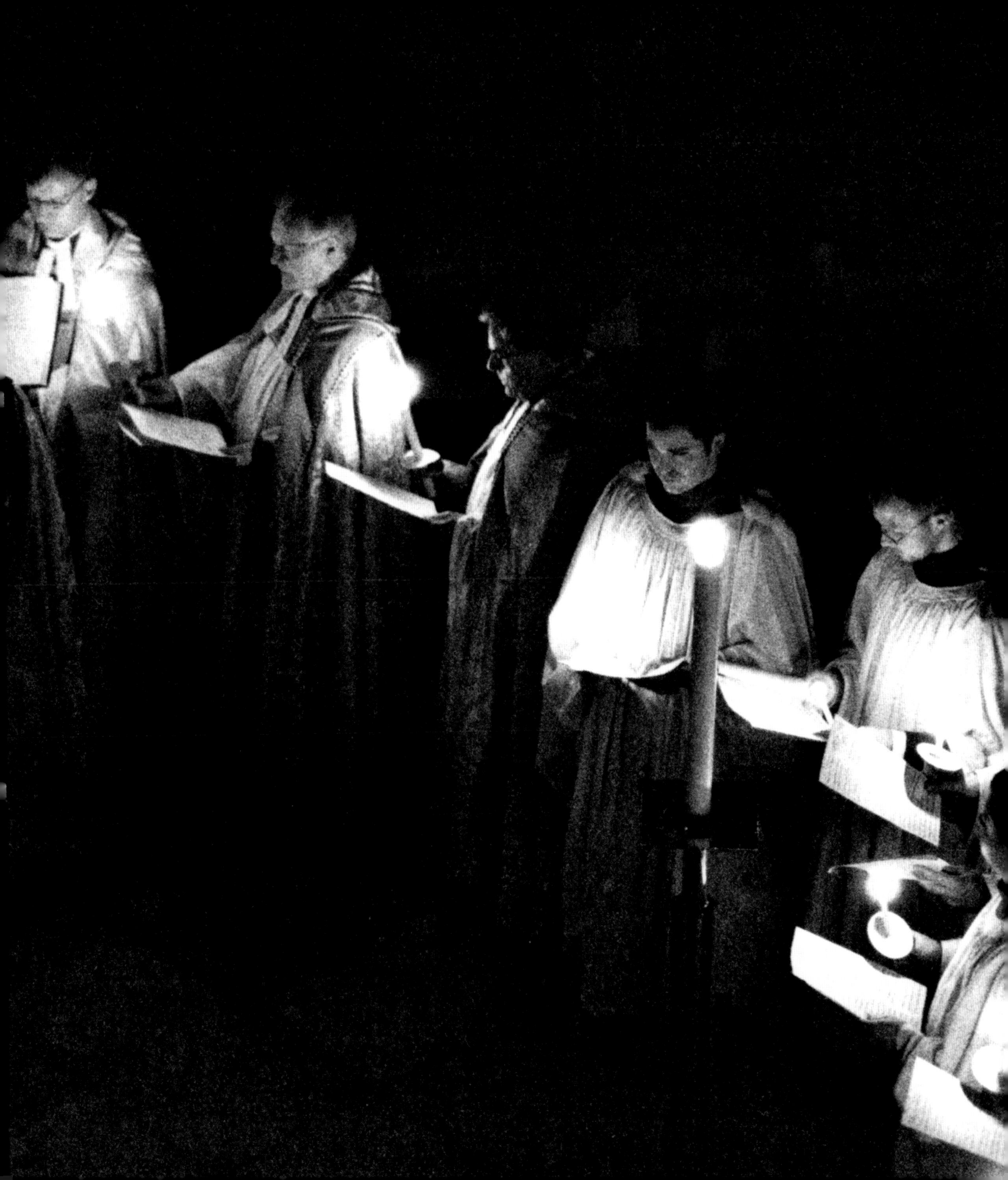

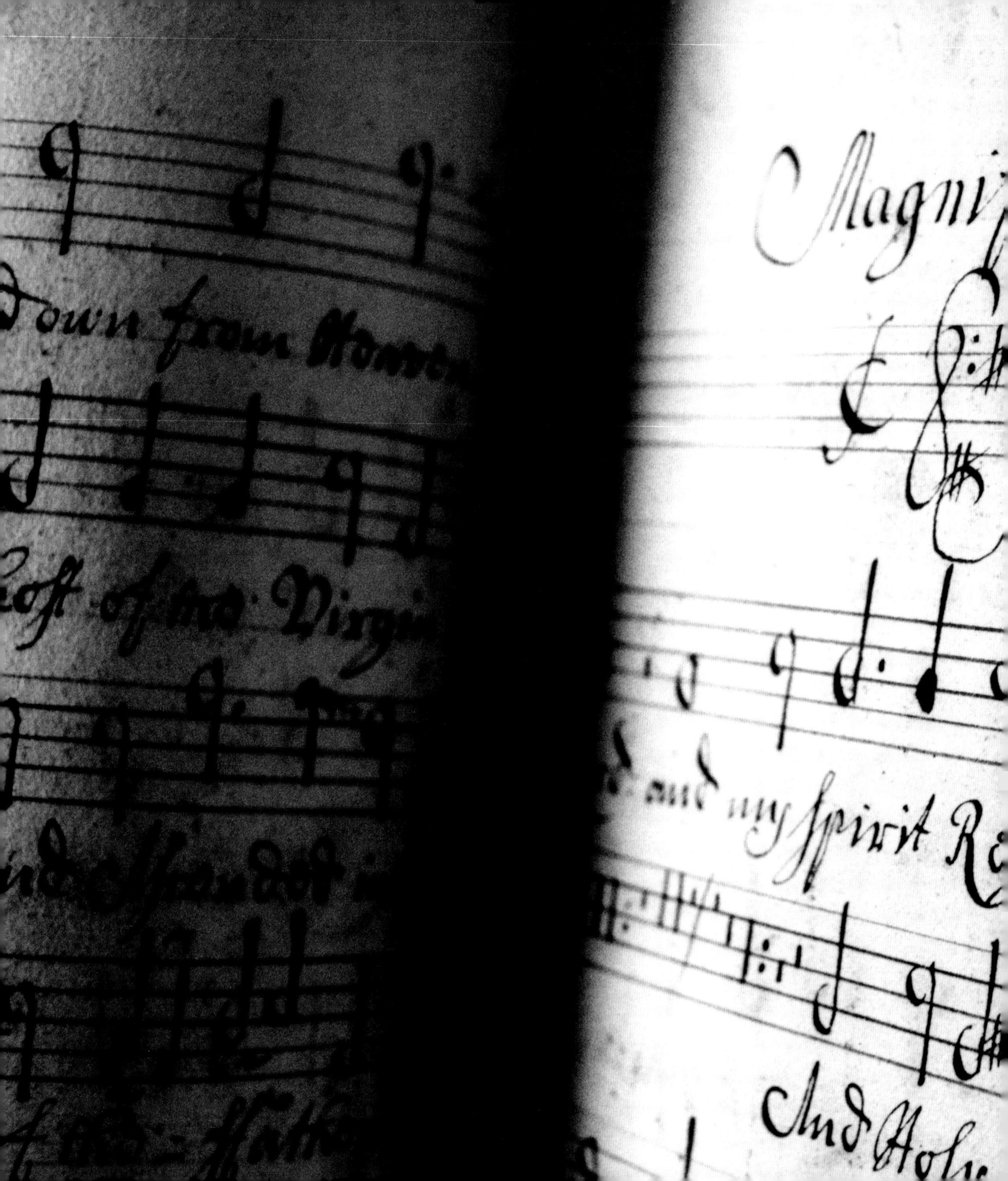
Down from
of the
Magni
and my Spirit
And

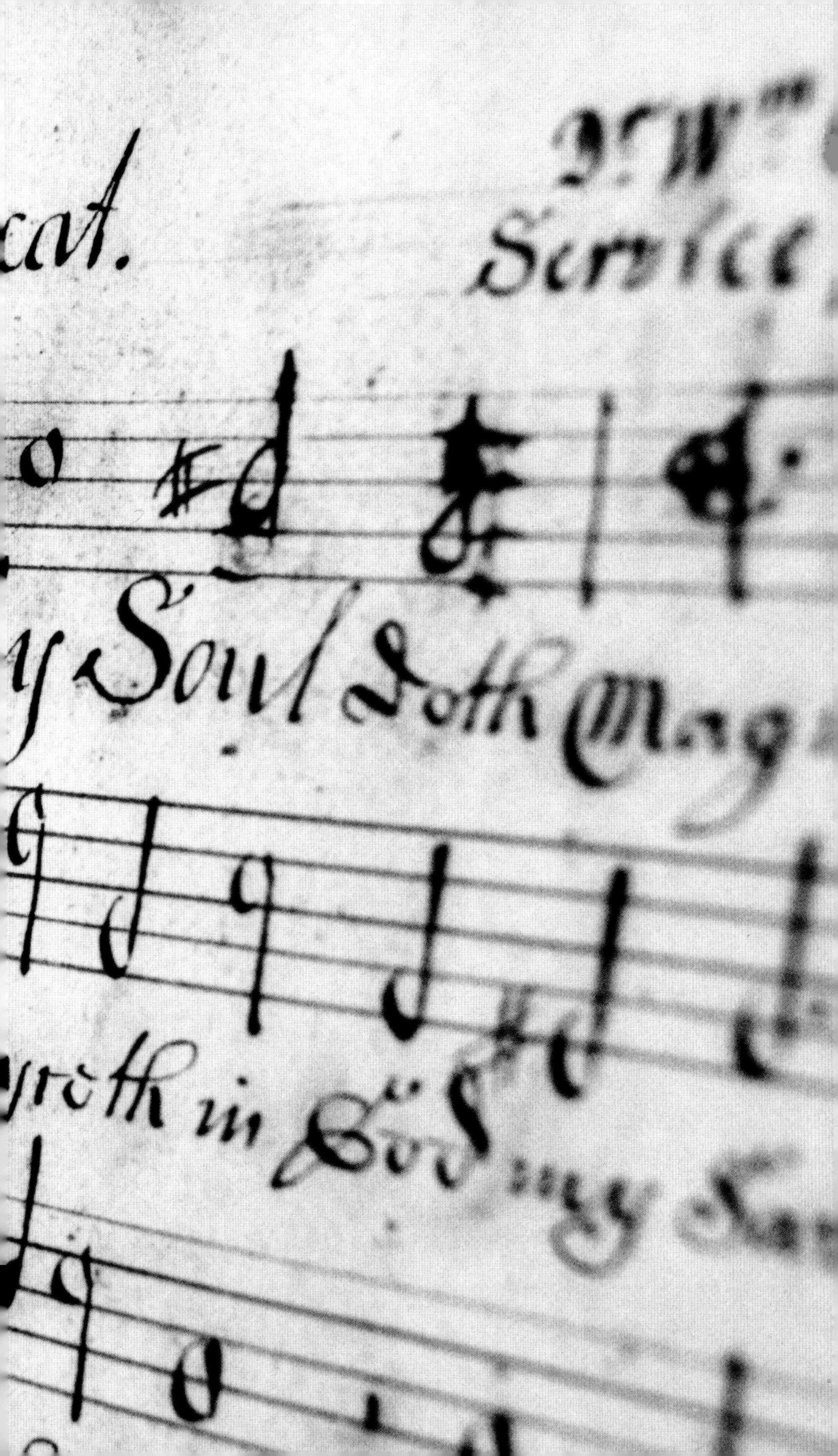

Service
Soul doth
in God

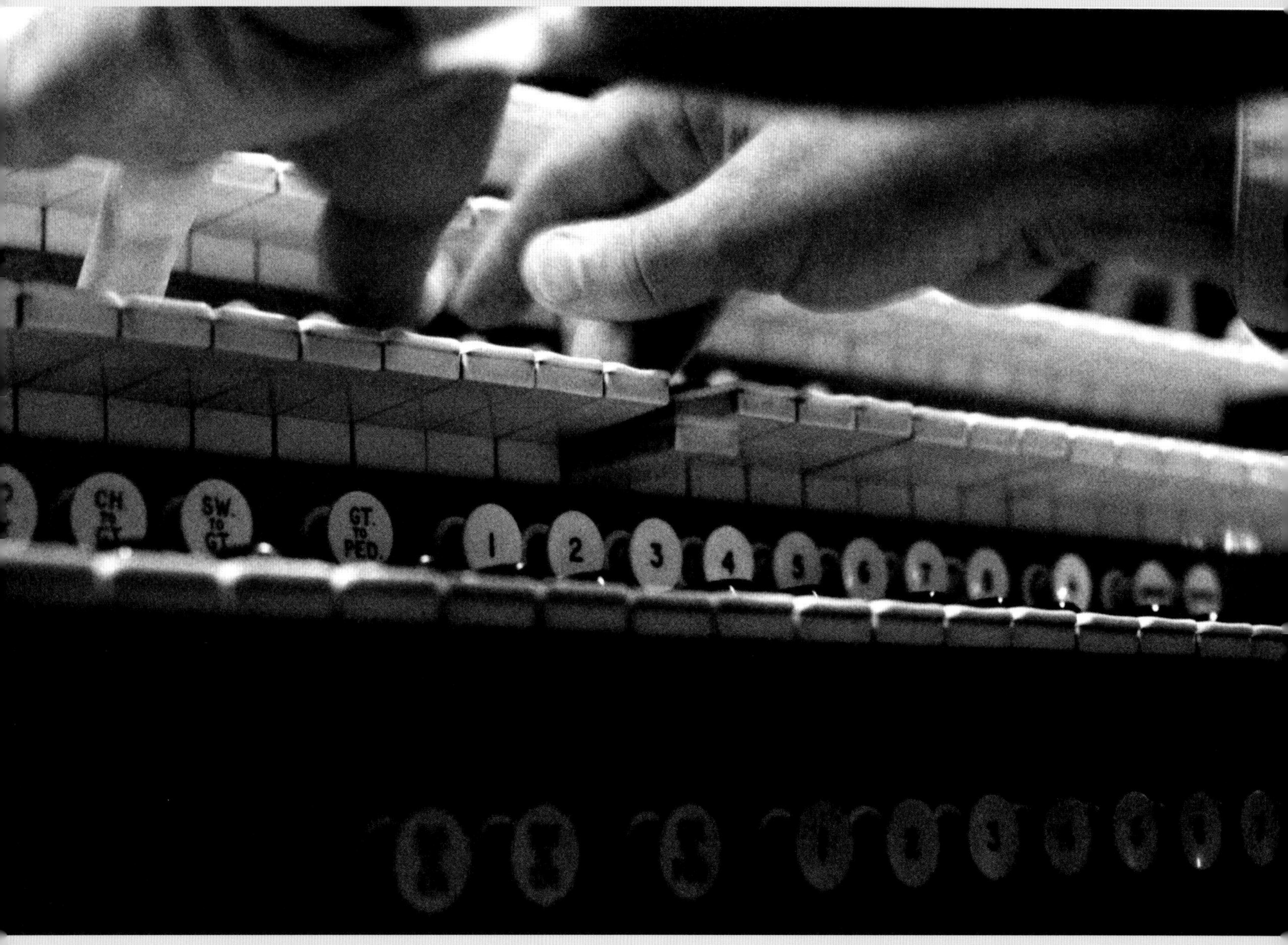

Above: The manuals of the organ as played by the Assistant Organist of St George's Chapel, Roger Judd.
Right: Pipes in the organ loft. The organ of St George's has approximately four thousand pipes.

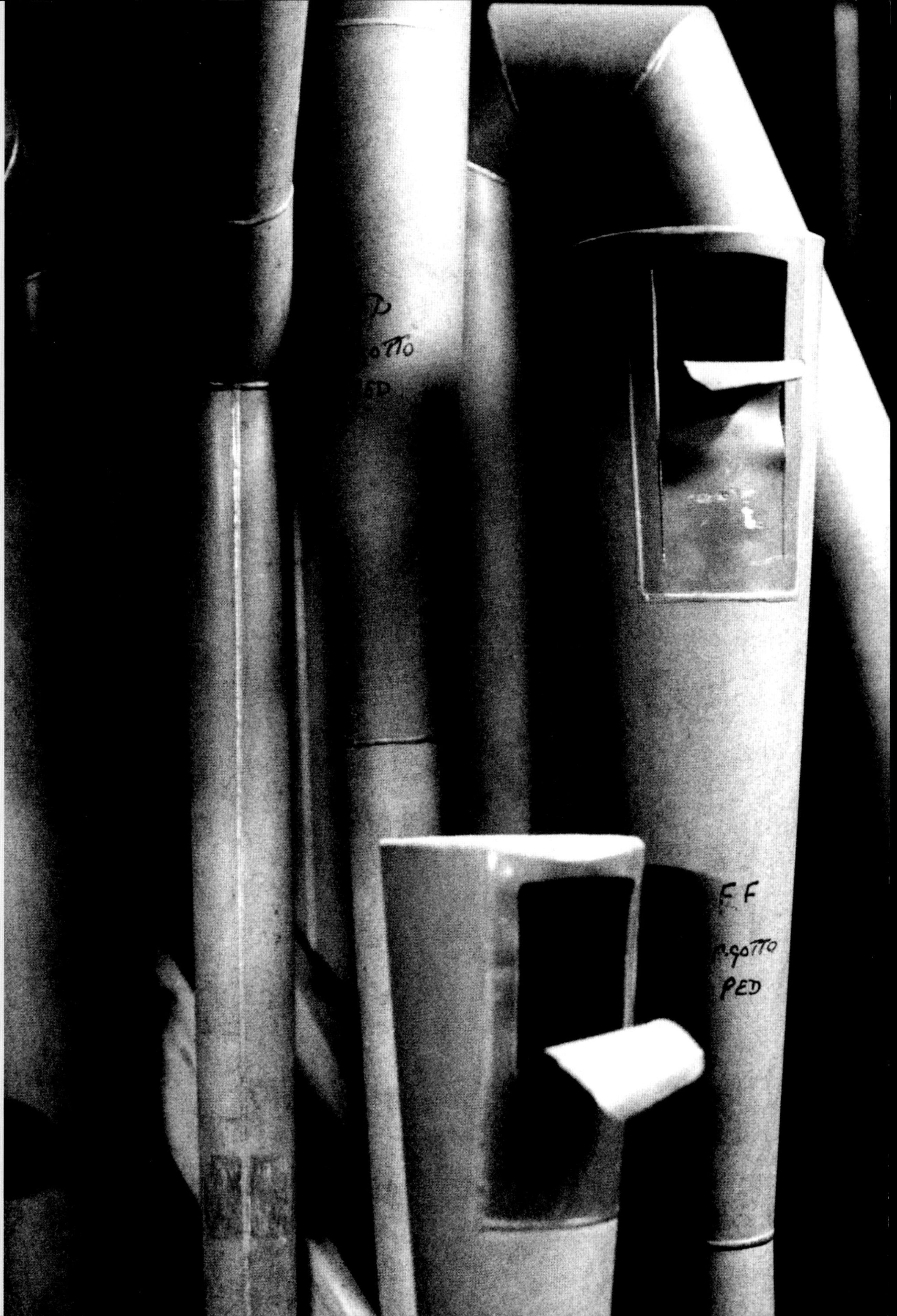

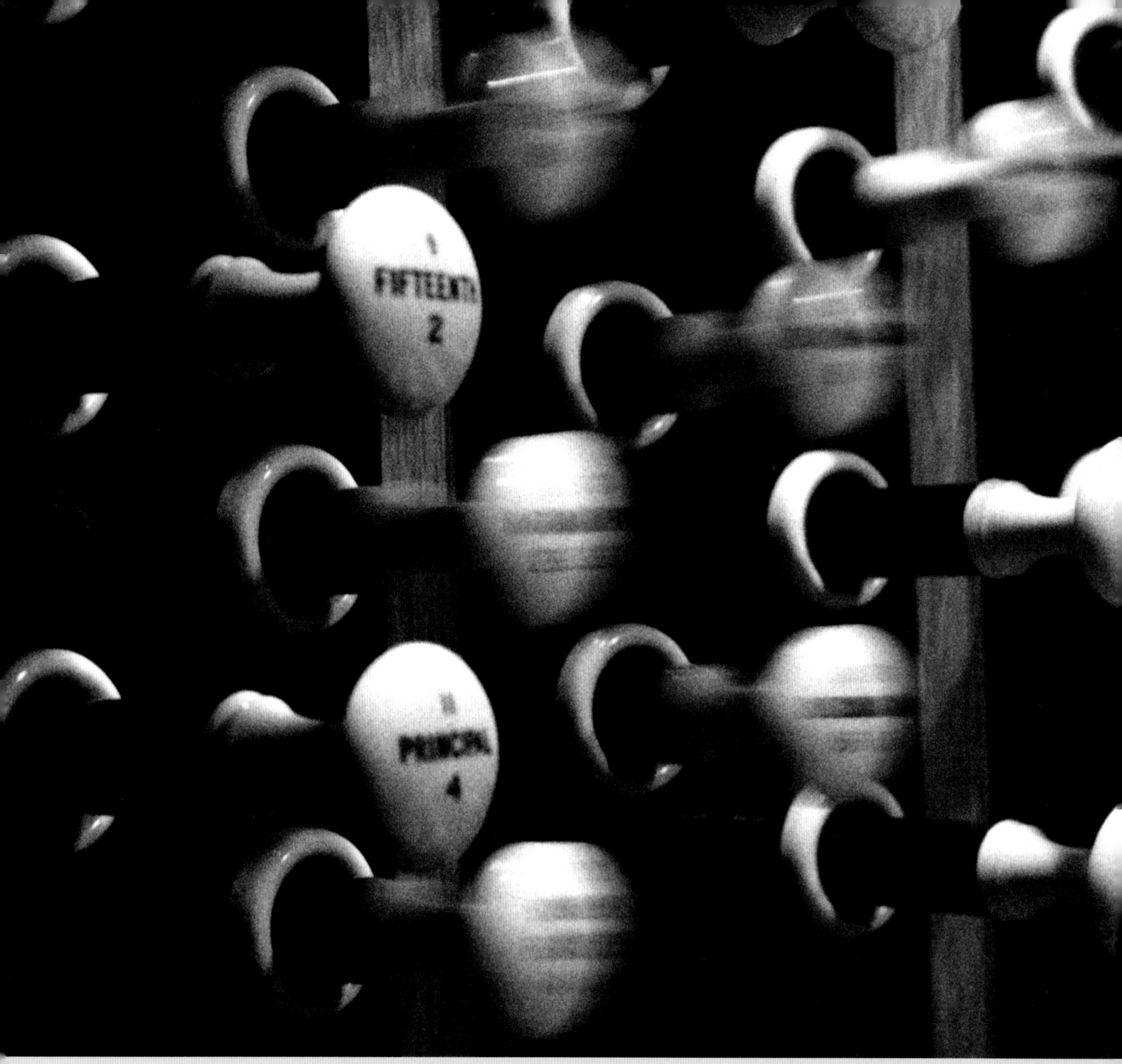

Above: The stops of the organ in action.
Right: Tuning the pipes prior to an important service at the Chapel.

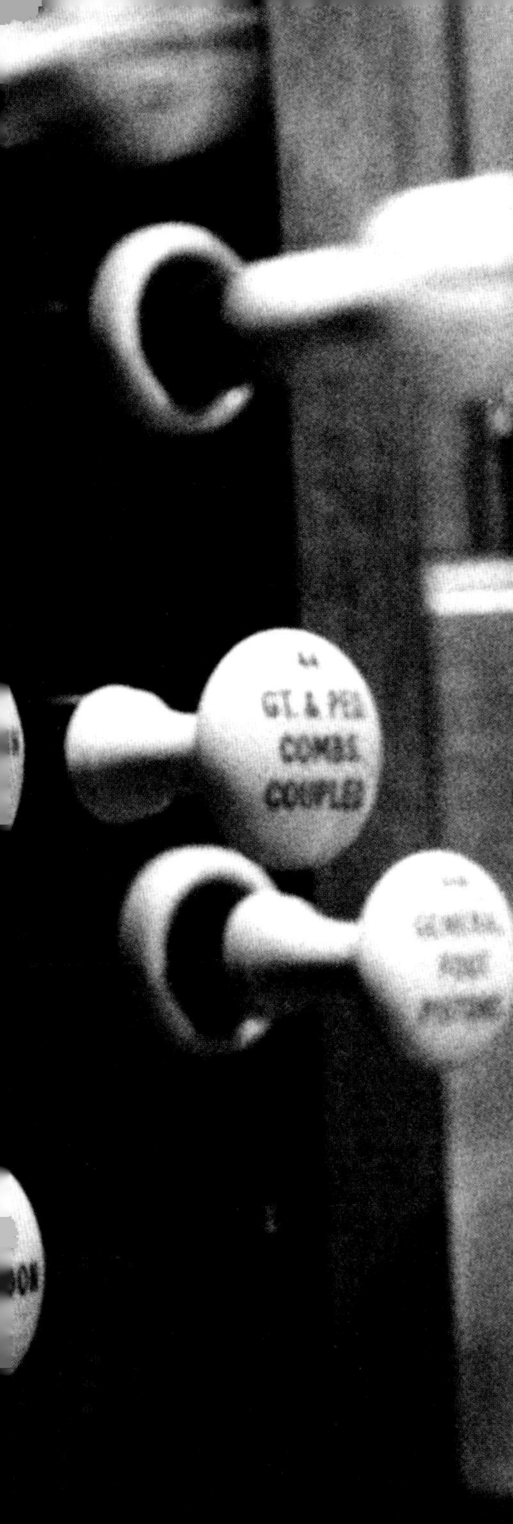
GT. & PED.
COMBS.
COUPLED

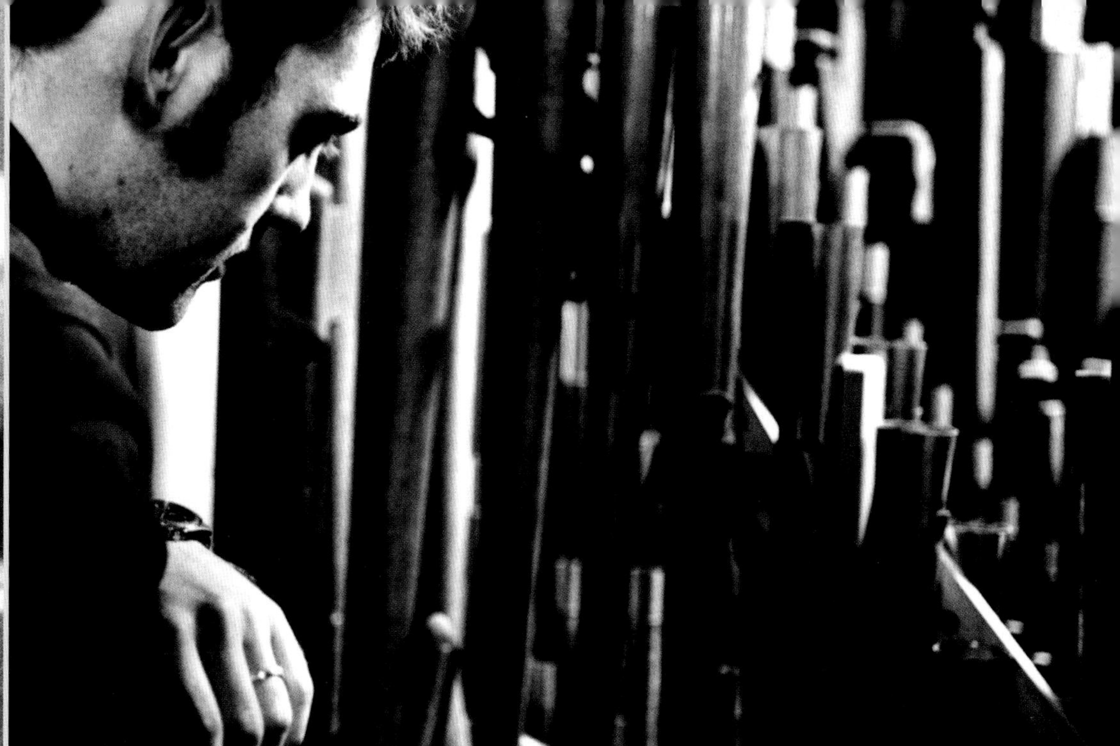

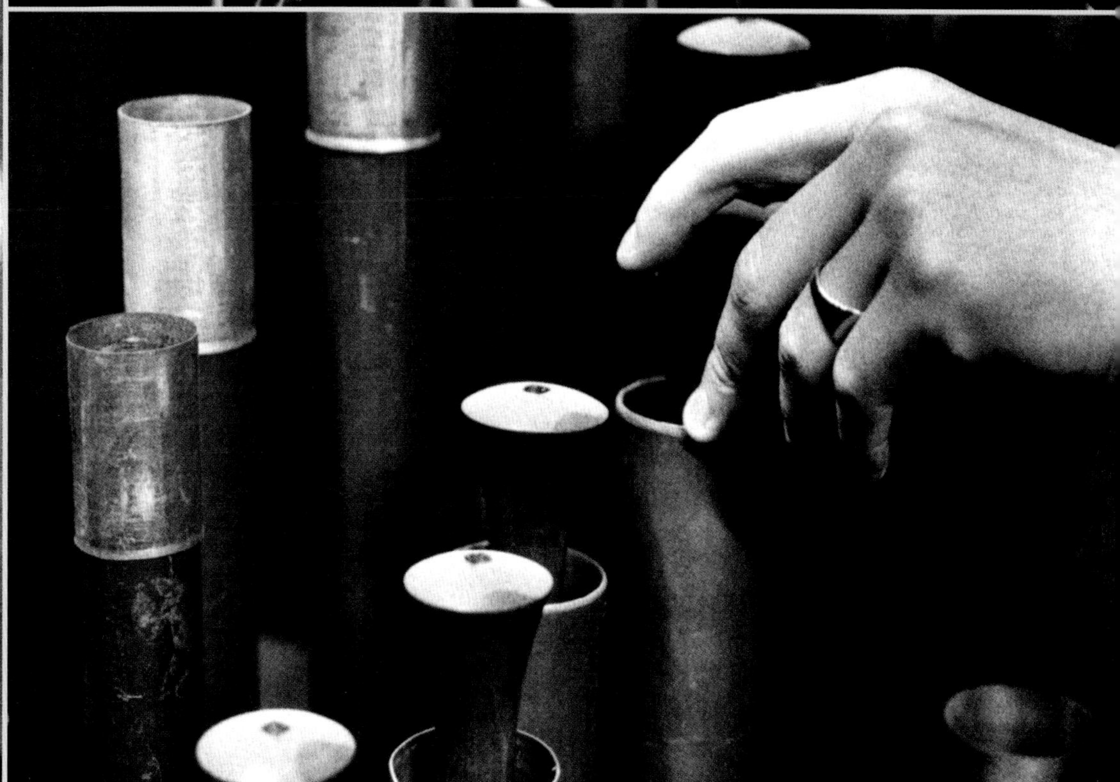

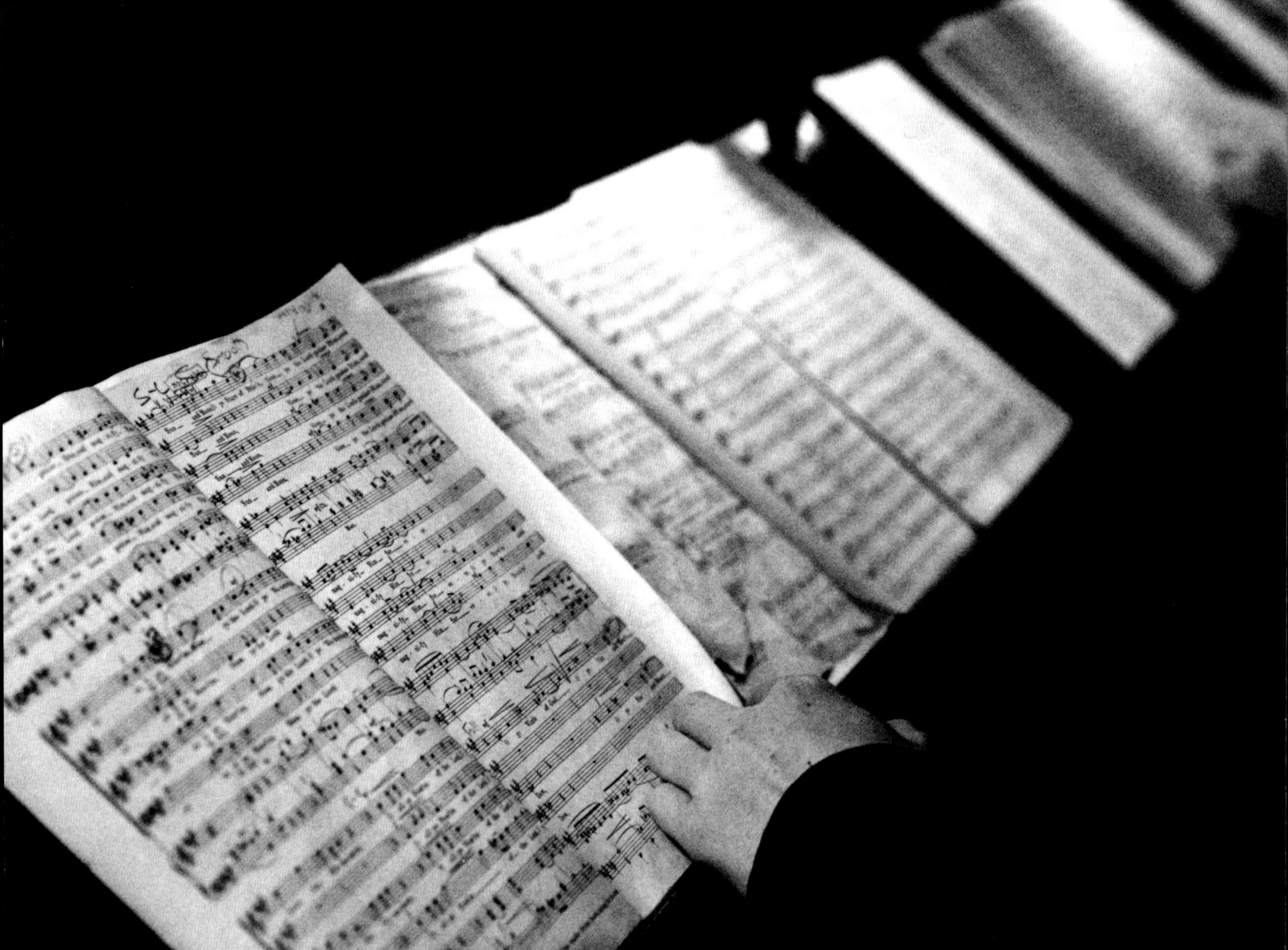

Above and right: Lay Clerks in their places in the quire during practice before Evensong. The choir of St George's comprises 16 choristers, some

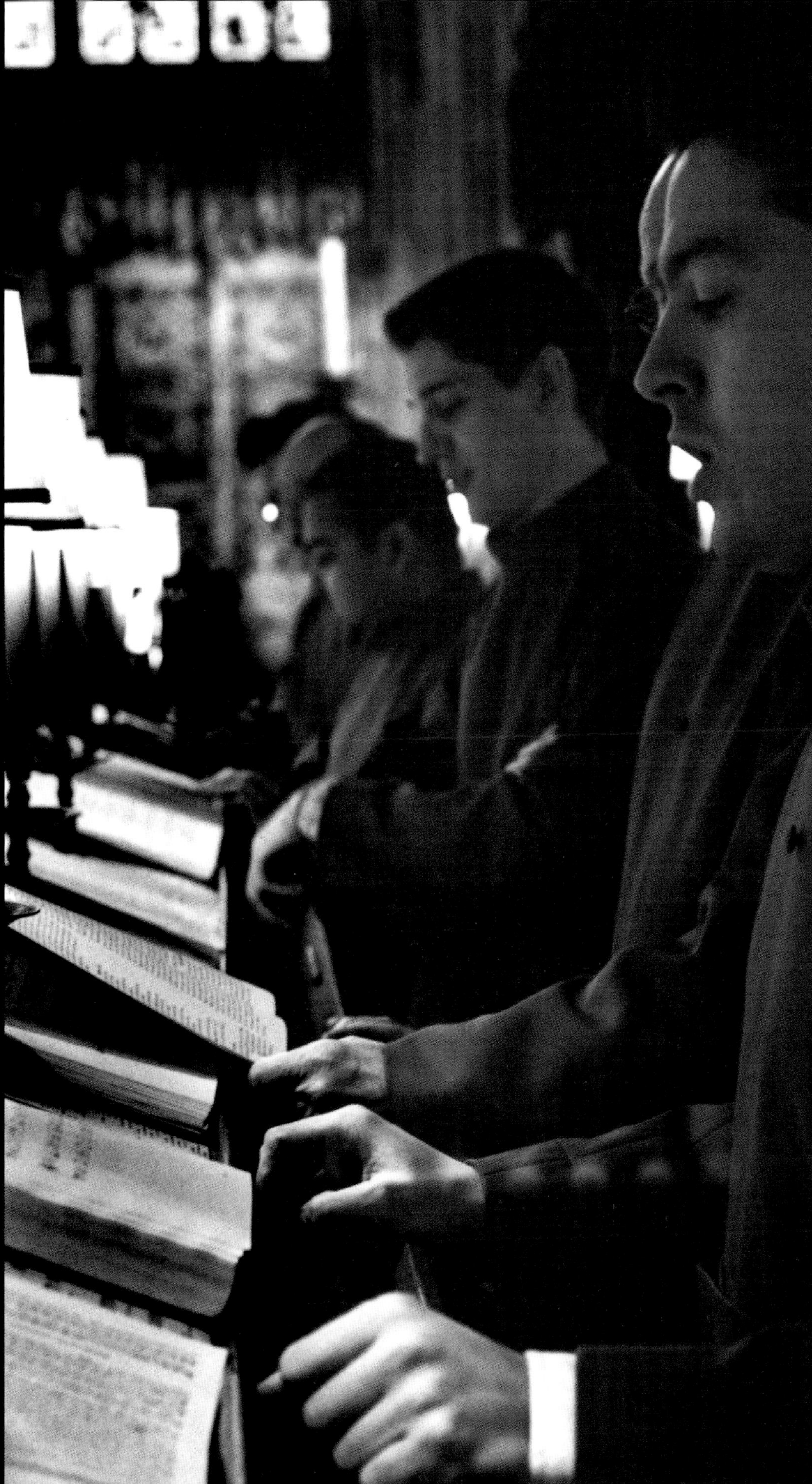

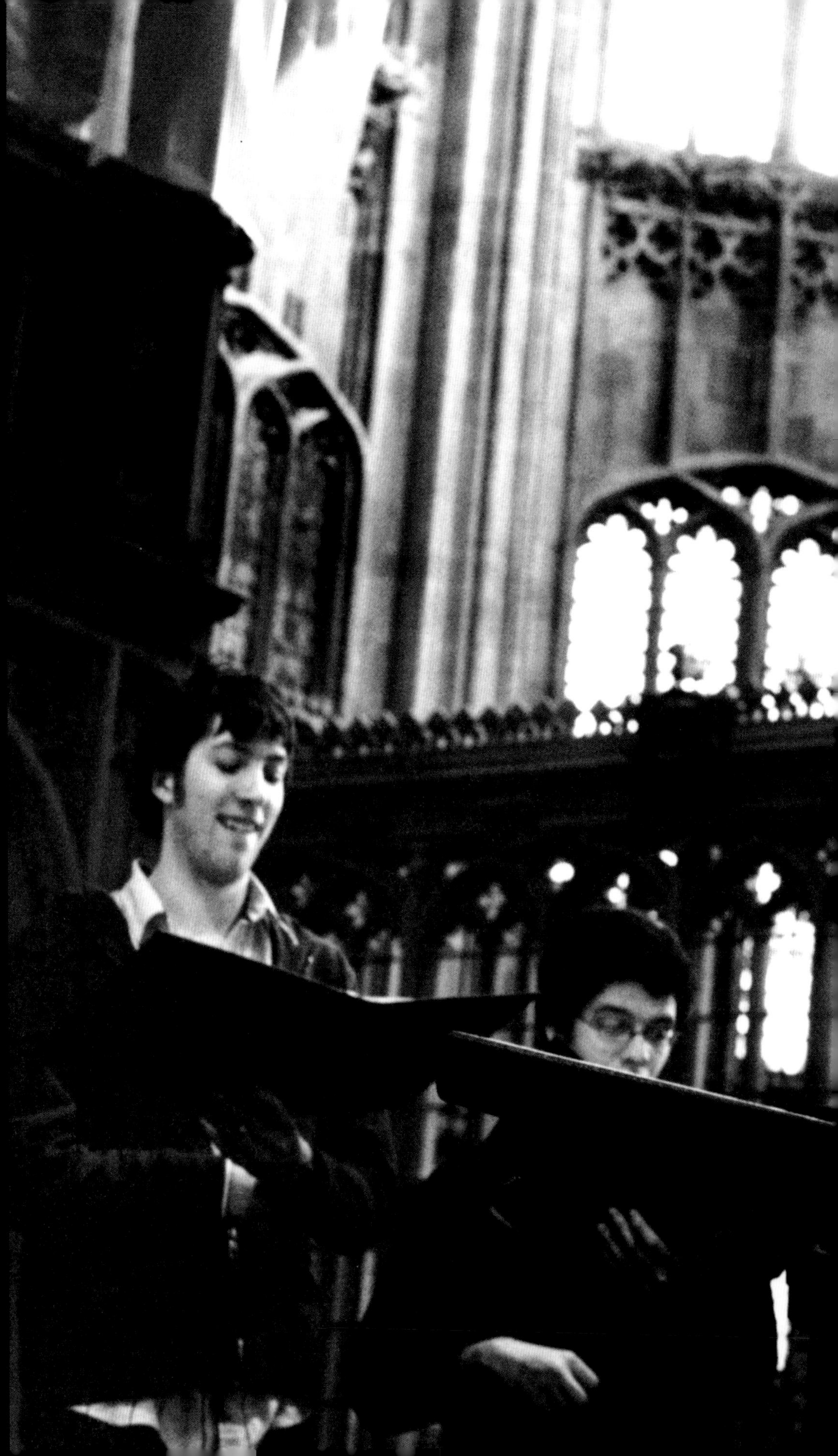

The Choir of London rehearses in the nave for the Interfaith Concert given as part of a consultation at St George's House involving the three main Abrahamic faiths.

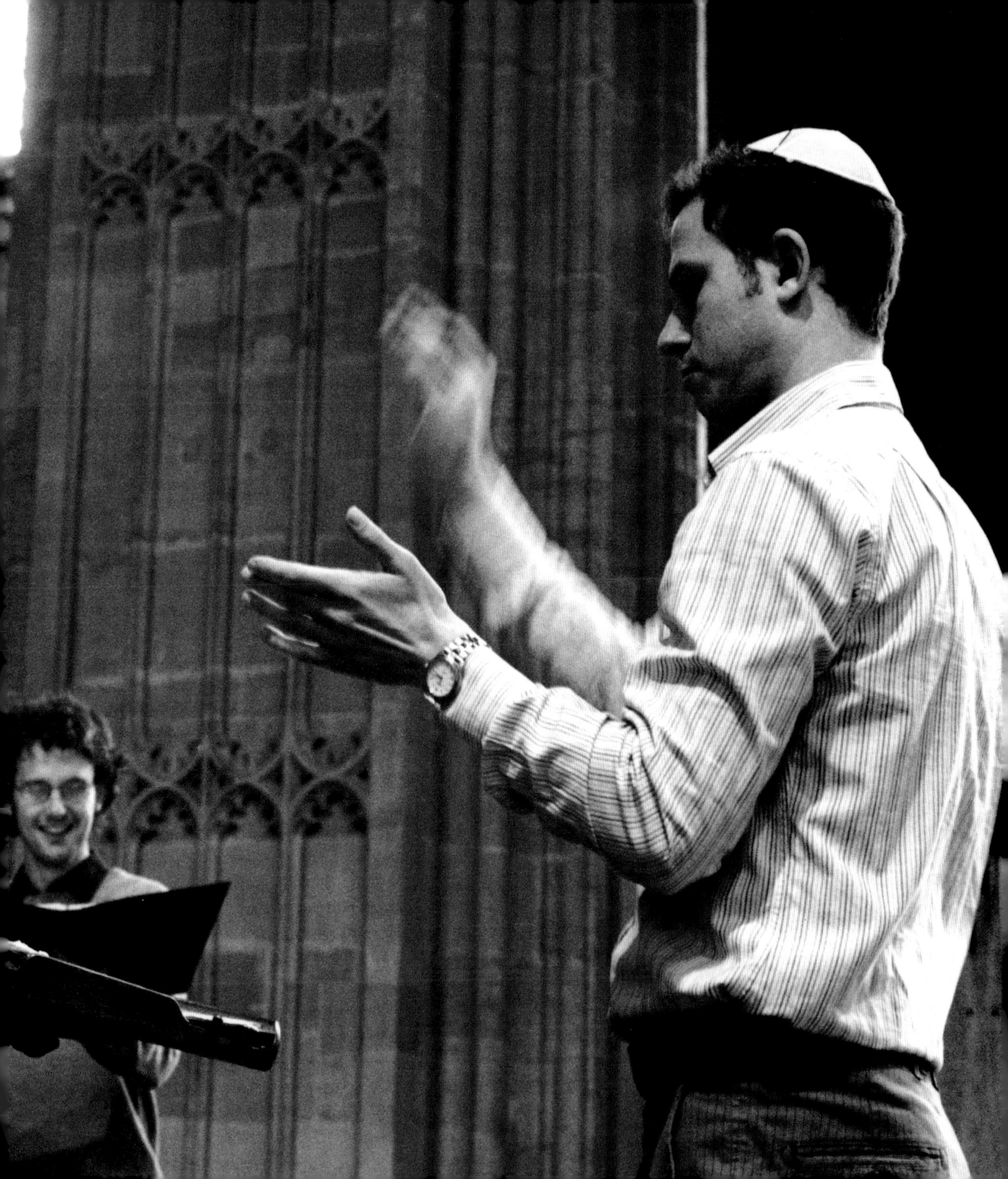

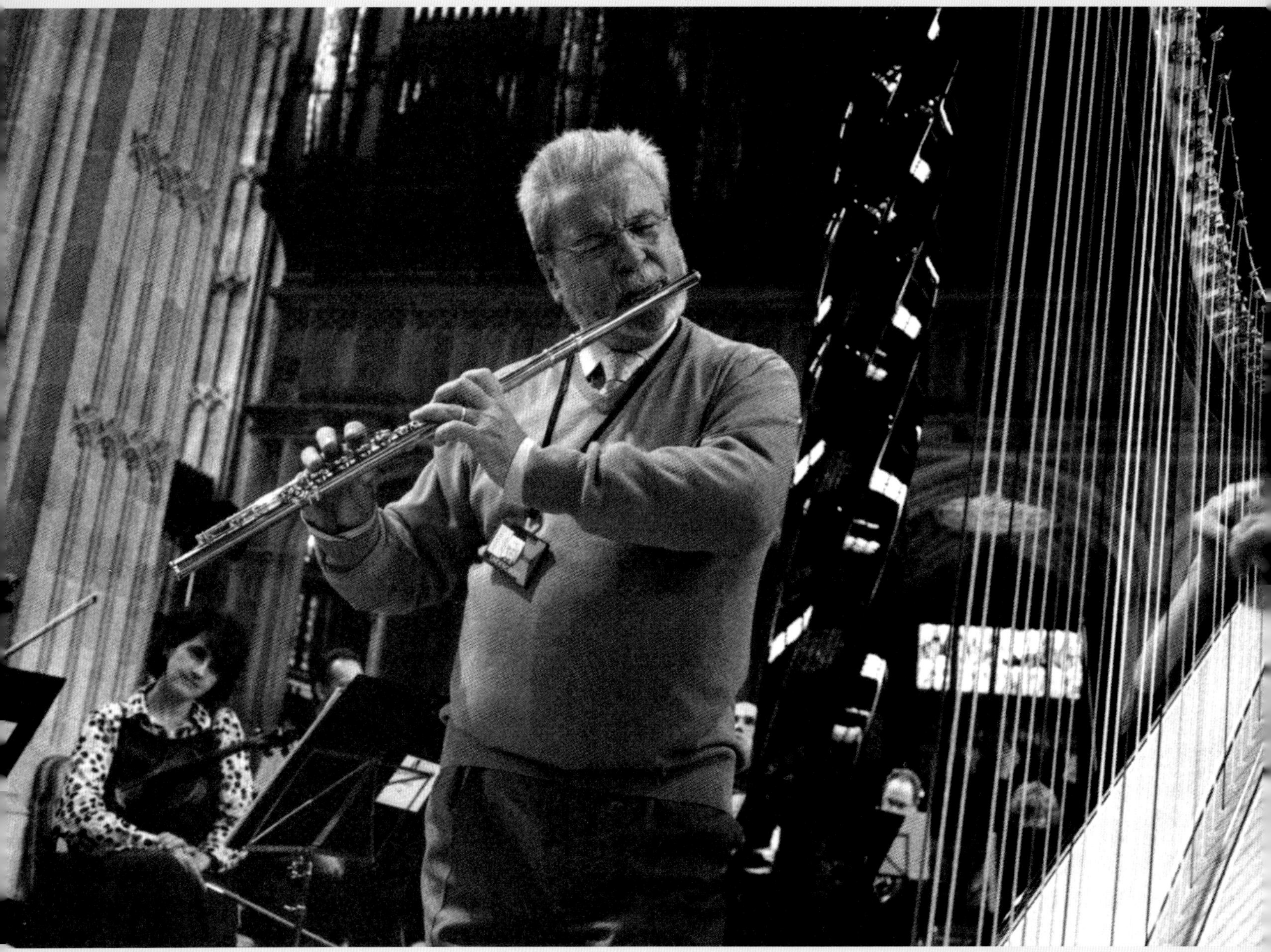

Above: The flautist James Galway rehearses in the nave with the London Mozart Players.
Right: Peter Maxwell Davies consulting his score of *The Golden Rule*, commissioned for HM The Queen's 80th Birthday, during a rehearsal for the Windsor Festival.

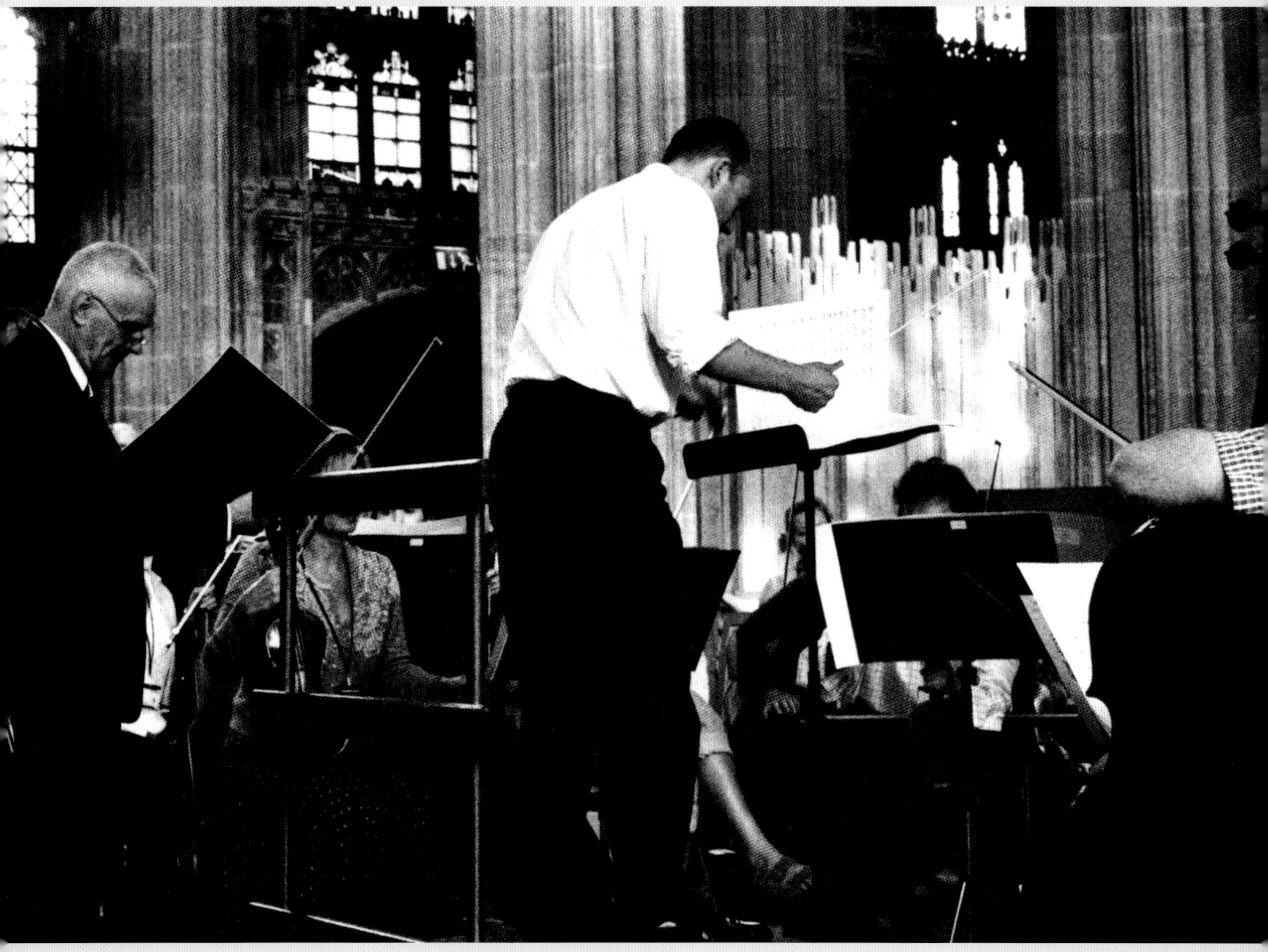

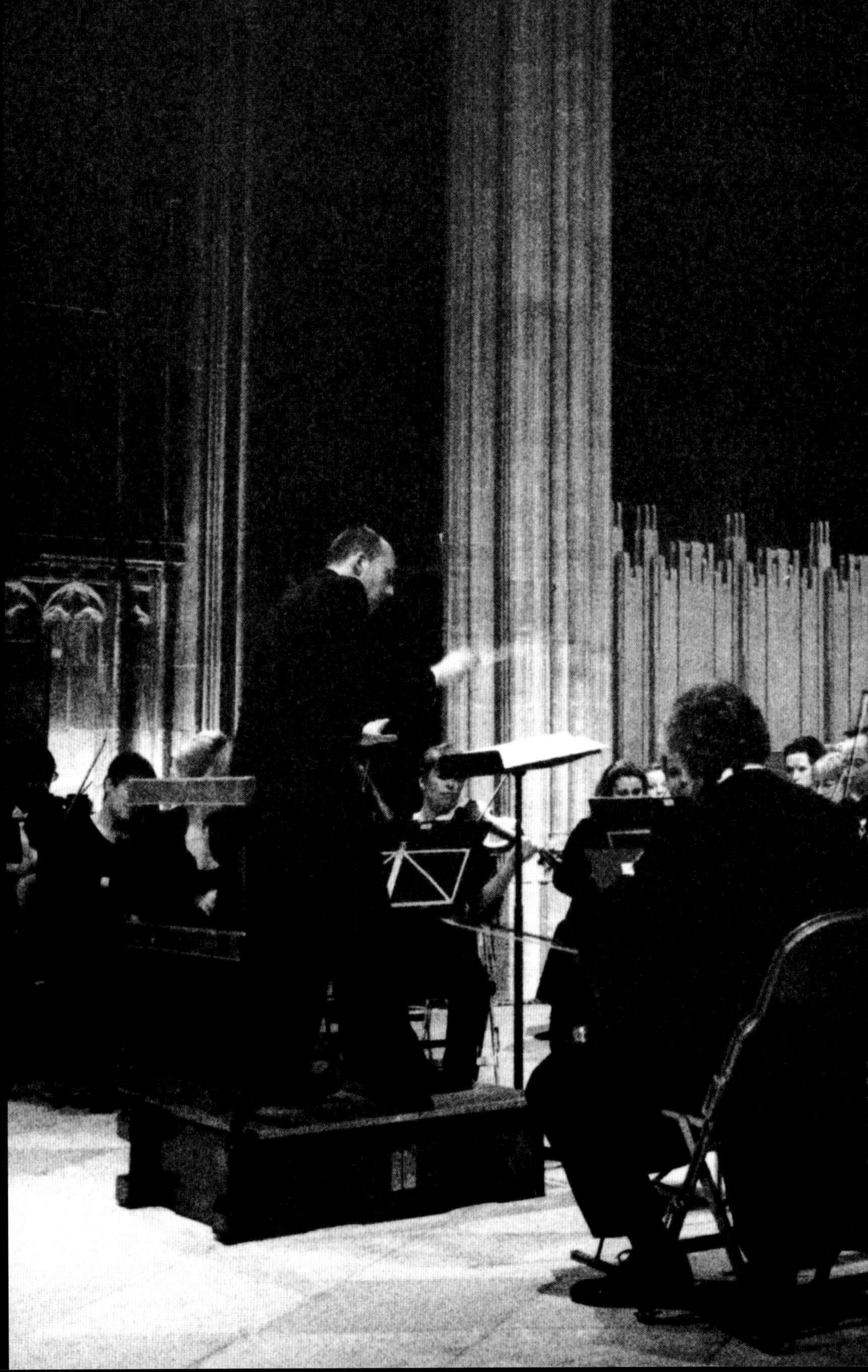

Timothy Byram-Wigfield, Director of Music at St George's Chapel, leads St George's Choir and the London Concert Orchestra at a performance for the Windsor Festival of *The Golden Rule*. A work by Sir Peter Maxwell Davies, Master of The Queen's Music, with words by Andrew Motion, Poet Laureate, it was commissioned by the Friends of St George's and the Windsor Festival for HM The Queen's 80th Birthday celebrations earlier that year.

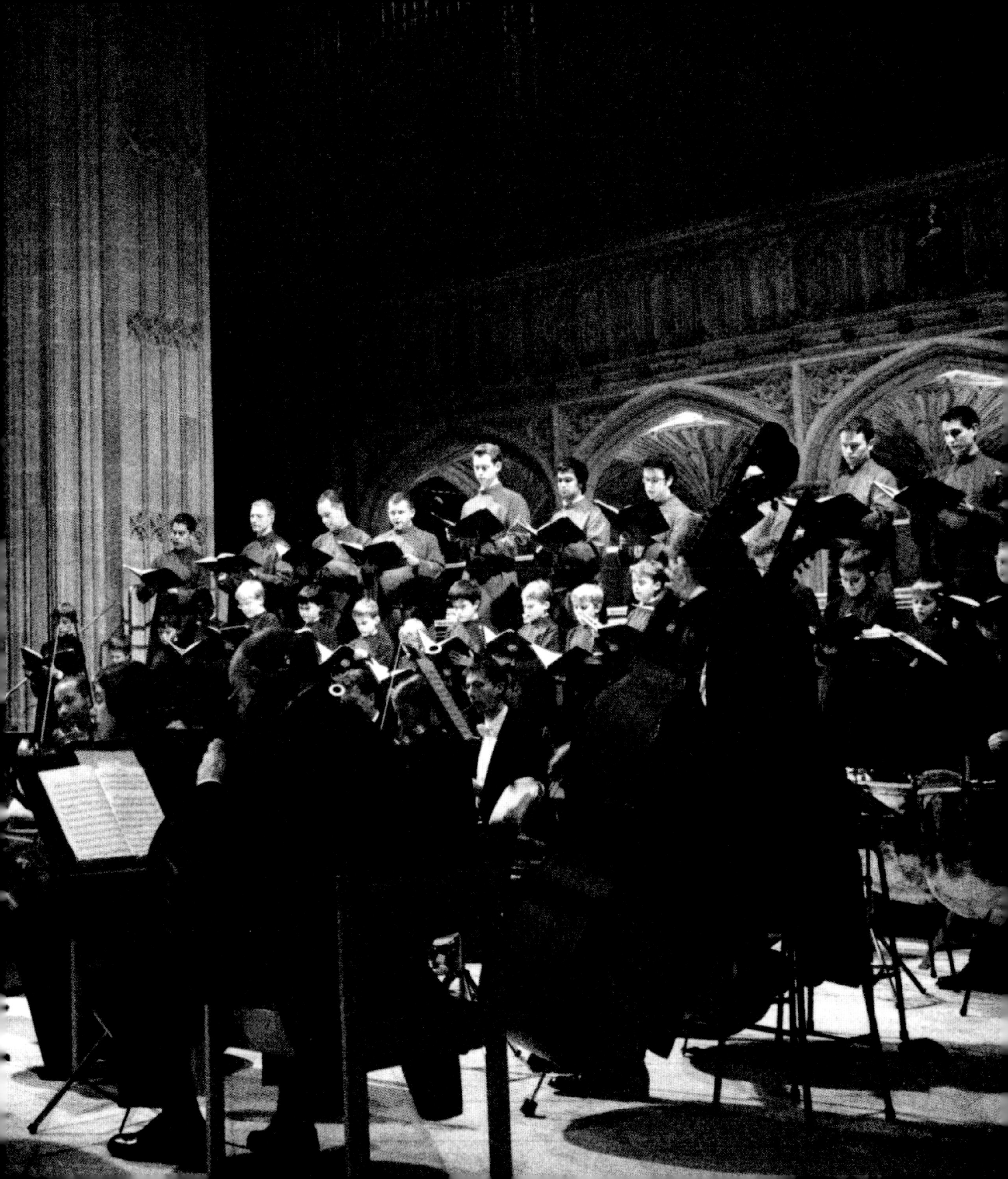

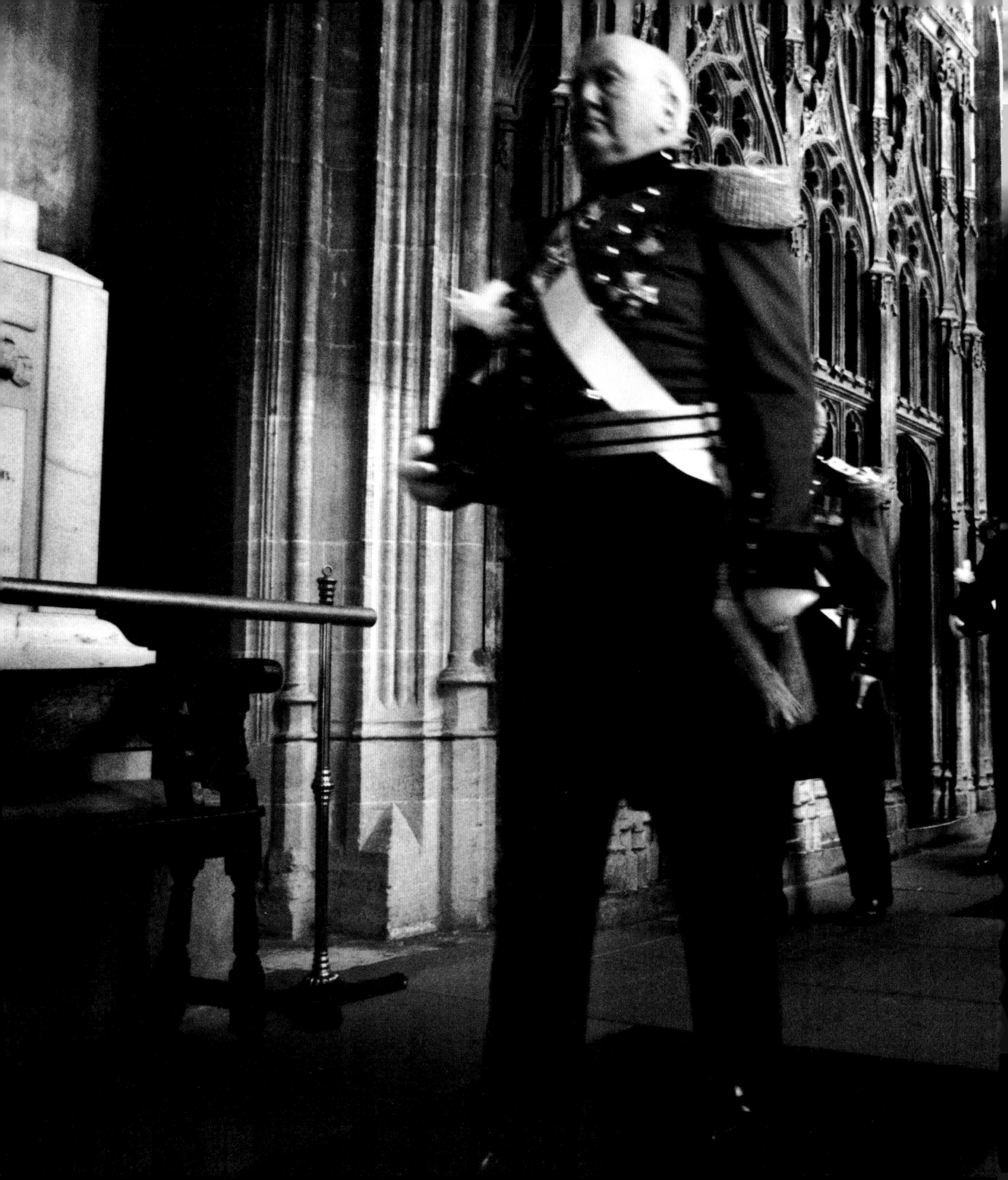

Military

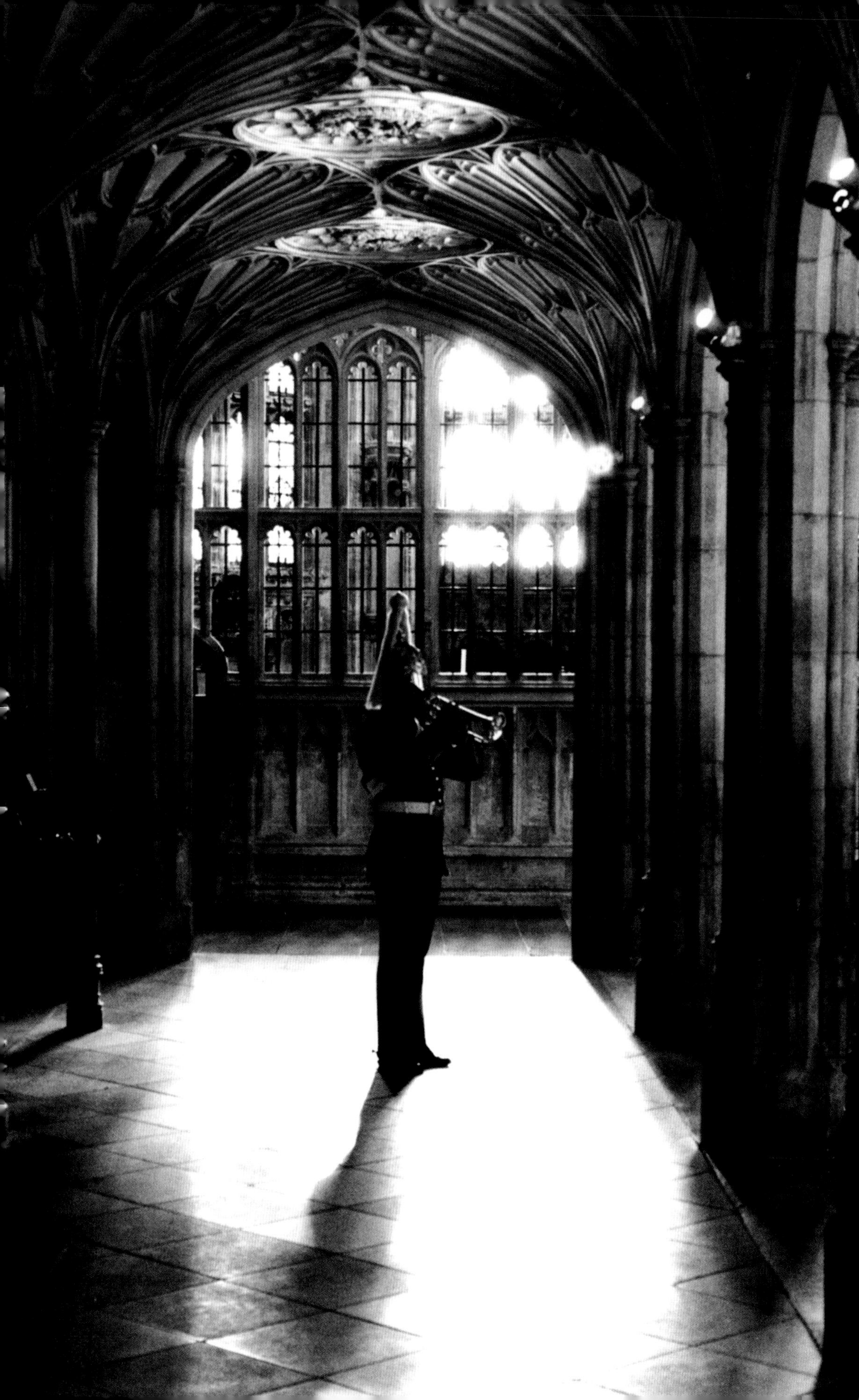

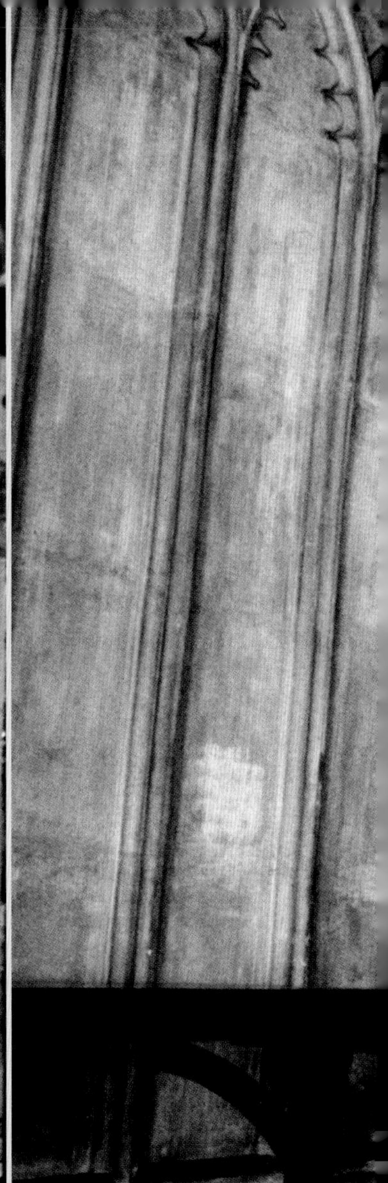

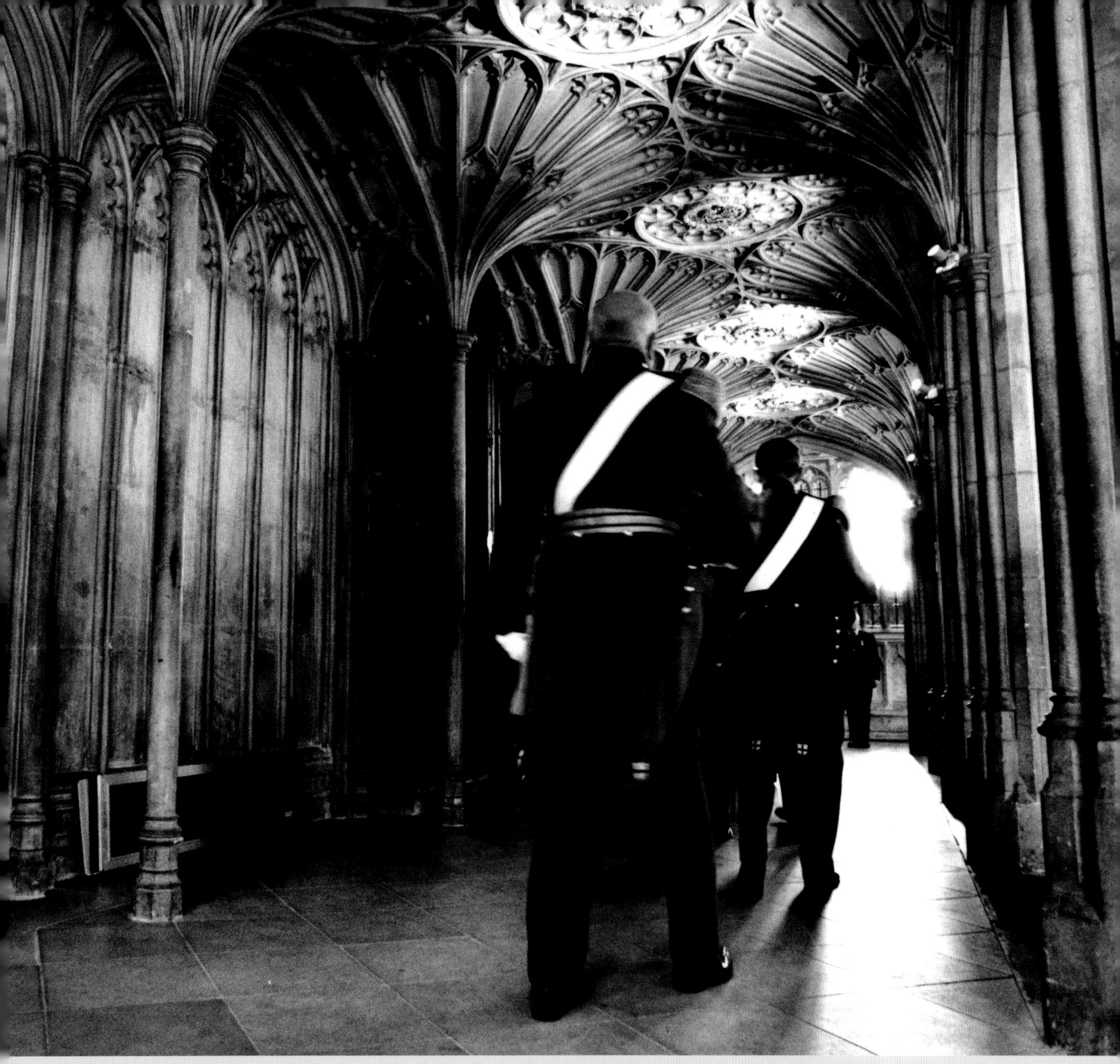

Remembrance Sunday: *Left*: The bugle player, standing beneath the organ screen between the nave and the quire, sounds 'Reveille' at the end of the two minutes' silence observed during Mattins on Remembrance Sunday.

Above and Preceding Pages: The Military Knights of Windsor process in and out of the quire prior to the Service. The Military Knights are retired officers who live in the castle and attend Mattins every Sunday on behalf of the Knights of the Garter. Led by their Governor, Sir Michael Hobbs, they march in pairs dressed in their uniforms.

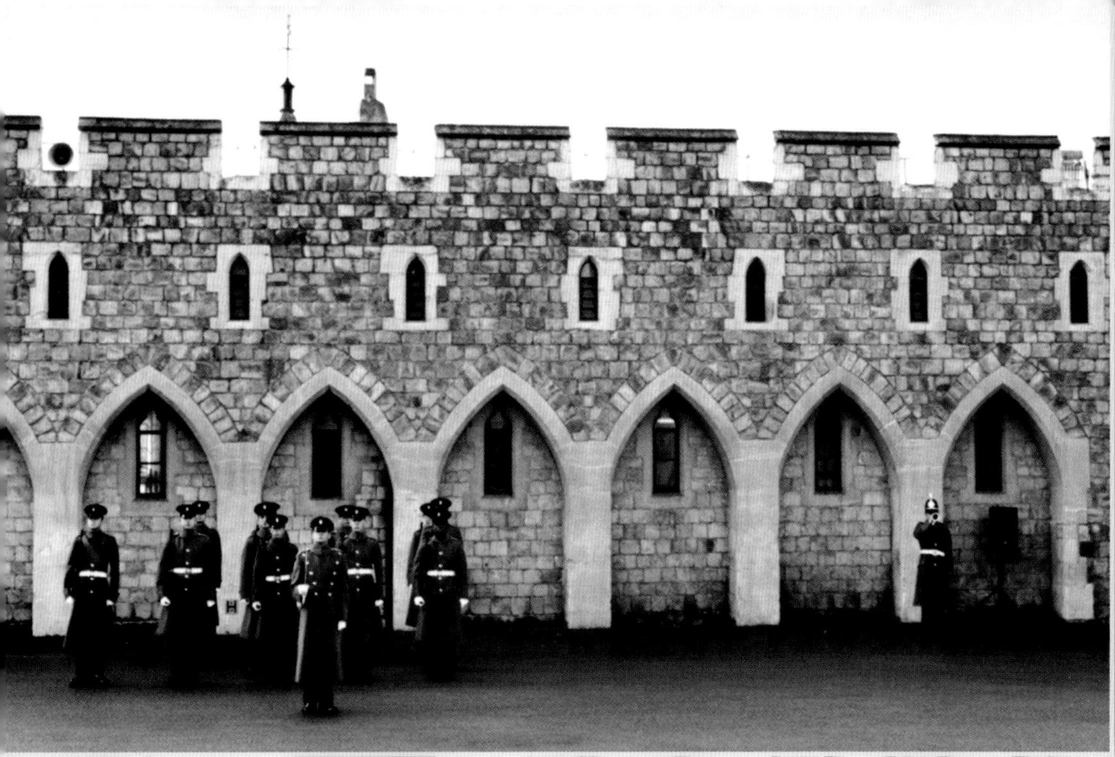

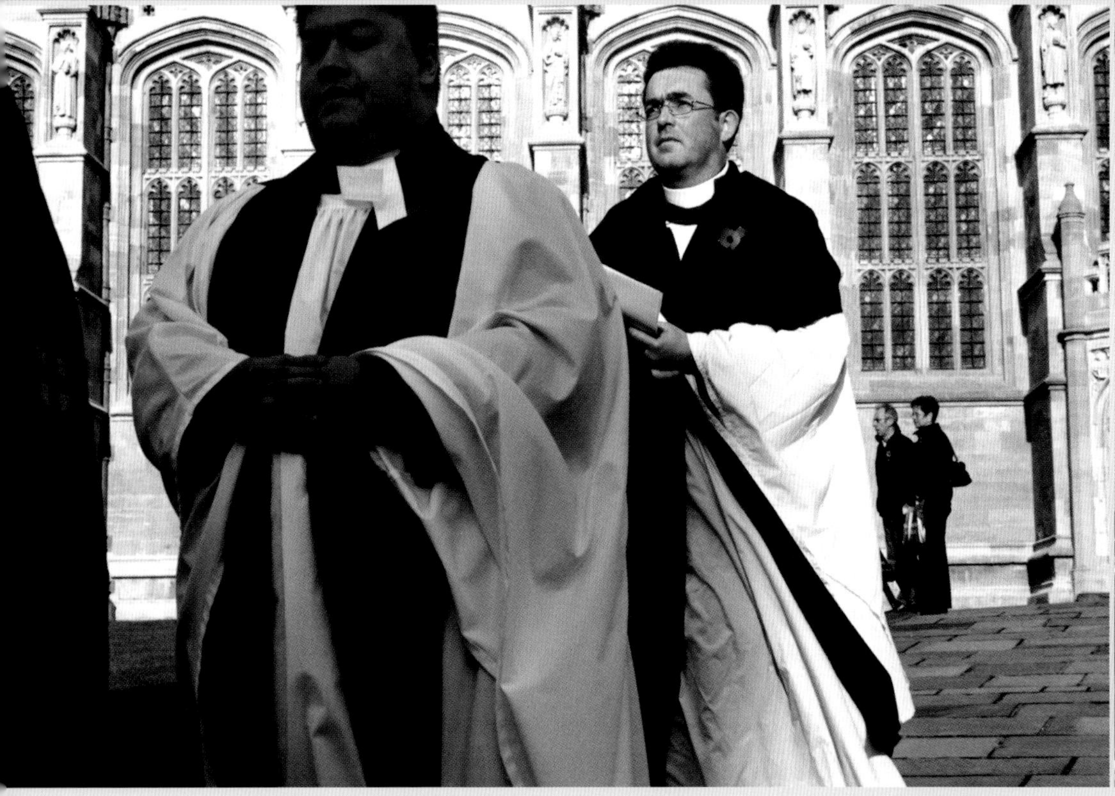

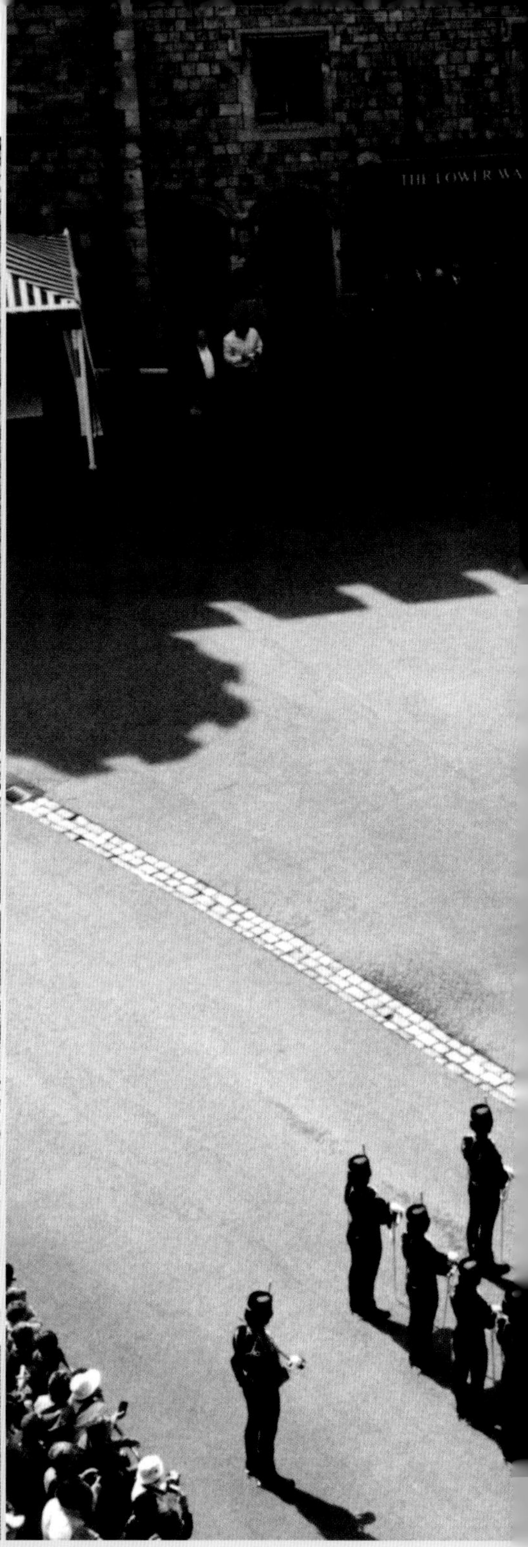

Top Left: Part of the Windsor Castle Guard turned out in front of the Guard Room on 11 November.
Bottom Left: The Reverend Canon Dr Hueston Finlay on his way to the parade ground from the Chapel to lead the prayers outside the Guard Room for members of the public.

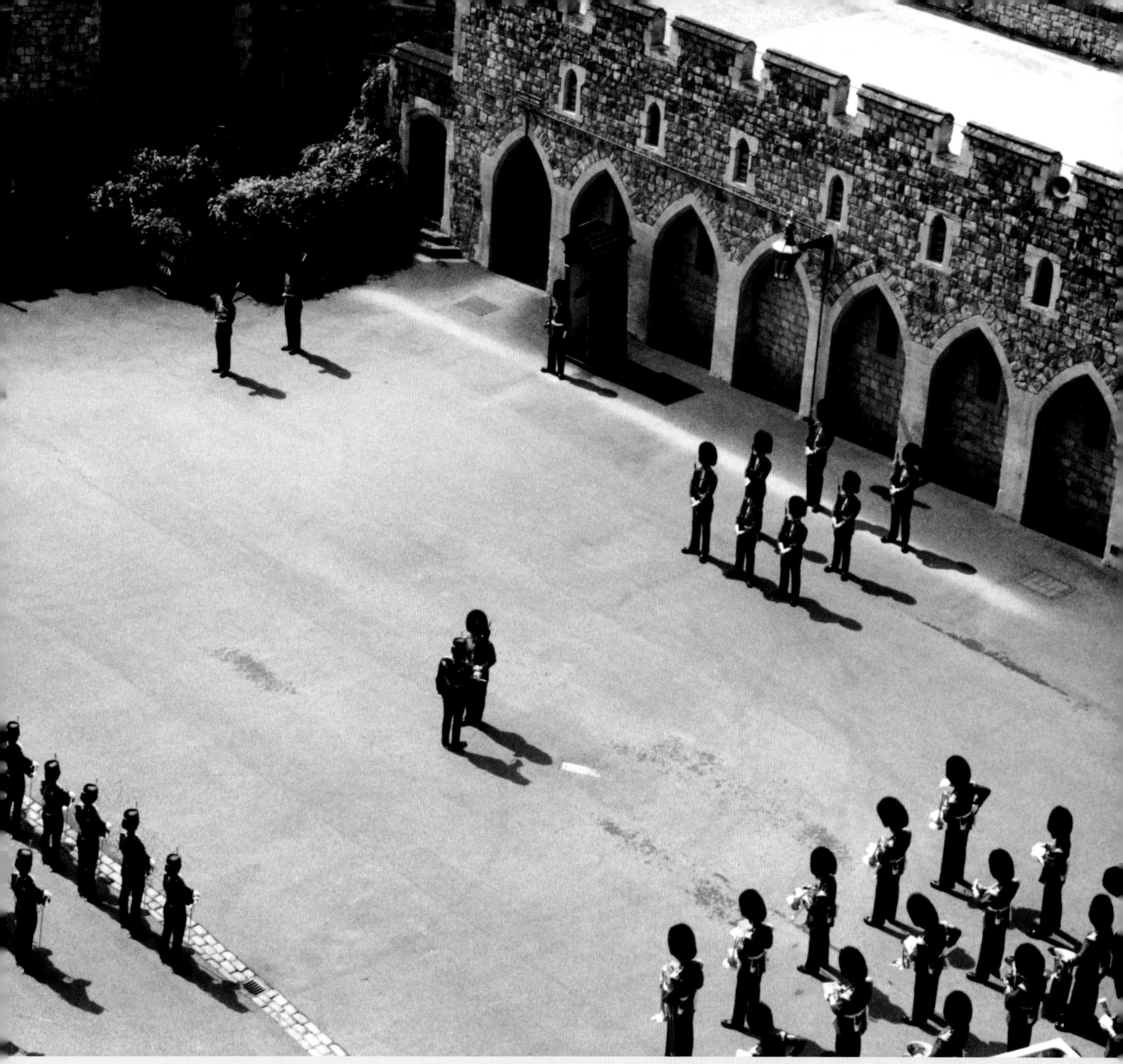

Above: The Changing of the Guard as seen from the roof of the west front. The ceremony takes place outside the Guard Room in the Lower Ward all year round, weather permitting. The Guards march on alternate days from August to March and daily during April, May, June and July, but never on Sundays. A band, as seen here, usually accompanies the Guards.

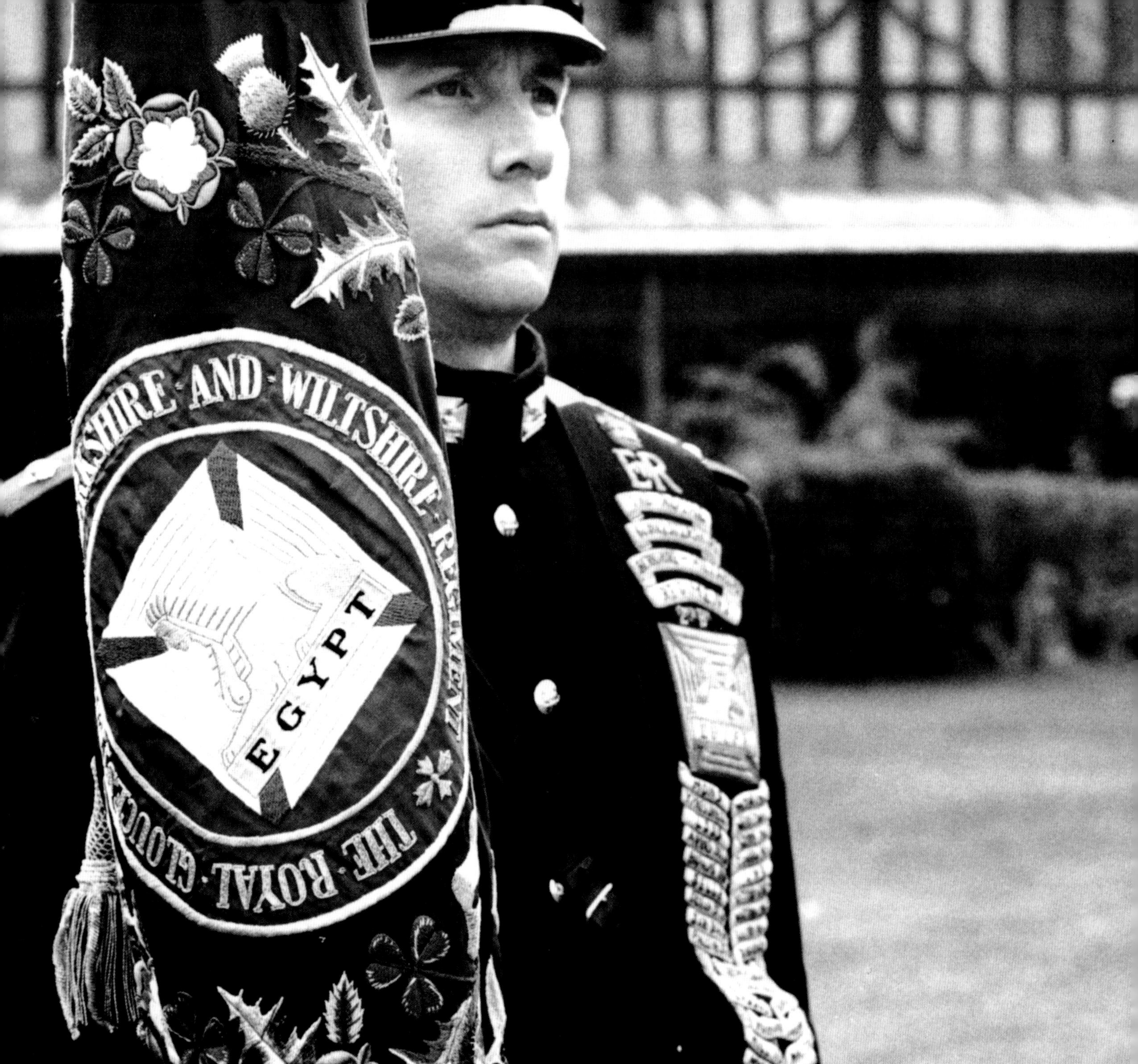

A Thanksgiving Service for the Disbanding of the Royal Gloucestershire, Berkshire and Wiltshire Regiment at St George's Chapel. Members of the Regiment are seen here marching through the Horseshoe Cloisters and on the West Steps prior to the Service.

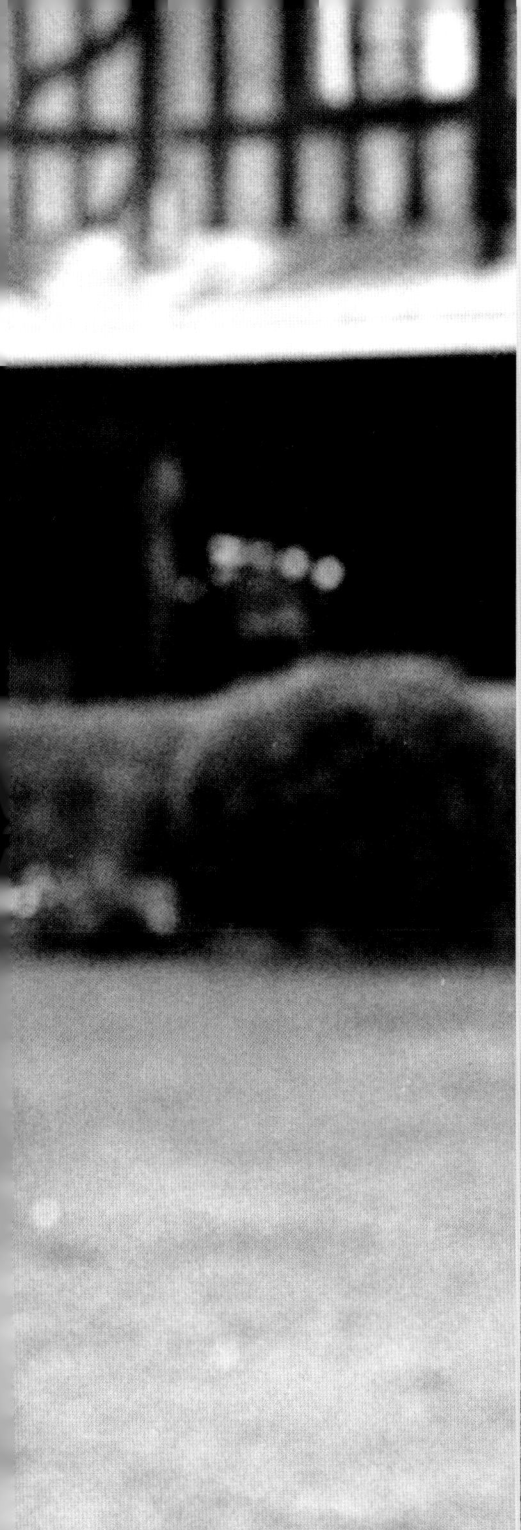

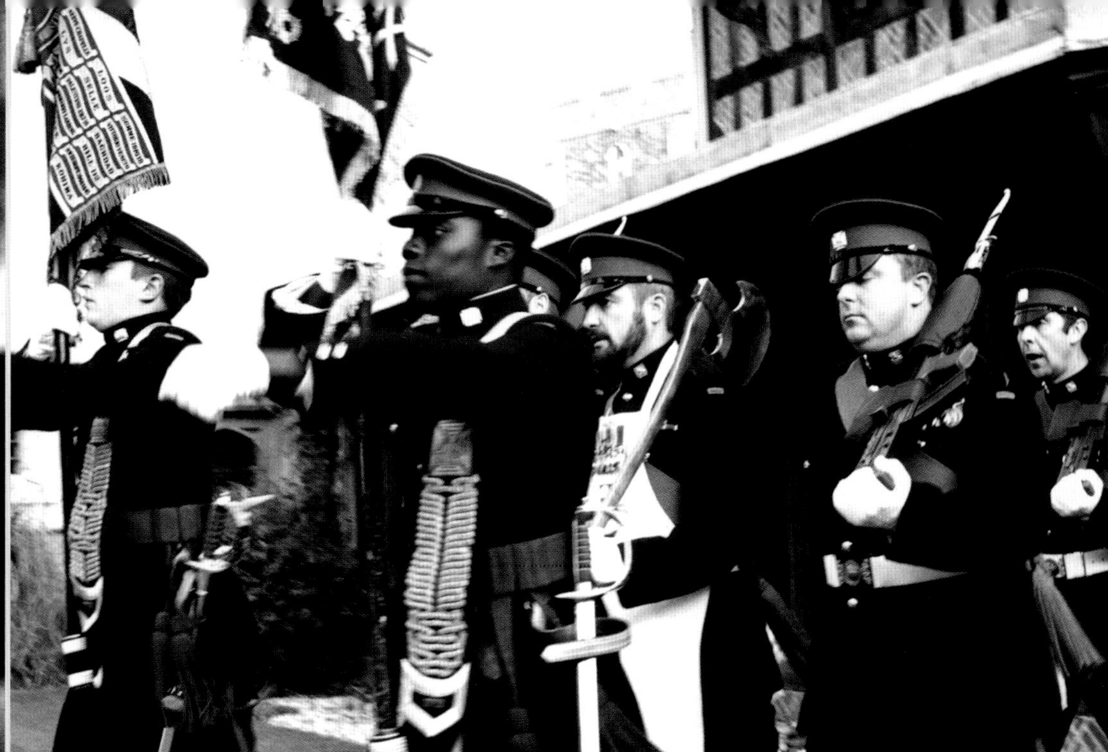

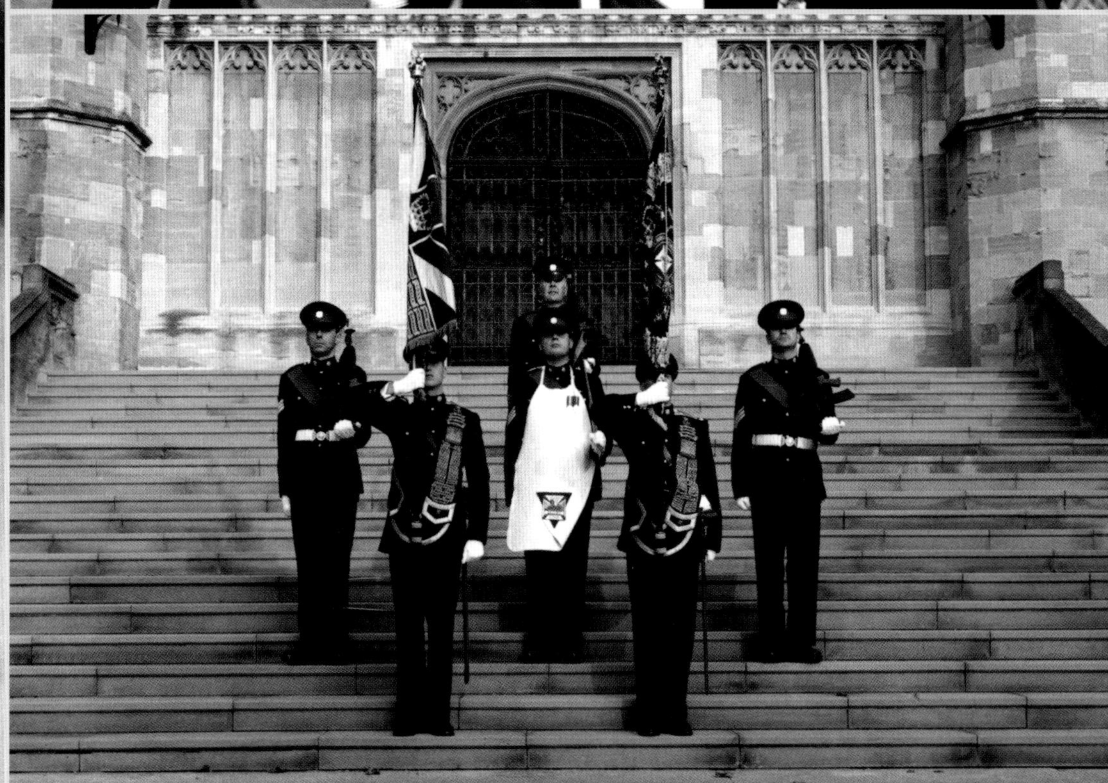

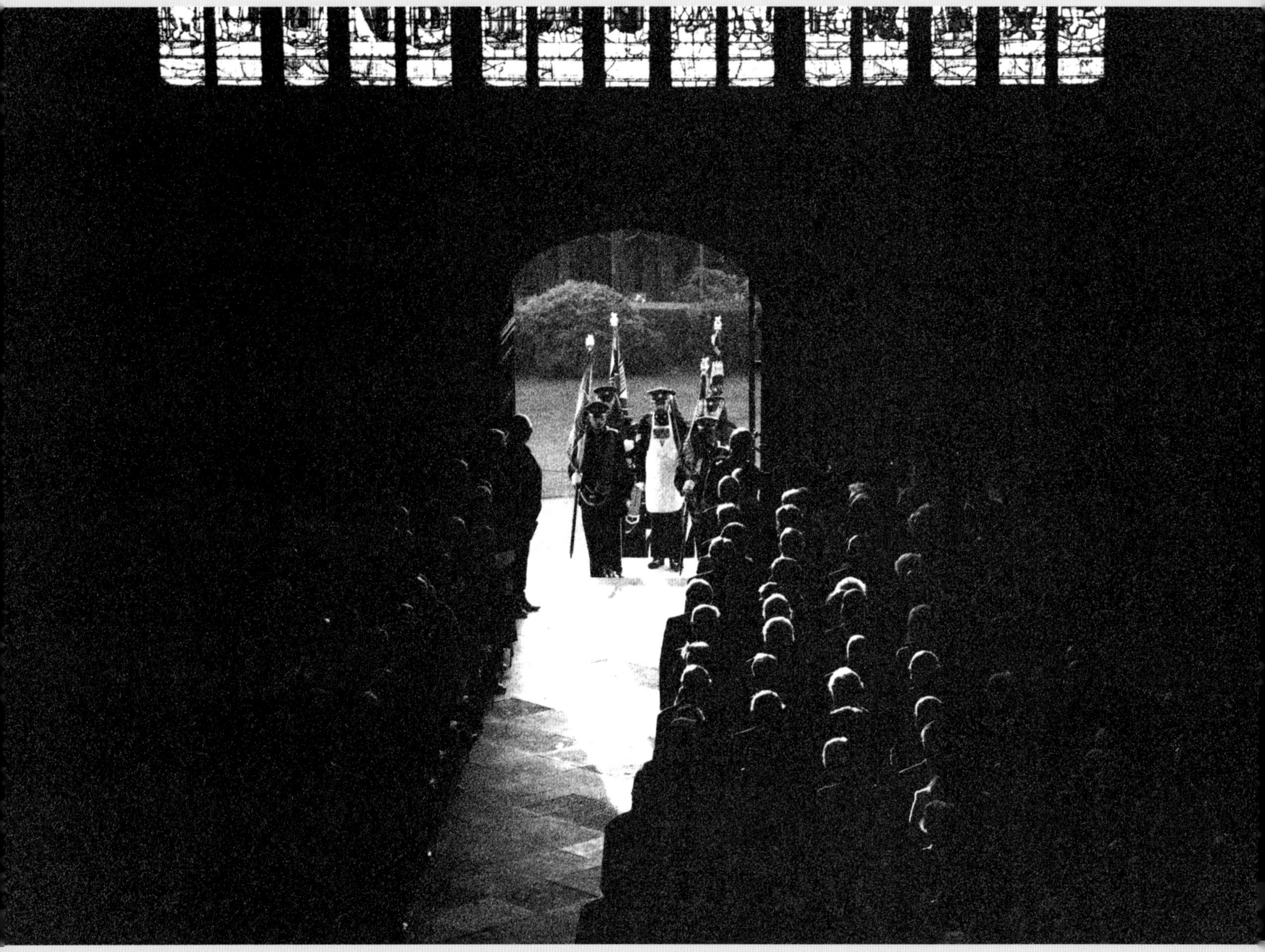

Above: The Royal Gloucestershire, Berkshire and Wiltshire Regiment enter the Chapel via the West Doors with their Colours.
Right: The Dean leads the Service in the nave.

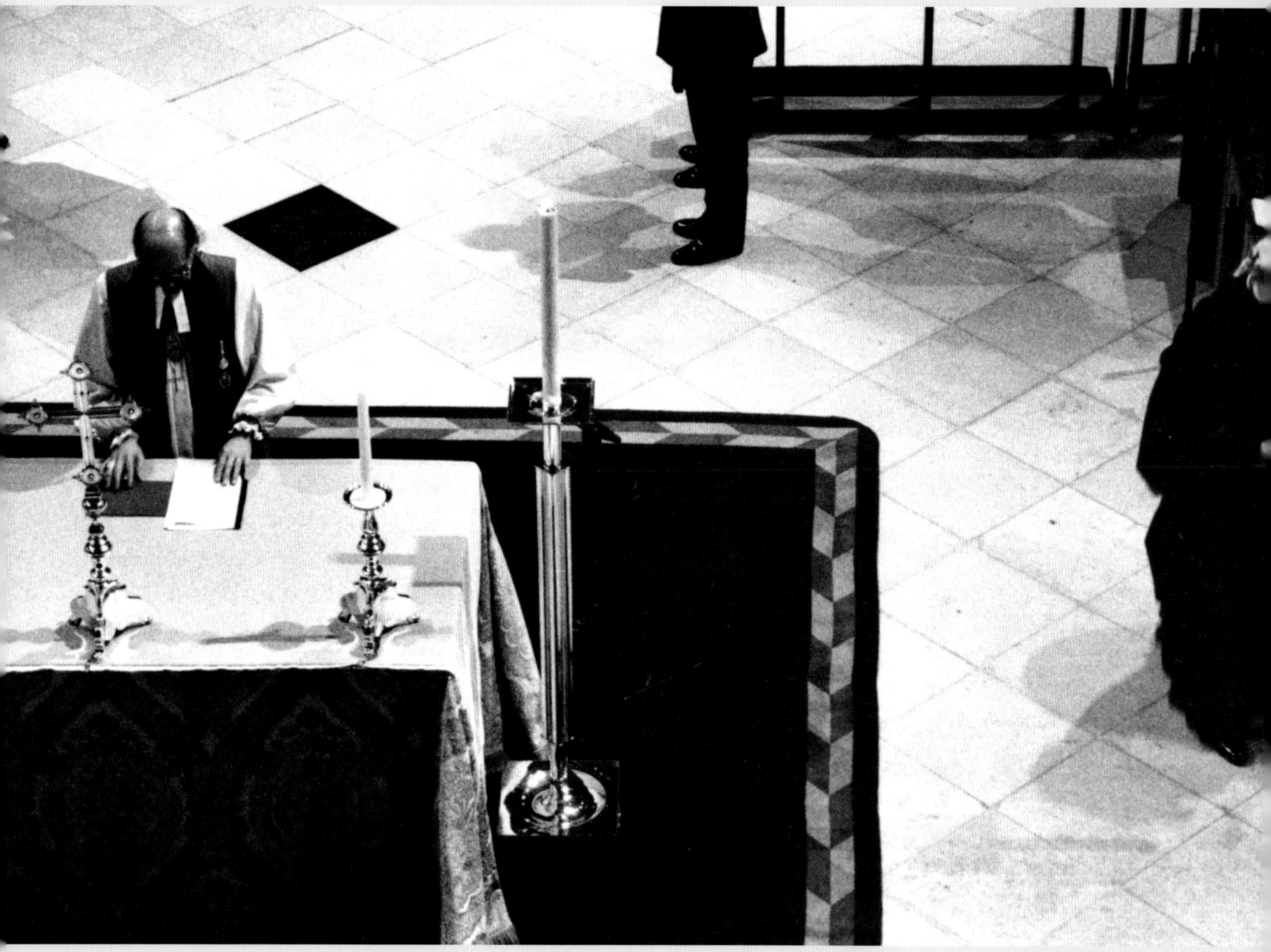

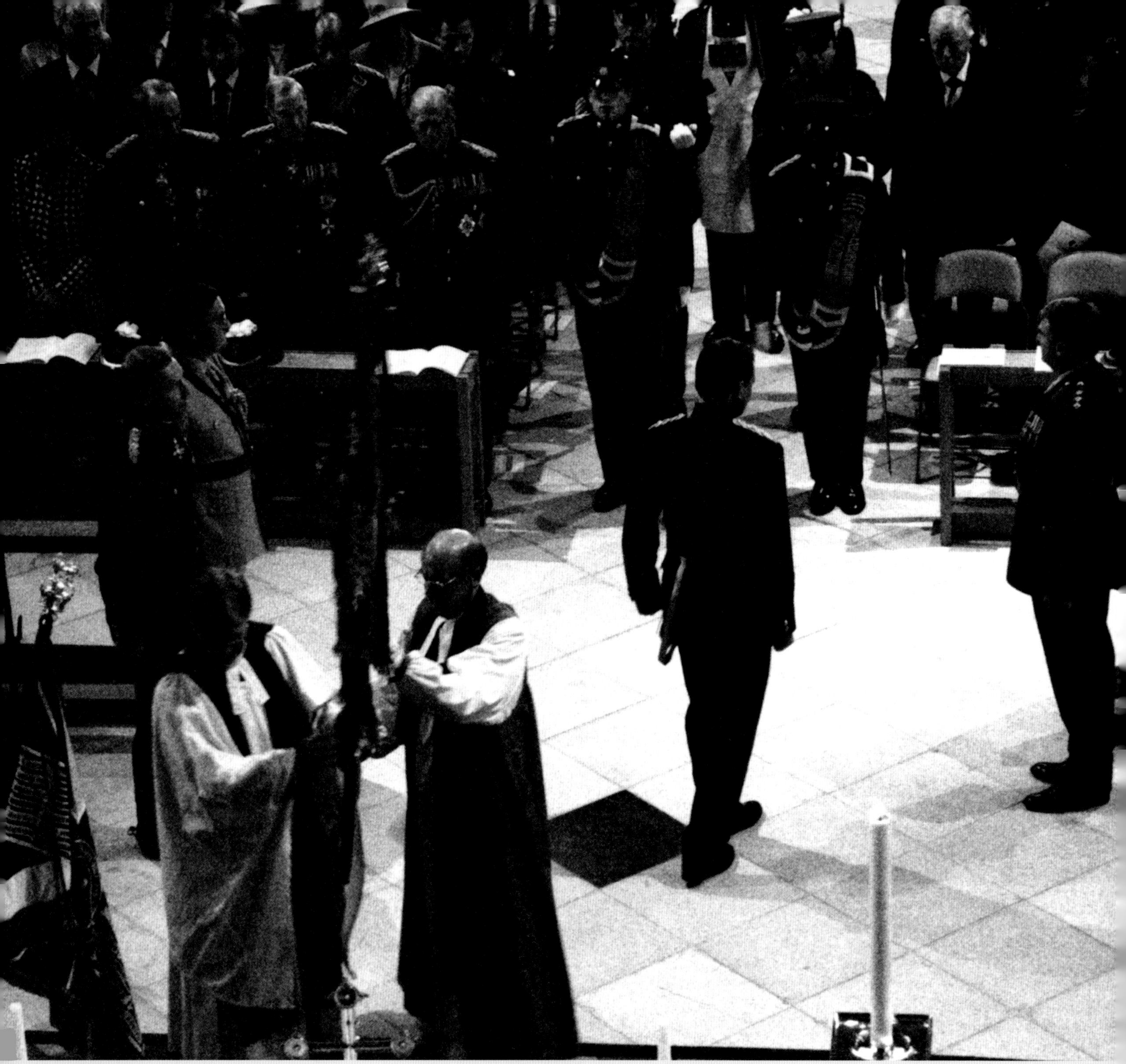

Above: HRH The Duke of Edinburgh looks on from the front row as the Dean receives the Regiment's Colours.
Right: The Queen's Scouts parade from the Quadrangle in the Castle to St George's Chapel for their National Scout Service. The Scouts' St George's Day is an annual event established in 1934 by King George V. The service is prepared and led by a small group of Queen's Scouts under the guidance of one of the Canons.

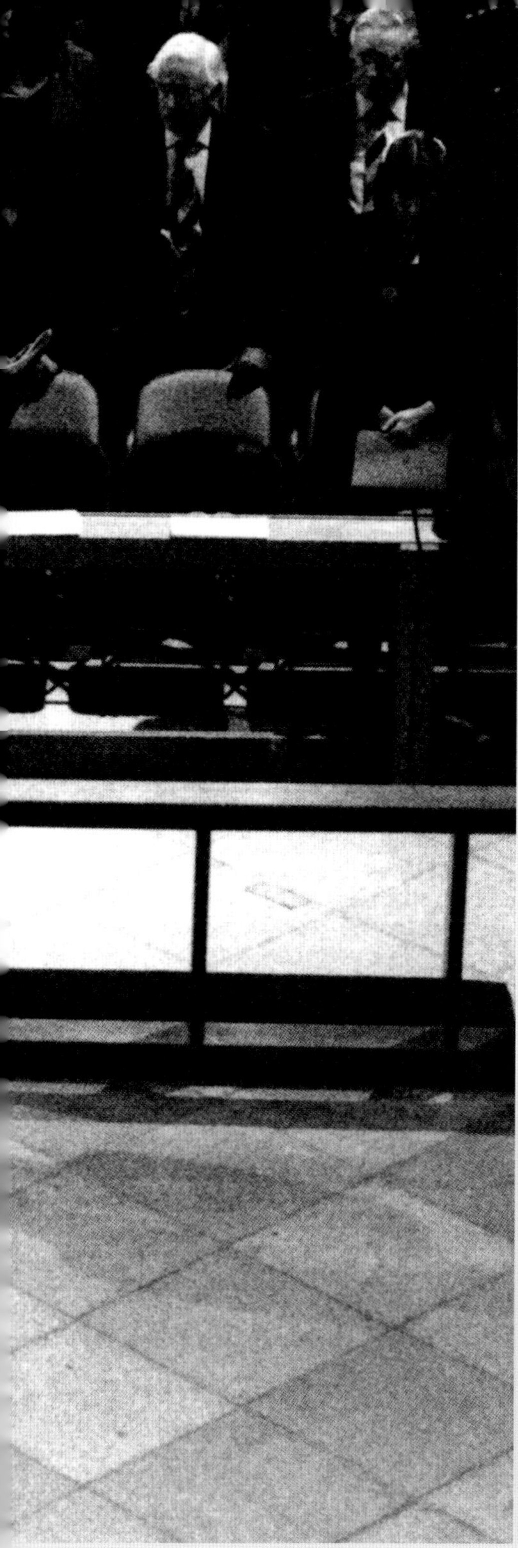

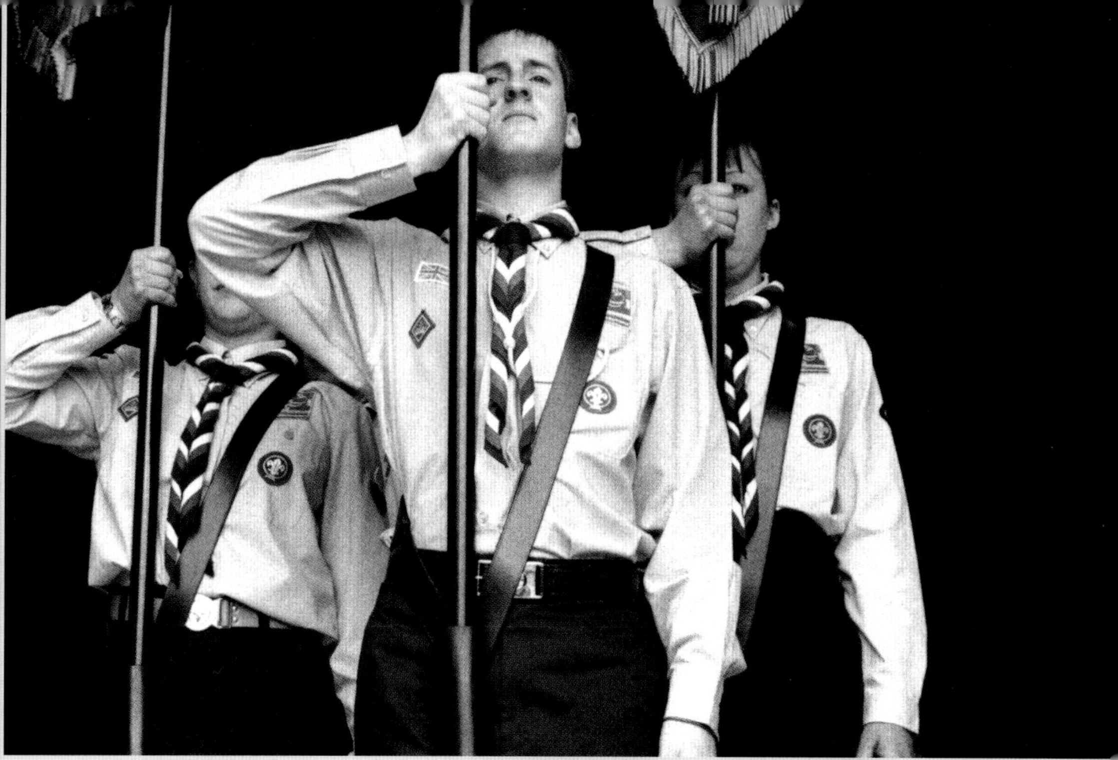

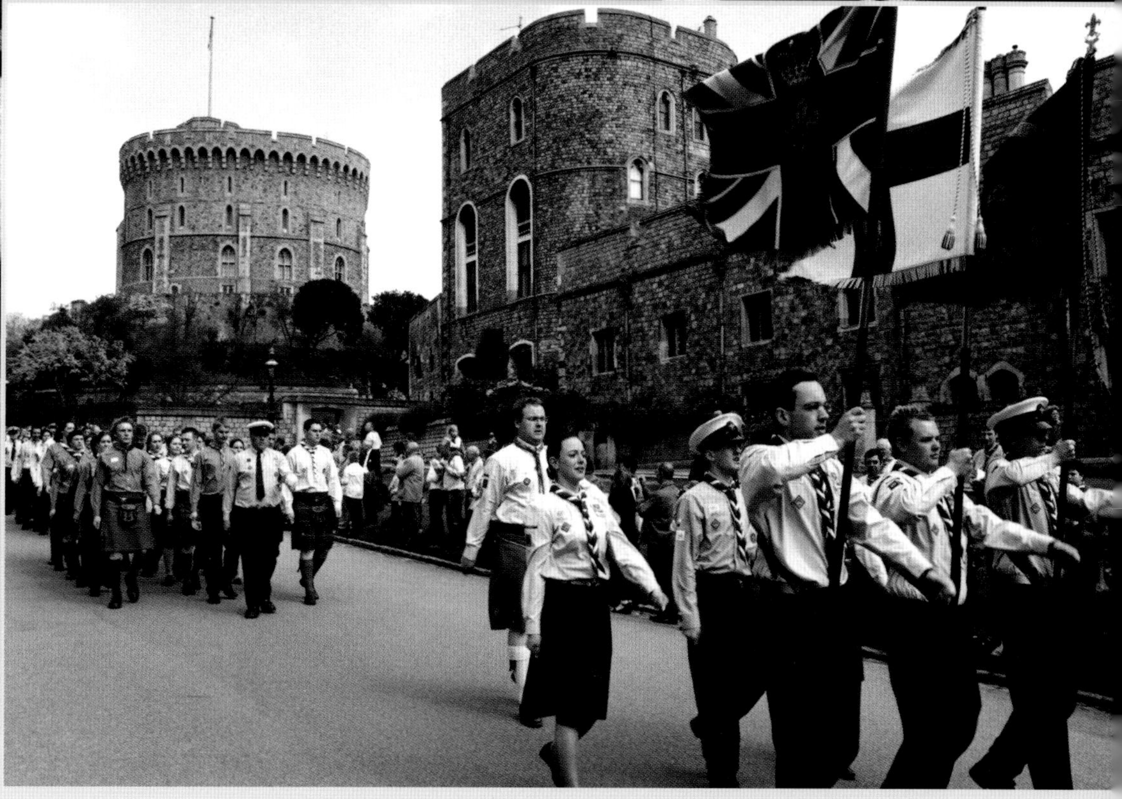

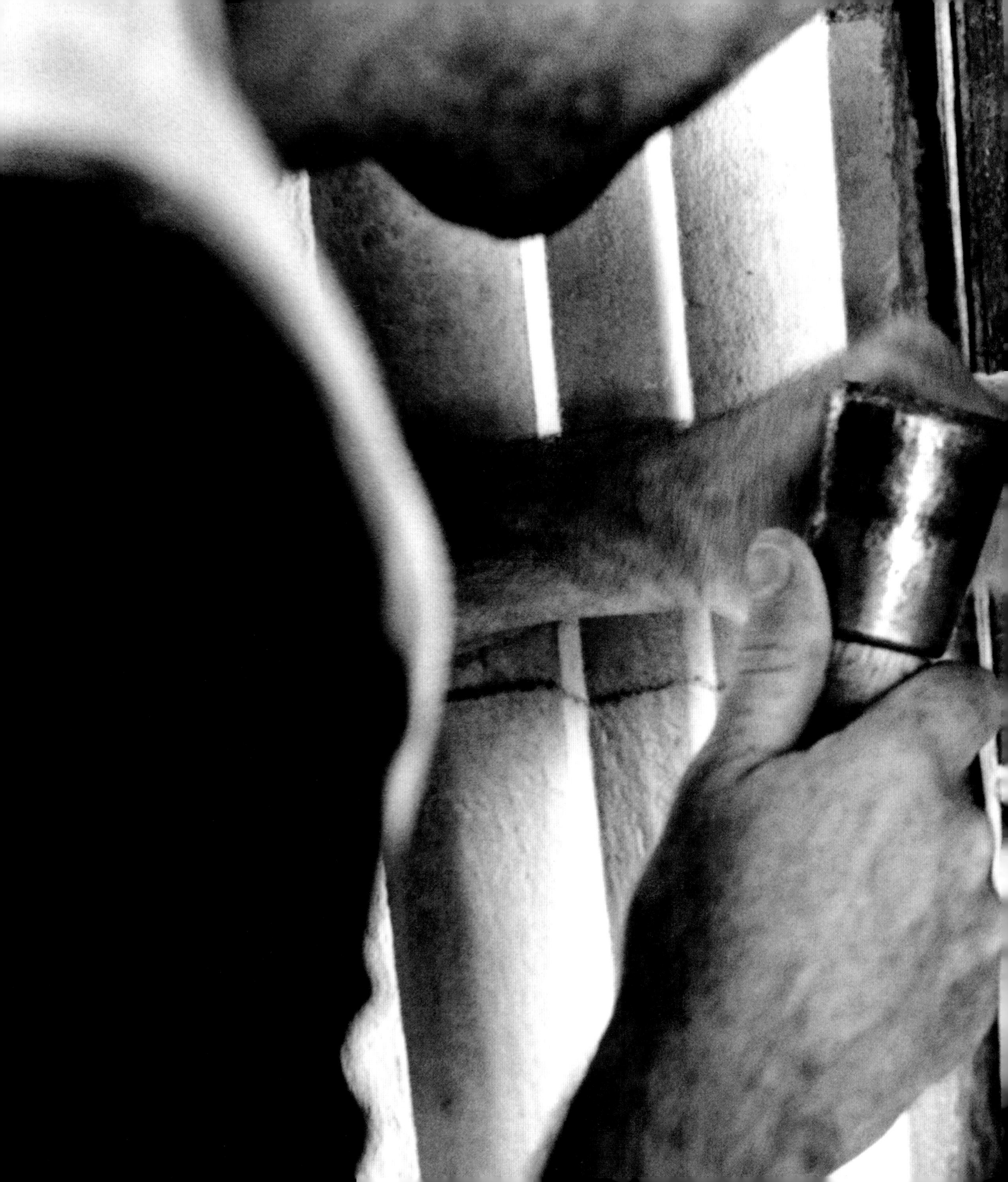

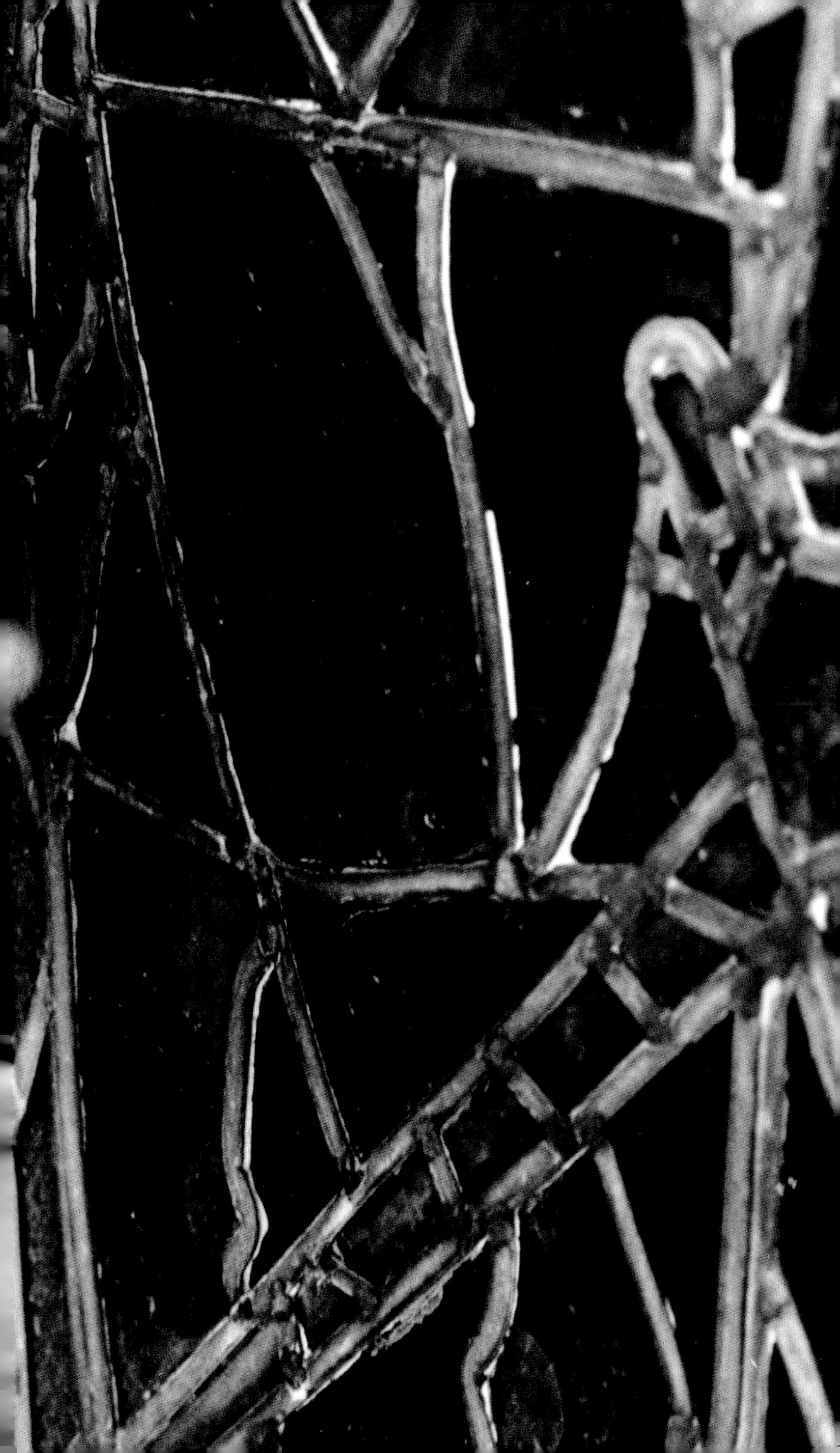

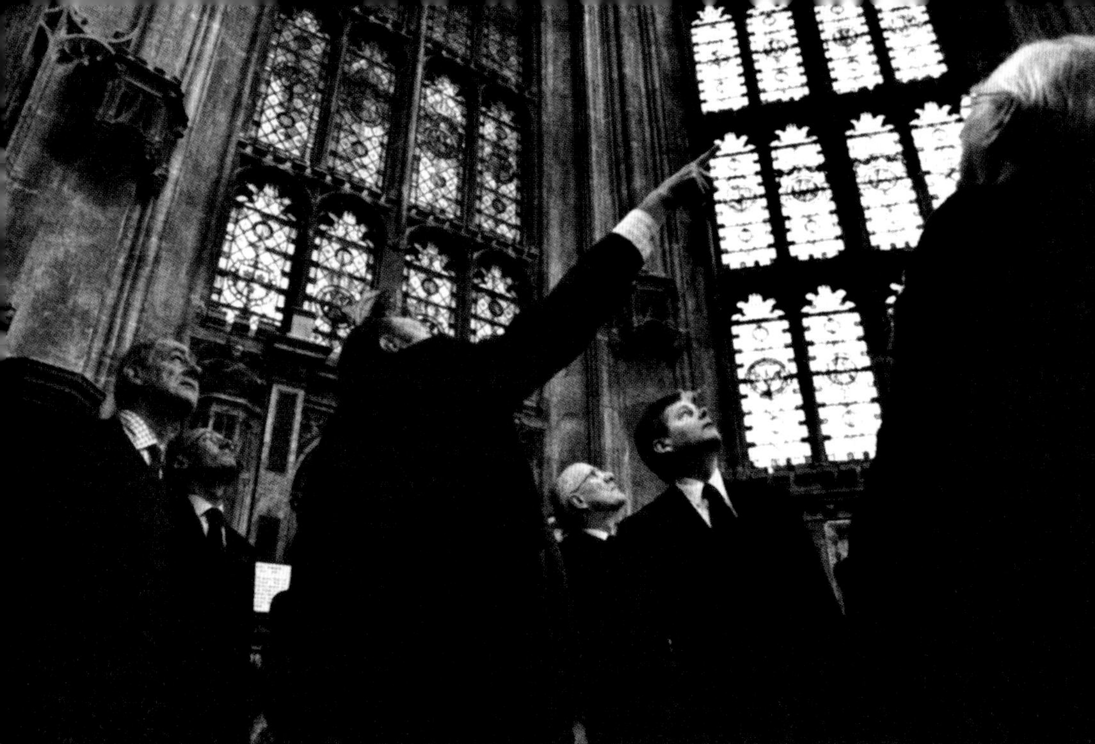

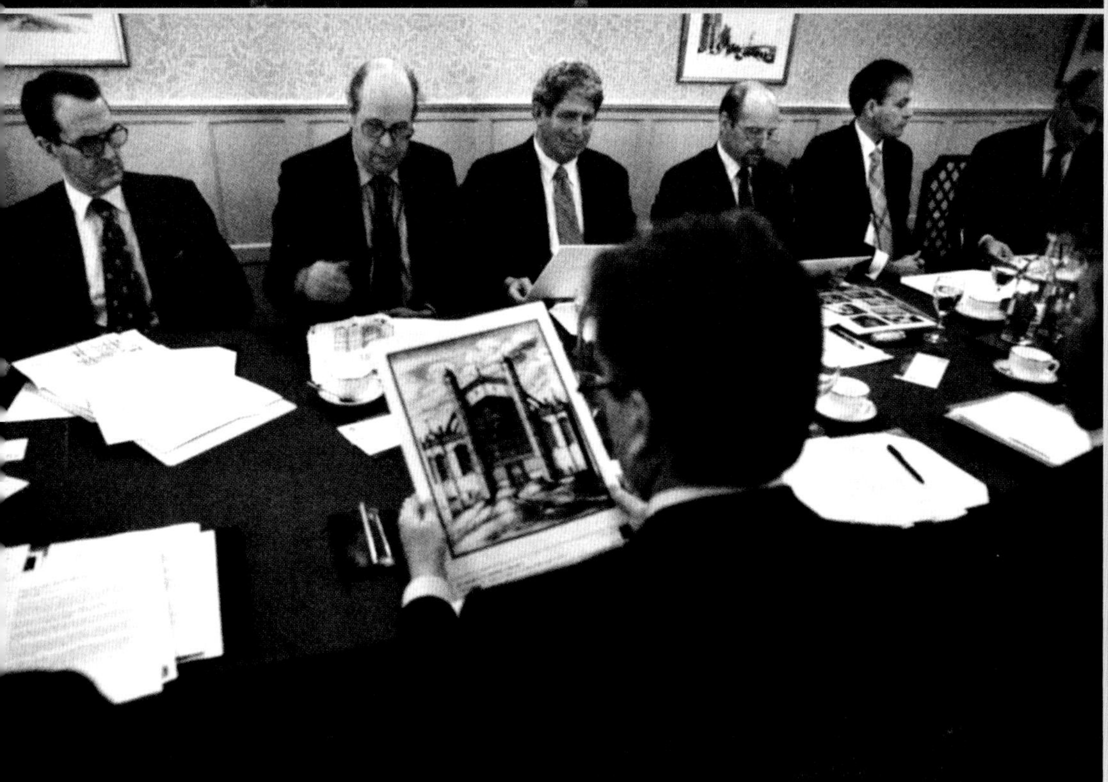

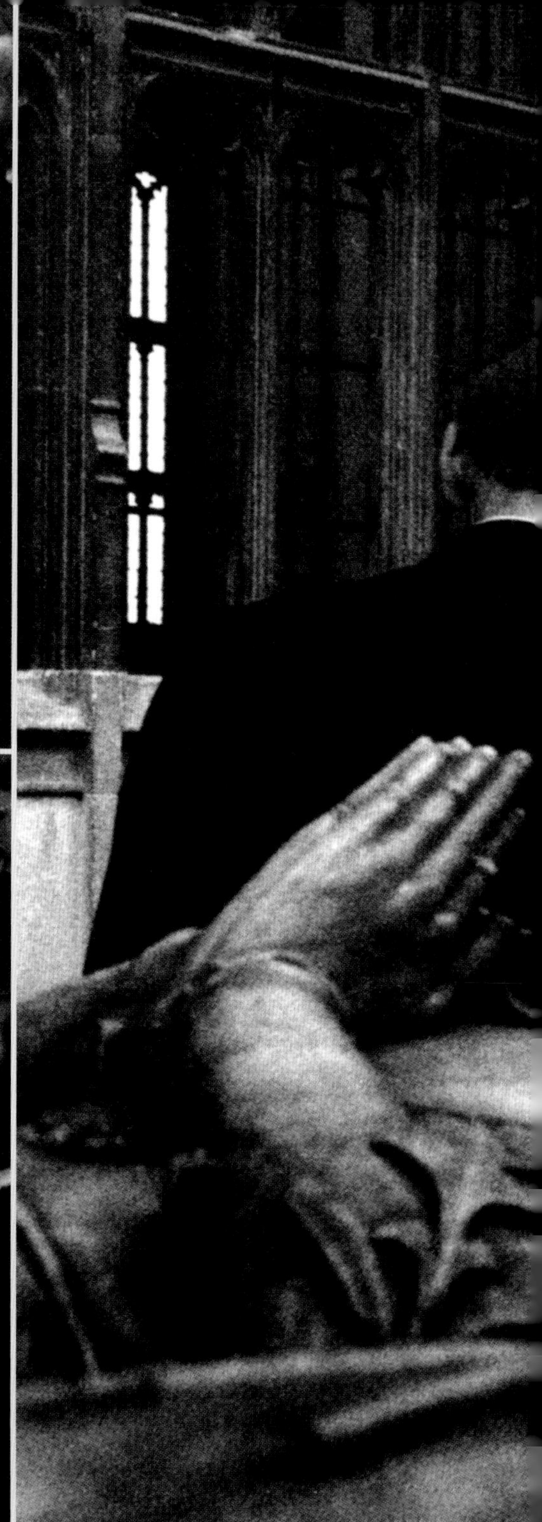

Preceding pages: A conservator gently taps to loosen the glass from the outside of the west window as part of the refurbishment of the west front of the Chapel.

Top: The Fabric Advisory Committee in the Bray Chantry on the south side.
Above: The Committee meet to discuss the current restoration and conservation concerns and projects.

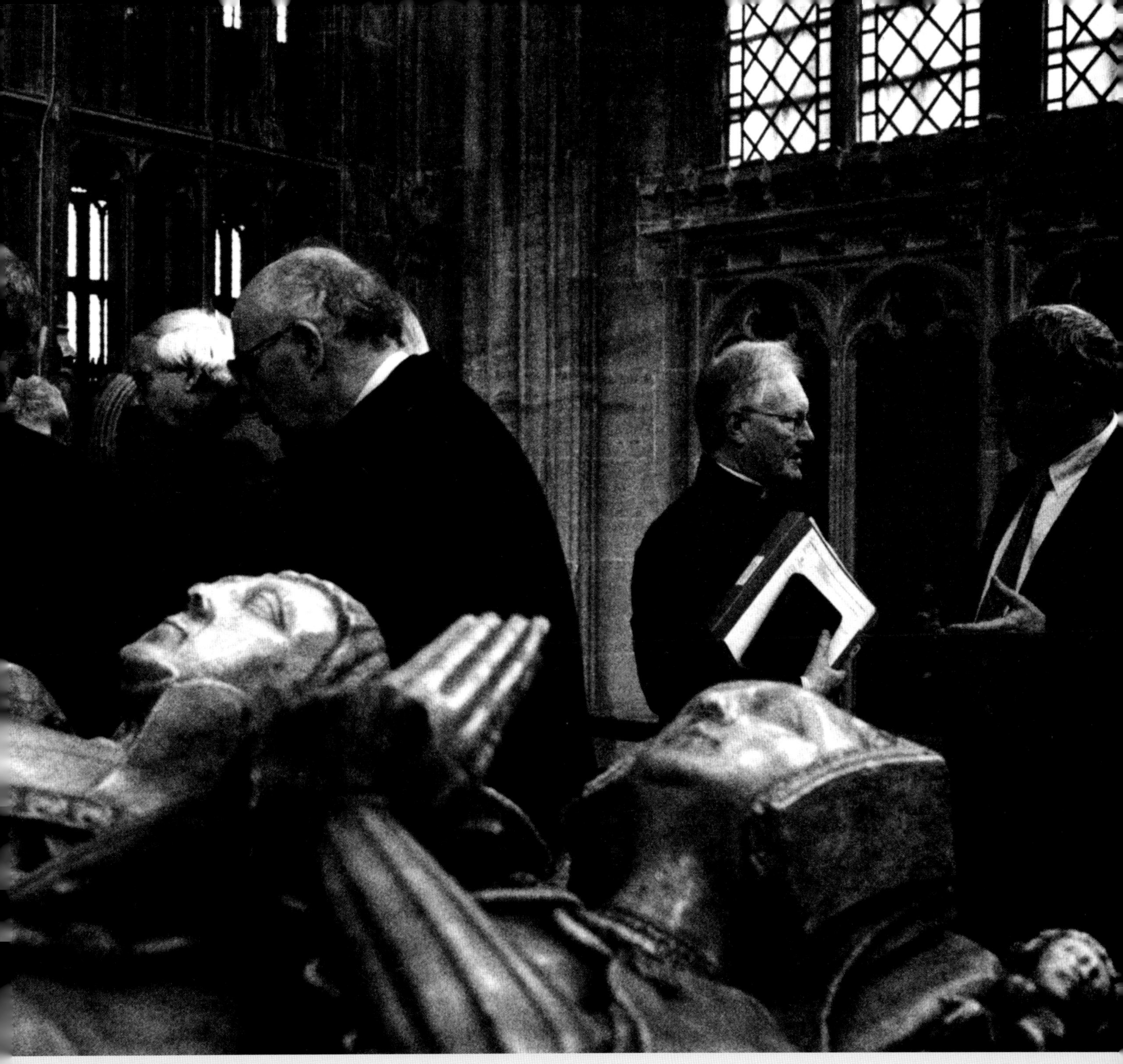

Above: The Committee in mid-discussion in the Rutland Chapel on the north side. The Rutland Chapel contains the tomb of George Manners, Lord Ros, who died in 1513, and his wife Anne, daughter of Anne of York, Dowager Duchess of Exeter.

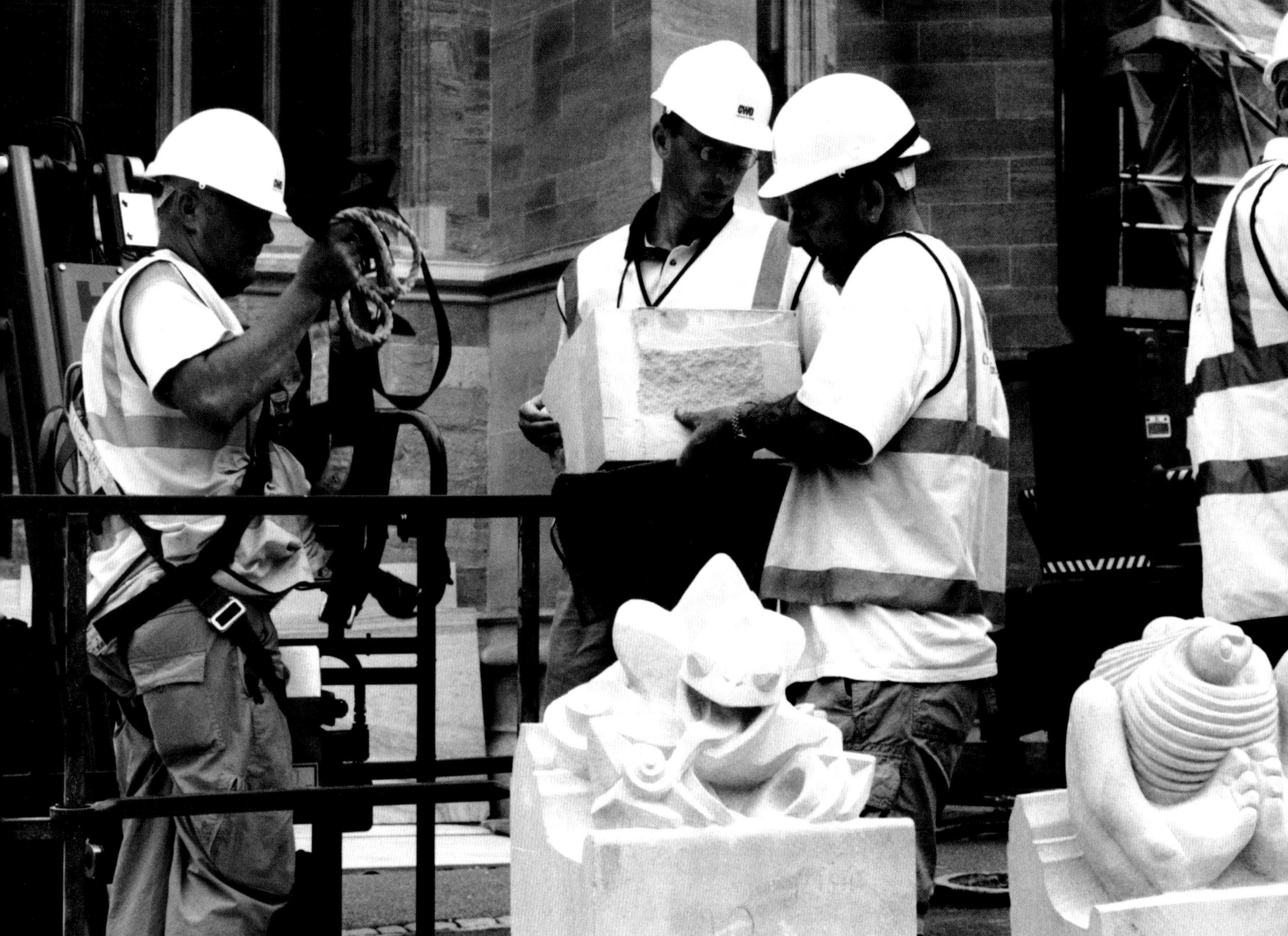

The installation of new grotesques onto the outer wall of the Bray Chantry. These grotesques were part of a larger commission by St George's and have resulted in the creation of new stonework projects at the London City and Guilds Institute.

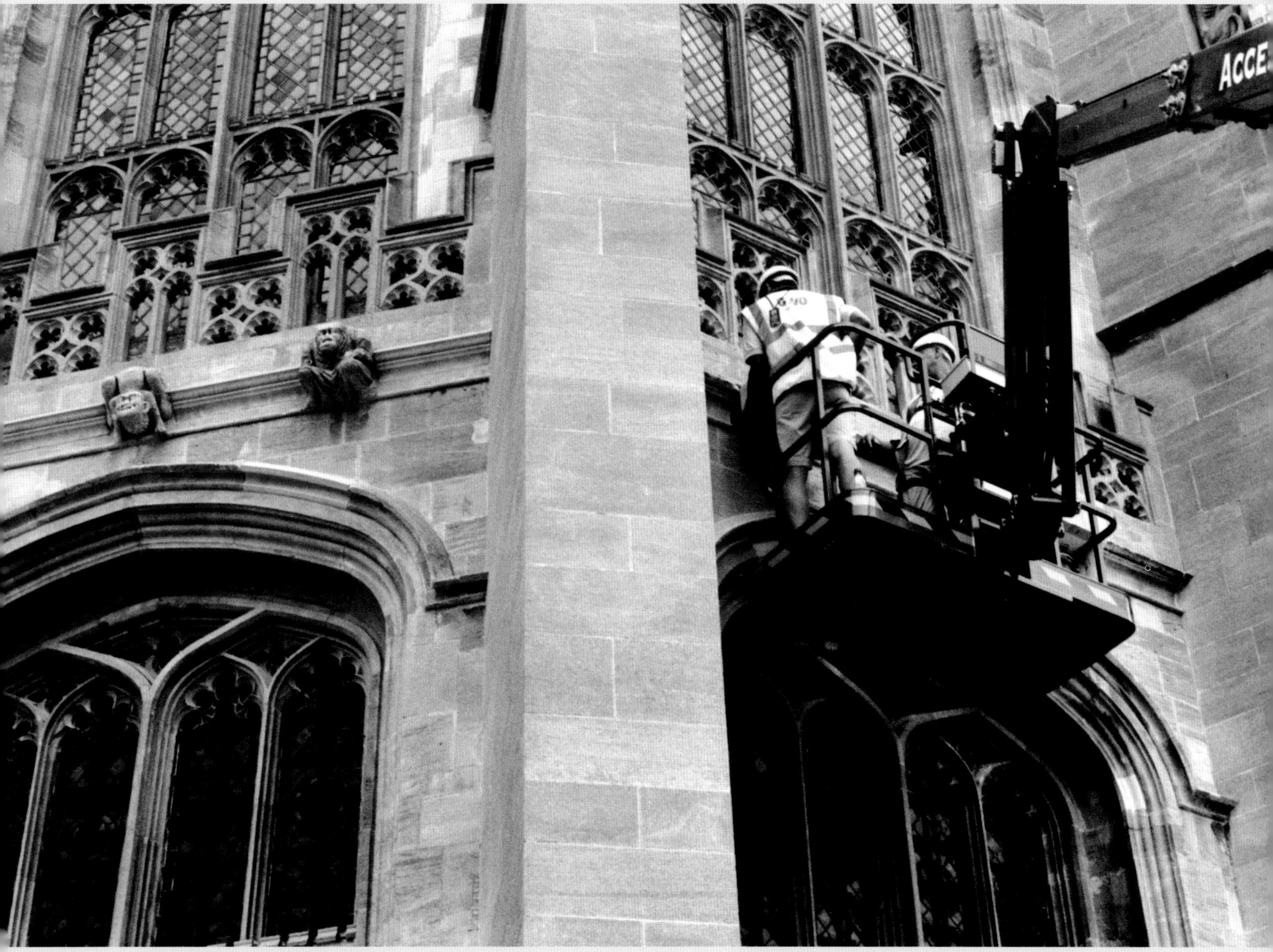
ACCE

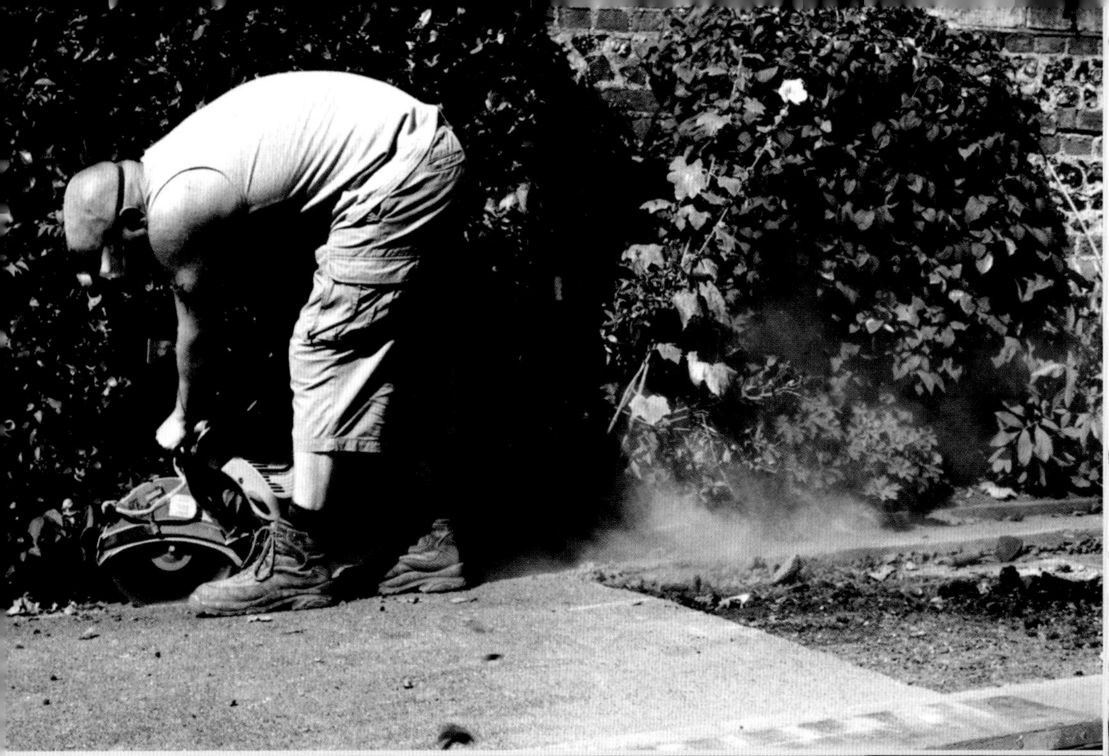

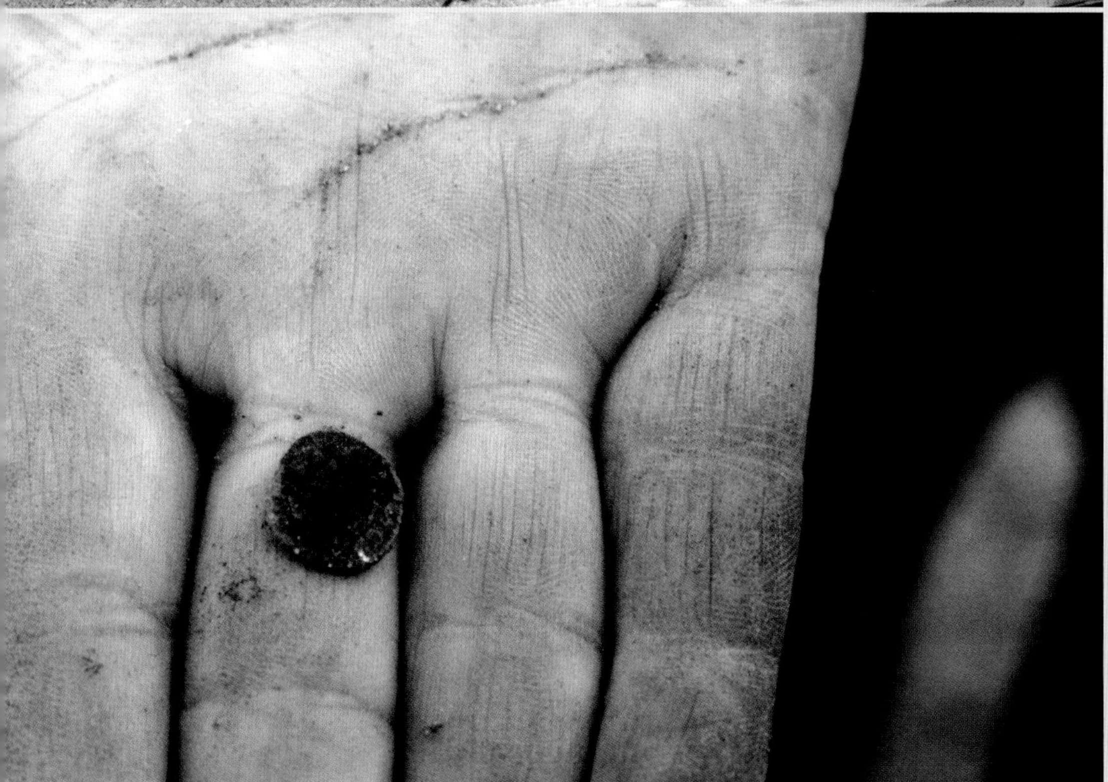

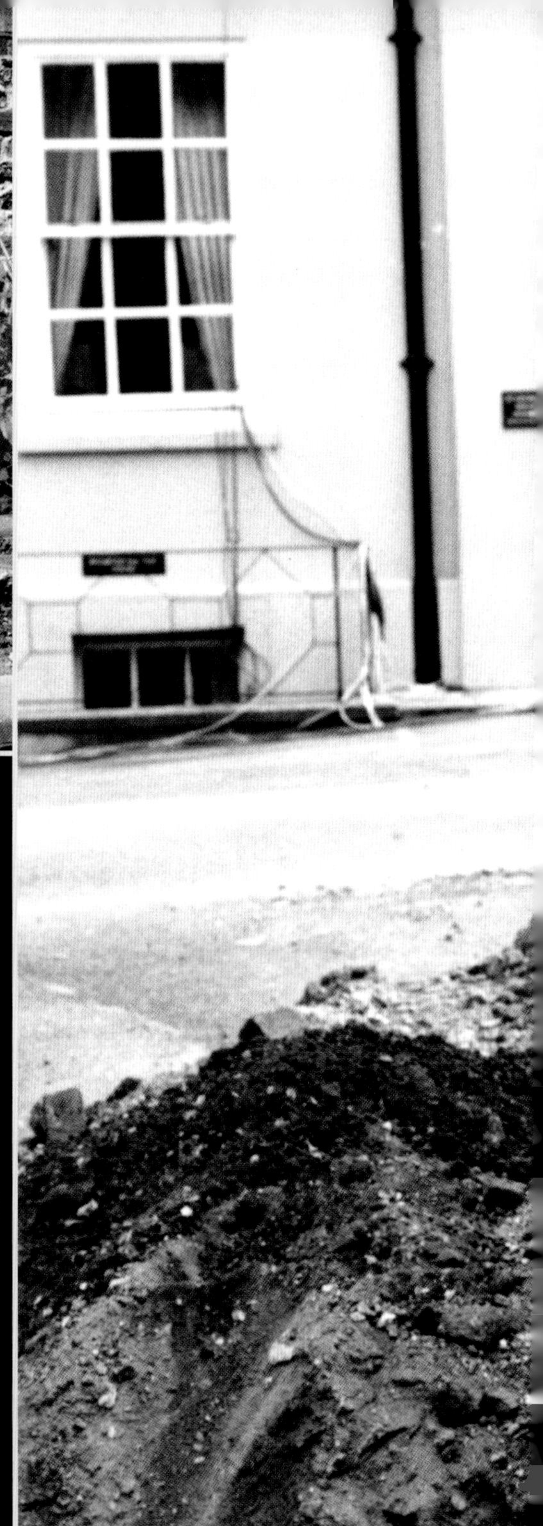

Top and Above: Channel 4's *Time Team* digs up the foundations of Denton's Common on the north side of St George's Chapel, looking for the origins of the 'Great Hall'.
Right: Team members inspecting a rare find.

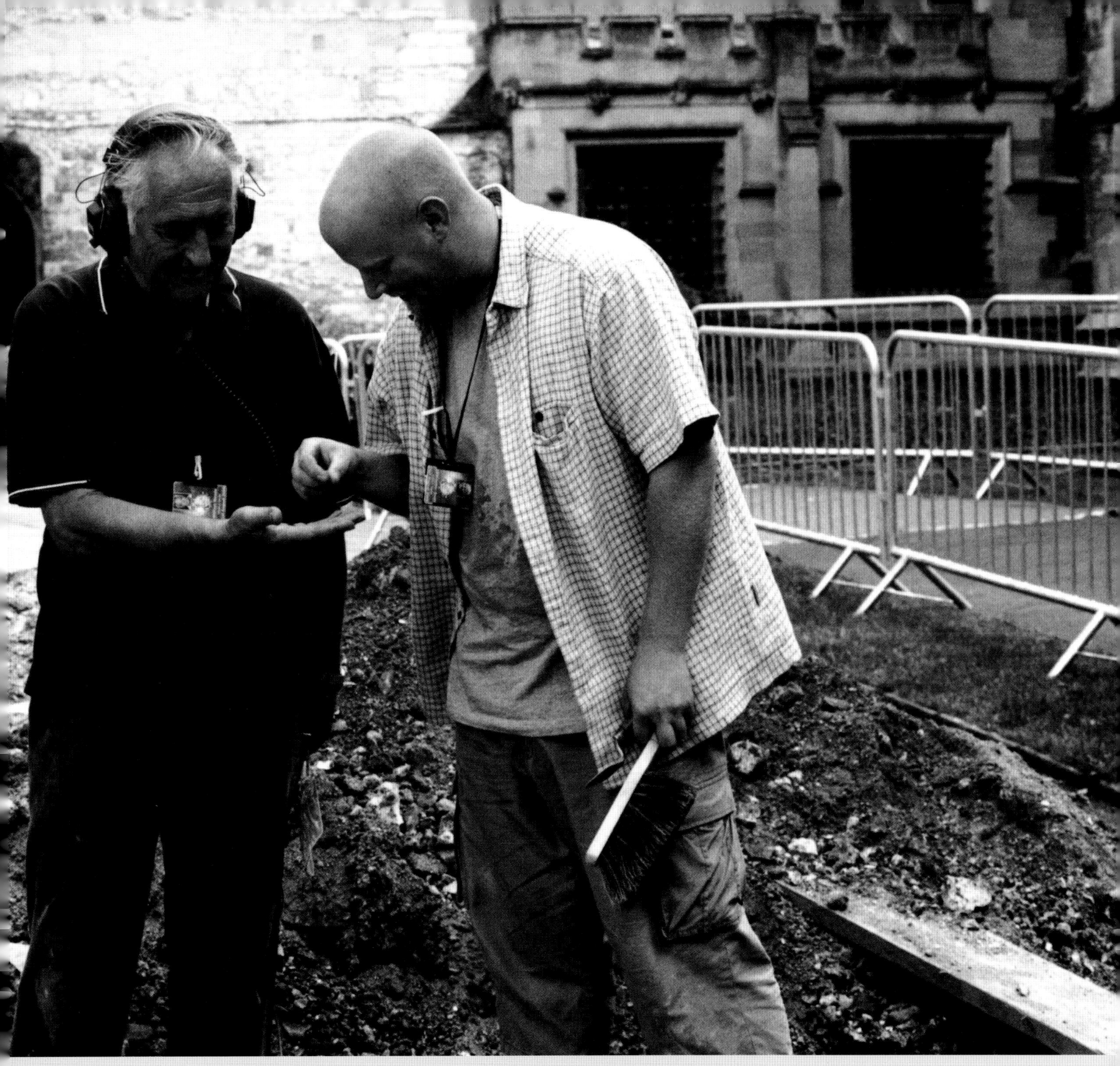

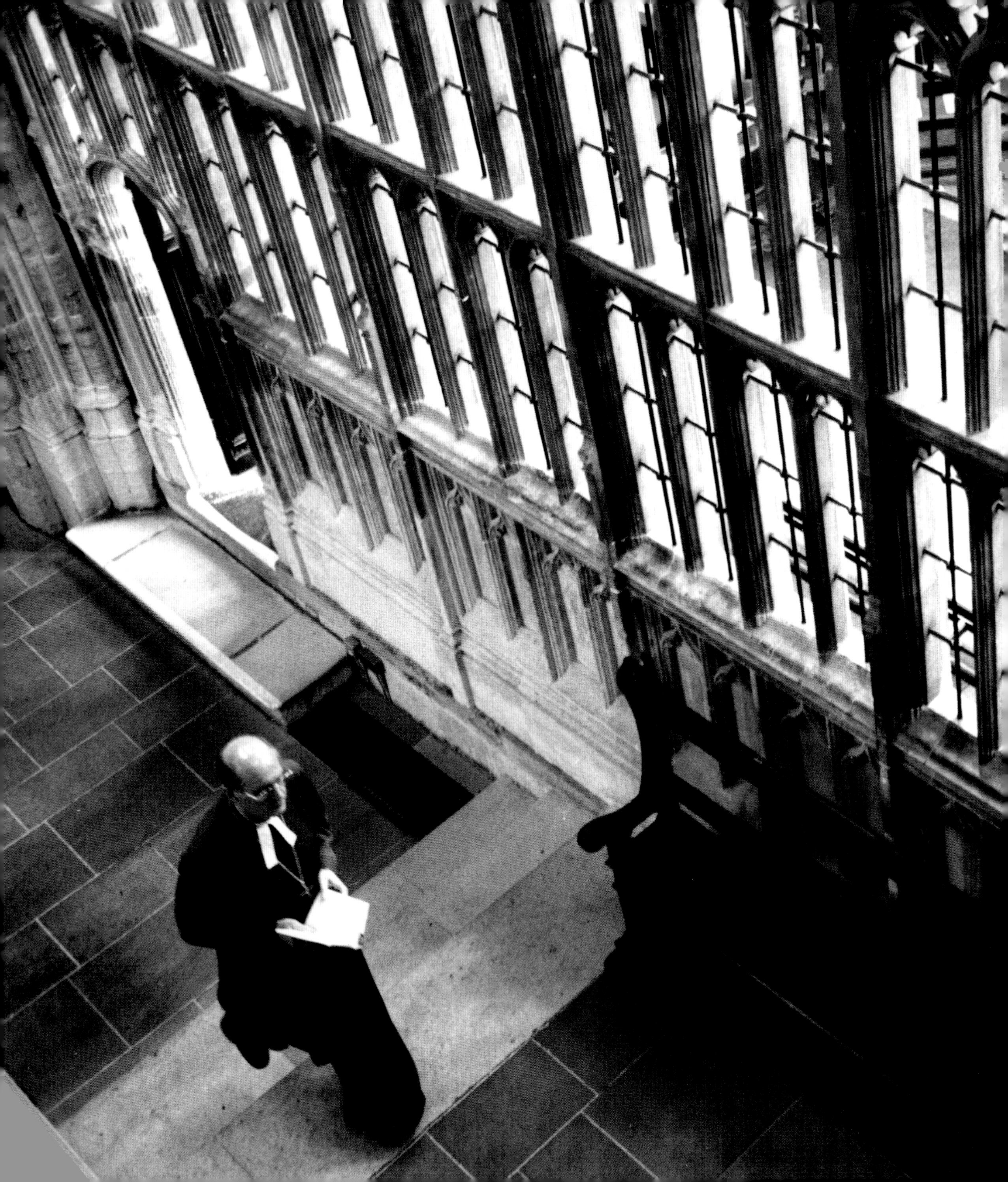

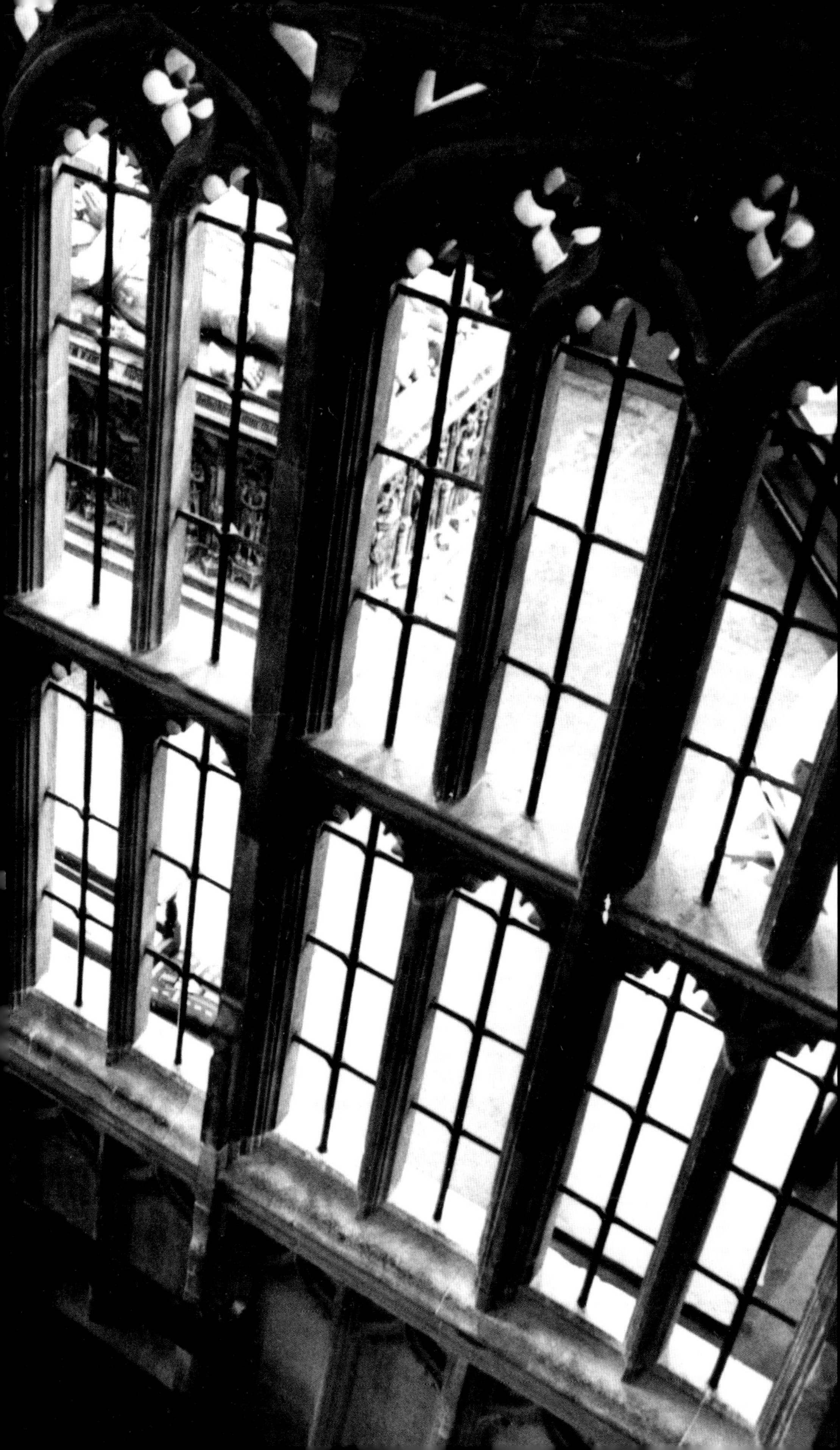

Daily Life

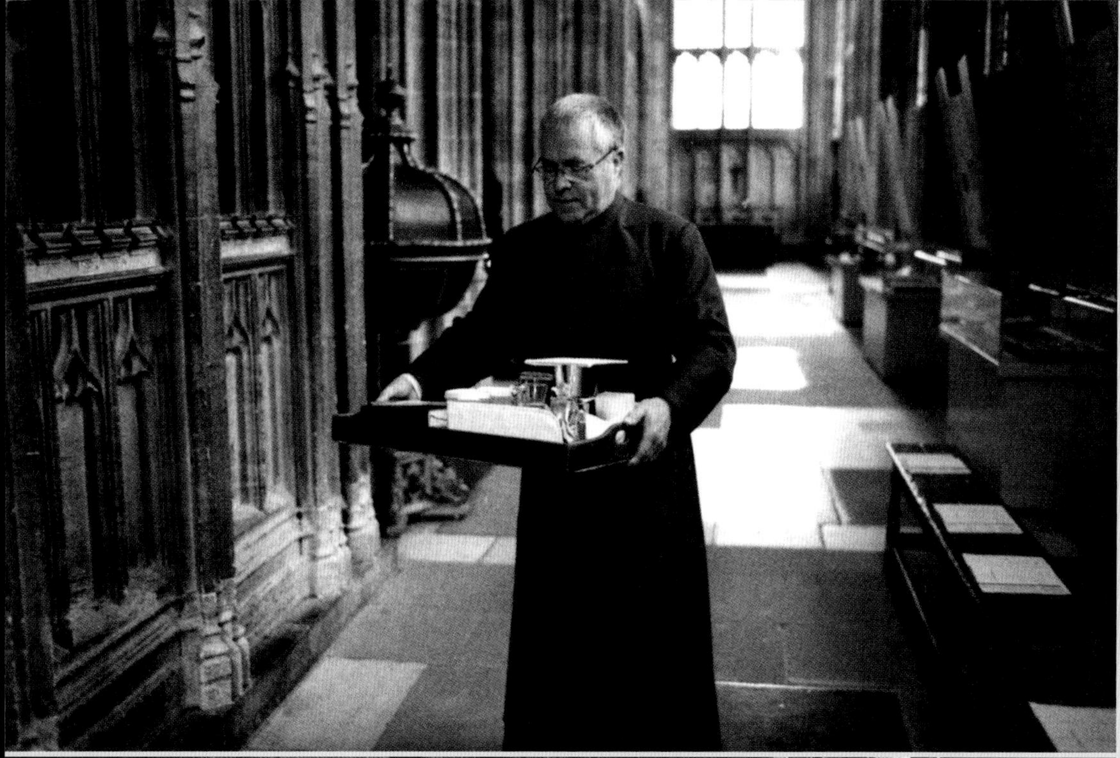

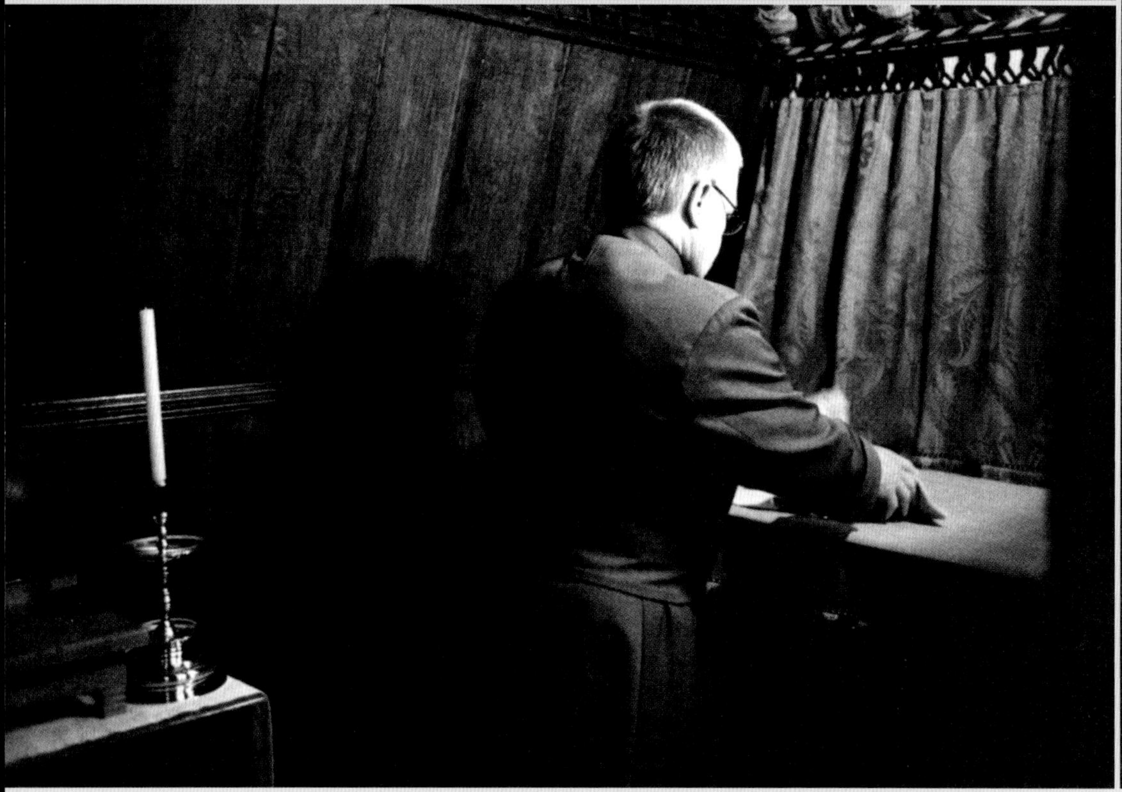

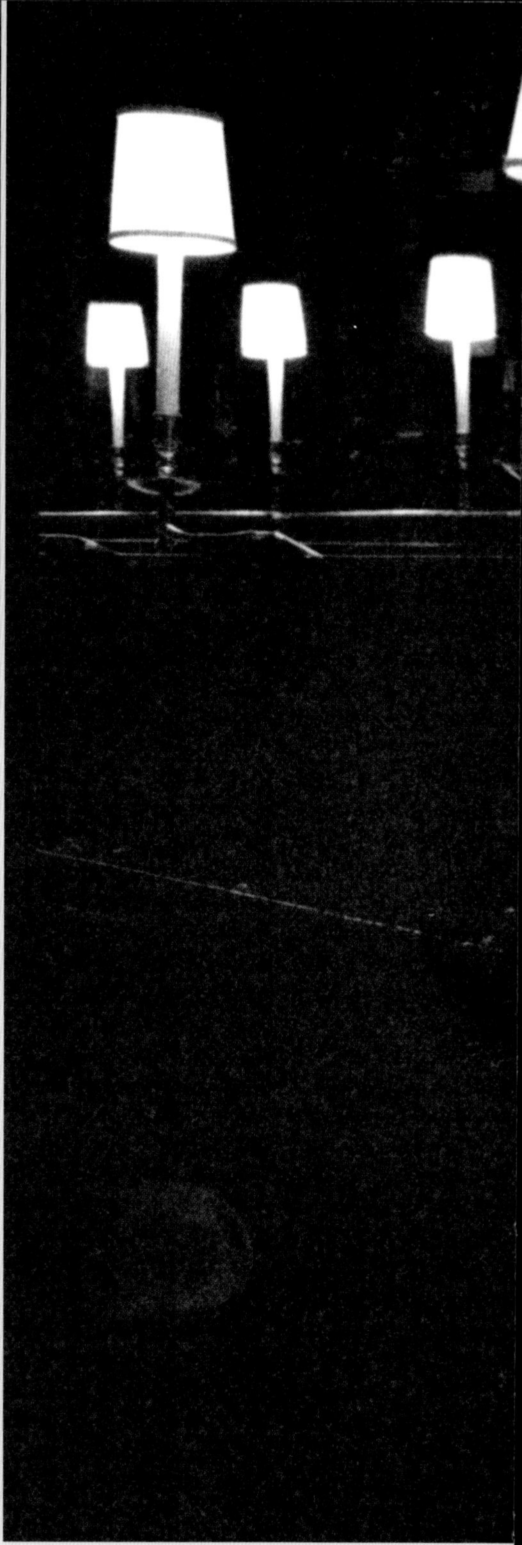

Early morning preparations of the Chapel.
Top and Above: The Virger seen carrying the 'communion tray' – of plate, chalice, wafers, service book and water – into the Oxenbridge Chantry, which dates back to 1522.
Right: The Virger checking the service sheets in the quire.

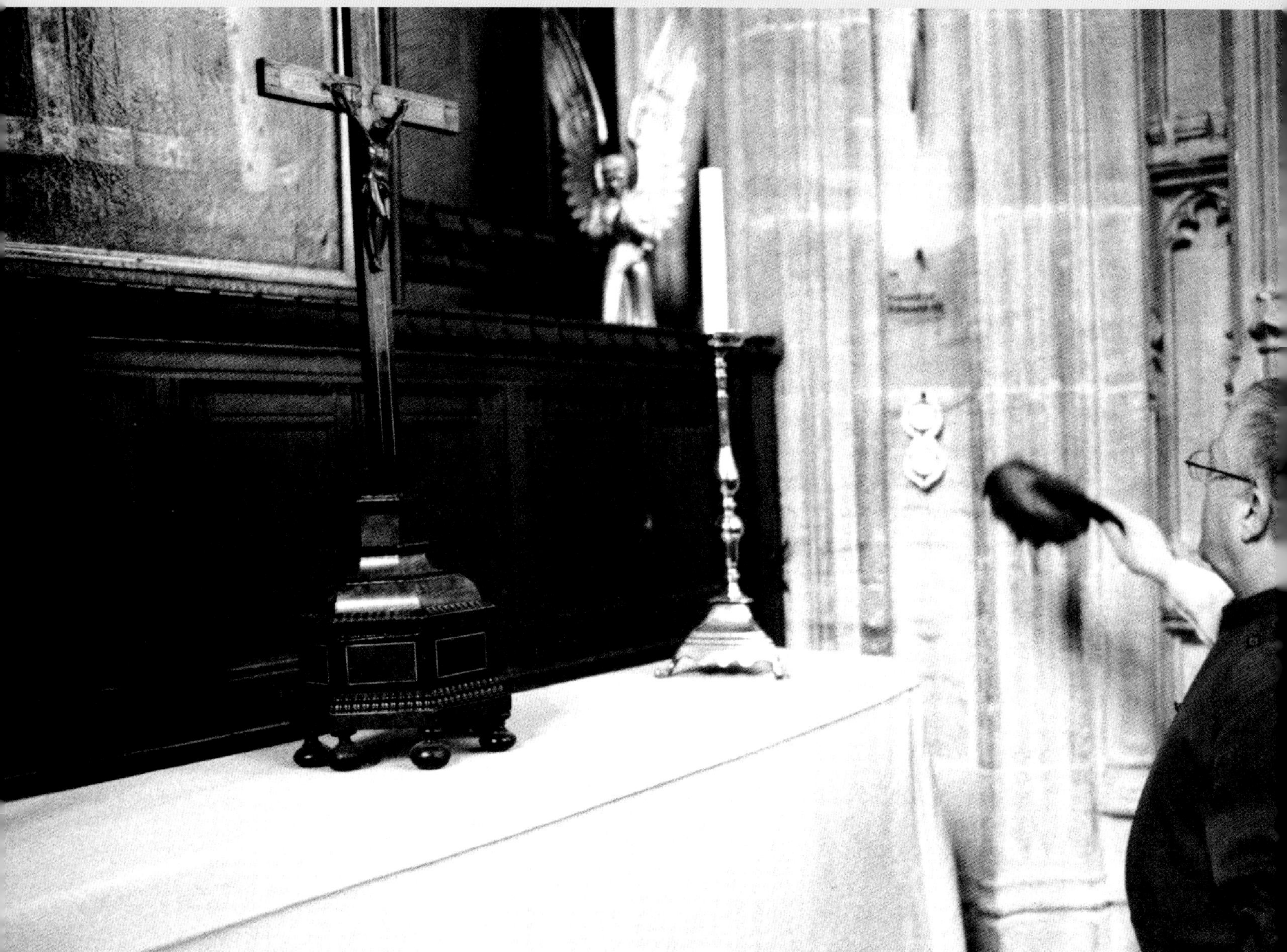

Above: Keeping the Chapel clean, the Virger wipes the dust off cross and angel. The tip of Edward III's sword may be seen in the background. Edward III was the founder of the Order of the Garter and the College of St George and his sword, which measures six feet eight inches long, was made to be used in battle.

Right: The Virger lays out the patten in the Oxenbridge Chantry as part of the preparations for Communion.

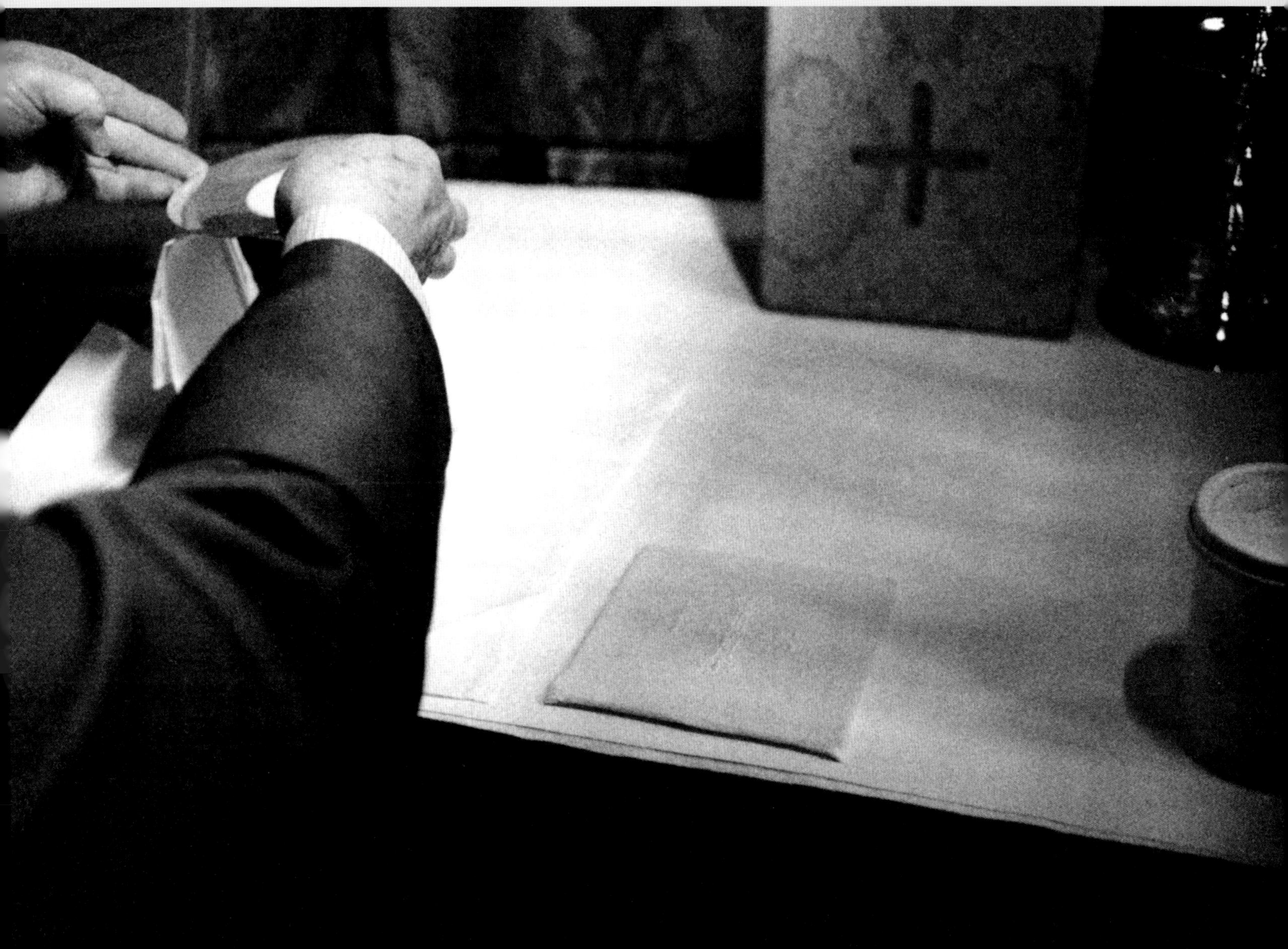

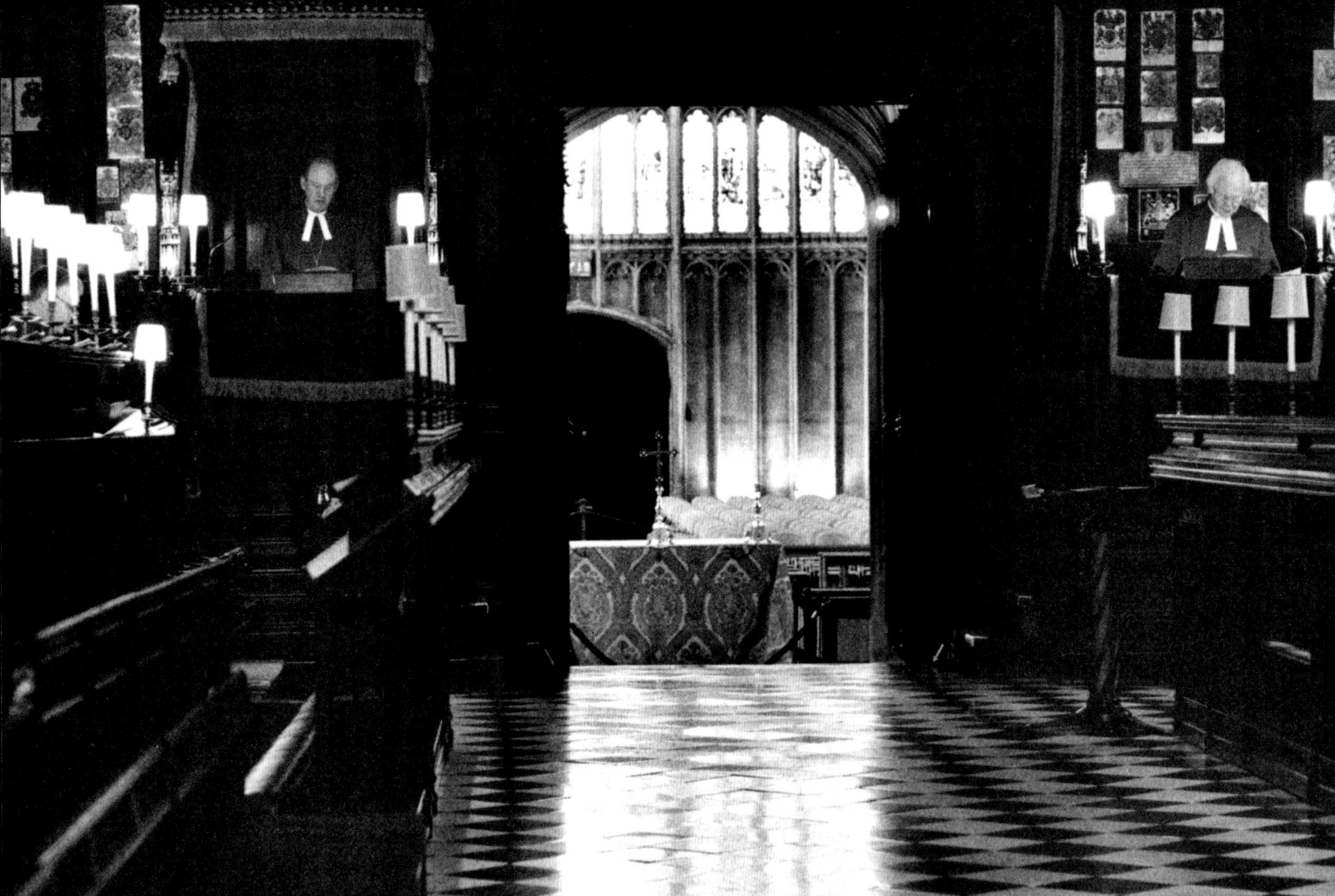

Above: Mattins in the quire. The Dean stands in the Sovereign's Stall on the left, and the Canon-in-Residence in the Prince of Wales's Stall on the right. *Right*: Detail of an attendance register from 1384–86 recording the monthly register of daily attendance of the Dean, Canons, Poor Knights, Priests, Vicars, Clerks and Bell Ringers.

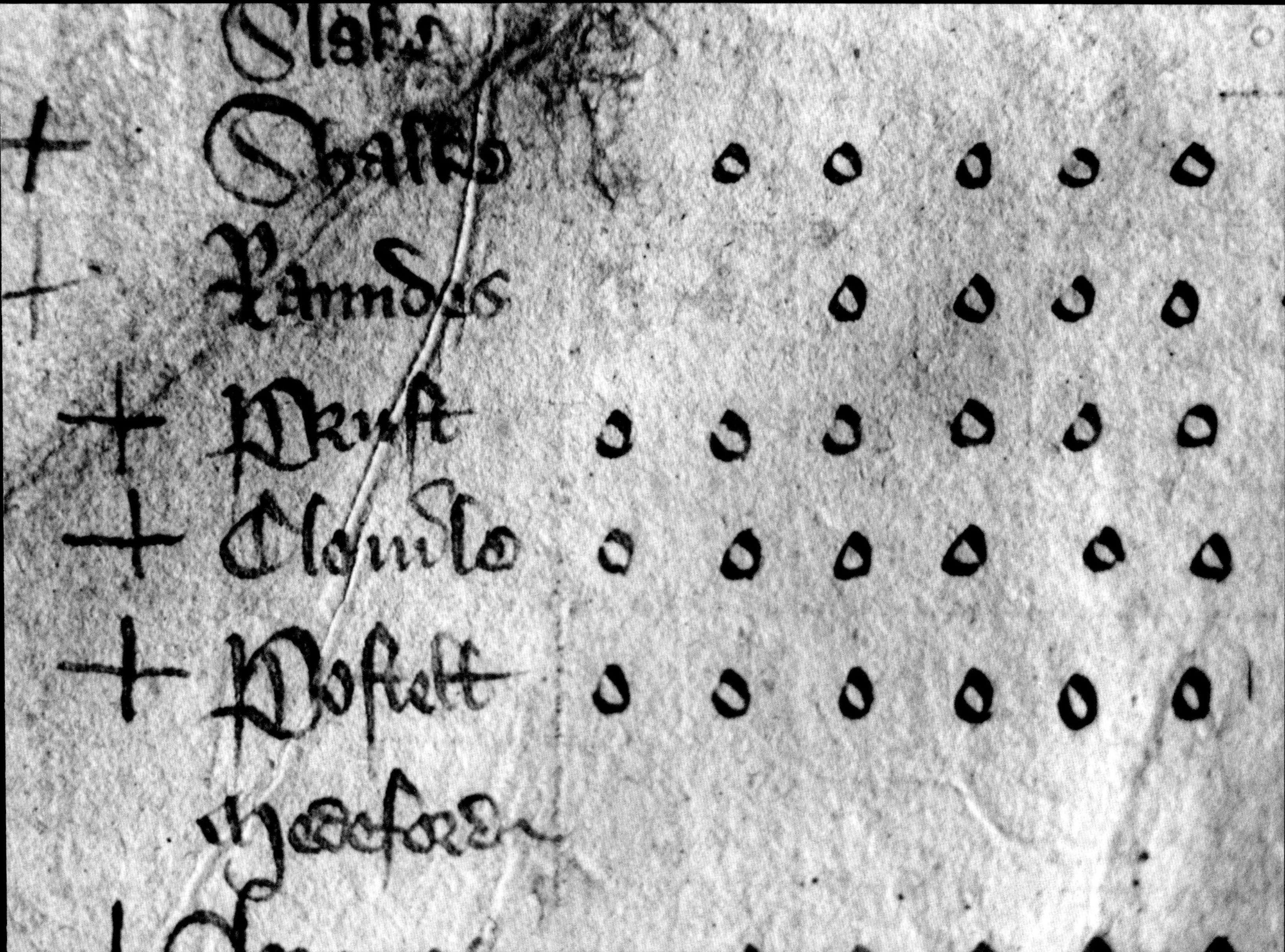

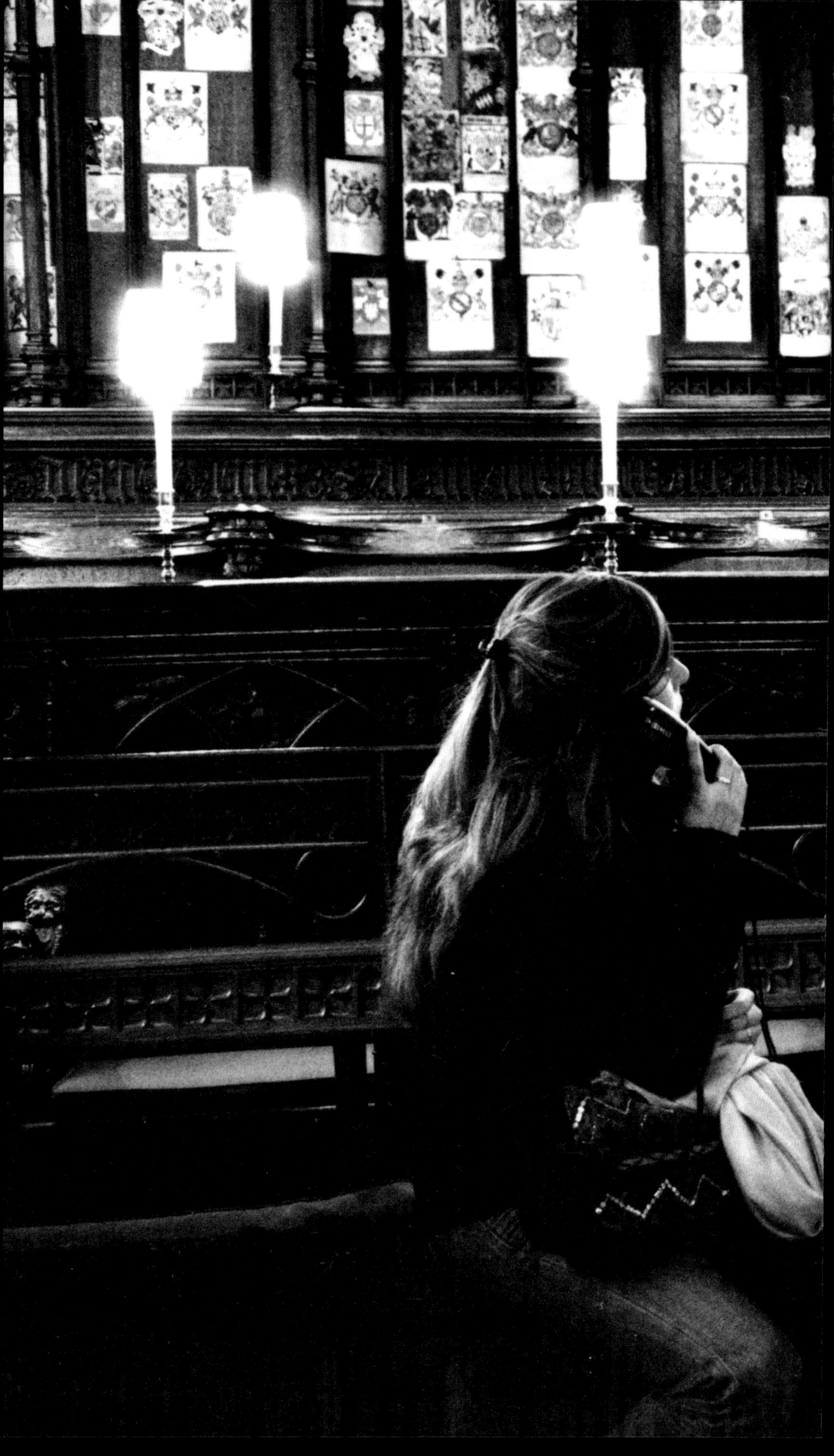

Tourists in the quire listen to their audio-guides and gaze up at the banners, crests and stallplates of the Knights of the Order of the Garter.

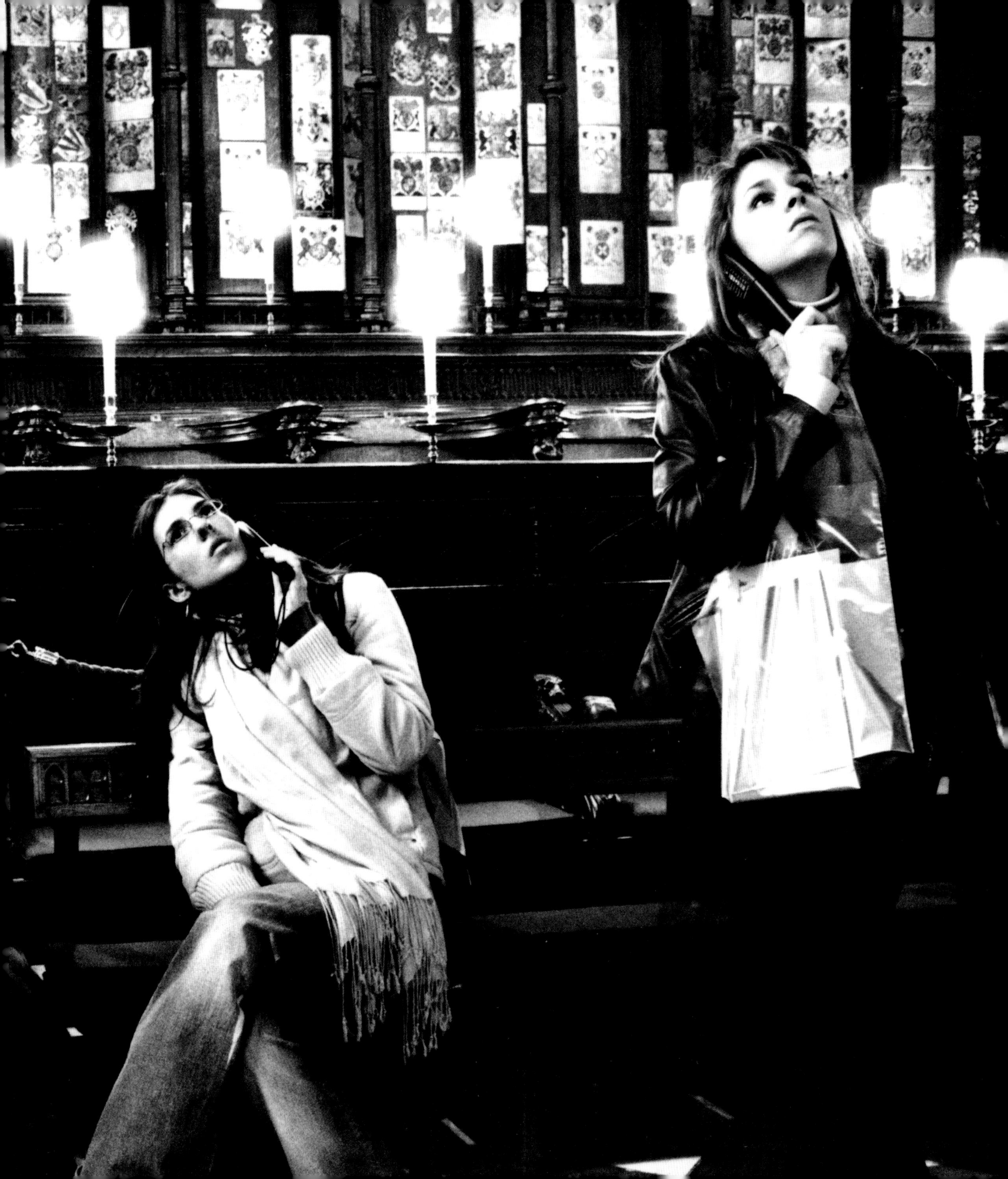

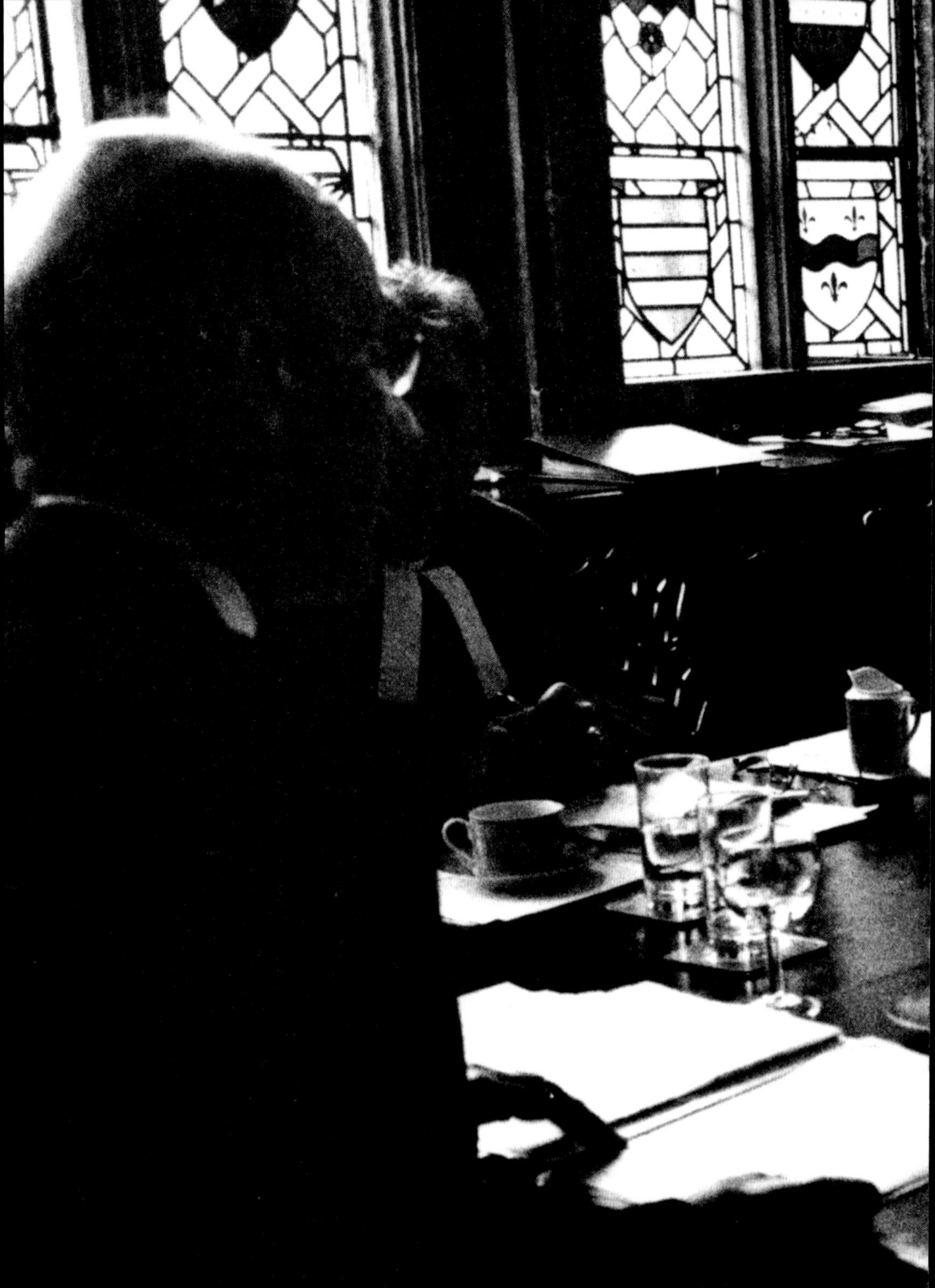

The Surveyor of the Fabric presents a report to Chapter, the Governing Body of the College of St George, which meets monthly in the Chapter Room.

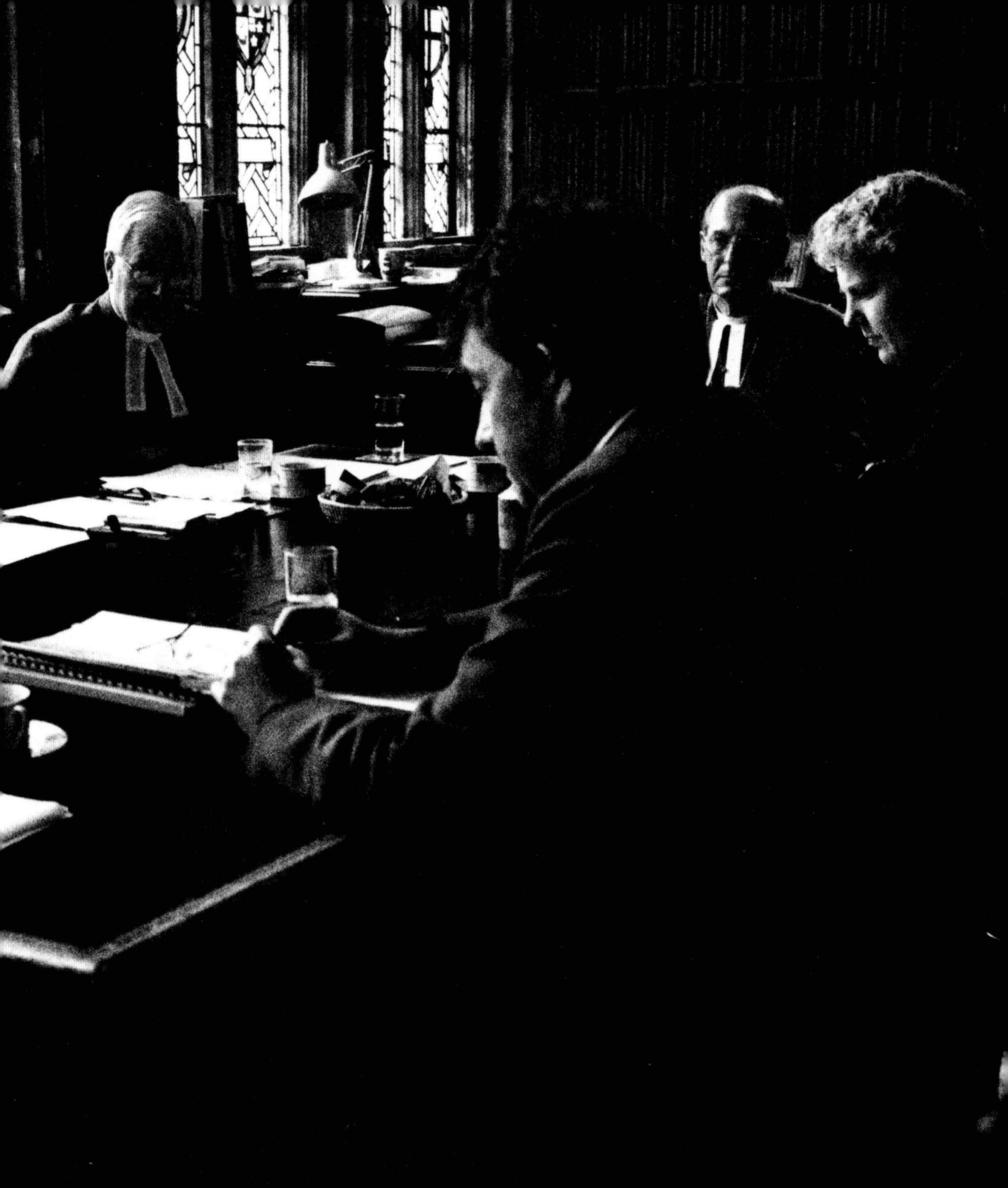

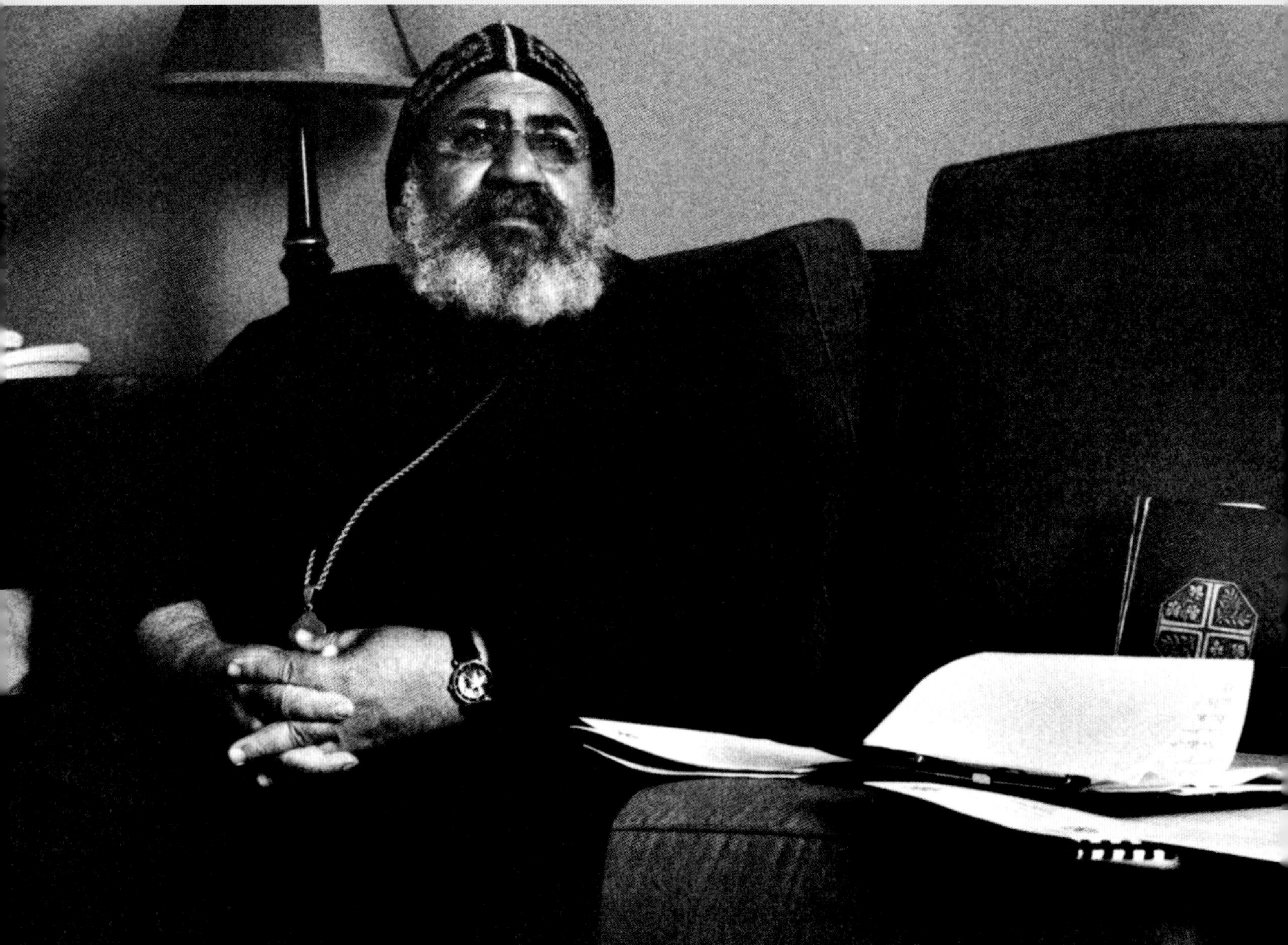

Participants at the International Conference on AIDS at St George's House. These three participants were from Egypt, the US and South Africa. St George's House is dedicated to conferences and consultations, both general and clerical, and deals with a wide range of contemporary and international issues. It was established in 1966 and is an integral part of the College of St George.

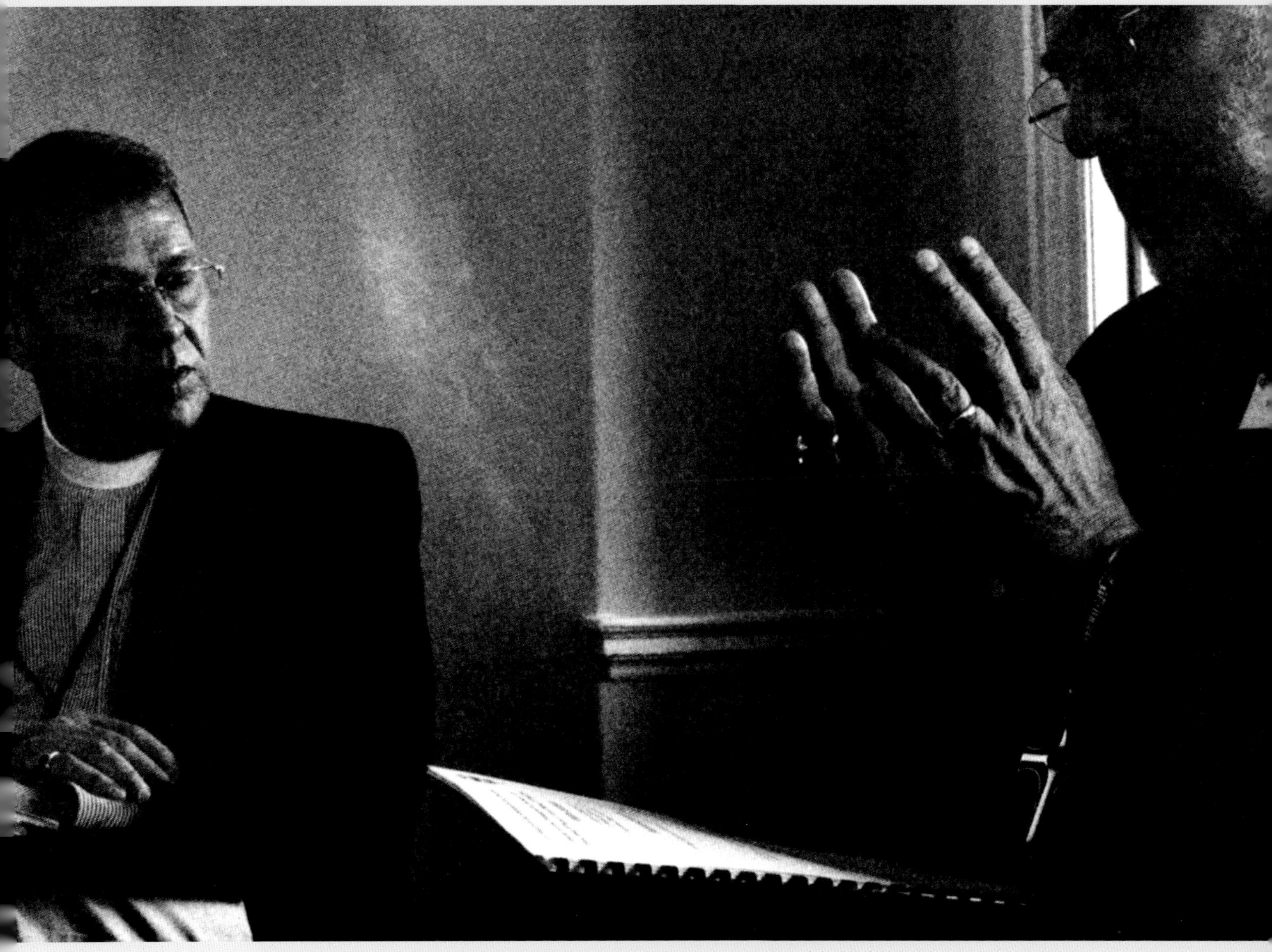

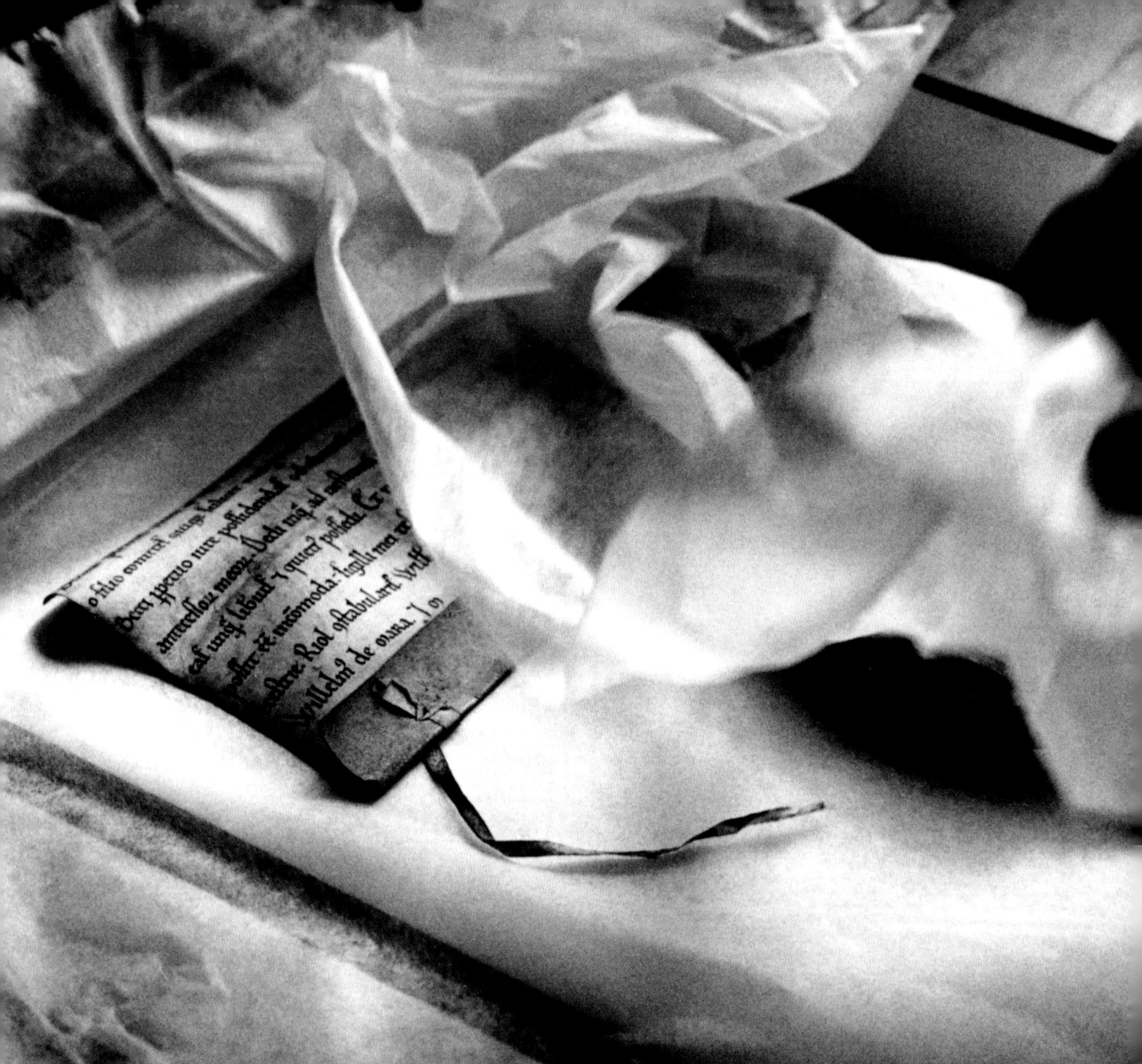

The Archives and Chapter Library hold a collection of rare books and manuscripts dating back to the early twelfth century. Today they are used not only by dedicated scholars but also as a resource for current architectural projects.

Above and right: An archivist unveils a twelfth-century wax seal and scroll. This unusual wax seal is of Matilda of Wallingford (1122–33), granting money to the monks for making cloaks in Ogbourne Priory, Wiltshire, which belonged to the Abbey of Bec in Normandy.

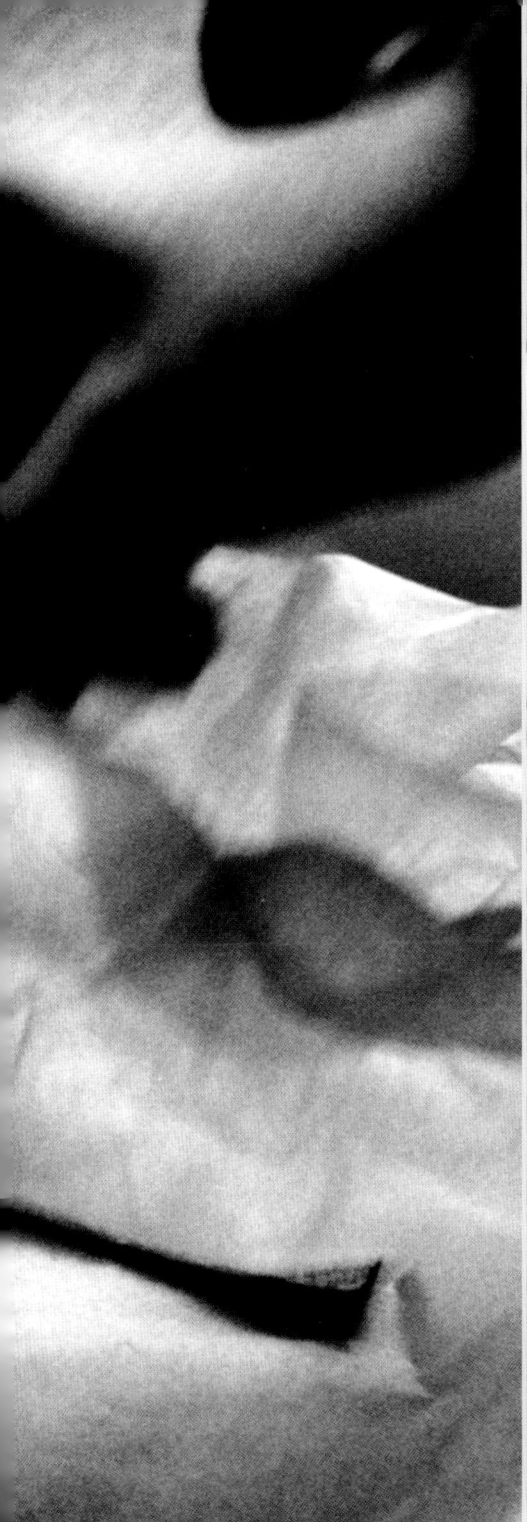

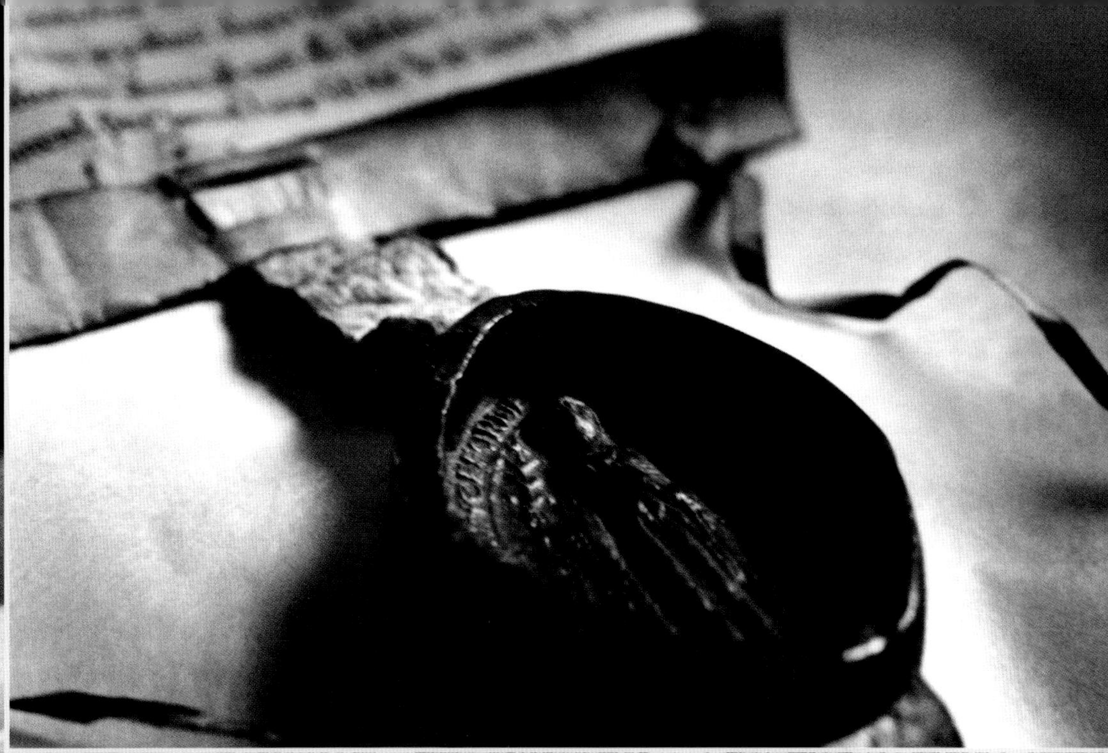

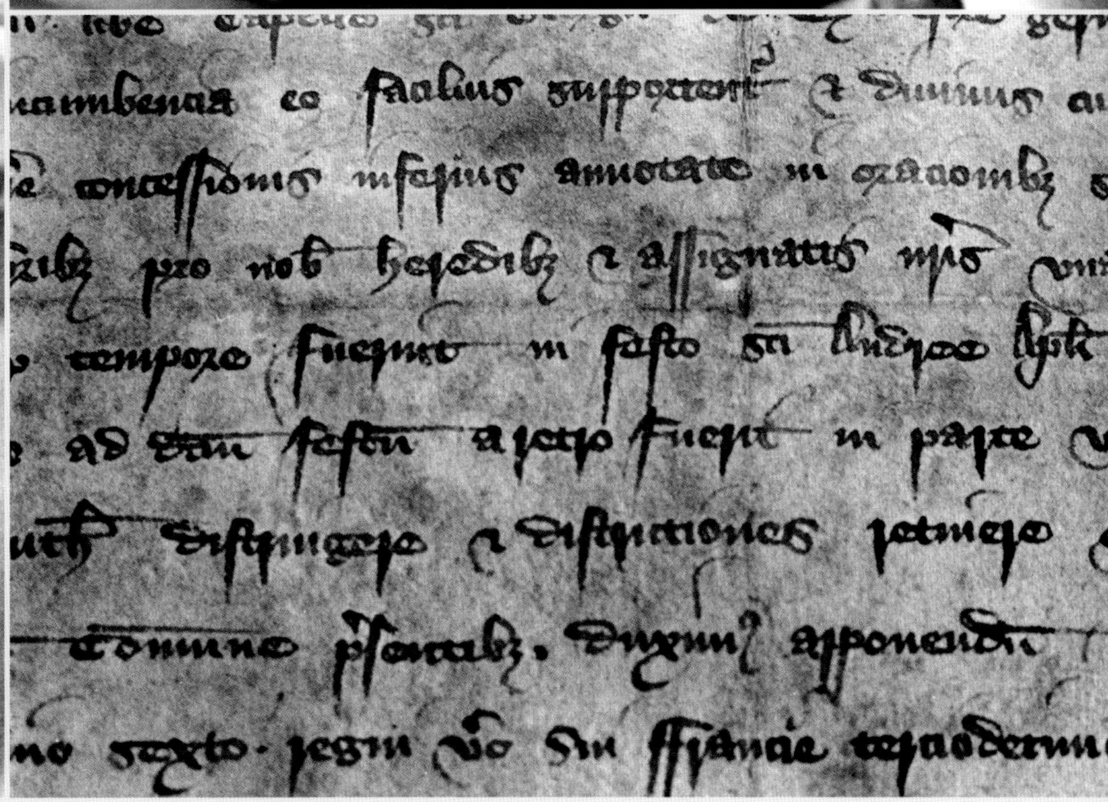

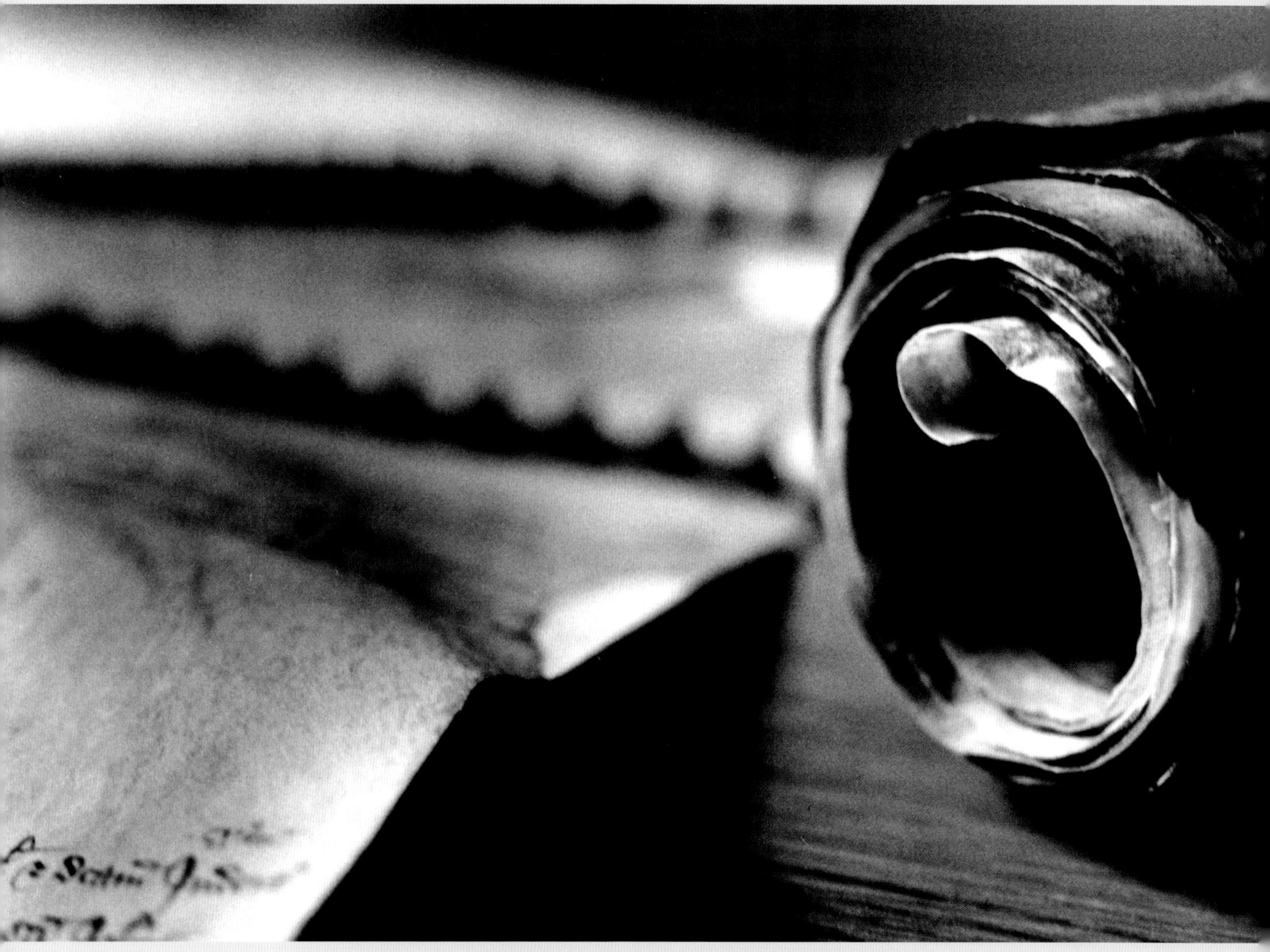

Above: A Treasurer's Roll from 1406–07 on goat skin. Some of the scrolls may measure up to 20 metres in length.

Right: Opening page, with the emblem of St George, of the first volume of the Denton Black Book, which dates back to 1517 and details the setting up of Denton's Commons. The fancy script is Gothic Bookhand.

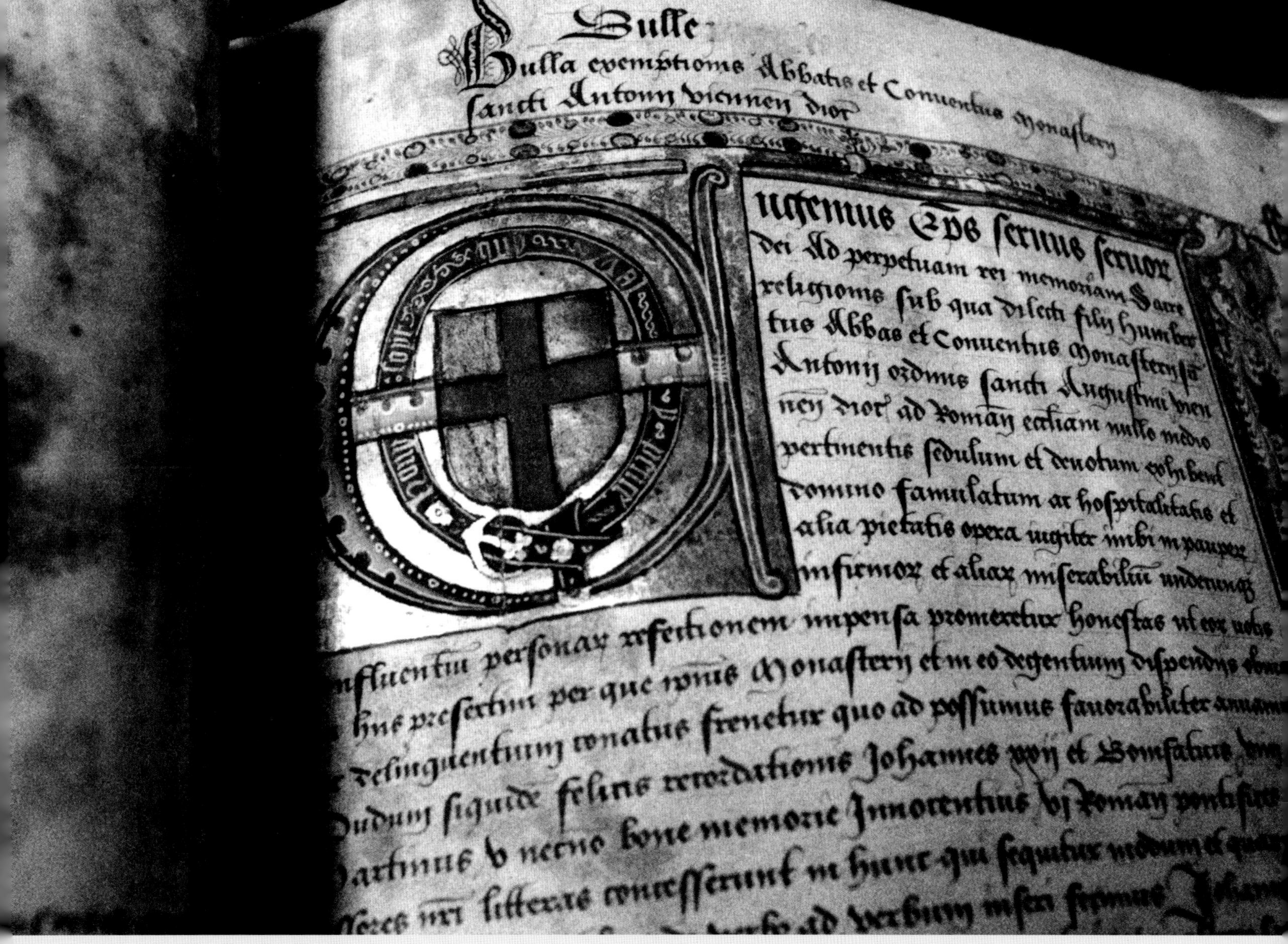

Chronology

1348 King Edward III establishes the Order of the Garter and the College of St George at Windsor, including the Choir

1475 Building of St George's Chapel commences under King Edward IV

1477 Curfew Tower converted to belfry. Eight bells, the majority dating from the 17th century, hang there today.

1503-09 59 of 75 lights within West Window made and stone vaulting over nave and quire completed

1528 St George's Chapel completed under King Henry VIII

1649-60 Commonwealth Period

(The date of Charles I's execution was in 1648 according to the Julian calendar then in use, when the year started on 25 March; or 1649 according to the Gregorian calendar, used in England since 1752. Charles I is buried in the same vault as Henry VIII and Jane Seymour (and an infant child of Queen Anne) in the centre of the quire.)

1780/90s Refurbishment of Chapel and organ under Henry Emlyn including new organ screen and four new stalls in the Quire

1863-73 Restoration of Henry III Chapel on the east side by Queen Victoria as a memorial to Prince Albert. (The Chapel was built in 1240 but fell into decay when St George's Chapel was built in 1475.)

1896 Queen Victoria institutes the Royal Victorian Order. (The Chapel of the Order is at The Chapel of the Savoy but it holds its annual event every fourth year at St George's Chapel.)

1948 King George VI reinstates annual Garter Service of Thanksgiving and Installation at the Chapel for the 600th Anniversary of the Order of the Garter

1966 St George's House founded

1969 King George VI Chapel off north quire aisle completed

2004 Twelve year refurbishment project of St George's Chapel and all surrounding buildings in the College of St George begun

2005 Service of Dedication and Prayer following the marriage of The Prince of Wales and The Duchess of Cornwall

2006 80th Birthday of Queen Elizabeth II

2006 Archaeological dig to the north of St George's Chapel to establish the exact position of the Great Hall begun by King Henry II

Acknowledgments

I would like first to acknowledge with thanks the Dean, David Conner, and the Canons of Windsor for giving me permission to undertake this project; it has been a great privilege to have experienced St George's Chapel in this way. Secondly, I would like to extend my gratitude to the Chapter Clerk, Charlotte Manley, for all of her time, effort and energy; none of this work would have been possible without her dedication and efficiency. In addition I would like to acknowledge the many individuals that make up the community of the College of St George who have been consistent in their interest and support for my work over these years, and who have allowed me to bring my cameras into their working life within the College. Outside of the Castle walls, I would like to mention Mike Dyer & Associates in central London, who have been consistently professional in their processing and printing of my films; my thanks to all of the team in WC1 who have worked and managed my negatives and prints. And lastly, I would like to thank family and friends who have offered valuable comments, insights and suggestions with regards to the many aspects of this project.

Eleanor Curtis